APPLIED TIME SERIES ECONOMETRICS

APPLIED TIME SERIES ECONOMETRICS

*A Practical Guide for Macroeconomic Researchers
with a Focus on Africa*

Alemayehu Geda

Njuguna Ndung'u

Daniel Zerfu

University of Nairobi Press

African Economic Research Consortium

First published 2012 by
University of Nairobi Press
Jomo Kenyatta Memorial Library
University of Nairobi
P.O. Box 30197 – 00100 Nairobi

Email: nup@uonbi.ac.ke   website: **www.uonbi.ac.ke/press**

Reprinted 2014

The University of Nairobi Press supports and promotes the University's objectives of discovery, dissemination and preservation of knowledge, and stimulation of intellectual and cultural life by publishing works of the highest quality in association with partners in different parts of the world. In doing so, it adheres to the University's tradition of excellence, innovation and scholarship.

University of Nairobi Library CIP Data

Applied time-series econometrics: a practical guide for macroecomic researchers with a
      focus on Africa / by A. Geda, N. Ndung'u and D. Zerfu. – Nairobi: University of
      Nairobi Press, 2012.
      205P.
ISBN–10–9966–792–11–2
ISBN–13–978–9966–792–11–2
      1. Time-series analysis   2. Econometrics   I. Geda, Alemyehu
II. Ndung'u, Njuguna   III. Zerfu, Daniel
QA 280 .A66

Printed by:

Aliki Printers.
P.O. Box 9434 – 00300, Nairobi, Kenya

Table of Contents

Chapter 1

Chapter 2

Chapter 3

Chapter 4

Chapter 5

Chapter 6

List of Figures

List of Tables

List of Illustrations

List of Boxes

About Authors

Alemayehu Geda is Professor of Economics at the Department of Economics, Faculty of Business and Economics, Addis Ababa University. He is also a Research Associate of the University of London (SOAS, London), the UN Economic Commission for Africa (ECA), Addis Ababa, African Economic Research Consortium (AERC), Nairobi, The Kenyan Institute for Public Policy Research and Analysis (KIPPRA), Nairobi, Central Bank of Kenya, Nairobi, African Development Bank, Tunis and Economic Policy Research Center (EPRC), Kampala. He has worked as a consultant for a number of international organizations including the UN ECA, The United Nations Development Programme (UNDP), the World Bank, Swedish International Development Cooperation Agency (SIDA), Department for International Development (DfID) as well as the governments of Ethiopia, Kenya, Uganda, Tanzania, and Zambia.

Njuguna Ndung'u is Governor, Central Bank of Kenya and Associate Professor of Economics at the School of Economics, University of Nairobi. He holds a PhD from the University of Gothenborg. He was the Director of Training at African Economic Research Consortium (AERC), immediately before his current post. He also worked as the Regional Program Specialist for the Eastern and Southern Africa Regional Office, of the International Development Research Center (IDRC), Canada and Head of the Macroeconometric and Modelling Division of the Kenya Institute for Public Policy Research and Analysis (KIPPRA) before his current job. He has taught macroeconomics, macroeconometric modelling and econometrics at the University of Nairobi, regional training centres such as Microeconomic and Financial Management Institute (MEFMI) network and at AERC.

Daniel Zerfu is a senior research economist at the African Development Bank, Tunis. Before joining the Bank, he was an assistant professor of economics at the School of Economics, Addis Ababa University. He taught macroeconomics and macroeconometric modeling at the Addis Ababa University. He also worked as a consultant for a number of international organizations, including the World Bank, United Nation Economic Commission for Africa (UNECA), United Nations Development Program (UNDP), and Department for International Development (DfID) of the UK.

Preface and Acknowledgment

Writing a book like this represents the work of a number of people, friends and colleagues. It is also basically a compilation of ideas from great econometric textbooks. We would like to record our gratitude to those superb authors whose classic textbooks we have used extensively in the course of writing this book. We saw some value-added in the current book – relevance to the students and researchers of developing countries and its self-teaching style which is quite relevant for macroeconomic experts working in ministries of finance and economic development as well as central banks in Africa and beyond.

Drawing from our experience as educators in African universities, we see the need to progressively present such books by beginning with simple intuitive ideas using diagrams, descriptive analysis and less algebra. Instructors can then progressively move to more sophisticated, and rigorous levels with more of the techniques being given at later stages. We have attempted to do that in this book. We believe the book could be relevant for advanced econometric courses at undergraduate level and for a time series course at graduate (MA/MSc) level. First year PhD candidates could also use the book as a refresher course to pursue their advanced econometrics and macroeconomic studies.

A number of people, including our students at the University of Addis Ababa, University of Nairobi and at African Economic Research Consortium (AERC) in Nairobi, contributed to this work by being the first users of its first draft and offering comments. We thank them all and would in particular like to thank, William Lyakurwaa, Olu Ajakaiye, Marios Obwana, Grace Omodho, Abebe Shimeless and Marc Wuyts for the inspiration and the intellectual support they gave us at various stages of this book. We have received constructive comments from the two referees of the University of Nairobi Press which enormously improved the book. Getachw Yirga of Baherdar University offered us excellent research assistance and we are very grateful.

We would also like to thank The African Economic Research Consortium (AERC) for financing this study and its publication through its textbook grant.

Alemayehu Geda
Njuguna Ndung'u
Daniel Zerfu
February 2012

Chapter 1

INTRODUCTION

Econometric analysis entails an economic theory-inspired dialogue with nonexperimental economic data with a view to arriving at a model which presents an adequate, yet parsimonious model of the underlying phenomenon. Econometrics of time series has a long history from its formative stage at the Cowles Commission for Research in Economics founded in 1932 and based on five tenets; zero restrictions, invariance in time, structural invariance, causal ordering and the fact that models can only be tested with the use of classical (Neyman-Pearson) tests against "nature". In the 1950s and 1960s there was a great spirit of optimism and confidence in econometrics. Large scale structural multi-equation models were constructed based on the five Cowles Commission assumptions: the 24 equation model of the Dutch economy build by Jan Tinbergen in 1936 and the six equation of the inter-war economy of the USA published by Lawrence Klein in 1950, among others. Computing advances and availability of national accounts data, however, made applied researchers to systematically abuse the Cowles Commission methodology (e.g. through data mining), which caused disquiet in econometrics. Additionally, the forecasting ability of several large-scale macroeconometric models was outperformed by the univariate Box-Jenkins approach. This created self-doubt in the 1960s, which divided econometricians into three groups: those who dismissed econometrics, those who stuck to the traditional econometrics, and those struck by the new direction who sought to re-look at the five basic tenets of the Cowles Commission (Charemza and Deadman, 1992). This has seen developments in time series econometrics on several fronts, all attempting to revise the five Cowles Commission assumptions: Sims (1980) on Vector autoregressions (revising causal ordering assumption), Dickey and Fuller (1981) on unit roots, Engle and Granger (1987) on cointegration and error correction representation theorem, Hendry (1995) on "general-to-specific modelling", Johansen (1988, 2002) on test of cointegrating rank in a VAR. Modern macroeconometric models (e.g. the KIPPRA Treasury Macromodel for Kenya-KTMM) incorporate the new developments in applied time series econometrics; unit roots, cointegration and error correction mechanisms. The theoretical concepts of cointegration have found some practical use in policy oriented papers in research institutions in Sub-Saharan Africa and in the African Economic Research Consortium (AERC) network. At the same time, the availability of macro-panel data to study for instance Purchasing Power Parity (PPP) and growth convergence generated interest in panel unit roots and panel cointegration in the late 1990s.

The job of an applied macroeconometrician working on African data is complicated by several factors. First, the researchers are confronted with huge and complicated literature on time series econometrics spanning well over eight decades. Few of these researchers have formal training in time series econometrics and have limited access to appropriate text books and journals. Second, most countries in Sub-Saharan Africa have poor quality data owing to limited resources for the national statistical agencies as well as structural breaks reflecting policy regime switches and turf wars, among others. Modelling such data therefore requires extra care and extensive exploratory data analysis (EDA). Third, the applied macroeconometricians work in environments where there are still remnants of senior macroeconomists who do not believe in the new direction in econometrics.

In writing this book, we are cognizant of the above challenges faced by applied macroeconometricians working on African data. First, we attempt to demystify time series econometrics so as to equip macroeconomic researchers focusing on Africa with solid but accessible foundation in applied time series techniques that can deal with the challenges of developing economic models using African data.

Second, the book is a self-instruction handbook owing to the fact that most governments in Africa do not have funds to send the experts working on economic analysis for training. In addition, most students of economics do not have access to journals. This book thus helps to summarise and bring the frontiers of knowledge in this area closer to the researchers and students. The book is not meant to be a specialised text for econometricians and therefore those who want a more rigorous treatment are referred to, Charemza and Deadman (1992), Banerjee, Dolado, Galbraith and Hendry (1993), Hamilton (1994), Harris and Solis (2003), Enders (2003), Baltagi (2005), Juselius (2006) and, appropriate journals.

Third, there has been an increasing realisation by policy makers in most African countries that macroeconometric models play a significant role in policy analysis and forecasting. This has also received a major boost from the success stories of models such as KTMM in Kenya and regional macroeconomic modelling courses that were held by KIPPRA for participants from eastern and southern African countries. Building a macroeconometric model entails the following steps: model specification, data analysis and estimation, model diagnostics, forecasting and policy simulations. In this process, applied econometrics play a crucial role. There, are, however, two challenges in building a macroeconometric model in Africa: (i) how to structure the model to serve the unique characteristics of African countries; and (ii) how to customise economic theory concepts and advanced time series econometrics to be useful in an African context. It is also important to note that for effective use of financial programming (the mantra in IMF, which has been widely in use in Africa), the identities in the model need to be supplemented by behavioural equations. The same applies to modern Computable General Equilibrium (CGE) models.

The book provides a basic introduction of time series treatment and application macroeconomic data. More specifically, the book provides a demonstration of the advancement of time series, how it can be applied to African macro data and how the applicable software in the analysis can be handled. This is supplemented with practical data and examples.

The book also targets graduate students as well as researchers who are constantly confronted with research and policy issues but the proxy data available requires some skills and priors to interpret results.

The book is not meant for those wishing to specialize in econometrics or those who cherish econometric models, but rather, it should be an added reference to aid research, modelling, estimation, and interpretation of data and providing safeguards on interpretation and reliance on results generated.

The rest of the book is organized as follows: Chapter two focuses on model specification and data exploration. The main message is that model specification in an environment where data are seldom normal in shape is a task that requires skill and experience. This is indeed the case in Sub-Saharan Africa, where, in most cases, data is of poor quality. Upon studying this chapter the macro econometrician will be equipped with appropriate skills for model specification for using data that is rarely normal. First, it shows how to specify a focused research question and relate it to relevant economic theories. Second, it shows how to perform fruitful Exploratory Data Analysis (EDA) and extract key message in the process of dialogue with data regarding model specification and what to anticipate in subsequent econometric analysis. Specifically, the reader is taken through steps of how to perform graphical inspection, data transformations and diagnostic analysis in the spirit of Tukey's (1977) ladder of transformations and Box-Cox transformations. The chapter illustrates the fundamental steps of model specification using examples from Ethiopia, Kenya and Ghana, among others. Specifically, a research problem is formulated and all the steps of model specification are carried out sequentially, including EDA using STATA econometrics software.

Chapter three focuses on testing of unit roots. If variables are nonstationary, unless it combines with other nonstationary series to form a stationary cointegrating relationship, then regressions involving the series can falsely imply the existence of a meaningful economic relationship. The key message in this chapter is that while it is necessary to test for the presence of unit roots, this is by no means a simple exercise. One needs to follow a systematic strategy that takes into consideration structural breaks, data frequency and sample size, among others. The chapter presents some basic time series theoretical concepts and illustrates them using Monte Carlo simulations in EVIEWS econometrics software. Ethiopian data is used to illustrate how to perform the Augmented Dickey Fuller test in PCGIVE software and Phillips-Perron test in EVIEWS software. This includes an exposition on how to interpret unit root results correctly. The chapter also illustrates how to perform unit root tests with structural breaks using Clemente, Montañés and Reyes (1998) in STATA software.

Chapter four is devoted to cointegration analysis. The key message in this chapter is that since almost all macroeconomic variables exhibit stochastic trends (nonstationary), a regression carried out with such variables is at best spurious, unless they are cointegrated. This follows the classic works of Engle and Granger (1987) and subsequent developments that include the econometrics team in the UK led by David Hendry and his colleagues at the London School of Economics. The chapter covers the theory and practical issues on cointegration analysis using Engle-Granger (EG) two-step procedure as well as Johansen's cointegrated VAR framework. The chapter recognises that modelling time series requires some basic concepts in matrix algebra and tries to simplify these concepts by picking the most relevant for cointegration analysis, namely rank and eigen values and vectors. Illustrative examples are presented using PCGIVE/PcFiml econometrics software on consumption data from Ethiopia, Purchasing Power Parity (PPP) data for Mozambique and exchange rate data for Kenya, used in Were *et al.* (2001). After studying this chapter, the reader should be able to perform cointegration analysis using EG and Johansen cointegrated VAR approaches. With regard to the cointegrated VAR approach, the reader should be able to estimate a reduced-form VAR, perform diagnostics on it, test for cointegration using the trace test, impose long-run restrictions, impose short-run restrictions on the loading matrices (weak exogeneity test) and estimate a Vector Error Correction Model (VECM). The chapter also underscores the importance of the Gausianity of the residuals in the reduced form VAR for the validity of Johansen cointegration results.

Chapter five deals with issues regarding modelling with I(2) variables. The key message here is that the common practice of ignoring trends in data that exhibit two roots near the unit circle may lead economists to draw erroneous inferences from their statistical inferences. Instead of forcing such data into an I(1) framework, as is always done, it would be more useful to construct an economic model that is consistent with I(2) behaviour. An illustration that is presented employs an I(2) framework to address the issue of I(2)-ness in estimating aggregate production function using Ethiopian data for the period 1960/61 to 2001/02.

Chapter six presents the econometrics of forecasting time series variables. Forecasting economic variables is important for policy design and analysis in any country. The chapter notes that understanding the behaviour of variables is a fundamental starting point for univariate and multivariate forecasting. Specifically, the chapter starts with how to model trends, deterministic shifts, seasonalities and cycles. It then proceeds to show how to use Box-Jenkins univariate techniques and the multivariate VAR techniques for forecasting. It presents how to evaluate model forecasts using the Theil's inequality and other statistics. Illustrative examples are presented with Kenyan exchange rates and Ethiopian rainfall data using EVIEWS and PCGIVE econometrics software.

Chapter six concludes with the presentation of an introduction to panel data tests for unit roots and cointegration. It is noted that one advantage of panel unit root tests, over the time series counterpart, is that, they have a higher power and emanate from the introduction of the cross-section dimension. Additionally, the tests have asymptotically standard normal distribution as opposed to the non-limiting distributions in time series. The chapter presents two types of panel unit roots. First, is the tests that assume common unit root such as Levin and Lin (1992, 1993), Hadri (2000) and Breitung (2000). Second are tests that assume individual unit roots such as Im, Pesaran and Shin (1995, 1997 and 2003) and Fisher-type ADF test. The chapter presents two types of panel cointegration tests: Residual based tests (Pedroni and Kao panel cointegration tests) as well as the multi-equation-based test (Johansen Fisher test). The concepts are illustrated using oil consumption data for 11 African countries.

The book has an appendix which briefly summarizes the fundamentals of statistics and probability (distribution) theories relevant for time series analysis. It is advisable to begin the book by reading that appendix so as to refresh ones understanding of the basic statistics that will be used in the main text of the book.

In all the chapters, an attempt has been made to use data, the software and the theoretical relationships to generate some results. The idea is to provide practical examples without being stuck with the software or the line of reasoning. Using the examples throughout the book helps to illustrate the pitfalls of empirical work, the pains a researcher has to go through to replicate the neighbourhood of the data generating process under the backdrop of policy and empirical pressures to provide practical results.

Increased use and reliance of macroeconomic modelling and consistency checks in policy analysis is forcing our knowledge of empirical estimation to be revised. We do not, however, advocate that these models are an end to themselves but rather to emphasize that since economists think through structural relationships, the macro modelling, estimation and testing empirical estimations approach in this book is an appropriate starting point.

Chapter 2

MODEL SPECIFICATION

The Theoretical Model

Motivating Your Model

Suppose a researcher wants to examine the determinants (or conditions) of investment in Kenya. When working on this topic one has to have knowledge of econometrics to investigate the macroeconomic determinants of private investment in Kenya. The researcher may have observed the available data and trends in the data and perhaps asked an empirical question: what determines the pattern of private investment in Kenya? The researcher needs to know the type and frequency of the data and should have econometrics knowledge, especially of the time series, required in carrying out the investigation.

Investment is central to the growth experience of any country. One may be required to empirically investigate the determinants of investment. From macroeconomic theory, there are different theories about investment functions. Keynesian theory, for example, explains the dynamics of investment through the accelerator principle, which puts the emphasis on the demand side. In contrast, neoclassical theory emphasizes the supply side by looking at the user cost of capital. Another approach, associated with James Tobin, looks at the discrepancy between the market value of productive assets *vis-à-vis* their replacement costs to explain new investments.

A further perspective on the dynamics of private investment can be obtained by investigating the interaction between public and private investment in an economy. A key question here is, whether public investment has a crowding-out or a crowding-in effect on private investment: that is, whether public investment goes on at the expense of private investment or, whether it stimulates private investment. One of the currently celebrated empirical regularities is the complementarities between forms of public investment such as infrastructure and private investment. Finally, in a country like Kenya, determining to what extent institutional and political factors influence investment behaviour and investment decisions is uncertainty that causes complications.

Hence, we can tackle this topic in various ways. In a nut shell, suffice it to say that to write a research paper on this topic you will need to carry out a number of steps:

1.   Specify a focused question within this general topic and relate it to relevant theories;

2.   Study and summarize the relevant literature on your chosen question;

3.   Carry out econometric estimation and hypothesis testing, and evaluate the results in the light of the research question.

So far, we have emphasized the role of investment in growth and theories of investment as possible motivation for your research. Another source of motivation is an examination of the pattern of the data under analysis. For instance, you may take up a good section of your research paper to analyse the macro variable in question using descriptive analysis and graphs. One aspect to enrich such an analysis is to break down the variable into its various components: in case of investment this could be into fixed investment, inventory, infrastructure (for public investment), and so on. Such detailed descriptive and trend analysis is important to focus on major turning points and the source of such events.

Locating Your Study in the Literature and Formulating Testable Empirical Questions

To carry out your research, you will need to broaden your theoretical reading, say, about investment through a literature survey. Your readings should enable you to formulate your econometric model on the investment function, say, for Kenya or South Africa. This reading needs to be complemented by general reading on the Kenyan and South African economy and on investment behaviour in Kenya and South Africa.

Successful research requires formulating the question you want to investigate in a way that makes investigation possible. At the start of your work, you should spend time thinking about the research question you wish to study and how to make that question manageable. Then, after you have read basic literature and thought through the way authors have set out their research questions, you should try to formulate your questions. You may wish to repeat their research questions and relate them to your data. That is a legitimate scientific procedure. But in most cases, you will need to establish clear value added, in the research questions you propose. This is not difficult. It may be that you want to update the data and include a recent period of analysis; it may be that there have been major policy shifts during the update period (such as the 1993 liberalization in Kenya, or the demise of apartheid in South Africa in 1994 or the fall of "Socialism" in 1991 in Ethiopia, etc); or it may be that you have discovered weaknesses in other research works.

A further constraint on the type of research questions you can deal with in an econometric study relates to the data at your disposal. Clearly, the way you formulate your research question will depend also on your empirical implementation and whether or not the data is available. For example, the database may not allow you to estimate sectoral investment functions (that is, separate functions for agriculture, mining, manufacturing, and so on), but you may distinguish between private and public investment. Similarly, you may find it more difficult to estimate Tobin's (1969) q-model for Kenya because data on replacement costs are not usually available but, they can be done for South Africa. Hence, when thinking about a research question, take account of the data at your disposal and decide how to make the best use of them.

Data Exploration with STATA: A Brief View

As noted by Wuyts (1992), many published articles convey the message that the researcher began with clear cut hypothesis, tested it, and obtained the reported result. Any *ad hoc* tampering with the hypothesis is taken as data mining and carefully left out. Such a research method is rooted in the methodology which is referred as Popperian (following the works of Karl Popper). The real process, however, is a bit messy and involves a lot of trial and error. The latter is hardly reported, however. In fact, as Wuyts noted, when researchers and students fail to find a confirmation to their initial hypothesis they begin to get frustrated. Even getting a confirmation on the initial hypothesis doesn't confirm the impossibility of having an alternative explanation which fits the data just as well (Wuyts 1992). Such problems could be, however, avoided by resorting to another approach to data analysis which is rooted in the method of "inference to the best explanation" whose essential ingredient is proper data exploration.

'Inference to the best explanation' departs from the Popperian methodology in favour of a realist approach. It is our view that the adoption of such an approach represents a much more fruitful avenue of research in developing countries. This methodological framework is informed by the works of Harman (1965), Lipton (1991), Mukherjee and Wuyts (1991), Wuyts (1992a, 1992b) and Lawson (1989). The overall framework is Harman's (1965) "inference to the best explanation" (contrastive inference), which looks for residual differences in similar histories of facts and foils as a fruitful method for determining a likely cause (Lipton, 1991:78; Mukherjee and Wuyts 1991). This approach entails testing competing hypotheses in the process of research.

At a practical level, this general approach could be narrowed down to a more refined one proposed by Mukherjee and Wuyts (1991) in which "a working hypothesis" is confronted with the evidence and various rival explanations. Wuyts (1992b) argues that "the best way to test an idea (wrapped up as a hypothesis) is not merely to confront it with its own evidence, but to compare it with rival explanations. It then becomes easier to detect which explanation has more loose ends or will need to resort to *ad hoc* justifications to cope with criticism" (Wuyts, 1992b:4). Once a working hypothesis has been arrived at, the dialogue between data and alternative explanations may best be handled by exploratory data analysis, which comprises graphical display, techniques of diagnostic analysis and transformation of data (Mukherjee and Wuyts, 1991:1). This does not imply that theory has no role to play. Rather, that theory is important "as a guide to pose interesting questions which we shall explore with data" (Wuyts, 1992a:2).

The generation of working hypotheses, and the subsequent examination of these, may be pursued along Kaldorian lines (Lawson 1989, Lawson *et al* 1996). In this realist approach to economic analysis, the researcher is free to start from 'stylized' facts – broader tendencies ignoring individual details – and to construct a working hypothesis, which fits with these facts. The final stage of the analysis entails subjecting the entities postulated at the modelling or explanatory stage to further scrutiny (Lawson 1989).

In sum, data exploration is a pre-requisite for good model formulation and econometric estimation. This is because one has to know the pattern of the data in order to give it a mathematical form (i.e., to model it). Data exploration and inference, as we noted above, comprises three major techniques:

1. Graphical inspection,
2. Data transformation, and
3. Diagnostic analysis.

Graphical Inspection and Transformation

Data exploration needs to be guided by two guiding principles (Wuyts 1992):

1. Use numerical summaries along with graphical displays: they complement each other and allow the data to talk back to you;

2. Pay attention to outliers and influential points. They are not necessarily a nuisance but can be a source of valuable hints and clues.

In their excellent, but unfortunately not widely used book, "Econometrics and Data Analysis for Developing Countries", Mukherjee *et al* (1998), noted that "graphical method allows us to see our abstraction in the context of the full range of variation, and to asses whether further clues and hints can be gleaned from the data which may suggest novel ideas or things we overlooked in our analysis". For these authors, good data analysis involves theory-inspired dialogue in which data play an active part in the process of arriving at an appropriate specification of a model, and not in just testing it". Mukherjee *et al* (1998) noted that it is no use to force the data into a straitjacket and ignore the signs which tell us that our model is clearly inadequate, as most of our graduate students at African Economic Research

Consortium (AERC) and elsewhere do when they fail to get the signs that they were expecting, nor should we just discard bad results in the waste basket without asking the data why the result obtained are contrary to our expectation. Such questioning of the data, using both graphic and non-graphic approach is central for modelling.

Graphical analysis can be done using scattered plots, plots of variable on time and similar data inspection techniques. Transformation of the variable, in particular to a logarithmic form, not only helps to show influential points in a very sharp manner, but also corrects skewed to the right distribution towards normality – a correction relevant in the context of regression analysis. Before going to the use of graphic analysis using real African data, we have used below a fictious data that could easily demonstrate the power of data exploration analysis in general and the graphic approach in particular[1].

Simple classic example of the central role that graphics play in terms of providing insight into a data set is given by the following data sets:

	Data Set I		Data Set II		Data Set III		Data Set IV	
	X1	Y1	X2	Y2	X3	Y3	X4	Y4
	10	8.04	10	9.14	10	7.46	8	6.58
	8	6.95	8	8.14	8	6.77	8	5.76
	13	7.58	13	8.74	13	12.74	8	7.71
	9	8.81	9	8.77	9	7.11	8	8.84
	11	8.33	11	9.26	11	7.81	8	8.47
	14	9.96	14	8.1	14	8.84	8	7.04
	6	7.24	6	6.13	6	6.08	8	5.25
	4	4.26	4	3.1	4	5.39	19	12.5
	12	10.84	12	9.13	12	8.15	8	5.56
	7	4.82	7	7.26	7	6.42	8	7.91
	5	5.68	5	4.74	5	5.73	8	6.89
N	11	11	11	11	11	11	11	11
Mean	9.00	7.50	9.00	7.50	9.00	7.50	9.00	7.50
b_0	3		3		3		3	
b_1	0.5		0.5		0.5		0.5	
SD (e)	1.237		1.237		1.237		1.237	
Cor	0.816		0.816		0.816		0.817	
R^2	0.66		0.66		0.66		0.66	

---

[1] We are grateful to Dr. Getenet Alemu of Institute of Development Research, Addis Ababa University who provided us this data from his lecture notes. The discussions are based on his lecture notes. It is also based and inspired by Marc Wuyts' great work on data exploration.

11

Descriptive or quantitative statistics for all data sets 1, 2, 3, and 4 remarkably yields identical values for mean, slope, intercept, standard deviation of residuals and correlation coefficient (except insignificant difference for data set 4 for correlation coefficient). If the goal of the analysis is to compute summary statistics plus determine the best linear fit for Y as a function of X, the results obtained are identical for all data sets. One might naively assume that the four data sets are "equivalent" since that is what the statistics tell us; but what do the statistics not tell us? Or does this quantitative analysis give us the complete insight into the data?

To see that, we use a scatter plot of the first data (A scatter plot is a plot of the values of Y [dependent variable] on the corresponding values of X [independent variable]):

Figure 2.1:   Scatter plot: Y1 on X1

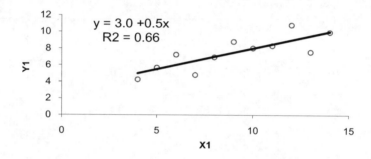

The scatter plot tells us that:

1.   The data set 'behaves like' a linear curve with some scatter (Y and X are linearly related);

2.   There is no justification for a more complicated model (e.g., quadratic);

3.   There are no outliers;

4.   The vertical spread of the data appears to be of equal height irrespective of the X-value (i.e. It is homoskedastic); this indicates that the data are equally precise throughout and so a 'regular' (that is, equi-weighted) fit is appropriate.

Coming to the second data set, unlike the statistics, the following simple scatter plot of the data set II (Y2 on X2) suggests a different story:

Figure 2.2: Scatter plot: Y2 on X2

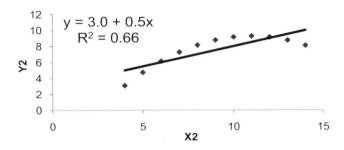

In fact, unlike the statistics, the two data sets are far from "equivalent" and a scatter plot of each data set, which would be step 1 of any Exploratory Data Analysis (EDA) approach, would tell us that immediately. Data set two – clearly shows a non-linear relationship.

Similarly, scatter plot of Y3 on X3 suggests a different story.

Figure 2.3: Scatter plot: Y3 on X3

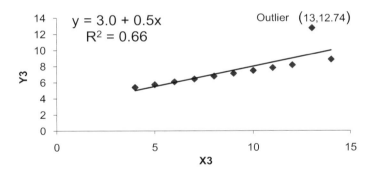

The scatter plot here reveals a basic linear relationship between X and Y for most of the data, and a single outlier (at X = 13). An outlier is defined as a data point that emanates from a different model than do the rest of the data. The data here appear to come from a linear model with a given slope and variation except for the outlier which appears to have been generated from some other model. Outlier detection is important for effective modelling. Outliers should be excluded from such model fitting. If all the data here are included in a linear regression, then the fitted model will be poor virtually everywhere. If the outlier is omitted from the fitting process, then the resulting fit will be excellent almost everywhere (for all points except the outlying point). Thus, removing the outlier will give us a different slope, intercept, etc as can be seen from Figure 2.3a. We have to note however that outliers do give us a hint or clue about an invent. It gives us an opportunity to scrutinize the data. Thus, you need to ask yourself why this outlier? What happened in that specific period? etc, to get to the bottom of the issue at hand.

Figure 2.3a: Scatter plot: Y3 on X3 by removing the outlier

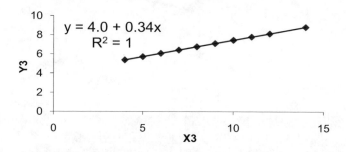

Finally, scatter plot of Y4 on X4 suggests a different story. Data set 4 is obviously the victim of a poor experimental design with a single point far removed from the bulk of the data "wagging the dog".

Figure 2.4:   Scatter plot: Y4 on X4

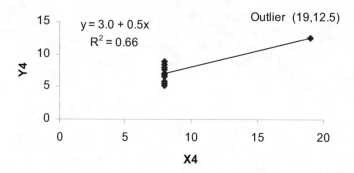

Removing the outlier will give us a different slope, intercept, etc. This is done in Figure 2.4a. This graph or relationship has no slope. Y4 has different values for fixed value of X. The association has no slope {Slope=(y2–y1)/(x2–x1) and x2–x1=0}

Figure 2.4a: Scatter plot: Y4 on X4 by removing the outlier

We hope that this factious data set provides an illustration of the need for "insight" and "feel" for a data set. They are the goals and the fruits of an open EDA approach to the data. Quantitative statistics could not be wrong per se, but they are incomplete. They are incomplete because they are numeric summaries, which in the summarization operation do a good job of focusing on a particular aspect of the data (e.g., location, intercept, slope, degree of relatedness, etc.) by judiciously reducing the data to a few numbers. Doing so also filters the data, necessarily omitting and screening out other sometimes-crucial information in the focusing operation. Quantitative statistics focus and filter; and filtering is exactly what makes the quantitative approach incomplete at best and misleading at worst. The estimated intercepts (= 3) and slopes (= 0.5) for data sets 1, 2, 3, and 4 are misleading because the estimation is done in the context of an assumed linear model and that linearity assumption is the fatal flaw in this analysis (Getenet, 2008).

A very versatile graph in STATA software is the scatter plot. You may have the scatter plot using the simple STATA command "graph" followed by the name of the variables to be plotted, such as X and Y. Thus, go to your STATA file and type the command: graph X, Y. This will offer you the following graph (see Figure 2.5). STATA has also a facility to weight (analytical weight: aweight; frequency weight: fweight; sampling weights: pweight and importing weight: iweight) your data and label the plot. For instance if you like to have the importance weight by density and also want to label the Y axis by 0, 10, 20, 30, 40 and 50; while the X axis by 0, 10, 20, and 30; and have the title 'Weighted Scatter Plot', you may use the following command:

graph X Y[iweight=density], ylable (0,10,20,30,40,50) xlable (0,10,20,30) tiltle (Weighted Scatter Plot).

Figure 2.5: Scatter plot of Ethiopian debt (1970–2001)

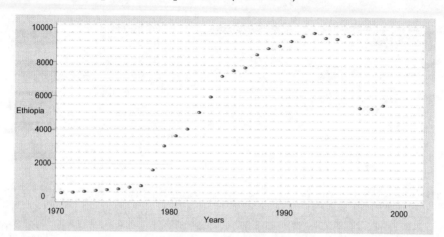

Another interesting scatter plot which is excellent for data exploration is the scatter plot matrix (see Figure 2.6) which can be generated using the command:

Graph X Y Z G F, matrix labor symbol(p)

Figure 2.6: Scatter plot matrix of debt for some African countries (1970–2001)

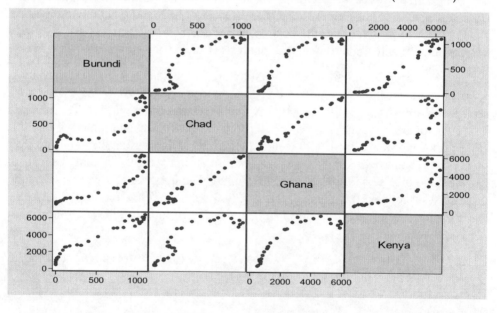

Another extremely important scatter plot is what is called "a two-way scatter plot" which can have box plots in the margin. Such scatter plots are important to make an inference about the nature of the distribution of the variable in question. This latter

16

information is important to help decide on whether the variable needs transformation to come to normality or not. You may use the following command to generate such scatter plots and box plots:

graph X Y, twoway oneway box title (Scatterplot with Marginal Boxplot and Oneway Scatterplot).

You may also generate box plots directly by using the command: *graph X, box*

Such box plots (see Figure 2.7) are helpful to understand the distribution characteristic of a series such as debt by African countries shown as Figure 2.6. Note for instance that the Ethiopian and Kenyan debt is relatively normally distributed while the other variables show some degree of skewness. When you run a regression and you want to check whether the error term (which is a linear combination of the dependent and explanatory variables) is normally distributed – which is the requirement in classical regression – you could learn a great deal from the box plot which of the variables could be possible sources of non-normality.

Figure 2.7:   Box plots of debt for some African countries (1970–2001)

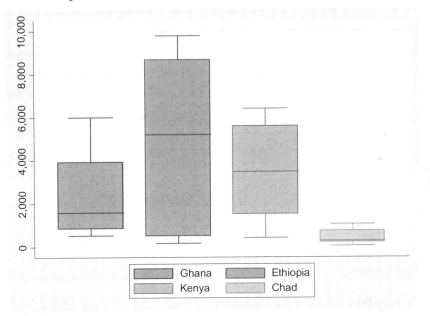

Use of summary statistics (such as mean and median, quintiles, etc.) creatively is another dimension of data exploration. We illustrate this from Alemayehu and Alem's (2006) study of the labour market in Ethiopia using household level data. As can be read from the summary statistic given in Table 2.1, median wage income was unchanged between the two rounds of the survey (1994 and 2000) at about 250.00 Birr, while mean incomes changed from about Birr 331.00 to Birr 386. The stagnation in median incomes, however, hides the changes that occurred at the lower and higher ends of the wage distribution. A more disaggregated comparison of changes in income across the rounds indicates that the largest percentage change in wage income occurred in the first (lowest) and fifth (richest) quintiles, and the smallest change in the third quintile. This pattern of change has important implications for the evolution of indicators of poverty. Given the observed level of head-count ratios, larger changes in poverty indicators would have occurred if changes in incomes were concentrated around the middle of the distribution instead of the extremes. In simple words, the growth that took place in the period doesn't seem to be pro-poor or distributional neutral as can be read from Table 2.1 below.

Table 2.1:   Level and inequality of wage incomes: Changes between 1994 and 2000

	Gini				Mean				Median			
	1994	2000	Change	%	1994	2000	Change	%	1994	2000	Change	%
Q1	30.96	23.71	-7.25	-23.41	42.45	64.11	21.66	51.02	38.44	65.99	27.55	71.66
Q2	10.69	10.15	-0.54	-5.04	136.99	146.20	9.21	6.72	134.56	142.99	8.43	6.27
Q3	8.95	9.38	0.43	4.81	249.42	254.84	5.41	2.17	250.00	246.50	-3.50	-1.40
Q4	8.31	8.75	0.44	5.28	405.55	448.94	43.39	10.70	400.00	441.70	41.70	10.43
Q5	23.56	27.10	3.54	15.02	857.08	1025.08	168.00	19.60	689.70	759.49	69.79	10.12

Figure 2.8:   Changes in the distribution of wage income per month (1994–2000, by quintile)

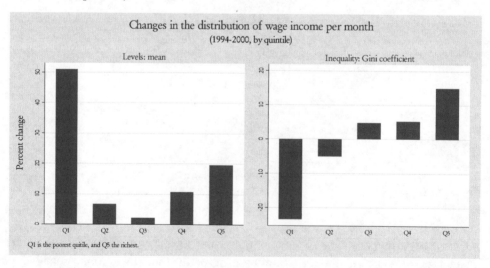

Inequality in individual-level wage incomes over the whole sample has changed only slightly. The change in inequality indicated by alternative indicators differed at this level of aggregation. A careful comparison of all indicators showed that those indicators that give greater weight to the left-hand side of the distribution indicated a decline, while the others indicated no change or an increase in inequality. Further investigation of changes in inequality by levels of income shows that the aggregate results hide interesting patterns of change at different levels of income. Inequality has declined substantially at the lower end of the distribution, remained unchanged in the middle, and increased at the upper end. Inequality among the lower-earning 40 percent of wage-workers declined (Gini coefficient falling from 34 to 27) while it increased in the remaining 60 percent (Gini coefficient rising from 32 to 36). The changes were such that inequality among the lower-earning 40 percent has become lower not only relative to its level in 1994, but also relative to the higher-earning 60 percent. Consistency between different indicators is also achieved once the analysis is done with income disaggregated by levels.

Another important tool in such data exploration is the use of a Kernel density estimation, which is a nonparametric way of estimating the probability of a random variable. Kernel density estimation makes it possible to extrapolate the data to the entire population. Figure 2.9 shows Kernel density estimates of wage income at two different periods at individual and household levels.

Figure 2.9: Kernel density estimates of wage income (1994 and 2000)

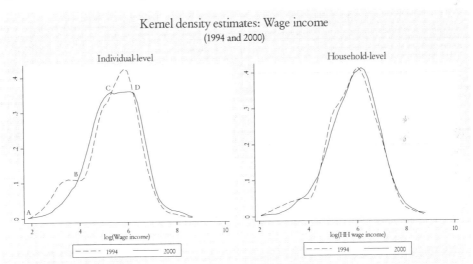

Once you have explored your data using data exploration techniques outlined in your STATA manual, you need to move towards modelling the pattern of data that you have observed thus far. Transformation is also crucial when we plan to model (or give a mathematical form) the pattern of data that we managed to read from carrying out data exploration using various techniques such as scatter plots. STATA's function "gladder", followed by the name of the variable of interest, offers an array of functional forms and their possible distribution in the process of searching for a function form for your model (see Figure 2.10). This is done in the spirit of Tukey's ladder of transformations or the Box-Cox transformation. From Figure 2.10 we note that the logarithmic transformation of the variable seems to offer the best approximation for normal distribution.

Figure 2.10: Functional forms that may fit Ghana's pattern of debt (1970–2001)

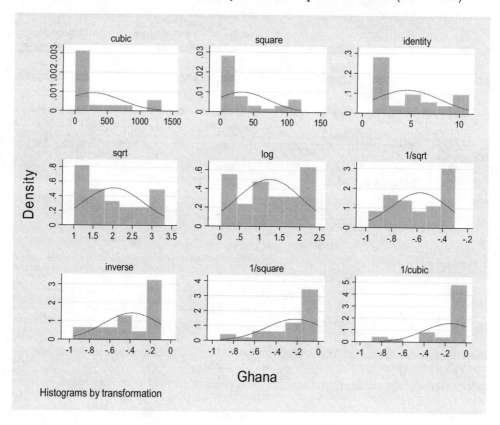

Thus, before you read how to formulate a more specific research question, we suggest that you take the time to have a good look at the evolution of the variable you seek to explain: for example, private investment in Kenya or South Africa. If we are interested in the evolution of the volume of investment, it is best to use investment at constant prices. Some authors, however, also use investment as a share of GDP as their dependent variable. You might wish to consider both variants, although we suggest you use the former variant: investment at constant prices. Now plot this variable against time and take a good look at it. Better still, plot the logarithms (which means transform the data) of this variable against time. Why is this better? Recall from your econometrics study why a plot of the logarithm of an economic time series against time is superior for detecting trends and its implication for distribution. Figure 2.7 below shows the scatter plot of

Ethiopian debt before and after transformation to a logarithmic form. In such a plot you need to inspect the graphs by paying attention to outliers, influential points and points of leverage.

Figure 2.11: Box plots of Ethiopia's debt and its logarithmic form (1970–2001)

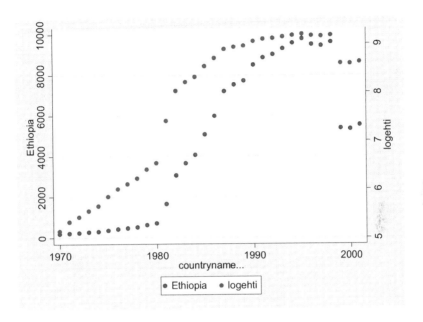

Let us attempt to use the discussion above to study the pattern of investment in Kenya. If you have looked at the evolution of Kenya's investment (and even more the logarithm of its investment) over time (see Figure 2.12), you will have noted that the 1990s (the grey-coloured area) witnessed a marked upsurge in private investment (note, however, the degree of this upturn in the log version). That is, the growth rate picked up. This is not surprising in view of the extensive reform and a major shift in major macro aggregates following the intensification of liberalization. One would expect that this might affect private investment behaviour. This gives you an interesting clue: do you expect the investment function to be stable over the period as a whole? Or might there have been a structural break in the 1990s that political and economic reform factors caused? These are questions you may want to investigate econometrically once you have decided on a particular model.

Figure 2.12: Pattern of investment in Kenya: 1972–1999

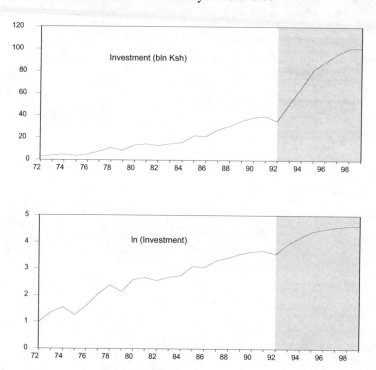

Another question you may want to ask is why investment seems to have surged upward at this time (note the outlier or influential points). Is it the type of investment? Here you may want to separate short-term investment in financial assets from fixed investments. One could also separate fixed investment into "productive" investment—machinery, and so on, from simply building. A further question would be to ask why investment is surging upward but the economy sinking into a recession in this period. Then the question of productivity becomes relevant.

Diagnostic Analysis

This technique is also referred to as "influence diagnostics and residual analysis". A number of researchers are familiar with residual analysis in the context of confirmatory analysis as argued by Mukherjee and Wuyts (1991); but diagnostic analysis are extremely useful tools of exploratory data analysis too. There are various residual plots that you may get using your STATA. This includes commands such as "avplot", "cvrplot", "lvr2plot", etc, which help carry out a diagnostic analysis on the residual. In your STATA such commands do function after running regression equation. It offers residual graphs such as Figures 2.13 and 2.14. You can learn a lot by focusing on influential points in the residual plot by examining the source of such influential points in the residual plot.

22

Figure 2.13: Residuals and fitted values from STATA

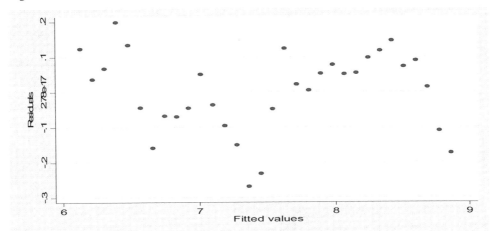

Figure 2.14: Normalised residuals and leverage from STATA

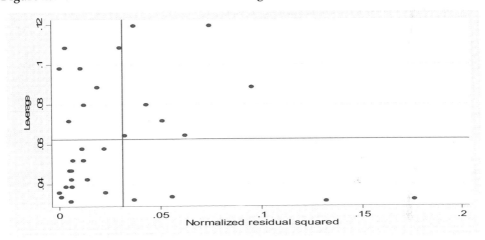

Narrowing Down the Research Question and Coping with Model Specification

Narrowing Down the Research Question

Let's assume your general question concerns the determinants of private investment in Kenya. Depending on the nature of your work, you may be expected to deal with the issue in all of its forms, or you may not be expected to deal with this question exhaustively. If the latter, it is best to narrow down your task by setting yourself a more specific task within the confines of this general question. Here are two broad suggestions as to how you might do this.

1. One possible avenue is to compare and contrast demand-side with supply-side theories of investment. In this case, we suggest that you compare the accelerator and the user cost models in terms of how well they explain private investment behaviour in the Kenyan economy. You might even decide to end up with a mongrel (= mixed) specification that borrows elements from each in a single specification;

2. Another avenue is to examine whether public investment crowds out or crowds in private investment. That is, your specific research question will be to assess the impact of public investment on private investment.

Each of these avenues gives your research a more limited task. The former involves comparing how well different theories of investment explain the empirical evidence; the latter investigates a specific policy question. In each case, however, it is important to think carefully about the specification of your model. Which variables should you include? Should you use log-transformed variables or not? How should you deal with lagged variables? What are the expected signs of the coefficients in the model? Which hypotheses are interesting to test? Is the model stable across the period as a whole?

As to the last question, we suggest that you investigate specifically whether model stability pertained during the 1990s. To do this, you can use Chow's test or some other technique. Alternatively, you may wish to use dummy variables to single out the 1990s. The important point is not just to introduce dummies but also to explain their meaning. Before you introduce dummies, it is always advisable to estimate the model recursively, understand the profile of the coefficients estimated, and then locate the effect the dummies will have in stabilizing the coefficients. You should note that if dummies cannot be explained/motivated, it may be construed as a data mining exercise.

Coping with Model Specifications

Specifying a model is a task that requires skill and experience. This is particularly true when we work with time-series data, where we often use lagged variables to denote that what happened in the past has repercussions for the present. From theory, it depicts the process of adjustment towards some level. For example, in dealing with investment functions, you may wish to try out a specific type of models that aims to capture the fact that adjustment is neither smooth nor immediate. This is the partial adjustment model. On the other hand, to be able to deal with the problem of crowding in or out of private investment by public investment, it is necessary to bring public investment explicitly into the picture as an explanatory variable. You may do this in the context of a mixed specification using a partial adjustment model. You may wish to try out your own pet theory instead.

When dealing with the crowding-in-crowding-out hypothesis, it matters what assumptions you make about the lags of the explanatory variables. The important point is that your assumptions about these lags should be reasonable. For example, on the one hand, private investors may immediately react to initiating construction of new infrastructure that may take time to complete, or they may respond with a certain lag after its completion. On the other hand, high levels of government investment may reduce private capital's access to finance. For these reasons, it is advisable to try out various lags (say, zero to five years) to check the effect of public investment on private investment. In Kenya, for instance, we found current and five-year lagged public investment have statistically significant (positive) impact on private investment.

From Model Specification to Estimation

It is one thing to have specified your theoretical model but quite another to estimate it. Estimation requires not only skill but also patience. Since most macro models rely on time-series data, we will focus on estimation based on time series data, that is, on macroeconometrics. We will use data from Kenya, Mozambique and Ethiopia to motivate the exposition.

The first main point to note at estimation stage is that econometrics is not a mechanical procedure. You need to withdraw yourself from the mechanics of it and see the whole issue from a wider perspective, and in particular, in light of the questions posed at the beginning of your inquiry. The second important point is that since you are confronting your theory with data at this stage, you have a lot of room to modify it in light of those data—you should repeatedly move back and forth between data and theory. This means going back to your original theory to revise it further, coming back to your data with the revised theory . . . and so on. In this interactive process, you need to make sure that each of your move back and forth is a justifiable move. You should not simply move mechanically from unit root test, to cointegration, to error-correction modelling, to theory and so on. Each step should justify your conclusions at every stage. The details of this estimation technique and its application are taken up in the next chapter.

Chapter 3

TIME SERIES PROPERTIES OF MACRO VARIABLES: TESTING FOR UNIT ROOTS

Introduction

The last three decades 1970–2000, witnessed a revolution in time series econometrics. This followed the classic work of Engle and Granger (1987) and its subsequent development by important contributors that include the econometric team in UK which is led by David Hendry. Their fundamental contribution is to question the validity of the "stationarity" assumptions of classical regression technique in light of the time series property of macro variables. The classical regression technique, the Ordinary Least Squares (OLS), assumes that the variables under consideration are 'stationary', which means, in simple words, their mean, variance and covariance are time invariant. It is found that almost all macroeconomic variables are non-stationary. Unfortunately, a regression carried out with such non-stationary series gives spurious results and is referred to as "spurious" or "non-sense" regression. The rest of this chapter is devoted to how detect such problems as well as how to address them in a satisfactory manner.

Theoretical Time Series Issues

Before we proceed to the actual testing of the assumption of stationary (also called the unit root test) using actual African data, let us briefly state the formal concept of stationarity and unit root.

Covariance and Difference Stationarity

Covariance stationarity: if (y_t) is a stationary series (i.e., time invariant variable), it would have a finite mean, variance, and the covariance between any two consecutive periods which are time invariant or constant. That is,

$$E(y_t) = \mu \text{ and } Var(y_t) = \sigma_y^2$$

$$Cov(y_t, y_{t-s}) = Cov(y_{t-j}, y_{t-s-j}) = \gamma_s \qquad [3.1]$$

Where μ, σ_y^2 and γ_s are all constants. μ is the mean, σ_y^2 is the variance and γ_s is the covariance.

In simple words, a stationary variable is mean reverting while a non-stationary one diverts from its mean with time. A stationary variable doesn't contain a unit root. A nonstationary variable, on the other hand, is said to contain unit root in the autoregressive process. That is,

$$y_t = \phi y_{t-1} + \varepsilon_t \quad \text{and} \quad \phi \geq |1| \qquad [3.2]$$

Figure 3.1: Stationary and nonstationary time series variable

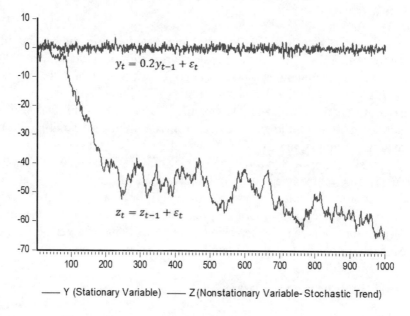

—— Y (Stationary Variable) —— Z (Nonstationary Variable- Stochastic Trend)

Perhaps in economic interpretation, ϕ is the memory strength of the variable so that, as it tends to unity, the variable predicts itself from history. In such non-stationary case, it is easy to show that $E(y_t) - t\mu$ and $Var(y_t) t\sigma_y^2$. Thus, a test for a unit root is fundamentally a test for whether $\phi \leq 1$. This could be shown using a data generating process (DGP) of pth order autoregressive (AR) formulation given by:

$$y_t = \phi_1 y_{t-1} + \phi_2 y_{t-2} + \ldots + \phi_p y_{t-p} + u_t \qquad [3.3]$$

Collecting all the y terms to the left-hand side and using a polynomial lag operator, equation 3.3 could be written as,

$$\Phi(L)y_t = u_t \quad \text{where} \quad \Phi(L) = 1 - \phi_1 L - \phi_2 L^2 - \ldots - \phi_p L^p \qquad [3.4]$$

If the roots of the characteristic equation $\left(1 - \phi_1 L - \phi_2 L^2 - \ldots - \phi_p L^p\right) = 0$ are all greater than unity in absolute value then y_t is stationary. For instance for the simple AR(1) process, if the root of $1 - \phi_1 L = 0$ is greater than unity in absolute value, then y_t will be stationary. Stated alternatively, the AR(1) model is stationary if $|\phi_1| < 1$, since the root is simply $L = \dfrac{1}{\phi_1}$ which will be > 1 if $|\phi_1| < 1$.

We may generalize this formulation for a general AR(p) process, involving up to 'p' unit roots by reformulating [3.3] in terms of change in $y_t [= \Delta y_t]$ (or the first difference of y):

$$\Delta y_t = \phi^* y_{t-1} + \phi_1^* \Delta y_{t-1} + \phi_2^* \Delta y_{t-2} + \cdots + \phi_{p-1}^* \Delta y_{t-p+1} + u_t \qquad [3.5]$$

We would expect that if $\phi^* = 0$, there is a unit root in equation [3.5]. This can be shown vividly if we formulate equation [3.5] as an AR(3) process. This AR(3) process could be given by [3.6a]

$$\left(1 - \phi_1 L - \phi_2 L^2 - \phi_3 L^3\right) y_t = u_t \qquad [3.6a]$$

If a unit root exists, the coefficient (the lag operator term) in the left hand side of equation [3.6a] could be factorized as [3.6b], which is equivalent with [3.6c].

$$\left(1 + \alpha L + \beta L^2\right)(1 - L) y_t = u_t \qquad [3.6b]$$

$$\left(1 + \alpha L + \beta L^2\right) \Delta y_t = u_t \qquad [3.6c]$$

Equation [3.6b = 3.6c] in turn could be solved for Δy_t to make it similar, and hence comparable, with equation [3.5]. This is given as equation [3.6d],

$$\Delta y_t = -\alpha L \Delta y_t - \beta L^2 \Delta y_t + u_t = -\alpha \Delta y_{t-1} - \beta \Delta y_{t-2} + u_t \qquad [3.6d]$$

We know that equation [3.6d] has a unit root because we have assumed that it can be factorized as equation [3.6b]. Given the similarity of equation [3.6d] and [3.5], there will be a unit root in equation [3.5] if only $\phi^* = 0$, which in turn implies that $\phi_1 + \phi_2 + \phi_3 = 1$. On the other hand, if $\phi^* < 0$, then $\phi_1 + \phi_2 + \phi_3 < 1$, and y_t must be stationary. Thus, testing for stationarity is essentially testing the hypothesis that $\phi^* = 0$ against the alternative $\phi^* < 0$.

Exposition of Some Time Series Characteristics Using Monte Carlo Simulation

The underlying philosophy of Monte Carlo simulation is that the behaviour of a statistic in random samples can be assessed by the empirical process of actually drawing lots of random samples and observing this behaviour. The key steps are as follows:

(i)   Specify the "pseudo population in symbolic terms in such a way that it can be used to generate samples. We do this by developing a computer algorithm to generate data in a specified manner;

(ii)   Calculate statistic of interest;

(iii)   Repeat the process several times;

(iv)   Assess the statistic and make conclusions.

We use this approach to analyse some concepts in time series econometrics. One important key concept is that for stationary variables, the covariance between any two consecutive periods depends on the distance between the lags (for instance lag 1 and lag 2 should be same as lag 5 and lag 6). This is not the case for nonstationary variables. We can illustrate this using Monte Carlo simulation in EVIEWS as follows:

(i)   Open a blank file in EVIEWS to store the series generated using file→new→workfile. You can use undated series with 1000 observations.

(ii)   Write a small program. This can be done by opening a new program as shown in Illustration 3.1 and typing appropriate commands using EVIEWS syntax.

Illustration 3.1: How to create a new program in EVIEWS

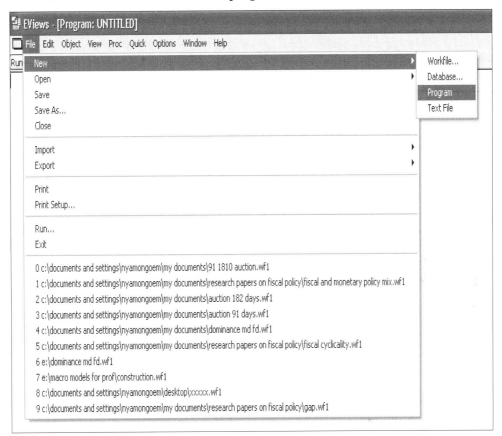

When you click on the program, you will have a blank screen where you can type your commands.

(i)   Save the program using a name of your choice;

(ii)   Run the model by clicking on the run icon;

(iii)   Generate lags 1,2, …5 or any other number;

(iv)   Repeat the process several times;

(v)   Assess the properties.

We need to understand what to type on the program. To generate variables with specific characteristics, we use nrd command in EVIEWS which generates (pseudo) random draws from a normal distribution with zero mean and unit variance. We can then change that to reflect other characteristics. For instance, let's generate a variable called y with an initial value of 0 and vary the autoregressive coefficient. For a stationary variable, say with an AR parameter of 0.2, the commands are as follows:

```
smpl @first @first
series y = 0
smpl @first+1 @last
series y = .2*y(-1)+nrnd
```

This is equivalent to generating $y_t = 0.2y_{t-1} + \varepsilon_t$, $\varepsilon_t \sim \text{Niid}\left(0, \sigma_t^2\right)$. Notice that the initial value is zero i.e. $y_0 = 0$.

Let's also generate a nonstationary variable by changing the AR root as follows:

```
smpl @first @first
series y = 0
smpl @first+1 @last
series y = 1*y(-1)+nrnd
```

This is equivalent to a pure random walk variable $y_t = y_{t-1} + \varepsilon_t$, $\varepsilon_t \sim \text{Niid}\left(0, \sigma_t^2\right)$. In this case, we are playing the role of nature by specifying the DGP ourselves. Let's now assess our data to see whether they meet our theoretical priors about stationary and nonstationary data.

Assessment

We need to generate lags by using the generate command in EVIEWS. You can do this from the workfile by clicking on *gen* and type y_1 = y(-1). To generate y lagged two periods, you can use y_2 = y(-2), etc. You can then open the series as a group and compute the correlation for stationary series and nonstationary series. Ideally the process should be repeated several times but we simply illustrate with one sample. The results are as shown in Table 3.1.

Table 3.1: **Monte Carlo simulation for stationary time series**

$$Cov(y_t, y_{t-3}) = Cov(y_{t-1}, y_{t-4}) = Cov(y_{t-2}, y_{t-5})$$
$$Cov(y_t, y_{t-1}) = Cov(y_{t-1}, y_{t-2}) = Cov(y_{t-2}, y_{t-3}) = Cov(y_{t-3}, y_{t-4}) = Cov(y_{t-4}, y_{t-5})$$

	Y	Y_1	Y_2	Y_3	Y_4	Y_5
Y	**0.9935**	**0.2356**	0.0044	*-0.0168*	-0.04345	-0.0586
Y_1	0.2357	**0.9937**	**0.2362**	0.0035	*-0.0166*	-0.0492
Y_2	0.0044	0.2362	**0.9931**	0.2364	0.0036	*-0.0152*
Y_3	-0.0168	0.0035	0.2364	**0.9939**	0.2360	0.0083
Y_4	-0.0434	-0.0166	0.0036	0.2360	**0.9940**	0.2339
Y_5	-0.0586	-0.0492	-0.0152	0.0083	0.2339	**1.0219**

As expected, the variance is approximately the same for all lags and covariance depends on the difference between the lags only.

For nonstationary data, the situation is quite different as shown in Table 3.2. The variances for the various lags differ and the covariances differ for each lag. It is this characteristic that makes modelling nonstationary time series a challenging task.

Table 3.2: **Monte Carlo simulation for nonstationary time series**

	Z	Z_1	Z_2	Z_3	Z_4	Z_5
Z	**45.3965**	45.683	45.9953	*46.3282*	46.6273	47.0240
Z_1	45.6834	**46.9092**	47.2666	47.5603	*47.8499*	48.2162
Z_2	45.9953	47.2666	**48.5630**	48.9030	49.1523	*49.5106*
Z_3	46.3282	47.5603	48.9030	**50.1813**	50.4769	50.7950
Z_4	46.6273	47.8499	49.1523	50.4769	**51.7118**	52.0748
Z_5	47.0240	48.2162	49.5106	50.7950	52.0748	**53.3792**

$$Cov(z_t, z_{t-1}) \neq Cov(z_{t-1}, z_{t-2}) \neq Cov(z_{t-2}, z_{t-3}) \neq Cov(z_{t-3}, z_{t-4}) \neq Cov(z_{t-4}, z_{t-5})$$

$$Cov(z_t, z_{t-3}) \neq Cov(z_{t-1}, z_{t-4}) \neq Cov(z_{t-2}, z_{t-5})$$

Trend Stationarity

We can also generate a variable to assess trend stationarity. This is done by simply amending our program by introducing trend in the stationary variable and plotting both variables. You can generate a trend variable in EVIEWS by using @trend (starting date) command. For instance to generate trend called t, we go to gen and in the equation menu type t=@trend(0).

The program can then be amended by including @trend(0).

> **smpl @first @first**
> **series y = 0**
> **smpl @first+1 @last**
> **series y = .2*y(-1)+@trend(0)+nrnd**

This is equivalent to $y_t = 0.2y_{t-1} + t + \varepsilon_t$, $\varepsilon_t \sim \text{Niid}(0, \sigma_t^2)$. The results for 100 observations are as in Figure 3.2.

Figure 3.2: Covariance stationary and trend stationary variables

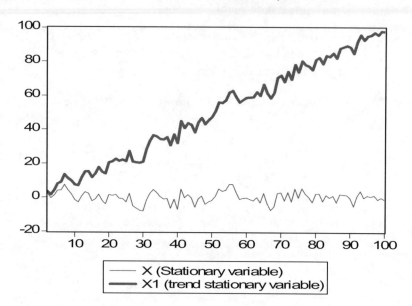

Difference Stationarity

This is a variable that has a stochastic trend but when it is differenced, it becomes stationary. We plot the nonstationary variable in levels and first difference in Figure 3.3.

Figure 3.3: Nonstationary variable in levels and first difference

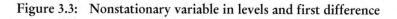

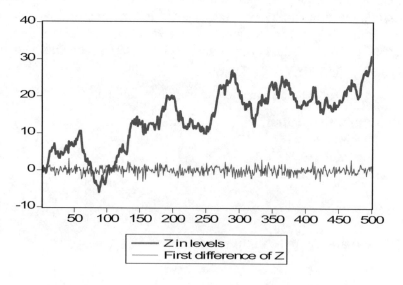

Unit Root Tests

The most commonly used unit root tests in applied work, such as the Dickey-Fuller test (DF), the Augmented Dickey-Fuller test (ADF) and the Phillips-Perron test (PP) that are also used in this text, are based on the exposition given thus far.

The Dickey FullerTest

The simplest version of the DF test is based on the following estimate:

$y_t = \phi y_{t-1} + u_t$ or $\Delta y_t = (\phi - 1)y_{t-1} + u_t$. It then tests for

$$H_0 : \phi = 1 \big[\equiv (\phi - 1) = 0\big] \quad \text{against} \quad H_1 : \phi < 1 \big[\equiv (\phi - 1) < 0\big] \qquad [3.7]$$

The ADF test augments the formulation by adding generous lagged levels of the change in the dependent variable to produce a better white-noise error term. It could be given by:

$$\Delta y_t = \phi^* y_{t-1} + \phi^*_1 \Delta y_{t-1} + \phi^*_2 \Delta y_{t-2} + \cdots + \phi^*_{p-1} \Delta y_{t-1+1} u_t \qquad [3.8]$$

Where

$\phi^* = \phi_1 + \phi_2 + \phi_3 + \cdots + \phi_p - 1$ and $= (\phi - 1)$ for the case of [3.7] where $p = 1$

$\phi^*_i = -(\phi_{i+1} + \cdots + \phi_p)$ and $= -\phi_2$ for the case of [3.7] where $p = 1$

Finally, the ADF type test includes additional higher order lagged terms to account for the fact that the underlying data generating process is more complicated than a simple AR(1) process and this augmentation will "whiten" the error term. Phillips (1987) and Phillips and Perron (1988) suggested a non-parametric correction to the test statistics which are basically used in such tests to account for the autocorrelation, and hence, possible non-white noise processes, that will be present when ADF type augmentation is done. Phillips and Perron (1988) have generalized the ADF test to the case where the disturbance terms are serially correlated by introducing a correction term to the test statistics of ADF test, instead of whitening the error term by adding the differenced lagged dependent value of the unit root test regression equation as is estimated by Dickey and Fuller (see, among others, Patterson 2000 for detail and the formula). The Phillips and Perron correction is sometimes referred as "a nonparametric" approach while the ADF procedure is referred as "a parametric approach". Note also the notation in the literature that a variable that needs to be differentiated d times to be stationary is referred as an I(d) series. In the rest of this section we demonstrate the use of these tests in applied work.

Hands on About Unit Root Test With PCGIVE

Let us now help you to carry out unit root test using PCGIVE and EVIEWS. In PCGIVE we can test for unit root. The first step is to import the data from any spread sheet program like EXCEL to GiveWin. To import the data from Excel use the following procedure:

(i)   Open GiveWin;

(ii)   Go to file.

Once the data is imported, the next step is to go to modules in GiveWin and select PCGIVE menu ➔ Model➔Descriptive statistics. This procedure will take you to a dialog table which prompts you to select the variables of interest and the lag length. Next, select the variables that you want to test for unit root and click OK. This will take you to another dialog table as shown below. Check COMPUTE UNIT-ROOT TESTS. (See Illustration 3.2 below.)

Illustration 3.2:   Descriptive statistics

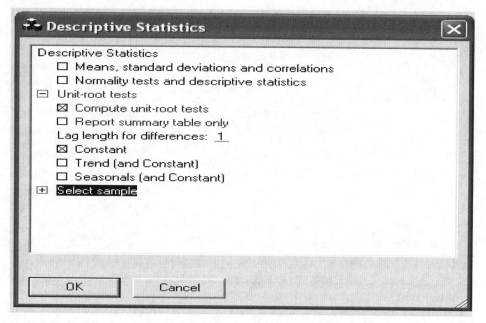

After the lag length for the ADF test is determined, another important step is to make decision about the inclusion of a constant, trend or constant and trend term together in the ADF equation. The decision whether to include these terms or not depends on the nature of the data. For example, if the variable is supposed to have a zero mean (as in the case of the error term), there is no need to include either a constant or a trend. Otherwise, it is wise to include a constant and/or a trend to capture any drift and/or time trend in the data. This can be done by checking the appropriate box as shown in Illustration 3.2. Table 3.3 presents a unit root test results for our data for logarithm of real private consumption (LRCP) in Ethiopia.

Table 3.3: **Unit root test using Ethiopian data**

```
Unit-root tests for 1965 (1) to 2001 (1)
Augmented Dickey-Fuller test for LRCP; regression of DLRCP on:

                  Coefficient        Std.Error          t-value
LRCP_1            -0.012329          0.036643           -0.33646
Constant           0.14852           0.32654            0.45484
DLRCP_1           -0.17593           0.17001            -1.0348

sigma = 0.0733862  DW = 2.064  DW-LRCP = 0.05504  ADF-LRCP = -0.3365
Critical values used in ADF test: 5%=-2.942, 1%=-3.617
RSS = 0.1831082894 for 3 variables and 37 observations
```

The interpretation of unit root results follows a standard Neyman-Pearson framework where the parameter space is divided into "acceptance" and "rejection" regions as shown in Figure 3.4. Generally unit root tests are left tailed. The exception is the test by Kwiatkowski *et al.* (1992) referred to as KPSS, which has a null of stationarity. If the computed ADF statistic falls in the rejection region, we reject the null hypothesis of unit roots and conclude that the series is stationary. Conversely, if the ADF statistic falls in the acceptance region we fail to reject the null hypothesis and conclude that the series is nonstationary.

Figure 3.4: **Nonstationary variable in levels and first difference**

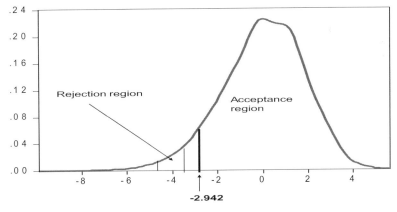

Table 3.4 shows that LRCP is non stationary since the computed ADF *t*-value (-0.3365) falls in the acceptance region for at 1% and 5% critical values. This necessitates differencing LRCP until the data becomes stationary. To difference LRCP, go to GiveWin → tools and calculator. In calculator, select LRCP, then click the button DIFF, choose the level of difference (i.e., differencing once or twice) and click '=' button. This would prompt you for the desired variable name.

By default GiveWin gives a name such as DLRCP. Click the button OK and the variable would be created. To test for stationarity of DLRCP use the same procedure as above and you would get the result given in Table 3.4. The result shows that DLRCP is stationary as the computed ADF *t*-value is greater than the critical value (in absolute terms) at 1% and 5% levels of significance. Thus, LRCP is an I(1) series.

Table 3.4:   Augmented Dickey Fuller test for DLRCP

```
Augmented Dickey-Fuller test for DLRCP; regression of DDLRCP on:

                  Coefficient        Std.Error          t-value
DLRCP_1            -1.4715            0.25568            -5.7551
Constant            0.047798          0.014171           3.3730
DDLRCP_1            0.24459           0.16669            1.4674

sigma = 0.0712858  DW = 1.976  DW-DLRCP = 2.341 ADF-DLRCP = -5.755**
Critical values used in ADF test: 5%=-2.942, 1%=-3.617
RSS = 0.1727765045 for 3 variables and 37 observations
```

Similar procedure could also be used to test for stationarity of the remaining variables. The unit root test for real income (RY) and price level (P) shows that the variables are non-stationary in levels while their first difference is stationary. Hence all of our variables for our consumption equation are I(1) series.

ADF is not the only test statistics to test for stationarity. Among others, the Phillips-Perron test for unit root is also another test statistics for unit root having its own peculiar features such as being non-parametric. PCGIVE does not have this test. Thus, we need to switch to EVIEWS for this test statistics. In EVIEWS, once the data is loaded go to: Quick ➔ series statistics➔ unit root test. This would take you to a dialog box illustratration 3.3.

Illustration 3.3:   Unit root test

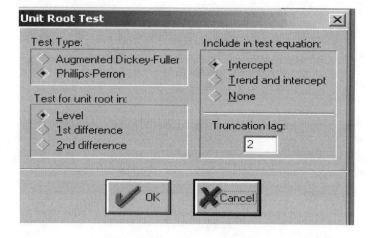

In the dialog box, check Phillips-Perron, determine whether the test would apply to the level or the difference of the variable and choose the lag length for truncation and the inclusion of intercept and/or trend terms. The result of the Phillips-Perron test for LRCP shown in Table 3.5 also tells us that LRCP is non-stationary in levels.

Table 3.5:   PP test LRCP

```
PP Test Statistic   -0.075775      %    Critical Value*           -3.6067
                                   5%   Critical Value            -2.9378
                                   10%  Critical Value            -2.6069
*MacKinnon critical values for rejection of hypothesis of a unit root.

Lag truncation for Bartlett kernel: 3  (Newey-West suggests: 3)
Residual variance with no correction                            0.004903
Residual variance with correction                               0.002892

Phillips-Perron Test Equation
Dependent Variable: D(LRCP)
Method: Least Squares
Date:   08/24/03        Time: 18:29
Sample(adjusted): 1963 2001
Included observations: 39 after adjusting endpoints
```

Variable	Coefficient	Std. Error	t-Statistic	Prob.
LRCP(-1)	-0.010436	0.033056	-0.315709	0.7540
C	0.124902	0.294176	0.424582	0.6736
R-squared	0.002687	Mean dependent var	0.032099	
Adjusted R-squared	-0.024268	S.D. dependent var	0.071034	
S.E. of regression	0.071890	Akaike info criterion	-2.377432	
Sum squared resid	0.191224	Schwarz criterion	-2.292121	
Log likelihood	48.35992	F-statistic	0.099672	
Durbin-Watson stat	2.334978	Prob(F-statistic)	0.753997	

The above analysis shows that the presence of a unit root in macro variables is not uncommon. If left uncorrected, this will lead to the problem of spurious regression when there is need to model relationships suggested by a researcher. The question is what is the solution?

Differencing the I(1) series above would tackle the non-stationary problem, however, you would lose the long-run information in the data, which is central to your theoretical model. Thus, you need to think of a mechanism by which you can tackle the problem of spurious regression and have the long-run information as well. This basically requires combining the short-run (differenced) equation with the long-run (level-based) equation in one model. This can be done provided you can find a vector that renders a linear combination of the level variables that is stationary. Such vector is referred as the cointegrating vector, and the method of using it to generate a stationary linear combination is termed as "cointegration analysis". It is one of the recent developments in time-series econometrics and is discussed in the next chapter.

Problems With Unit Root Testing

Testing for unit roots is not that straightforward as we have done. There are some important issues that must be taken into consideration. First, there is a concern that if structural breaks exist and are not taken into consideration, they may lead to under-rejection of the null hypothesis. Second, it is necessary to take into account the correct data generating process (DGP) in terms of pure random walk, random walk with drift and random walk with drift and time trend. Third, when dealing with small samples, the standard tests for unit roots are biased towards accepting the null hypothesis of non-stationarity when the true DGP is stationary i.e. low power of the tests. Fourth, it is possible to have multiple unit roots. One needs to follow the "Pantula principle" to identify the level of integration. Finally, unit root test may be affected by the frequency at which data is observed (i.e. seasonal unit roots). It is therefore important to include centred seasonal dummies or deseasonalise the data. Let us focus mainly on the structural breaks as they are the most common problems of data from developing countries.

Unit Roots and Structural Breaks

The Dickey-Fuller type tests of unit root are sensitive to structural breaks in the data. Such tests confuse structural break with non-stationarity. A truly stationary variable with some structural breaks may be labelled to be non-stationary. Fortunately, there are some tests that take structural breaks into consideration in testing for unit root.

Andrews and Zivot (1992) provided the test for unit root in the presence of one structural break while Clemente, Montañés and Reyes (1998) introduced the test for unit root in the case of two breaks and they distinguished between additive outliers (which captures a sudden change in a series) and innovational outliers (allowing for a gradual shift in the mean of the series). These tests are not yet available in PCGIVE. However, they can be implemented using STATA[2]. We illustrate the problem of structural break in testing for unit root using Ethiopian data on agricultural output per capita.

We first test for unit root using the Augmented Dickey Fuller test. The result presented in Table 3.6 shows that the null of non-stationarity cannot be rejected. Let's now plot the log of per capita agricultural output to check for structural breaks.

---

[2] See for detail: BAUM, C. F. (2001): "Stata: The Language of Choice for Time Series Analysis", *The Stata Journal*, 1, 1–16.

Table 3.6:   Augmented Dickey Fuller test of log of per capita agricultural output

```
Unit-root tests for 1964 (1) to 2003 (1)
Variable: Log of Per Capita Agricultural Output
LPCI: augmented Dickey-Fuller tests (T=40, Constant)

D-lag     t-adf beta Y_1     sigma  t-DY_lag  t-prob      AIC   F-prob
2       -0.04942  0.99707   0.06335   -4.195   0.0002   -5.424
1        -0.7059  0.95056   0.07624  -0.01828  0.9855   -5.076   0.0002
                        0   -0.7365   0.95028 0.07523   -5.126   0.0008
```

Figure 3.5 presents the actual and HP filtered log of per capita agricultural output. It shows that there are at least two structural breaks in the series. As our data (1960/61 to 2002/3) covers, three different regimes with different agricultural policies, structural breaks are expected to be an important feature of agricultural output per capita. With this information, we proceed to test for unit root in the presence of these breaks.

Figure 3.5:   Actual and HP Filter of per capita agricultural output

The Clemente, Montañés and Reyes (1998) test in STATA identified two structural breaks and the null of unit root is rejected (see Table 3.7 and Figure 3.7). That is, agricultural output per capita is a mean reverting process that fluctuates randomly around a certain stationary level implying that its growth is zero over a long period of time. Figure 3.6 shows the trends in the growth of the actual and smoothed levels of agricultural output per capita. Once the structural breaks and the erratic fluctuations are filtered out, the growth in agricultral output per capita flatten out as shown by the broken line.

41

Table 3.7:   Clement-Montañés-Reyes double IO test for unit root

```
Clemente-Montañés-Reyes unit-root test with double mean shifts, IO
model

Log of Agricultural output per   T = 39      optimal breakpoints: 1975/6,
capita                                       1982/3

AR(2)            dul     dul2     (rho -1)  const
Coefficients:   -0.0939 -0.1992  -0.7630    3.9246
t-statistics:   -2.492  -2.952   -3.059
P-values:        0.018   0.006   -5.490 (5% crit.value)

Null of Unit root is rejected
```

Another interesting result is that the structural breaks tally with the regime change in 1975/76 and the period just after policy changes, 1982/83, that introduced "incentive non-compatible" policies such as compulsory grain delivery and socialization of production in the form of producers' cooperation as well as the severe drought that hit the country in 1983/84. though there was a major regime shift in 1991 that introduced many pro-agricultural policies, the data do not show any structural break following the regime change. This may indicate the absence of substantial innovative shock that changed per capita agricultural output and persists over time after the regime shift in 1991.

Figure 3.6:   Growth rate of agricultural output per capita

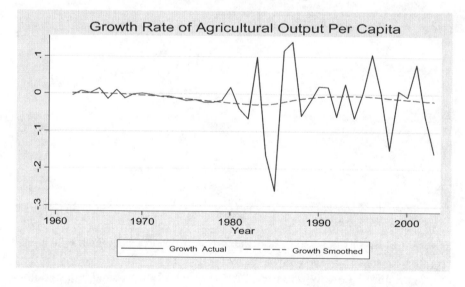

Figure 3.7: Clement-Montañés-Reyes double IO test for unit root

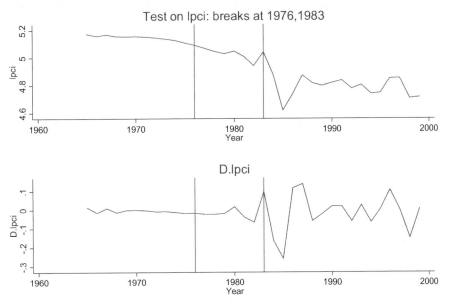

This exercise emphasizes taking structural breaks seriously. Disregarding structural breaks may give a completely different conclusion that is far from the reality. One should take a serious look on structural breaks especially when there are some reasons to believe that the series is stationary.

Another common problem relates to trend stationary variables whose normal testing using unit root tests would difference the series and then render the tests weak due to the problem of over-differencing. This problem can easily be detected by graphing the data over time to see if it oscillates around a trend. Most I(1) variables will exhibit a stochastic trend.

Chapter 4

COINTEGRATION ANALYSIS

Introduction to Cointegration (CI) and Error Correction Models (ECM)

The classical regression model assumes that the dependent and independent variables are stationary over time. Most economic variables, however, exhibit long-run trend movement and only become stationary after they are differenced. Applying the classical regression techniques to the levels of variables leads to a spurious correlation, particularly when the variables involved exhibit consistent trend, either upward or downwards, over time [see Thomas, 1993]. The empirical literature for unit root shows that almost all macro variables are non-stationary in level while their difference is stationary. This implies that almost all variables are integrated of degree one i.e. are I(1). A special case would be targeted variables like budget deficit to Gross Domestic Proudction (GDP) ratio-then such variables would oscillate around their target (mean) and so stationary over time.

To take care of the non-stationarity of the variables and confirm whether there exists a long run equilibrium relationship, the cointegration concept is used. This concept basically refers to the condition that even if individual series are non-stationary (i.e. are I(1) series), if there exists a linear combination of these I(1) series in the regression equation and is stationary, then the regression is not a spurious regression. From economic theory, a group of variables may be tied together by the same theory. In empirical work, this relationship can be uncovered by cointegration analysis. There are two basic ways of testing the existence of cointegration between variables of interest and estimating the co-integrating vector: the Engle-Granger or EG Approach and the Johansen Approach. We begin our exposition by the relatively simpler EG Approach. This will be followed by the relatively advanced Johansen Methodology. The application of the two approaches is shown using PCGIVE econometrics software.

The Engle-Granger (EG) Two-Step Approach

Following Engle and Granger (1987), two or more time series are cointegrated of order d,b; and they are denoted CI (d,b) if they are integrated of order d, but a linear combination of these variables exists that is integrated of order b, where $b < d$.

The first approach (the Engle-Granger two-stage approach) begins by testing whether the variables of interest are stationary or not. If variables contemplated in the model follow an I(1) process, then in the first stage, estimates of the long-run equilibrium equation (using OLS) are made. Then an ADF test on the residual of the long-run equation, which is equal to the linear combination of the variables of interest, is conducted to determine if the variables in question are cointegrated— that is, whether the error term follows a stationary process. If the error term is stationary (taken as proof of cointegration), in the second stage, we could combine the error term with the first difference of the variables (short-run indicators) to estimate the final model. This last model is called an Error Correction Model (ECM). This formulation helps to show the deviation from the equilibrium position and how an adjustment towards the equilibrium is made by combining both the long and short run versions of the model in one regression.

The explanation above can be shown using Keynesian theory of consumption. Current consumption, c_t, depends on current disposable income y_t:

$$c_t = \alpha + \beta y_t + \varepsilon_t \qquad [4.1]$$

Where α is autonomous consumption that does not depend on disposable income and should be positive and β is the marginal propensity to consume and is a positive fraction.

Using EG approach and assuming $[c_t, y_t] \sim I(1)$ then $\varepsilon_t = c_t - \alpha - \beta y_t$ is a linear combination of the variables in the model; and if $\varepsilon_t \sim I(0)$, then this linear combination of the variables, which is ε, forms a cointegrating vector. This allows a reparameterisation (even with lags) of the consumption model as in equation 4.2:

$$\Delta c_t = \beta_0 + \beta_1 \Delta y_t + \beta_2 \varepsilon_{t-1} + u_t \qquad [4.2]$$

Where ε_{t-1} is an error correction term and can be seen as;

$$\Delta c_t = \beta_0 + \beta_1 \Delta y_t + \beta_2 [c_{t-1} - \alpha - \beta y_{t-1}] + u_t \qquad [4.3]$$

The linear combination is the error correction term and β_2 will show the speed of adjustment.

This approach has a number of shortcomings. In particular, when we have more than two variables in an equation, the residual-based technique no longer has a unique vector. It should be understood that with k variables in the system, there must be at most $k - 1$ possible vectors (see Engle and Granger, 1991; Banerjee *et al.* 1993, Enders 1996). Second, unless one has a clear theory, as for example a long-term money-demand equation that specifies the direction and magnitude of the coefficients, the interpretation of the outcome vector in this residual-based method is problematic. Finally, one has to make a strong assumption about a unique cointegration vector in the analysis. These factors have led to the popularity of the Johansen approach, which handles multivariate systems in a better way (see Johansen, 1988, 1991; Johansen and Juselius, 1990).

In the rest of this section, we will explore the EG approach using PCGIVE. In the EG approach, the first step is to estimate a long run static model. Using PCGIVE, go to "model" and formulate your model. This will take you to a dialog table shown below. As we don't know the data generating process, a good starting point is to formulate an over parameterized model that includes lags of all of the variables. Then, we can reduce the model until we reach to a model that describes the data very well i.e. congruent model. This approach is referred as Hendry's general-to-specific modelling. We specify the model with two lags of all the variables[3]. On the bottom of the right most part of the "Data selection" window, set the lag length to 2. Then, double click on the dependent variable followed by the independent variables and click OK. This will take you to another dialog box in which you have to choose the method of estimation. Check the ordinary least square box and click OK. The estimation result is reported in Table 4.1.

Illustration 4.1: Selecting variables in PCGIVE

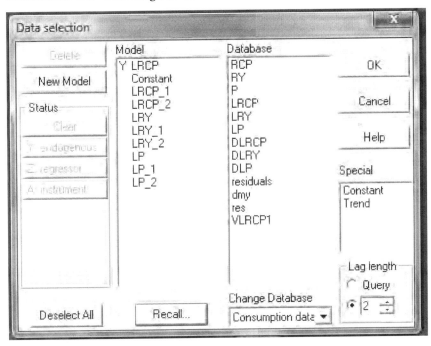

---

[3] Note that there is no specific rule that determines the lag length in specifying the general model. While it is mostly better to include as many lags as possible, the theoretical model may guide us on the selection of the lag length.

Table 4.1: Model of consumption using Ethiopian data

```
EQ(1) Modelling LRCP by OLS (using Ethiopian Consumption data)
The estimation sample is: 1964 to 2001
```

	Coefficient	Std.Error	t-value	t-prob	Part.R^2
LRCP_1	0.318957	0.1741	1.83	0.077	0.1038
LRCP_2	0.284785	0.1851	1.54	0.135	0.0755
Constant	0.144747	0.8056	0.180	0.859	0.0011
LRY	0.788777	0.1024	7.70	0.000	0.6718
LRY_1	-0.108775	0.2014	-0.540	0.593	0.0100
LRY_2	-0.322834	0.1864	-1.73	0.094	0.0938
LP	0.111066	0.09207	1.21	0.237	0.0478
LP_1	0.157123	0.1534	1.02	0.314	0.0349
LP_2	-0.241286	0.1084	-2.23	0.034	0.1458

```
sigma                0.0316011   RSS                 0.0289602025
R^2                  0.99355     F(8,29) =      558.4 [0.000]**
log-likelihood       82.4893     DW                          2.01
no. of observations       38     no. of parameters              9
mean(LRCP)           8.93965     var(LRCP)                0.118148
```

The model gives a marginal propensity to consume of around 0.79 and the lags of real income do not seem to be significant. It also suggests that the contemporaneous price levels do not significantly affect private consumption while the effect of the second lag of price is negative and significant. We now turn to reducing the general model to obtain the data congruent model following the same procedures as above. Go back to "model" then formulate to obtain the "Data selection" window. Select the second lags of all the variables while holding the control key; then press the delete button to remove all the second lags from the model. This gives us the result presented in Table 4.2.

Table 4.2: Model of LRCP using Ethiopian data

```
EQ(2) Modelling LRCP by OLS (using Consumption data2.in7)
        The estimation sample is: 1964 to 2001
```

	Coefficient	Std.Error	t-value	t-prob	Part.R^2
LRCP_1	0.420465	0.1656	2.54	0.016	0.1678
Constant	0.867978	0.7308	1.19	0.244	0.0422
LRY	0.853228	0.1036	8.24	0.000	0.6796
LRY_1	-0.412119	0.1606	-2.57	0.015	0.1707
LP	0.105268	0.08633	1.22	0.232	0.0444
LP_1	-0.0344577	0.1108	-0.311	0.758	0.0030

```
sigma                0.0332332   RSS                 0.0353422798
R^2                  0.992128    F(5,32) =      806.6 [0.000]**
log-likelihood       78.7053     DW                          2.15
no. of observations       38     no. of parameters              6
mean(LRCP)           8.93965     var(LRCP)                0.118148
```

We can further reduce the model by removing all the lags from the model. The reduction process basically imposes zero restrictions on the selected lags which are testable hypothesis. We can thus test the validity of our restriction and the selection of the data congruent model would be based on the validity of the restriction along with the AIC, SBC and the HQ statistics[4]. PCGIVE has its own routine of doing so. Go to model, click on progress and click OK.

Illustration 4.2: Assessing model formulation progress in PCGIVE

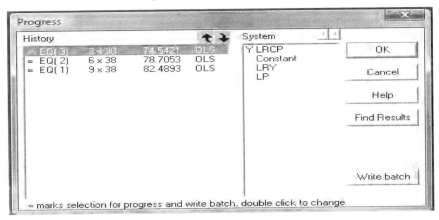

The result of this exercise is presented in Table 4.3. The results show that the reduction from lag 2 to lag 1 is statistically valid while the reduction from lag 2 to lag 0 is rejected. The HQ and AIC statistics are also the lowest in the case of the lag 1 model. It seems reasonable to consider the lag 1 model as the data congruent model.

Table 4.3: Lag reduction from 2 to 1

```
Progress to date
Model        T        p        log-likelihood       SC        HQ        AIC
Lag 1        38       6 OLS          78.705304     -3.5680   -3.7346   -3.8266
Lag 2        38       9 OLS          82.489294     -3.4800   -3.7299   -3.8679
Tests of model reduction (please ensure models are nested for test validity)
Lag 2--> Lag 1: F(3,29)  =   2.1303 [0.1180]
```

Reduction from lag 2 to lag 0

```
Progress to date
Model        T        p        log-likelihood       SC        HQ        AIC
Lag 0        38       3 OLS          74.542051     -3.6361   -3.7194   -3.7654
Lag 1        38       6 OLS          78.705304     -3.5680   -3.7346   -3.8266
Tests of model reduction (please ensure models are nested for test validity)
Lag 1 --> Lag 0: F(3,32)  =   2.6131 [0.0682]
Lag 2 --> Lag 0: F(6,29)  =   2.5101 [0.0443]*
```

---

[4] AIC is Akaike information criteria of Hurwich and Tsai (1989); SBC is Shwartz Bayesian criteria; and HQ is Hannan-Quinn statistics. A congruent model is a model that has the minimum value of these criteria.

The next step is to save the residual from the long run equation, which we have just estimated, and test it for stationarity. To save the residual in PCGIVE, go to test and click store in data base. This would prompt you to choose what you want to store in data base. Check the box residual and click OK. This would again prompt you for a variable name. Assign the name of your choice and click OK. Now the residual series would be saved in the data base. Following the same procedure we used when testing for the stationarity of the residual series above, we will do the same here and obtain the unit-root test for the residual series which is presented below in Table 4.4. Note that the test for unit root does not include constant and trend as the residual is supposed to have a mean of zero. The unit-root test shows that the residual series is stationary in levels and hence there exists a cointegrating vector that ties the variables in the regression equation (i.e. the variables are cointegrated).

Table 4.4:   Unit root test for residuals

```
Unit-root tests for 1964 (1) to 2001 (1)

Augmented Dickey-Fullertest for residuals; regression of Dresiduals
on:

                  Coefficient        Std.Error        t-value
residuals_1        -0.50210          0.17693          -2.8377
Dresiduals_1       -0.15908          0.16464          -0.96621

sigma = 0.0316123  DW = 1.902  DW-residuals = 1.184
ADF-residuals = -2.838**
Critical values used in ADF test: 5%=-1.95, 1%=-2.624
RSS = 0.03597604666 for 2 variables and 38 observations
```

To estimate the error correction model, go to model and check single equation dynamic modeling. Going back to model, select "formulate" to see the window (Illustration 4.3):

Illustration 4.3:   Selecting variables for VECM

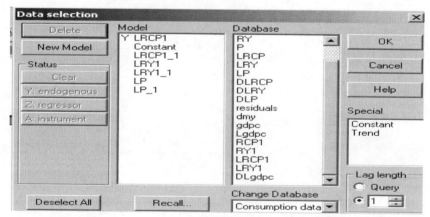

First press "new model" to clear any previous selected variables. Next, double click on the variables of interest which are already differenced. Following Hendry's general-to-specific method, it is important to include some lags in the specification. Once all the variables are included, double click on residuals. Select the contemporaneous component of the residual and delete it. The specification looks like the following:

Illustration 4.4: Selecting variables for VECM with residual lagged

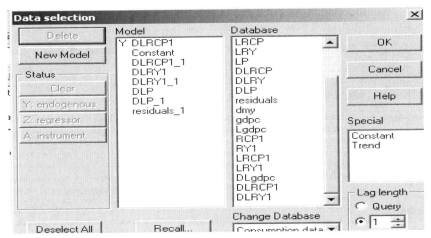

The result of this estimation is given in Table 4.5 as:

Table 4.5: ECM model for LRCP

```
Modelling DLRCP by OLS (using Consumption data2.in7)
The estimation sample is: 1964 to 2001

                 Coefficient   Std.Error   t-value   t-prob   Part.R^2
DLRCP_1            0.0217493      0.2762    0.0788    0.938     0.0002
Constant          -0.0126424     0.009728  -1.30     0.203     0.0517
DLRY               0.761867      0.09068    8.40      0.000     0.6948
DLRY_1             0.0346101     0.2694     0.128     0.899     0.0005
DLP                0.100192      0.08786    1.14      0.263     0.0403
DLP_1              0.189466      0.09945    1.91      0.066     0.1048
residuals_1       -0.717436      0.3145    -2.28      0.030     0.1437

sigma              0.0307937    RSS              0.0293957572
R^2                0.846681     F(6,31) =        28.53 [0.000]**
log-likelihood    82.2057       DW                           1.95
no. of observations      38     no. of parameters              7
mean(DLRCP)        0.0320216    var(DLRCP)        0.00504553

AR 1-2 test:       F(2,29)   =     1.4056   [0.2614]
ARCH 1-1 test:     F(1,29)   =     0.026441 [0.8720]
Normality test:    Chi^2(2)  =     0.23644  [0.8885]
hetero test:       F(12,18)  =     1.5077   [0.2092]
Not enough observations for hetero-X test
RESET test:        F(1,30)   =     0.69037  [0.4126]
```

Our diagnostic results in Table 4.5 show that none of the classical assumptions are violated in statistical terms. The adjustment term (*residuals_1*) has the right sign and it is also significant implying that there is a reasonable adjustment towards the long run steady state. Using the same procedure discussed above, we can reduce the model by removing some of the lags. For instance, estimating the model with no lags gives the result in Table 4.6. It seems that the model with no lag is the congruent model and the reduction is acceptable as the test of reduction in the last raw of Table 4.6 shows. This in a nut shell is the two step Engle-Granger approach. In the next section, we will move to the most advanced and widely employed approach to cointegration analysis called the Johansen approach. Before that section, however, we need to revise some basic mathematical concepts relevant for cointegration analysis.

Table 4.6: ECM model for LRCP

```
Modelling DLRCP by OLS (using Consumption data2.in7)
The estimation sample is: 1964 to 2001

                  Coefficient   Std.Error   t-value   t-prob   Part.R^2
Constant          -0.00595254   0.007615    -0.782    0.440    0.0177
DLRY               0.858390     0.07755     11.1      0.000    0.7828
DLP                0.162560     0.07322     2.22      0.033    0.1266
residuals_1       -0.658679     0.1707      -3.86     0.000    0.3046

sigma              0.031785     RSS              0.0343496618
R^2                0.820844     F(3,34) =   51.93 [0.000]**
log-likelihood     79.2466      DW                      1.85
no. of observations      38     no. of parameters          4
mean(DLRCP)        0.0320216    var(DLRCP)        0.00504553

AR 1-2 test:       F(2,32)   =   0.98363 [0.3850]
ARCH 1-1 test:     F(1,32)   =   0.010478 [0.9191]
Normality test:    Chi^2(2)  =   3.9591 [0.1381]
hetero test:       F(6,27)   =   1.1448 [0.3641]
hetero-X test:     F(9,24)   =   0.83917 [0.5883]
RESET test:        F(1,33)   =   0.049508 [0.8253]
```
Test of Reduction
```
Lag 1 --> Lag 0: F(3,31)     =   1.7414 [0.1790]
```

Box 4.1: Alternative methods of estimating long run parameters

There are alternative methods of estimating the long run parameters where there is only one cointegrating relationship. The Stock and Watson's (1993) dynamic OLS (DOLS), Phillips and Hansen's (1990) fully modified OLS (FMOLS), and the autoregressive distributed lag (ADL) dynamic model are among the usual alternatives. The alternative approaches provide consistent estimates of the long run parameters solving the defects of the simple OLS approach.

DOLS Estimation of Cointegrating Relationship

Let the cointegrating relationship be given as:

$$y_t = \alpha + \beta x_t + u_t \qquad [1]$$

and

$$x_t = x_{t-1} + \varepsilon_t \qquad [2]$$

Cointegration of y_t and x_t implies that u_t and ε_t are correlated and hence u_t and x_t are also correlated. This will make the least square estimator of [1] asymptotically inefficient. The DOLS modifies the OLS estimator to derive asymptotically efficient estimator.

Assume u_t is correlated with at most k leads and lags of ε_t :

$$u_t = \sum_{s=-k}^{k} \delta_k \varepsilon_{t-k} + v_t \qquad [3]$$

From equation [2],

$$\varepsilon_t = x_t - x_{t-1} = \Delta x_t \qquad [4]$$

Substituting [4] into [3],

$$u_t = \sum_{s=-k}^{k} \delta_k \Delta x_{t-k} + v_t \qquad [5]$$

Note that v_t is orthogonal with all leads and lags of x by construction.

Substituting [5] into [1],

$$y_t = \alpha + \beta x_t + \sum_{s=-k}^{k} \delta_k \Delta x_{t-k} + v_t \qquad [6]$$

Equation [6] is the asymptotically efficient DOLS estimator of the cointegrating relationship in [1]. By the stationarity of v_t, one would expect that the values of Δx_{t-k}, in the very remote past and future can only have a negligible impact on y_t and can therefore be ignored. Their main purpose in the model is to remove the effect that the short-run dynamics of u_t may have on the estimation of β.

Unlike the EG approach that handles the cointegration relationship among $I(1)$ variables, the Stock and Watson (1993) DOLS approach can handle cointegrating regressions among general $I(d)$ variables with general deterministic components. This method is implemented in Eviews 7.

Fully Modified OLS

Phillips and Hansen (1990) propose an estimator which employs a semi-parametric correction to eliminate the problems caused by the long run correlation between the cointegrating equation and stochastic regressors' innovations as in equation [1] and [2]. The resulting Fully Modified OLS (FMOLS) estimator is asymptotically unbiased and has fully efficient mixture normal asymptotic distribution allowing for standard Wald tests using asymptotic Chi-square statistical inference. This method is available in some statistical packages such as Microfit 4.0 and Eviews 7.

ADL or Dynamic Model

Rather than estimating equation [1] that throw away all the short run dynamics into the error term, this approach suggests using over-parameterized dynamic model as in equation [7] below:

$$y_t = \alpha + \sum_{r=0}^{n} a_r y_{t-r} + \sum_{r=0}^{p} b_r x_{t-r} + \in_t \qquad [7]$$

Using lag operators,

$$A(L)y_t = \alpha + B(L)x_t + \in_t \qquad [8]$$

where $A(L)$ is the polynomial lag operator $1 - a_1 L^1 - a_2 L^2 - ... - a_n L^n$

and $B(L) = 1 - b_1 L^1 - b_2 L^2 - ... - b_p L^p$.

The long run parameters can be solved from [8] by dividing both sides by $A(L)$ and taking expectations, i.e.,

$$E(y_t) = \beta_0 + \beta_1 E(x_t)$$

where $\beta_0 = \dfrac{\alpha}{A(L)}$ and $\beta_1 = \dfrac{B(L)}{A(L)}$.

The standard errors of βs can be obtained using a non-linear algorithm. This method is implemented in some statistical packages such as PcGive and Microfit.

Some Relevant Mathematical Concepts: Matrices and Eigen Values

Points on Matrix Algebra for Cointegration Analysis

Time-series analysis, which is important in macroeconometric modelling, requires some basic concepts in matrix algebra. This section is aimed at providing such input by simplifying the treatment of these concepts in major textbooks and picking the most relevant ones for cointegration (CI) analysis.

Linear dependence and rank of a matrix

The two concepts of linear dependence and rank of a matrix are widely used in CI analysis. Solution to a matrix requires that the matrix is non-singular. Non-singularity implies that the determinant of the matrix is different from zero. This in turn requires that each row or column of the matrix is linearly independent. A row or column is linearly independent if it cannot be formulated as a linear combination of another row or column. The number of linearly independent rows or columns[5] of a matrix is referred as the rank of a matrix. The most important question in the context of CI analysis is how do we know that a matrix has linearly independent rows?

One important method is to check whether its determinant is equal to or different from zero. If it is equal to zero (that is, $|A| = 0$) definitely matrix **A** has linearly dependent rows. If on the other hand $|A| \neq 0$, then matrix **A**'s rows are said to be linearly independent. Thus, a non-singular matrix (a matrix with a non-zero determinant) is said to have a full rank. Note also that for a matrix of dimension ($n \times m$) the rank can have a maximum value of n or m, whichever is the minimum. It should be the minimum, because a determinant is defined only for a square matrix. Thus, $r(A) = \leq Min(m,n)$. So we require that $m = n$ at all times in the type of analysis we consider.

Another important concept in matrix algebra, which is widely used in cointegration analysis and related to the discussion above, is the characteristic root (Eigen values) and the characteristic vector (Eigen vector).[6]

The concept of Eigen values (and Eigen vectors)

Given an $n \times n$ matrix **D**, we may find a scalar r and an $n \times 1$ vector **X**, **X** $\neq 0$ such that the matrix equation below is satisfied, that is,

---

[5] Since using either a row or a column makes no difference, we will use the row in the exposition.
[6] Characteristic roots (vectors), Eigen values (vectors), and latent roots (vectors) are synonymous. Time-series literature often uses the term Eigen value (vector). Every Eigen value will be related to an Eigen vector of the variables in the analysis.

$$\underset{n \times n \ n \times 1}{D \ X} = \underset{n \times 1}{r \ X} \qquad [4.4]$$

If expression [4.4] is satisfied, then the scalar r is referred to as the characteristic root (Eigen value) of matrix **D** and the vector **X** is referred as the characteristic vector (Eigen vector) of matrix **D**.

Equation [4.4] can be rewritten as

$$(\mathbf{D} - r\mathbf{I})X = \mathbf{O} \qquad \text{where } \mathbf{O} = \text{n} \times 1 \text{ matrix} \qquad [4.5]$$

If we need a non-trivial solution, the determinant of the coefficient matrix $(\mathbf{D} - r\mathbf{I})$, called the *characteristic matrix* of matrix **D**, needs to be singular (that is, its determinant vanishes):

$$|\mathbf{D} - r\mathbf{I}| = \begin{vmatrix} d_{11} - r & d_{12} & \cdots & d_{1n} \\ d_{21} & d_{22} - r & \cdots & d_{2n} \\ \cdot & \cdot & \cdot & \cdot \\ d_{n1} & d_{n2} & \cdots & d_{nn} \end{vmatrix} = 0 \qquad [4.6]$$

The expression in equation [4.6] is what is referred as the characteristic equation of matrix **D**. This determinant, upon Laplace expansion gives an nth-degree polynomial in the variable r. This will have n roots $(r_1, r_2 \ldots r_n)$, each of which is a characteristic root (Eigen value).

Inserting such Eigen values into the equation system $(\mathbf{D} - r\mathbf{I})\mathbf{X} = \mathbf{O}$ will produce a vector that we term as Eigen vector (note that the determinant of the equation $|\mathbf{D} - r\mathbf{I}|$ will vanish). The $(\mathbf{D} - r\mathbf{I})\mathbf{X} = \mathbf{O}$ system, however, generates an infinite number of vectors corresponding to the Eigen values r_i because it is a homogenous system.[7] Through normalization, however, a characteristic root can be selected from this set of infinite solution. Imposing a unit circle function on the solution usually does such normalization. The latter gives stability to the function. If the characteristic roots lie outside the unit circle, the solution for the polynomial in question will be explosive. Since this concept is important in CI analysis, we have illustrated its derivation using a numerical example (see Chiang 1984:327).

$$\text{If D} = \begin{bmatrix} 2 & 2 \\ 2 & -1 \end{bmatrix} \qquad [4.7]$$

$$|\mathbf{D} - r\mathbf{I}| = \begin{vmatrix} 2 - r & 2 \\ 2 & -1 - r \end{vmatrix} = r^2 - r - 6 = 0 \qquad [4.8]$$

with characteristics roots (Eigen values) $r_1 = 3$ and $r_2 = -2$

---

[7] A matrix system is homogenous when it has zero (as opposed to a constant) on the right-hand side of the equality sign.

When these roots are used in equation $(\mathbf{D} - r\mathbf{I})\mathbf{X} = \mathbf{O}$ we get

$$\Rightarrow \begin{bmatrix} 2-3 & 2 \\ 2 & -1-3 \end{bmatrix}\begin{bmatrix} X_1 \\ X_2 \end{bmatrix} = \begin{bmatrix} -1 & 2 \\ 2 & -4 \end{bmatrix}\begin{bmatrix} X_1 \\ X_2 \end{bmatrix} = \begin{bmatrix} 0 \\ 0 \end{bmatrix} \quad [4.9]$$

Note that the rows are linearly dependent. The system in [4.9] results in

$$X_1 = 2X_2 \quad [4.10]$$

A unique solution can be found out of this infinite solution possibility by imposing the unit circle function $X_1^2 + X_2^2 = 1$

$\Rightarrow X_1^2 + X_2^2 = (2X_2)^2 + X_2^2 = 1$. (Inserting $2X_2$ in place of X_1 as given by equation [4.10])

$$\Rightarrow 5X_2^2 = 1 \quad \text{and, hence,} \quad X_2 = \frac{1}{\sqrt{5}} \quad \text{and} \quad X_1 = \frac{2}{\sqrt{5}}$$

Thus, the first characteristic vector (Eigen vector) is given by

$$V_1 = \begin{bmatrix} \frac{2}{\sqrt{5}} \\ \frac{1}{\sqrt{5}} \end{bmatrix} \quad [4.11]$$

You can do the same using $r_2 = -2$.

The concept of rank and Eigen value or vector is central to the cointegration test using the Johansen approach. This is because testing the existence of a non-zero Eigen value is tantamount to testing the rank of a matrix. The latter in turn indicates the number of linearly independent rows. This follows from the fact that the rank of a matrix is equal to the number of non-zero Eigen values.[8]

---

[8] If all rows of a matrix are linearly independent, the determinants of this matrix are not equal to zero. It follows that none of the Eigen values can equal zero when the determinants of the matrix are different from zero. If the rank equals zero, on the other hand, each element of the matrix must equal zero and all Eigen values will be equal to zero. In the intermediate case, r linearly independent rows ($0 <$ rank of the matrix $= r < n$) will contain r Eigen values (the other $(n - r)$ Eigen values being zero). So the Johansen procedure requires testing for the most significant non-zero Eigen value, which has a corresponding linear combination of the variables in the system, the Eigen vector (see Enders, 1995:412–418 for detail).

Johansen's Multivariate Approach: Identification of the Beta-coefficient and Restriction Tests

An Introduction to VAR

The structural approach to time series modeling uses economic theory to model the relationship among the variables of interest. In the structural approach, "one assumes that the model is given. The observations are used to estimate the parameters of the model. In practice, however, econometricians derive the model at least in part from the data. When specifying an initial model, the investigator makes use of economic theory, knowledge about institutional arrangements, and other subject-matter considerations. Sometimes a heavily – perhaps too strongly – restricted model is chosen as an initial model because the estimation of its parameters is straightforward" (Palm, 2004:97–98).

Unfortunately, economic theory is not mostly capable of providing all the dynamic specification that identifies relationships among different variables of interest. Sims (1980) argued that structural models embodied "incredible" identifying restrictions: the restrictions needed to claim exogeneity for certain variables would not be valid in an environment where agents optimize intertemporally. Furthermore, estimation and inference are complicated by the fact that endogenous variables may appear on both the left and right sides of equations (Sims, 1980). These problems lead to alternative, non-structural approaches to modeling the relationship among several variables, i.e., the vector autoregression (VAR) model. This chapter describes the estimation and analysis of VAR models and their use for Cointegraton analysis and Error Correction Modelling.

VAR is multivariate stochastic time series model in which each variant is expressed as a function of lagged values of its own and other variables in the system. In these models all variables are often treated as being a *priori* endogenous, and allowance is made for rich dynamics. The VAR approach bypasses the need for structural modeling by treating every endogenous variable in the system as a function of the lagged values of all of the endogenous variables in the system. The VAR model of a simple bivariate system is given as[9]:

$$y_t = \beta_{10} - \beta_{12}x_t + \gamma_{11}y_{t-1} + \gamma_{12}x_{t-1} + u_{yt} \tag{1}$$

$$x_t = \beta_{20} - \beta_{21}y_t + \gamma_{21}y_{t-1} + \gamma_{22}x_{t-1} + u_{xt} \tag{2}$$

where it is assumed that both y_t and x_t are stationary, and u_{yt} and u_{xt} are uncorrelated white-noise disturbances.

---

[9] In applied empirical work, the order of the VAR or the lag length of the endogenous variables is determined based on data congruency judged by some information criteria such as Schwarz criterion (SC), the Hannan--Quinn (HQ) criterion, and the Akaike criterion (AIC), see sections 4.5 and 4.6.

These equations are not reduced-form equations since x_t has a contemporaneous impact on y_t through (β_{12}) and y_t has a contemporaneous impact on x_t through (β_{21}). As a result, u_{yt} is correlated with x_t and similarly u_{xt} is correlated with y_t, i.e., there is a problem of endogeneity. OLS estimates will not provide consistent estimates in this case. We can, however, transform the system to circumvent this problem. Rewriting the system in a matrix form:

$$\begin{bmatrix} 1 & \beta_{12} \\ \beta_{21} & 1 \end{bmatrix}\begin{bmatrix} y_t \\ x_t \end{bmatrix} = \begin{bmatrix} \beta_{10} \\ \beta_{20} \end{bmatrix} + \begin{bmatrix} \gamma_{11} & \gamma_{12} \\ \gamma_{21} & \gamma_{22} \end{bmatrix}\begin{bmatrix} y_{t-1} \\ x_{t-1} \end{bmatrix} + \begin{bmatrix} u_{yt} \\ x_{xt} \end{bmatrix}$$

Defining

$$B = \begin{bmatrix} 1 & \beta_{12} \\ \beta_{21} & 1 \end{bmatrix}, \quad x_t = \begin{bmatrix} y_t \\ x_t \end{bmatrix}, \quad \Gamma_0 = \begin{bmatrix} \beta_{10} \\ \beta_{20} \end{bmatrix}, \quad \Gamma_1 = \begin{bmatrix} \gamma_{11} & \gamma_{12} \\ \gamma_{21} & \gamma_{22} \end{bmatrix}, \quad u_t = \begin{bmatrix} u_{yt} \\ x_{xt} \end{bmatrix}$$

the system can be written in compact form as:

$$Bx_t = \Gamma_0 + \Gamma_1 x_{t-1} + u_t \tag{3}$$

Premultiplying the system by the inverse of the B matrix, B^{-1}, we obtain

$$x_t = A_0 + A_1 x_{t-1} + e_t \tag{4}$$

Where $A_0 = B^{-1}\Gamma_0, \qquad A_1 = B^{-1}\Gamma_1, \qquad e_t = B^{-1}u_t$

$$y_t = a_{10} + a_{11}y_{t-1} + a_{10}x_{t-1} + e_{yt}$$

Using the notations a_{i0} and a_{it} as the element i of the vector A_0 and e_t, respectively, and a_{ij} as the element in row i and column j, we can write the transformed system as:

$$y_t = a_{10} + a_{11}y_{t-1} + a_{12}x_{t-1} + e_{yt} \tag{5}$$

$$x_t = a_{20} + a_{21}y_{t-1} + a_{22}x_{t-1} + e_{xt} \tag{6}$$

The transformed system is usually referred as a standard form VAR while the previous one is referred as a structural VAR. Since only lagged values of the endogenous variables appear on the right-hand side of the standard VAR, simultaneity is not an issue and OLS yields consistent estimates. Since $e_t = B^{-1}u_t$, e_{yt} and e_{xt} can be computed as

$$e_{yt} = (u_{yt} - \beta_{12}u_{xt})/(1 - \beta_{12}\beta_{21}) \tag{7}$$

$$e_{xt} = (u_{xt} - \beta_{21}u_{yt})/(1 - \beta_{12}\beta_{21}) \tag{8}$$

Note that the error terms are the composites of the two shocks u_{yt} and u_{xt}. The error terms e_{yt} and e_{xt} are white-noise processes because of the white-noise property of u_{yt} and u_{xt}.

VAR, Granger Causality and Impulse Response Analysis

One of the attractive features of VAR models is that they allow us to test for the direction of causality in the form of Granger causality test. The Granger (1969) approach to the question of whether x Granger causes y is to see how much of the current y can be explained by past values of y and then to see whether adding lagged values of x can improve the explanation. y is said to be Granger-caused (not caused) by x if x helps in the prediction of y, or equivalently if the coefficients on the lagged x's are statistically significant. Note that two-way causation is frequently the case; x Granger causes y and y Granger cause x. Note also further that Granger-causality is more of an indicator of precedence than a real causal identification. One needs theory to come up with the latter.

Consider the two-variable VAR model as in (4)

$$y_t = a_{10} + a_{11}y_{t-1} + a_{12}x_{t-1} + e_{yt} \tag{9}$$

$$x_t = a_{20} + a_{21}y_{t-1} + a_{22}x_{t-1} + e_{xt} \tag{10}$$

The hypothesis that x does not Granger cause y could be tested simply by running the regression of equation (9) and examining whether the coefficient of the latter variable is significantly different from zero, i.e., test $a_{12} = 0$. Sigmilarly, that y does not Granger cause x could be tested simply by running the regression of equation (10) and examining whether the coefficient of y_{t-1} is significantly different from zero, i.e., test $a_{21} = 0$.

Consider a case of a VAR model with three variable

$$y_t = \alpha_0 + \alpha_1 y_{t-1} + \cdots + \alpha_n y_{t-n} + \beta_1 x_{t-1} + \cdots + \beta_n x_{t-n} + \gamma_1 z_{t-1} + \cdots + \gamma_n z_{t-n} + \varepsilon_t$$
$$x_t = \alpha_0 + \alpha_1 x_{t-1} + \cdots + \alpha_n x_{t-n} + \beta_1 y_{t-1} + \cdots + \beta_n y_{t-n} + \gamma_1 z_{t-1} + \cdots + \gamma_n z_{t-n} + u_t \tag{11}$$
$$z_t = \alpha_0 + \alpha_1 t_{t-1} + \cdots + \alpha_n z_{t-n} + \beta_1 y_{t-1} + \cdots + \beta_n y_{t-n} + \gamma_1 x_{t-1} + \cdots + \gamma_n x_{t-n} + v_t$$

For this system, we can test a pair-wise Granger causality test in the same fashion as in the previous model. We can also test the exogeneity of the variable of interest in the system. For instance, the exogeneity of z can be examined by testing the restrictions that $\gamma_1 = \gamma_2 = \cdots \gamma_n = 0$ in the first two equations of the VAR. This test is referred as block exogeneity test.

VAR is commonly used for forecasting systems of interrelated time series variables and for analyzing the dynamic impact of random disturbances on the system of variables (see Chapter 5 for detail). These require the identification of the parameters in the primitive VAR model from the estimated reduced form standard VAR. Identification, however, is not possible without restricting the primitive system. This is because the number of parameters in the primitive VAR is greater than the number of parameters estimated in the reduced form. In terms of the primitive VAR in (1 and 2) and the standard VAR in (4 and 5), there are ten parameters in the primitive system while the standard VAR has nine parameters including the variances and covariance of *x* and *y*. Identification, thus, requires imposing a zero restriction on one of the parameters in the primitive system.

One way of identification is to follow Sims' (1980) recursive approach. The approach involves ordering the variables in the system in such a way that the variable affected most by the others ordered last in the model. In the case of three variable VAR model, *y, x, z*, ordered in accordance of their contemporaneous effect where *z* is affected most by *y* and *x* the restrictions in the *B* matrix in the primitive system in equation (3) is given as:

$$
B_0 = \begin{bmatrix} 1 & 0 & 0 \\ \beta_{21} & 1 & 0 \\ \beta_{31} & \beta_{32} & 1 \end{bmatrix} \tag{12}
$$

The restriction on *B* is referred to as the Choleski factorization and ensures that there is a strict Granger-causal ordering in the contemporaneous relationships between the endogenous variables. Before wrapping up this section we briefly noted one important application of the VAR approach called the ***impulse response analysis*** (see for detail and illustration in Chapter 5).

Consider the two-variable VAR model as in (4)

$$
y_t = a_{10} + a_{11} y_{t-1} + a_{12} x_{t-1} + e_{yt} \tag{13}
$$

$$
x_t = a_{20} + a_{21} y_{t-1} + a_{22} x_{t-1} + e_{xt} \tag{14}
$$

A shock in e_{yt} has an immediate and one-for-one effect on y_t, but no effect on x_t. In period t+1, that shock in y_t affects y_{t+1} through the first equation and also affects x_{t+1} through the second equation. These effects work through to period t + 2, and so on. Thus a shock in one innovation in the VAR sets up a chain reaction over time in all variables in the VAR. Impulse response functions calculate these chain reactions.

To derive the impulse response function, we need to transform the VAR model into its vector moving average (VMA) representation. The VMA representation of the VAR model in equation (4) is given as:

$$x_t = \mu + \sum_{i=0}^{\infty} A_1^i e_{t-i} \tag{15}$$

Where $\mu = \begin{bmatrix} \bar{y} & \bar{x} \end{bmatrix}'$

In matrix form, the VMA representation of the VAR model in (13) and (14) is:

$$\begin{bmatrix} y_t \\ x_t \end{bmatrix} = \begin{bmatrix} \bar{y} \\ \bar{x} \end{bmatrix} + \sum_{i=0}^{\infty} \begin{bmatrix} a_{11} & a_{12} \\ a_{21} & a_{22} \end{bmatrix}^i \begin{bmatrix} e_{yt-1} \\ e_{xt-1} \end{bmatrix} \tag{16}$$

Using the relationship between e_{it} and u_{it} in equation (7) and (8),

$$\begin{bmatrix} e_{yt} \\ e_{xt} \end{bmatrix} = \frac{1}{1 - \beta_{12}\beta_{21}} \begin{bmatrix} 1 & -\beta_{12} \\ -\beta_{21} & 1 \end{bmatrix} \begin{bmatrix} u_{yt} \\ u_{xt} \end{bmatrix} \tag{17}$$

Substituting (17) into (16):

$$\begin{bmatrix} y_t \\ x_t \end{bmatrix} = \begin{bmatrix} \bar{y} \\ \bar{x} \end{bmatrix} + \frac{1}{1 - \beta_{12}\beta_{21}} \sum_{i=0}^{\infty} \begin{bmatrix} a_{11} & a_{12} \\ \beta_{21} & a_{22} \end{bmatrix}^i \begin{bmatrix} 1 & -\beta_{12} \\ -\beta_{21} & 1 \end{bmatrix} \begin{bmatrix} u_{yt-1} \\ u_{xt-1} \end{bmatrix}$$

To simplify the above expression, let us define a 2×2 matrix ϕ_i with elements $\phi_{jk}(i)$:

$$\phi_i = \frac{A_1^i}{1 - \beta_{12}\beta_{21}} \begin{bmatrix} 1 & -\beta_{12} \\ -\beta_{21} & 1 \end{bmatrix}$$

The VMA representation of 16 is thus given as:

$$\begin{bmatrix} y_t \\ x_t \end{bmatrix} = \begin{bmatrix} \bar{y} \\ \bar{x} \end{bmatrix} + \sum_{i=0}^{\infty} \begin{bmatrix} \phi_{11}(i) & \phi_{12}(i) \\ \phi_{21}(i) & \phi_{22}(i) \end{bmatrix}^i \begin{bmatrix} u_{yt-1} \\ u_{xt-1} \end{bmatrix}$$

Compactly, it can be written as:

$$x_t = \mu + \sum_{i=0}^{\infty} \phi_i u_{t-i} \tag{18}$$

The coefficient of ϕ_i can be used to generate the effect of u_{yt} and u_{xt} shocks on y_t and x_t. The four elements $\phi_{jk}(0)$ are impact multipliers. For example, $\phi_{21}(0)$ is the instantaneous impact of a one-unit change in u_{yt} on x_t. The four sets of coefficients $\phi_{11}(i), \phi_{12}(i), \phi_{21}(i),$ and $\phi_{22}(i),$ are called the impulse response functions.

Similar to the identification problem noted above, some restrictions are necessary to identify the impulse responses. That is, to derive the structural shocks of the primitive system from the reduced form VAR, the parameters of the primitive model need to be restricted. The Choleski decomposition discussed earlier is one way of identification. However, as this decomposition depends on the ordering of the variables, the impulse responses are also dependent on the ordering.

VAR, CI and ECM

Having understood the basic concepts about VAR and its application, we will now revert to the use of VAR for cointegration analysis in multivariate framework. This will be done in the rest of this chapter.

We have noted earlier that the rank of a matrix is equal to the number of non-zero eigen values. Thus if we have

$$X_t = A_1 X_{t-1} + \varepsilon_t \qquad\qquad [4.12]$$

we can generate equation [4.13] by subtracting X_{t-1} from both sides of equation [4.12].

$$\begin{aligned} \Delta X_t &= A_1 X_{t-1} - X_{t-1} + \varepsilon_t \\ &= (A_1 - I) X_{t-1} + \varepsilon_t \qquad\qquad [4.13] \\ &= \Pi X_{t-1} + \varepsilon_t \end{aligned}$$

where X_t and ε_t are $(n \times 1)$ vectors, A_1 and I $(n \times n)$ matrices of parameters and identity, respectively, and $\Pi = (A_1 - I)$. The rank of $(A_1 - I)$ equals the number of cointegrating vectors. If the rank = 0, all the X_t are unit root processes. They are not cointegrated for we lack the linear combination of X_t. The system [4.13] will also be a convergent system of difference equations if we rule out eigen values that are greater than unity (or if we impose the unit circle functional form for transformation). We hope you are now convinced that a test for non-zero eigen values is tantamount to the test for the rank of a matrix, which in turn is a test for the number of cointegration vectors. If yes, the next question is how are we going to conduct such a test?

It follows from the previous discussion that the major issue in testing is to check the statistical significance of the Eigen values (that is, whether they are statistically different from zero or not). Here we will use our knowledge that the rank of a matrix equals the number of its eigen values that differ from zero (see the discussion above). Suppose the n eigen values of the matrix Π are given in the following order: $\lambda_1 > \lambda_2 > ...\lambda_n$. If the rank of Π is 0, then all these eigen values (the λ_s) will equal zero. Applying our knowledge of logarithm that $\ln(1) = 0$, the expressions $(1 - \lambda)$ in matrix Π can be reduced to zero if we substitute the zero values of λ_s in the expression $(1 - \lambda)$ and take its logarithm (that is, $\ln(1 - \lambda_1) = 0$). If the rank of Π is unity and $0 < \lambda_1 < 1$, the first expression in $\ln(1 - \lambda)$ = negative (that is, log of a fraction is negative). In applied work we can get the estimates of Π and the eigen values. Then we can conduct a test for the number of eigen values that are not significantly different from unity using what are called the λ_{trace} and λ_{max} tests given by

$$\lambda_{trace}(r) = -T \sum_{i=r+1}^{n} \ln(1 - \hat{\lambda}_i)$$

$$\lambda_{max}(r, r+1) = -T \ln(1 - \hat{\lambda}_{r+1})$$

[4.14]

Where:

$\hat{\lambda}$ are estimated eigen values obtained from estimated Π matrix.

λ_{trace} tests the null hypothesis that the number of cointegrating vectors is $\le =$ r against a general alternative[10].

λ_{max} tests the null that the number of cointegrating vector is r against the alternative $r+1$.

T is the sample size.

The distribution of this test is non-standard and depends only on the degrees of freedom $(n - r)$. It is tabulated by Osterwald-Lenum (1992) and could be found in most recent econometrics textbooks. Most econometric software packages (such as EVIEWS or PCGIVE/PcFiml) will give you the critical values developed by Johansen and Juselius (1990, 1992) using Monte Carlo studies or using the Cointegration Analysis for Time Series (CATS) software which was developed for this purpose. To test the hypothesis, compare the calculated statistics above with the tabulated critical values and the usual rule of rejecting the null if the calculated t-value is greater than the critical value would apply.

Once this is done, noting the Granger representation theorem (Engle and Granger 1987) that states that a cointegrating system has an error-correction representation and vice versa, we can formulate an Error Correction Model (ECM) from the vector

---

[10] Notice that this statistics equals zero when $\lambda_s s = 0$. The further these Eigen values are from zero, the more negative the $\ln(1 - \lambda_i)$ will be; hence the higher the λ_{trace} statistics and hence the possibility of having cointegrating vectors.

auto-regressive (VAR) representation of the model. We outline below how one can transform a VAR model, into an error-correction representation. This two-step procedure borrows from Johansen and Juselius (1990, 1992) and Juselius (1991). Let us examine this issues using Johansen's (1988, 1991) VAR formulation.

Following Johansen (1988, 1991) we may consider a VAR model given by equation [4.15].

$$X_t = A_1 X_{t-1} + \ldots + A_k X_{t-1}\text{-}X_{t-k} + \mu + \phi D_1 + \varepsilon_t \quad (t = 1,\ldots T) \qquad [4.15]$$

Where X_t is an $n \times 1$ vector of macro variables of interest, D_1 is a vector of centred seasonal dummies, μ is a vector of constants and ε_t is a vector of $i.i.d(0,\Omega)$ error terms.

In general, an economic time series is a non-stationary process, and VAR systems like equation [4.15] can be expressed in the first-difference form. If we use $\Delta = 1 - L$, where L is the lag operator, we can rewrite equation [4.15] as

$$\Delta X_t = \Gamma_1 \Delta X_{t-1} + \ldots + \Gamma_{k-1} \Delta X_{t-k-1} + \Pi X_{t-k} + \varepsilon_t \qquad [4.16]$$

Where

$$\Gamma_i = -(I - A_i - \cdots A_i)(i = 1, \cdots k - 1) \text{ and } \quad \Pi = -(I - A_1 - \cdots A_k)$$

Model equation [4.16] is a traditional first-difference VAR model except for the term $\Pi \mathbf{X}_{t-1+k}$. The Johansen procedure is based on an examination of matrix Π, which contains information about a long-run relationship. The analysis of the long-run relationship in the model is based on examining the rank of this matrix. If this matrix has a full rank, the vector process Xt is stationary. If the rank equals zero, the matrix is a null matrix and the equation [4.16] remains a traditional VAR where the variables are not cointegrated and hence have no long-run solution. The third and most interesting possibility is when $0 < rank(\Pi) = r < p$. This implies that there are $p \times r$ matrices α and β such that $\Pi = \alpha\beta'$. The cointegration vector β has the property that $\beta'X_t$ is stationary even though Xt itself is non-stationary. The Johansen procedure helps to determine and identify this (these) cointegrating vector(s).

The question is then how this can be done in a single equation. The algebra follows the same logic, but outside matrix algebra it becomes messy. We can thus demonstrate this using two variables that are lagged one period each.

$$X_t = \beta_0 + \beta_1 X_{t-1} + \beta_2 Y_t + \beta_3 Y_{t-1} + \varepsilon_t \qquad [4.17]$$

Subtracting X_{t-1} from both sides, we get

$$X_t - X_{t-1} = \beta_0 + \beta_1 X_{t-1} - X_{t-1} + \beta_2 Y_t + \beta_3 Y_{t-1} + \varepsilon_t$$
$$\Delta X_t = \beta_0 + (\beta_1 - 1)X_{t-1} + \beta_2 Y_t + \beta_3 Y_{t-1} + \varepsilon_t$$

[4.18]

To have ΔX_{t-1} on the right-hand side, we need to subtract $(\beta_1 - 1)X_{t-2}$ on both sides:

$$\Delta X_t - (\beta - 1)X_{t-2} = \beta_0 + (\beta - 1)X_{t-1} + \beta_2 Y_t + \beta_3 Y_{t-1} + \varepsilon_t$$
$$\Delta X_t = \beta_0 + (\beta_1 - 1)X_{t-1} - (\beta_1 - 1)X_{t-2} + \beta_2 Y_t + \beta_3 Y_{t-1} + \varepsilon_t$$

[4.19]

The same can be done for Y_t and then we get X_{t-k} combined with Y_{t-k} to form a vector as per the theory (such as the demand for money or the purchasing power parity in this chapter) to be tested. The most important thing is to assemble the variables in the Π matrix (as in equation [4.16]) that provide the set of long-run information in a way that they are theoretically plausible, and the econometrics testing will follow to validate the relationship.

We may summarize the discussion thus far by pointing out two important concepts in time series econometrics. First, if a vector of variables, say, y_t are non-stationary but become stationary on differencing (i.e. they are I(1) variables), modelling them using a VAR in levels entails a unit root in the series and hence spurious regression. However, a linear combination of such variables could be stationary. We refer the latter as the existence of cointegration (i.e. CI(1,1)). Second, the Granger Representation Theorem states that if the $k \times 1$ vector of variables y_t is CI(1,1) then there exists an error correction representation of the general form,

$$\Delta y_t = \alpha z_{t-1} + \Gamma_1 \Delta y_{t-1} + \Gamma_2 \Delta y_{t-2} + \cdots + \Gamma_{p-1} \Delta y_{t-(p-1)} + \upsilon(L)\varepsilon_t$$

[4.20]

Where: $z_{t-1} = \beta' y_{t-1}$ are the t linear, cointegrating combination among the k variables, with β the $k \times r$ matrix of r cointegrating vectors.

Numerical Illustration of the VAR and ECM Model Formulation

In this sub-section we offer a numerical illustration of the VAR and ECM formulation above based on Patterson (2000). Let us take a simple ECM for y_{1t} and y_{2t} given as:

$$\Delta y_{1t} = -1/2(y_{1t-1} - 1/8 y_{2t-1}) + \varepsilon_{1t}$$
$$\Delta y_{2t} = 1/2(y_{1t-1} - 1/8 y_{2t-1}) + \varepsilon_{2t}$$

[4.21]

By setting $\Delta y_{1t} = \Delta y_{1t-1} \cdots = 0$, $\Delta y_{2t} = \Delta y_{2t-1} \cdots = 0$, and ε_{1t} and ε_{2t} to their expected value the steady state equilibrium could be given by: $\xi_t = y_{1t} - 1/8 y_{2t}$. To the extent that $\xi \neq 0$, there was a disequilibrium last period which cause Δy_{1t} and Δy_{2t} to change. The adjustment coefficient for Δy_{1t} equation is negative (-1/2) because $\xi > 0 \Rightarrow y_{1t-1} > 1/8 y_{2t-1}$ so that Δy_{1t} should decrease to move towards equilibrium. The converse process is true for the positive adjustment coefficient of Δy_{2t}, which is (1/2).

From [4.21], we can write the following formulation which helps to show the adjustment and error correction elements explicitly:

$$\Delta y_{2t} = 1/2(y_{1t-1} - 1/8 y_{2t-1}) = -1/16(y_{2t-1} - 8y_{1t-1})$$
$$\Delta y_{2t} = -1/16(y_{2t-1} - 8y_{1t-1}) + \varepsilon_{2t}$$

[4.22]

Here Δy_{2t} can be taken as correcting on its own disequilibrium. Using matrix notation this could be written as:

$$\begin{pmatrix} \Delta y_{1t} \\ \Delta y_{2t} \end{pmatrix} = \begin{bmatrix} -1/2 & 1/16 \\ 1/2 & -1/16 \end{bmatrix} \begin{pmatrix} y_{1t-1} \\ y_{2t-1} \end{pmatrix} + \begin{pmatrix} \varepsilon_{1t} \\ \varepsilon_{2t} \end{pmatrix}$$

[4.23]

Which might also be summarized as,

$$\Delta y_t = \Pi_1 y_{t-1} + \varepsilon_t$$

[4.24]

Where $\quad \Pi = \begin{bmatrix} -1/2 & 1/16 \\ 1/2 & -1/16 \end{bmatrix} \quad y_t = \begin{pmatrix} y_{1t-1} \\ y_{2t-1} \end{pmatrix} \quad \varepsilon_t = \begin{pmatrix} \varepsilon_{1t} \\ \varepsilon_{2t} \end{pmatrix}$

The coefficient matrix Π could be separated out into an "adjustment" (α) and "equilibrium" (β) coefficients, where $\alpha' = (-1/2, 1/2)$ and $\beta' = (1, -1/8)$. It is also true that the equilibrium combination is $\beta' y_t = \xi_t$ and $\Pi = \alpha\beta'$. Thus, we can write [4.22] as:

$$\Delta y_t = \Pi y_{t-1} + \varepsilon \qquad \Delta y_t \equiv \alpha(B'\Delta y_{t-1}) + \varepsilon_t$$

[4.25]

In the example above, this is

$$\begin{pmatrix} \Delta y_{1t} \\ \Delta y_{2t} \end{pmatrix} = \begin{bmatrix} -1/2 & 1/16 \\ 1/2 & -1/16 \end{bmatrix} \begin{pmatrix} y_{1t-1} \\ y_{2t-1} \end{pmatrix} + \begin{pmatrix} \varepsilon_{1t} \\ \varepsilon_{2t} \end{pmatrix}$$

[4.26]

Which is also equivalent to,

$$\begin{pmatrix} \Delta y_{1t} \\ \Delta y_{2t} \end{pmatrix} = \begin{bmatrix} -1/2 & (1,-1/8) \\ 1/2 & \end{bmatrix} \begin{pmatrix} y_{1t-1} \\ y_{2t-1} \end{pmatrix} + \begin{pmatrix} \varepsilon_{1t} \\ \varepsilon_{2t} \end{pmatrix} \qquad [4.27]$$

Note from equation [4.27] that because the two variables in level are an I(1) series, the left hand side being an I(0), the equation will balance only if we have a linear combination of the level variables in the right hand side of the equation which is I(0). When this happens we refer the two variables as cointegrating and the vector that ties them together $[\beta' = (1,-1/8)]$ as the cointegrating vector. It is interesting to ask whether there is always a cointegrating vector. This can be answered by studying the characteristics of the Π matrix. From equation [4.24] it can be shown that the first row of this matrix can be obtained by multiplying the second raw by -1; or the second column could be obtained by multiplying the first column by -1/8. Thus, Π is an example of a matrix which doesn't have independent rows or columns. It is a matrix less than full rank – is a matrix with reduced rank. It has only 1 independent row or column while having a dimension of 2 by 2. This reduced rank characteristics could also be inferred from the fact that the determinant of Π is zero (or Π is singular). One of its eigen values is also zero. This can be shown by its characteristic equation given as,

$$|\Pi - vI| = 0 \quad \text{where } v \text{ is a scalar. Hence,}$$

$$\Pi - vI = \begin{bmatrix} -1/2 & 1/16 \\ 1/2 & -1/16 \end{bmatrix} - \begin{bmatrix} v & 0 \\ 0 & v \end{bmatrix} = \begin{bmatrix} -1/2 - v & 1/16 \\ 1/2 & -1/16 - v \end{bmatrix} \qquad [4.28]$$

Which in turn implies,

$$\begin{aligned} |\Pi - vI| &= (1/2 + v)(1/16 + v) - (1/2)(1/16) = 0 \\ &= 1/32 + (9/16)v + v^2 - 1/32 = 0 \\ &= v^2 + (9/16)v = 0 \\ &= v(v + 9/16) = 0 \end{aligned} \qquad [4.29]$$

The last equation is satisfied by the root $v = 0$ and $v = -9/16$. That is there are two eigen values obtained as a solution to the characteristic equation, of which one is zero. The zero values indicate the possibility of reduced rank. In fact the number of non-zero eigen values offers the rank of a matrix. Thus, testing for non-zero eigen values is tantamount to testing for the rank of the matrix and hence the number of co-integrating vector. In our numerical example above the number of non-zero eigen values is one and hence the rank of the matrix as well as the co-integrating vector is one. The discussion thus far can now be generalized in two directions: (a) to extend the VAR to more than two variables and, (b) extending the VAR to have longer lags. The first extension helps to show the possibility of having more than one co-integrating vectors. The second extension offers a similar formulation as that of equation [4.22] except the addition of a matrix for lagged level of the dependent variables in equation [4.22]. You are advised to pursue this by your own. Note also that in the case of first order VAR, the condition for stability is that all eigen values of Π have a modulus less than 1 (i.e. the root of the [reverse] characteristics polynomial have modulus greater [smaller] than 1, referred as the root lying [outside] inside the unit circle). (Patterson, 2000).

The following two numerical examples taken from Patterson (2000) demonstrate the nature of ECM when the VAR is extended to more than two variables (case 1), and when the bivariate case of VAR is allowed to have longer lags (case 2).

Case 1: Extension to more than 2 variables

ECM   Equilibrium

$$\Delta y_{1t} = -1/2\xi_{1t-1} + 1/4\xi_{2t-1} + \varepsilon_{1t}$$
$$\Delta y_{2t} = -1/8\xi_{1t-1} - 5/8\xi_{2t-1} + \varepsilon_{2t}$$
$$\Delta y_{3t} = 1/4\xi_{1t-1} + 3/8\xi_{2t-1} + \varepsilon_{3t}$$

$$\xi_{1t} = y_{1t} - 1/8 y_{2t}$$
$$\xi_{2t} = y_{2t} - 1/4 y_{3t}$$

This can be written in matrix form as:

$$\begin{pmatrix} \Delta y_{1t} \\ \Delta y_{2t} \\ \Delta y_{3t} \end{pmatrix} = \begin{bmatrix} -1/2 & 1/4 \\ 1/8 & -5/8 \\ 1/4 & 3/8 \end{bmatrix} \begin{pmatrix} \xi_{1t-1} \\ \xi_{2t-1} \end{pmatrix} + \begin{pmatrix} \varepsilon_{1t} \\ \varepsilon_{2t} \\ \varepsilon_{3t} \end{pmatrix}$$

$$= \begin{bmatrix} -1/2 & 1/4 \\ 1/8 & -5/8 \\ 1/4 & 3/8 \end{bmatrix} X \begin{pmatrix} 1 & -1/8 & 0 \\ 0 & 1 & -1/4 \end{pmatrix} \begin{pmatrix} y_{1t-1} \\ y_{2t-1} \\ y_{3t-1} \end{pmatrix} + \begin{pmatrix} \varepsilon_{1t} \\ \varepsilon_{2t} \\ \varepsilon_{3t} \end{pmatrix}$$

Eigen values: (-0.7928, -0.4416)

$$\alpha \qquad \beta'$$

$$\Pi = \begin{bmatrix} -1/2 & 5/16 & -1/16 \\ 1/8 & -41/64 & 5/32 \\ 1/4 & -11/32 & -3/32 \end{bmatrix} \qquad [4.30]$$

The rank or the number of non-zero eigen values (hence the number of the CI vectors of) Π is 2 (i.e, the full rank is reduced by 1).

$$\text{Adjustment coefficients } \alpha = \begin{bmatrix} -1/2 & 1/4 \\ 1/8 & -5/8 \\ 1/4 & 3/8 \end{bmatrix}$$

$$\text{Cointegrating vectors } \beta' = \begin{pmatrix} 1 & -1/8 & 0 \\ 0 & 1 & -1/4 \end{pmatrix}$$

Case 2: Extension to an Extended Lag Structure

Suppose a bivariate ECM is given by equation [4.31]

$$\Delta y_{1t} = -1/2(y_{1t-1} - 1/8 y_{2t-1}) + 1/8 \Delta y_{1t-1} + 1/4 \Delta y_{2t-1} + \varepsilon_{1t}$$
$$\Delta y_{2t} = 1/2(y_{1t-1} - 1/8 y_{2t-1}) + 1/4 \Delta y_{1t-1} - 3/4 \Delta y_{2t-1} + \varepsilon_{2t}$$

[4.31]

In a matrix form this is written as:

$$\Delta y_t = \Pi y_{t-1} + \Gamma_1 \Delta y_{t-1} + \varepsilon$$

$$\Pi = \alpha \beta' = \begin{pmatrix} -1/2 \\ 1/2 \end{pmatrix}(1, \ -1/8) = \begin{bmatrix} -1/2 & 1/16 \\ 1/2 & -1/16 \end{bmatrix} \text{ and } \Gamma_1 = \begin{bmatrix} 1/8 & 1/4 \\ 1/4 & -3/4 \end{bmatrix} \text{ [4.32]}$$

$$\qquad \alpha \qquad \beta'$$

Assuming y_{1t} and y_{2t} are I(1) and their first difference is I(0) the time series balance of the equation will be maintained if $y_{1t-1} - 8 y_{2t}$ is the cointegrating vector. The corresponding VAR for this is:

$$y_{1t} = 5/8 y_{1t-1} + 5/16 y_{2t-1} - 1/8 y_{1t-2} - 1/4 y_{2t-2} + \varepsilon_{1t}$$
$$y_{2t} = 3/4 y_{1t-1} + 3/16 y_{2t-1} - 1/4 y_{1t-2} + 3/4 y_{2t-2} + \varepsilon_{1t}$$

Which is $y_t = \Pi_1 y_{t-1} + \Pi_2 y_{t-2} + \varepsilon_t$

Where $\Pi_1 = \begin{bmatrix} 5/8 & 5/16 \\ 3/4 & 3/16 \end{bmatrix}$ $\qquad \Pi_2 = \begin{bmatrix} -1/8 & -1/4 \\ -1/4 & 4/4 \end{bmatrix}$

The relationship in the coefficients of the VAR and ECM can be given by equation [4.33].

$$\Pi = \Pi_1 + \Pi_2 - I \text{ and } \Gamma_1 = -\Gamma_2$$

[4.33]

In general if the VAR is pth order and given by

$$y_t = \Pi_1 y_{t-1} + \Pi_2 y_{t-2} + \cdots + \Pi_p y_{t-p} + \varepsilon_t \qquad \text{then the ECM is given by,}$$

$$\Delta y_t = \Pi y_{t-1} + \Gamma_1 \Delta y_{t-1} + \Gamma_2 \Delta y_{t-2} + \cdots + \Gamma_{p-1} \Delta y_{t-(p-1)} + \varepsilon$$

With

$$\Pi = \Pi_1 + \Pi_2 + \cdots + \Pi_p - I \quad \text{and} \quad \Gamma_i = -(\Pi_{i+1} + \Pi_{i+2} + \cdots + \Pi_p) \quad \textit{for} \ \ i = 1, \cdots, p-1$$

An Application of the Johansen Approach Using Ethiopian Consumption Data

Estimation of Reduced-form VAR and Test for Cointegration

We noted that, in the Johansen approach, the starting point is to run unrestricted VAR. The first step in this direction is to determine the lag length of the VAR. To estimate unrestricted VAR using PCGIVE, go to model and select multiple equation dynamic modelling. This will take you to a dialog box in which you have to choose the variables to be included in the VAR. But before you select the variables first click on NEW MODEL to erase any other variable/s selected earlier. Next, determine the lag length of the VAR by choosing the appropriate lag length from the bottom right most corners. Then, double click on the variables of interest each at a time. Now the variables would enter with their selected lag. Click OK and choose the method of estimation- unrestricted system. Determine the sample size for estimation and click OK. This final command would display the result along with the diagnostic tests.

The diagnostic test in Table 4.7 shows that the first and second lags of LRY are statistically significant, the first lag of LP is also significant while the rest are not significant at least at 5% level of significance. This necessitates dropping the insignificant lags to make our VAR congruent with the data. We would not, however, drop LRCP_1 even if it is insignificant since the other first lags are significant and our cointegration test requires the VAR to be of the same order of lag.

Table 4.7:   F-test of retained regressors

```
F-tests on retained regressors, F(3,29) =
      LRCP_1     1.82299 [0.165]      LRCP_2     2.26677 [0.102]
       LRY_1     3.72588 [0.022]*      LRY_2     3.34289 [0.033]*
        LP_1     24.6119 [0.000]**      LP_2     2.64411 [0.068]

   Constant U     1.98482 [0.138]
```

Dropping the insignificant lags gives us the following diagnostic result where all the lags included are significant.

Table 4.8:   F-test of retained regressors

```
F-tests on retained regressors, F(3,32) =
      LRCP_1    3.54414 [0.025]*      LRY_1      7.05962 [0.001]**


      LP_1    117.142 [0.000]**Constant U      9.36337 [0.000]**
```

Again to make sure that our reduction of the model from lag 2 to lag 1 is admissible, we can use the AIC, SC and the HQ statistics following the routine of PCGIVE. Go to model, click on progress and click OK.

Illustration 4.5:   Model selection for single equation

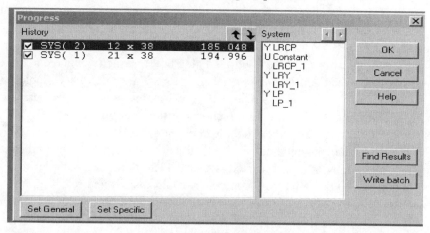

This will give you the result shown in Table 4.9. The result shows that reducing the model from VAR (2) to VAR (1)-i.e. SYS(1) to SYS (2), is acceptable based on the overall F-test at 5% level of significance. That is, it is possible to eliminate lag length 2 without losing much information.

Table 4.9:   Model reduction test

```
Progress to date
Model       T    p              log-likelihood        SC          HQ         AIC
SYS( 1)     38   21   OLS          194.99552       -8.2527     -8.8357     -9.1577
SYS( 2)     38   12   OLS          185.04756       -8.5906     -8.9238     -9.1078

Tests of model reduction (please ensure models are nested for test validity)
SYS( 1) --> SYS( 2): F(9,70)          =1.8863 [0.0682]
```

Once the order of the VAR is determined, we can go to the determination of the cointegration rank. Using PCGIVE, go to test and click on dynamic analysis and cointegration test. This will lead you to a dialog table in which you have to choose the level of integration of your data. In our case since all of our variables are I(1), check the box that reads as I(1) cointegration analysis. The result of the cointegration test is reported in Table 4.10.

Table 4.10:   Cointegration trace test

```
I(1) cointegration analysis, 1963 to 2001
          eigenvalue          loglik for rank
             162.3614                          0
              0.65010              182.8387     1
              0.24638              188.3546     2
              0.099513             190.3985     3

rankTrace test [ Prob] Max test  [ Prob]Trace test (T-nm)  Max test  (T-nm)
   0     56.07 [0.000]**  40.95  [0.000]**   1.76 [0.000]**   37.80 [0.000]**
   1     15.12 [0.224]    11.03  [0.258]    13.96 [0.299]    10.18 [0.329]
   2      4.09 [0.411]     4.09  [0.410]     3.77 [0.459]     3.77 [0.458]

Asymptotic p-values based on: Restricted constant
Restricted variables:
[0] = Constant
Number of lags used in the analysis: 1

beta (scaled on diagonal; cointegrating vectors in columns)
LRCP1      1.0000            -1.3878            0.38515
LRY1      -1.9866             1.0000           -2.7560
LP         0.34940            0.16547           1.0000
Constant   8.2994             2.6417           18.249

alpha
LRCP1      0.14527            0.38712           0.048681
LRY1       0.16302            0.029742          0.062492
LP         0.23210            0.24696          -0.070098

long-run matrix, rank 3
             LRCP1             LRY1                LP          Constant
LRCP1     -0.37322          -0.035636           0.16350         3.1167
LRY1       0.14582          -0.46634            0.12437         2.5720
LP        -0.13762          -0.020930           0.051862        1.2994
```

The cointegration test reports the eigen values, trace statistics, beta and alpha coefficients. The trace statistics (see the highlighted row in Table 4.10) suggest that the null hypothesis of zero cointegration relationship can be rejected in favour of one cointegrating vector.

Identification of β Coefficients

As the Johansen procedure only determines the number of stationary vectors that span the cointegration space, and any linear combination of stationary vectors is also stationary vector, the estimated β coefficients are not unique. As a result, once the cointegration rank is determined and the cointegrating relations are motivated based on some theory, we can impose a rank restriction in the cointegration space to obtain a unique relationship.

Select model, model setting, cointegrated VAR, to see Illustration 4.6:

Illustration 4.6:   Estimating cointegrated VAR

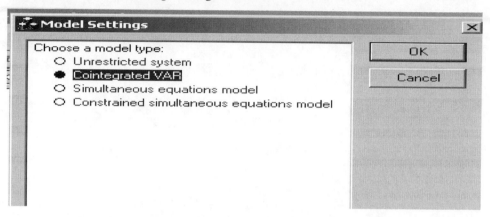

Click OK and the restricted cointegration analysis dialog table appears as:

Illustration 4.7:   **Estimating cointegrated VAR with no restrictions**

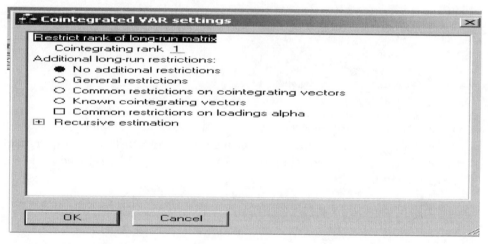

Set the cointegration rank to 1, select "No additional restrictions" and press OK. This prompts you to select the estimation method (which is by default, only reduced rank regression) and the sample period. Press OK to obtain the result in Table 4.11.

Table 4.11: Cointegration test

```
Cointegrated VAR (using Consumption data.in7)
The estimation sample is: 1963 to 2001
Cointegrated VAR (1) in:
[0] = LRCP1
[1] = LRY1
[2] = LP
Restricted variables:
[0] = Constant
Number of lags used in the analysis: 1
General cointegration restrictions:
beta
LRCP1          -0.11629
LRY1            0.23102
LP             -0.040631
Constant       -0.96512
alpha
LRCP1          -1.2492
LRY1           -1.4019
LP             -1.9959
Standard errors of alpha
LRCP1           0.33733
LRY1            0.31459
LP              0.40731

Restricted long-run matrix, rank 1
                LRCP1            LRY1              LP        Constant
LRCP1           0.14527       -0.28859        0.050758        1.2057
LRY1            0.16302       -0.32385        0.056960        1.3530
LP              0.23210       -0.46108        0.081096        1.9263

Standard errors of long-run matrix
LRCP1           0.039228       0.077929       0.013706       0.32557
LRY1            0.036583       0.072674       0.012782       0.30362
LP              0.047365       0.094094       0.016549       0.39310
Reduced form beta
LRCP1          -1.0000
LRY1            1.9866
LP             -0.34940
Constant       -8.2994
Standard errors of reduced form beta
LRCP1           0.00000
LRY1            0.36864
LP              0.14437
Constant        2.8967
Moving-average impact matrix
                2.4901         -2.9603         0.52066
                1.6722         -2.3220         0.58428
                2.3808         -4.7296         1.8319
log-likelihood       182.838716   -T/2log|Omega|        348.854524
no. of observations           39   no. of parameters              6
rank of long-run matrix        1   no. long-run restrictions      0
beta is not identified
No restrictions imposed
```

This process imposes a cointegration rank of 1 and produces the reduced beta coefficients from the reduced rank regression under the rank restriction. The beta coefficients extracted from Table 4.11 are shown in equation [4.34]:

$$LRCP = 8.2994 - 1.9866LRY1 + 0.3494LP \qquad [4.34]$$

The beta coefficients can be taken as the counterpart of the long run coefficients in our static long run equation except that the β coefficients are not structural parameters. As such we can see that income is positively related with private consumption while price is inversely related with private consumption. An important question at this point is whether this cointegrating vector is unique in the sense that all the variables span the cointegrating space. To answer this question it is possible to test the importance of each variable by dropping them one by one (or imposing zero restrictions) from the reduced form cointegrating vectors and testing the validity of these restrictions. This can also be considered as a hypothesis testing on the significance of the variables in the long run structural equation.

To carry out this procedure in PCGIVE, go to model, model settings, cointegrated VAR and press OK. Select the cointegration rank as before –i.e. 1, check the box "General restrictions" and click OK to see Illustration 4.8:

Illustration 4.8: General restrictions using PCGIVE

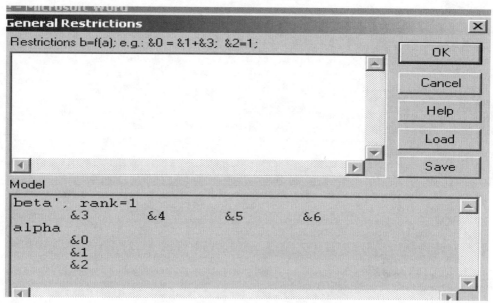

Using the restriction editor, we can impose different restrictions. The β coefficients are identified as &3, &4, &5 and &6 representing LRCP, LRY, LP and the constant. To test the significance of, for instance, LRY you can write **&4=0;** and press OK and choose restricted RRR to see the results in Table 4.12:

Table 4.12:   Testing long-run restrictions

```
Cointegrated VAR (using Consumption data.in7)
The estimation sample is: 1963 to 2001

Cointegrated VAR (1) in:
[0] = LRCP1
[1] = LRY1
[2] = LP
Restricted variables:
[0] = Constant
Number of lags used in the analysis: 1
General cointegration restrictions:
&4=0;
beta
LRCP1                        0.35108
LRY1                         0.00000
LP                          -0.13390
Constant                    -2.7367
alpha
LRCP1     -0.51294
LRY1      -0.49333
LP        -0.80341
Standard errors of alpha
LRCP1      0.12504
LRY1       0.12487
LP                           0.15027
Restricted long-run matrix, rank 1
              LRCP1          LRY1            LP          Constant
LRCP1      -0.18008       0.00000       0.068683        1.4037
LRY1       -0.17320       0.00000       0.066058        1.3501
LP         -0.28206       0.00000       0.10758         2.1987
Standard errors of long-run matrix
LRCP1       0.043900      0.00000       0.016743        0.34220
LRY1        0.043839      0.00000       0.016720        0.34172
LP          0.052758      0.00000       0.020122        0.41125

Reduced form beta
LRCP1      -1.0000
LRY1        0.00000
LP          0.38140
Constant    7.7950

Moving-average impact matrix
-1.4837 -8.0529e-017   0.94729
        -2.3888        1.0000         0.91108
-3.8903 -2.5576e-016   2.4837

log-likelihood               180.501634   -T/2log|Omega|          346.517442
no. of observations                  39   no. of parameters                5
rank of long-run matrix               1   no. long run restrictions        1
beta is not identified
LR test of restrictions: Chi^2(1) =4.6742 [0.0306]*
```

This procedure imposes zero restriction on LRY and estimates the reduced form cointegrating relationship without LRY. Then, it generates a likelihood ratio (LR) based test on the validity of the restriction. As the test in equation [4.35], Table 4.12, shows, the zero restriction on LRY is rejected implying that it is an important variable spanning the cointegration space. In terms of the long run structural relationship it is a significant variable in explaining private consumption. We can also do the same for LP. As the summary of the result shows below, LP is also an important variable in spanning the cointegration space.

$$\text{LR test of restrictions: Chi}^2(1) = 3.8761 \ [0.0490]^* \qquad [4.35]$$

The test results above suggest that our cointegrating vector is unique and in terms of the structural long run relationship, both income and price are significant variables in explaining private consumption in Ethiopia.

Testing for Weak Exogeneity

In the previous section, we managed to determine the cointegration rank and the uniqueness of the CI vector. Now we need to condition LRC on LRY and LP to represent the consumption function as LRC=f(LRY, LP) [$\log C = \beta_0 + \beta_1 \log Y + \beta_2 \log P$]. This representation presupposes classification of the variables as endogenous and exogenous. For this representation to be acceptable, we need to test for the weak exogeneity of LRY and LP. If we do not get this result, then our model is suffering from what is called an endogeneity problem. This in turn means we have no legitimate reason to make C the dependent variable as Y and P could also equally be such a candidate. Weak exogeneity requires the validity of zero restrictions on the α coefficients corresponding with the variables of interest. As illustration, consider the representation of a simple model composed of LRC and LRY:

$$\begin{bmatrix} \Delta LRC \\ \Delta LRY \end{bmatrix} = \Gamma_1 \begin{bmatrix} \Delta LRC_{t-1} \\ \Delta LRY_{t-1} \end{bmatrix} + \begin{bmatrix} \alpha_1 \\ \alpha_2 \end{bmatrix} \begin{bmatrix} \beta_1 & \beta_2 \end{bmatrix} \begin{bmatrix} LRC_{t-1} \\ LRY_{t-1} \end{bmatrix} \qquad [4.36]$$

When $\alpha_2 = 0$, then the equation for ΔLRY does not contain information about the long run beta parameters. That is, the beta parameters are not dependent on LRY and hence LRY is weakly exogenous. In this case as LRY is contemporaneous with LRC, we can write LRC as a function of LRY.

In PCGIVE, to test for weak exogeneity, we use a similar procedure of imposing restriction on the beta parameters except that in this case we impose restrictions on the α coefficients. For instance, by imposing a zero restriction on the α coefficient corresponding to LRY1, we can test for weak exogeniety of LRY1. In the restriction editor, type '**&1=0;**' and press OK to get the final result shown in Illustration 4.9.

Illustration 4.9: General restrictions

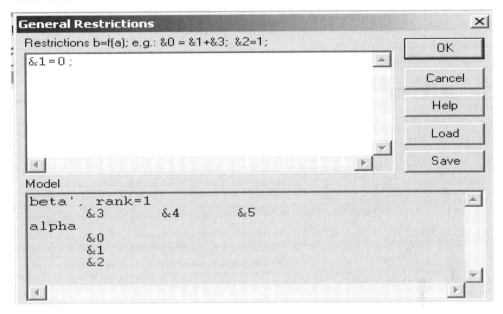

Weak exogeniety test for LRY1:   **LR test of restrictions: Chi^2(1) = 3.5580 [0.0593]**

Weak exogeniety test for LP: **LR test of restrictions: Chi^2(1) =0.48371 [0.4867]**

The result suggests that the zero restriction on LRY1 is not rejected implying that LRY1 is weakly exogenous in our consumption equation. Similarly, the weakly exogenous test for LP also suggests that it is weakly exogenous.

Once we establish the weak exogeneity conditions, we can write the cointegrating vector in equation format by classifying the variables into endogenous and exogenous. Imposing the zero restrictions on both LRY1 and LP, we can condition LRCP1 by LRY1 and LP as in equation [4.37]:

$$LRCP = -9.7557 + 2.1643LRY1 - 0.40416LP \qquad [4.37]$$

Finally, as we saved the residual from our static equation 4.47 [$\log C - (\beta_0 + \beta_1 \log Y + \beta_2 \log P) = error\ term$], we can save the cointegrating vector/s for our error correction estimation. In PCGIVE, go to test, store in data base, mark the check box "residual" and press OK and name the variable created.

Error Correction
Estimating the error correction model in this case is similar to the EG approach. Rather than the lag of the residual we will introduce the lag of the cointegrating vector that can be saved using the same procedure to save the residuals.

Modelling PPP using Data from Mozambique: The Nice Case of One Cointegration Vector

In this section, we use Mozambique's data to demonstrate how to model a time series variable using VAR and ECM formulation when there is only one cointegrating vector. The task will be a bit complicated when we encounter more than two cointegrating vectors. This is taken up in the next section.

We first tested for the time series properties of the variables (Lp, Ls and Lpsa, log of domestic price, exchange rate and foreign price, respectively) to be used in the Mozambique PPP model before proceeding to the cointegration test. The unit root test is carried out without a constant, with a constant and with a constant and trend using DF and ADF tests. From our DF test we observed that there is a problem of autocorrelation in the residuals as evidenced by the low DW statistics. We, however, switched to the ADF test. Using the AIC, we tried to determine the appropriate lag length to be included in our ADF test. A summary of our test is given in Table 4.13. We reported only the partial results which are relevant for our exposition here.

Table 4.13: Unit root test with trend and constant

```
The sample is 1991 (8) - 2001 (12)

DLp: ADF tests (T=125, Constant+Trend; 5%=-3.45 1%=-4.03)
D-lag    t-adf    beta Y_1    sigma   t-DY_lag   t-prob     AIC      F-prob
  6     -5.228**   0.11005    0.02390    1.476    0.1427   -7.399
  5     -5.061**   0.21772    0.02402    0.9611   0.3385   -7.396    0.1427
  4     -5.153**   0.28197    0.02401    0.7708   0.4423   -7.404    0.2155
  3     -5.368**   0.32913    0.02397    1.212    0.2281   -7.415    0.2996
  2     -5.355**   0.39388    0.02402    0.3148   0.7535   -7.419    0.2754
  1     -5.845**   0.40972    0.02393   -1.979    0.0501   -7.434    0.3877
  0     -8.785**   0.28800    0.02421   -7.418    0.1727

DLs: ADF tests (T=125, Constant+Trend; 5%=-3.45 1%=-4.03)
D-lag    t-adf    beta Y_1    sigma   t-DY_lag   t-prob     AIC      F-prob
  6     -4.124**   0.41554    0.03008    1.081    0.2821   -6.938
  5     -3.993*    0.46794    0.03010    0.5613   0.5757   -6.944    0.2821
  4     -4.083**   0.49544    0.03002    0.6432   0.5213   -6.958    0.4786
  3     -4.150**   0.52488    0.02994   -0.09175  0.9271   -6.970    0.5960
  2     -4.587**   0.52068    0.02982    0.3614   0.7184   -6.986    0.7534
  1     -4.936**   0.53708    0.02971   -0.8408   0.4021   -7.001    0.8436
  0     -6.208**   0.49742    0.02967                      -7.011    0.8412

DLpsa: ADF tests (T=125, Constant+Trend; 5%=-3.45 1%=-4.03)
D-lag    t-adf    beta Y_1    sigma   t-DY_lag   t-prob     AIC      F-prob
  6     -3.773*    0.27146    0.004051  -0.3835   0.7021   -10.95
  5     -4.231**   0.24401    0.004036  -0.3070   0.7594   -10.96    0.7021
  4     -4.783**   0.22175    0.004021   0.4568   0.6486   -10.98    0.8868
  3     -5.097**   0.25370    0.004007   0.8730   0.3844   -10.99    0.9303
  2     -5.252**   0.30988    0.004004  -0.3357   0.7377   -11.00    0.8788
  1     -6.362**   0.28707    0.003989  -0.6618   0.5093   -11.02    0.9338
  0     -8.637**   0.24121    0.003980                     -11.03    0.9417
```

The test result shows that the appropriate lag length can be one and the autocorrelation tests also do not detect autocorrelation among the residuals. With the critical values of -4.03 at 1% level of significance, the null hypothesis of the I(2) is rejected in favour of I(1). And hence, the variables are integrated variables-I(1). Since the order of integration of all the variables is I(1) we can proceed to test for cointegration.

In order to perform the Johansen test for cointegration among the variables, we first run the VAR model to determine the appropriate lag length to be included in our cointegrating equation. We started with a VAR of order 13 and performed restrictions tests to determine the data congruency of the VAR. First, we restricted in a way that only the first 8 lags are appropriate description of the data.

Table 4.14: Model reduction test

```
Model             T    p    log-likelihood       SC        HQ       AIC
Unrestricted     120  120        1088.1486   -13.348   -15.004   -16.136
Restricted       120   75        1074.7718   -14.921   -15.955   -16.663


Tests of model reduction (please ensure models are nested for test validity)
Unrestricted --> Restricted: F(45,232)=0.40266 [0.9998]
```

The result in Table 4.14 shows that the zero restrictions on the lags of 9–13 are not rejected. Now we proceed testing down by imposing restrictions on the lags of 4–8. The result is shown in Table 4.15.

Table 4.15: Model reduction test

```
Model             T    p    log-likelihood       SC        HQ       AIC
Unres(13)        120  120        1088.1486   -13.348   -15.004   -16.136
Res( 8)          120   75        1074.7718   -14.921   -15.955   -16.663
Res( 4)          120   39        1054.7365   -16.023   -16.561   -16.929


Tests of model reduction (please ensure models are nested for test validity)
Unr( 13) --> Res( 8): F(45,232)=0.40266 [0.9998]
Unr( 13) --> Res( 4): F(81,234)=0.59163 [0.9967]

Res( 8) --> Res( 4): F(36,275)=0.91568 [0.6111]
```

Our result shows that the reduction from both lag 13 to lag 4 and from lag 8 to lag 4 is not rejected. With this result, we tested if we could further reduce the lag length. This time we first experimented whether we can drop lag 4 and next lag three. The result shows that both lags can be dropped without any loss of information. However, the restrictions on lag 2 are rejected. Thus, the appropriate specification of our system is VAR of order 2. With lag length of 2 our VAR becomes a congruent representation of the data. The result of the reduction is reported in Table 4.16.

Table 4.16: Model reduction test summary

```
Model        T    p        log-likelihood       SC         HQ        AIC
Unr(13)    120  120  OLS        1088.1486    -13.348    -15.004    -16.136
RES( 8)    120   75  OLS        1074.7718    -14.921    -15.955    -16.663
RES( 4)    120   39  OLS        1054.7365    -16.023    -16.561    -16.929
RES( 3)    120   30  OLS        1052.7292    -16.349    -16.762    -17.045
RES( 2)    120   21  OLS        1044.7048    -16.574    -16.864    -17.062
RES( 1)    120   12  OLS        1014.1463    -16.424    -16.589    -16.702

Tests of model reduction (please ensure models are nested for test validity)

RES( 8) --> RES( 4): F(36,275)=0.91568 [0.6111]
RES( 8) --> RES( 3): F(45,277)=0.81047 [0.8009]
RES( 8) --> RES( 2): F(54,277)=0.94262 [0.5914]
RES( 8) --> RES( 1): F(63,278)=1.7805  [0.0009]**

RES( 4) --> RES( 3): F(9,255) =0.39325 [0.9378]
RES( 4) --> RES( 2): F(18,297)=1.0063  [0.4522]
RES( 4) --> RES( 1): F(27,307)=2.9667  [0.0000]**

RES( 3) --> RES( 2): F(9,262) =1.6507  [0.1012]
RES( 3) --> RES( 1): F(18,305)=4.3390  [0.0000]**

RES( 2) --> RES( 1): F(9,270) =6.9910  [0.0000]**
```

Once we have determined the appropriate lag length, we do diagnostic tests on residuals of the model for any misspecification. As the test, reported in Table 4.17, shows the residuals are not autocorrelated but they have a problem of normality.

Table 4.17: Model diagnostic tests

```
Lp        : Portmanteau(12): 16.8794
Ls        : Portmanteau(12): 9.96028
Lpsa      : Portmanteau(12): 5.05682
Lp        : AR 1-7 test:     F(7,106)  =  1.7054  [0.1154]
Ls        : AR 1-7 test:     F(7,106)  = 0.94600  [0.4746]
Lpsa      : AR 1-7 test:     F(7,106)  = 0.58169  [0.7695]
Lp        : Normality test:  Chi^2(2)  =  11.621  [0.0030]**
Ls        : Normality test:  Chi^2(2)  =  25.580  [0.0000]**
Lpsa      : Normality test:  Chi^2(2)  =  2.4115  [0.2995]
Lp        : ARCH 1-7 test:   F(7,99)   = 0.65048  [0.7131]
Ls        : ARCH 1-7 test:   F(7,99)   = 0.24482  [0.9727]
Lpsa      : ARCH 1-7 test:   F(7,99)   = 0.78689  [0.5999]
Lp        : hetero test:     F(12,100) = 0.86299  [0.5864]
Ls        : hetero test:     F(12,100) = 0.64668  [0.7974]
Lpsa      : hetero test:     F(12,100) = 0.70575  [0.7426]
Lp        : hetero-X test:   F(27,85)  =  1.0957  [0.3642]
Ls        : hetero-X test:   F(27,85)  = 0.54966  [0.9599]
Lpsa      : hetero-X test:   F(27,85)  = 0.70594  [0.8463]

Vector Portmanteau(12): 79.6945
Vector AR 1-7 test:      F(63,269)  = 0.92357  [0.6393]
Vector Normality test:   Chi^2(6)   =  37.073  [0.0000]**
Vector hetero test:      F(72,522)  =  1.0239  [0.4295]
Vector hetero-X test:    F(162,478) = 0.94961  [0.6476]
```

Noting the problem of normality, we proceed to testing for cointegration as, at least, we don't have autocorrelated residuals. The Johansen cointegration test result is reported in Table 4.18.

Table 4.18: Cointegration test using the trace statistic

```
I(1) cointegration analysis, 1992 (1) to 2001 (12)
      H0:rank<= Trace test  [ Prob]
        0              47.483 [0.000] **
        1              7.1420 [0.568]
        2              0.50135 [0.479]

Asymptotic p-values based on: Unrestricted constant
Unrestricted variables:
[0] = Constant
Number of lags used in the analysis: 2

β (scaled on diagonal; cointegrating vectors in columns)
Lp            1.0000        -0.67844       -0.25157
Ls           -0.75280        1.0000        -0.041383
Lpsa         -1.5067         1.2601         1.0000

α
Lp           -0.12192        0.00050259    -0.0040904
Ls           -0.014270      -0.035946      -0.0041932
Lpsa         -0.00069733    -0.00041408     0.0034732

long-run matrix, rank 3
                Lp              Ls            Lpsa
Lp           -0.12124        0.092456        0.18024
Ls            0.011172       -0.025030       -0.027989
Lpsa         -0.0012901     -3.2863e-005     0.0040020
```

As shown by the λ-trace statistics, the null hypothesis of no cointegrating relationship is rejected. The hypothesis that there, however, is one cointegrating relationship could not be rejected, and hence we have one cointegrating relationship among the variables. The resultant cointegrating vector normalized with respect to LP is shown in equation [4.38] separately.

$$
\begin{array}{lll}
\text{LP} & \text{LS} & \text{LPSA} \\
1.0000 & -0.67844 & -0.25157
\end{array}
\tag{4.38}
$$

The above vector can be viewed as the long run relationship among the variables. Now imposing a rank restriction, we can identify the beta and alpha vectors.

Table 4.19: Identifying long-run relationships

```
Beta
Lp              1.0000
Ls             -0.75280
Lpsa           -1.5067
Alpha                     Standard errors      t-stat (own calculation)
Lp             -0.12192        0.018445               6.6099
Ls             -0.014270       0.026518               0.5381
Lpsa   -0.00069733             0.0034727              0.2008
```

We also tested for exclusion of LS and LPSA from the cointegrating relationship. As the LR test shown in Table 4.20 implies, the zero restrictions on LS and LPSA are rejected suggesting that both variables span the cointegrating vector.

Table 4.20: Exclusion test of LS and LP

```
EXCLUSION TEST OF LS & LP
LR test of restrictions: Chi^2(1) = 22.868 [0.0000]
LR test of restrictions: Chi^2(1) = 19.422 [0.0000]
```

To test the PPP theory we have also imposed a restriction that the coefficients of LS and LPSA are equal to one. The result of the test is given in Table 4.21.

Table 4.21: Identified PPP relationship

```
beta                          Standard errors of beta

Lp              -1.0645            0.049328
Ls               1.0000            0.00000
Lpsa             1.0000            0.00000

Alpha                         Standard errors of alpha
Lp               0.074030           0.012788
Ls               0.011803           0.017774
Lpsa            -0.00026323         0.0023294

Restricted long-run matrix, rank 1
                 Lp                    Ls                   Lpsa
Lp              -0.078807          0.074030             0.074030
Ls              -0.012565          0.011803             0.011803
Lpsa             0.00028021       -0.00026323          -0.00026323

log-likelihood       1036.63876   -T/2log|Omega|         1547.45663
no. of observations        120    no. of parameters          16
rank of long-run matrix      1    no. long-run restrictions   1
beta is identified

LR test of restrictions: Chi^2(1) = 8.9902 [0.0027]**
```

The test result rejects the PPP hypothesis completely. The rejection of this hypothesis is not a surprise as it is consistent with most studies.

Handling Two Cointegrating Vectors: Kenya's Exchange Rate Model

In some theoretical settings, we may expect to get more than one cointegrating vector. Consider Were *et al's* (2001) exchange rate model of Kenya.

$$e_t = \alpha_0 + \alpha_1\left(p_t - p_t^*\right) + \alpha_2\left(i_t - i_t^*\right) + \alpha_3\left(\rho_t - \rho_t^*\right) + \alpha_4\int CA + u_i \qquad [4.39]$$

Where: $(p_t - p_t^*)$ is the price differential, $(i_t - i_t^*)$ is the interest rate differential, $(\rho_t - \rho_t^*)$ is the expected inflation rate differential between domestic and foreign prices and $\int CA$ is the cumulative current account balance.

With this specification, it is possible to have two cointegrating relationships. The first one may give the exchange rate relationship while the second one may represent the interest rate differential as a function of the rest of the variables. In such cases, once the long run relationships are determined, the error correction model may need to be estimated as there may be correlation between the residuals of the two equations (simultaneity bias). In what follows we demonstrate how we can handle such cases using Kenyan data and specification of Were *et al.* (2001).

Many of the practical procedures are similar to the case of one cointegrating vector in sections 4.4 and 4.5. We use the same procedures in estimating the unrestricted VAR, determining the lag length and testing for cointegration. Hence, only the results are reported here. The only different point introduced is the appearance of the seasonal terms. That is, since the data is a monthly data, seasonal terms are introduced to capture seasonal variation in the dependent variable.

Estimating the VAR

Illustration 4.10: Data selection

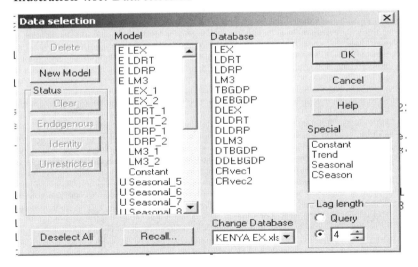

Table 4.22:   Estimated unrestricted reduced form model of LEX with four lags

```
Estimating the unrestricted reduced form by OLS (using KENYA EX.xls)
The present sample is:1993 (7) to 2000 (5)

URF Equation 1 for LEX
Variable      Coefficient   Std.Error    t-value      t-prob
LEX_1            1.1654       0.12873      9.053       0.0000
LEX_2           -0.17476      0.19860     -0.880       0.3827
LEX_3           -0.084749     0.19633     -0.432       0.6677
LEX_4            0.053594     0.13119      0.409       0.6845
LDRT_1          -0.12961      0.050707    -2.556       0.0134
LDRT_2           0.19751      0.083382     2.369       0.0214
LDRT_3          -0.12333      0.086717    -1.422       0.1606
LDRT_4           0.028929     0.051920     0.557       0.5797
LDRP_1           0.16609      0.41282      0.402       0.6890
LDRP_2          -0.23381      0.54544     -0.429       0.6698
LDRP_3           0.72298      0.52180      1.386       0.1715
LDRP_4          -0.76635      0.36475     -2.101       0.0402
LM3_1           -0.12376      0.31170     -0.397       0.6929
LM3_2            0.19406      0.41278      0.470       0.6401
LM3_3           -0.37367      0.38615     -0.968       0.3374
LM3_4            0.36796      0.26507      1.388       0.1707
Constant        -0.42985      0.84599     -0.508       0.6134
Seasonal_3       0.0045056    0.026582     0.169       0.8660
Seasonal_2       0.0023154    0.027772     0.083       0.9339
Seasonal_4       0.026277     0.026077     1.008       0.3180
Seasonal_1       0.024049     0.026721     0.900       0.3720
Seasonal_5      -0.0051753    0.025544    -0.203       0.8402
Seasonal_8      -0.0091009    0.023567    -0.386       0.7009
Seasonal_9       0.013072     0.025773     0.507       0.6140
Seasonal_6       0.034781     0.025376     1.371       0.1761
Seasonal_7       0.028620     0.024759     1.156       0.2527
Seasonal_10      0.040438     0.026449     1.529       0.1320
Seasonal_11      0.020383     0.023926     0.852       0.3980

\sigma = 0.0418292RSS = 0.09623239002
```

Table 4.23: Estimated unrestricted reduced form model of LDRT

```
URF Equation 2 for LDRT
Variable      Coefficient    Std.Error    t-value    t-prob
LEX_1           0.77112       0.34894       2.210     0.0313
LEX_2          -0.92622       0.53835      -1.720     0.0910
LEX_3           0.18064       0.53219       0.339     0.7356
LEX_4          -0.072658      0.35562      -0.204     0.8389
LDRT_1          1.2338        0.13745       8.976     0.0000
LDRT_2         -0.42407       0.22602      -1.876     0.0659
LDRT_3          0.19473       0.23506       0.828     0.4110
LDRT_4         -0.13489       0.14074      -0.958     0.3420
LDRP_1          1.0291        1.1190        0.920     0.3618
LDRP_2          0.33012       1.4785        0.223     0.8241
LDRP_3         -0.84132       1.4144       -0.595     0.5544
LDRP_4         -0.51675       0.98872      -0.523     0.6033
LM3_1           0.23991       0.84493       0.284     0.7775
LM3_2           0.22299       1.1189        0.199     0.8428
LM3_3          -0.29722       1.0467       -0.284     0.7775
LM3_4          -0.20499       0.71852      -0.285     0.7765
Constant        0.78914       2.2932        0.344     0.7321
Seasonal_3     -0.0042340     0.072055     -0.059     0.9534
Seasonal_2     -0.0056740     0.075282     -0.075     0.9402
Seasonal_4     -0.033769      0.070687     -0.478     0.6347
Seasonal_1     -0.061654      0.072434     -0.851     0.3984
Seasonal_5      0.055437      0.069241      0.801     0.4268
Seasonal_8      0.12210       0.063882      1.911     0.0612
Seasonal_9      0.030868      0.069863      0.442     0.6603
Seasonal_6      0.060978      0.068786      0.886     0.3792
Seasonal_7      0.020054      0.067113      0.299     0.7662
Seasonal_10     0.025108      0.071695      0.350     0.7275
Seasonal_11     0.054421      0.064855      0.839     0.4050

\sigma = 0.113386RSS = 0.7071004932
```

Table 4.24: Estimated unrestricted reduced form model of LDRP and LM3

```
URF Equation 3 for LDRP
```

Variable	Coefficient	Std.Error	t-value	t-prob
LEX_1	0.012768	0.038774	0.329	0.7432
LEX_2	0.033756	0.059821	0.564	0.5749
LEX_3	0.012145	0.059136	0.205	0.8380
LEX_4	-0.029151	0.039515	-0.738	0.4638
LDRT_1	0.027467	0.015273	1.798	0.0776
LDRT_2	-0.060354	0.025115	-2.403	0.0197
LDRT_3	0.038147	0.026120	1.460	0.1498
LDRT_4	0.0043546	0.015638	0.278	0.7817
LDRP_1	0.96636	0.12434	7.772	0.0000
LDRP_2	-0.15189	0.16429	-0.925	0.3592
LDRP_3	0.12322	0.15717	0.784	0.4364
LDRP_4	-0.093068	0.10986	-0.847	0.4006
LM3_1	0.072458	0.093886	0.772	0.4436
LM3_2	0.0094701	0.12433	0.076	0.9396
LM3_3	-0.22450	0.11631	-1.930	0.0588
LM3_4	0.21374	0.079841	2.677	0.0098
Constant	-0.75535	0.25482	-2.964	0.0045
Seasonal_3	-0.0016580	0.0080066	-0.207	0.8367
Seasonal_2	0.022557	0.0083651	2.697	0.0093
Seasonal_4	0.0020107	0.0078546	0.256	0.7989
Seasonal_1	0.010352	0.0080486	1.286	0.2038
Seasonal_5	0.0029017	0.0076938	0.377	0.7075
Seasonal_8	0.0086893	0.0070984	1.224	0.2261
Seasonal_9	-0.010724	0.0077630	-1.381	0.1727
Seasonal_6	-0.0030105	0.0076433	-0.394	0.6952
Seasonal_7	-0.011812	0.0074575	-1.584	0.1190
Seasonal_10	-0.0016801	0.0079665	-0.211	0.8337
Seasonal_11	0.014056	0.0072066	1.950	0.0562

```
\sigma = 0.0125992RSS = 0.008730640409
```

```
URF Equation 4 for LM3
```

Variable	Coefficient	Std.Error	t-value	t-prob
LEX_1	-0.00083797	0.053947	-0.016	0.9877
LEX_2	-0.0059823	0.083230	-0.072	0.9430
LEX_3	0.019557	0.082278	0.238	0.8130
LEX_4	-0.0087017	0.054979	-0.158	0.8748
LDRT_1	-0.026012	0.021250	-1.224	0.2261
LDRT_2	0.0017977	0.034943	0.051	0.9592
LDRT_3	0.068576	0.036341	1.887	0.0644
LDRT_4	-0.040187	0.021758	-1.847	0.0701
LDRP_1	-0.090819	0.17300	-0.525	0.6017
LDRP_2	-0.22905	0.22858	-1.002	0.3207
LDRP_3	0.44670	0.21868	2.043	0.0459
LDRP_4	-0.15071	0.15286	-0.986	0.3285
LM3_1	0.98356	0.13063	7.529	0.0000
LM3_2	0.19669	0.17298	1.137	0.2604
LM3_3	-0.28153	0.16183	-1.740	0.0875
LM3_4	0.091677	0.11108	0.825	0.4128
Constant	0.15635	0.35453	0.441	0.6609
Seasonal_3	-0.017355	0.011140	-1.558	0.1250
Seasonal_2	0.0011574	0.011639	0.099	0.9212
Seasonal_4	-0.010259	0.010928	-0.939	0.3519
Seasonal_1	-0.011915	0.011198	-1.064	0.2920
Seasonal_5	-0.014011	0.010705	-1.309	0.1960
Seasonal_8	-0.025620	0.0098763	-2.594	0.0121
Seasonal_9	-0.013601	0.010801	-1.259	0.2132
Seasonal_6	-0.016796	0.010634	-1.579	0.1200
Seasonal_7	-0.0062153	0.010376	-0.599	0.5516
Seasonal_10	0.0054523	0.011084	0.492	0.6247
Seasonal_11	-0.021706	0.010027	-2.165	0.0348

```
\sigma = 0.0175296RSS = 0.01690082882
```

Table 4.25:   Correlation of unrestricted form residuals

```
Correlation of URF residuals
                    LEX           LDRT          LDRP          LM3
  LEX             1.0000
  LDRT            0.016464      1.0000
  LDRP           -0.12722       0.011550      1.0000
  LM3             0.0087703    -0.082538     -0.0079435     1.0000

standard deviations of URF residuals
         LEX          LDRT          LDRP          LM3
      0.041829     0.11339       0.012599      0.017530

loglik = 1212.1317  log|\Omega| = -29.208   |\Omega| = 2.066e-013   T = 83
log|Y'Y/T| = -8.18231
R^2(LR) = 1R^2(LM) = 0.953044

F-test on all regressors except unrestricted, F(68,206) = 641.2 [0.0000] **
variables entered unrestricted:
Seasonal_3 Seasonal_2 Seasonal_4 Seasonal_1   Seasonal_5 Seasonal_8
Seasonal_9 Seasonal_6 Seasonal_7 Seasonal_10  Seasonal

F-tests on retained regressors, F(4, 52)
      LEX_1      20.8867  [0.0000] **    LEX_2    0.935230  [0.4509]
      LEX_3       0.0950147 [0.9836]     LEX_4    0.170023  [0.9527]
     LDRT_1      21.2577  [0.0000] **    LDRT_2   3.23341   [0.0192] *
     LDRT_3       1.96650 [0.1134]       LDRT_4   1.21271   [0.3166]
     LDRP_1      14.9338  [0.0000] **    LDRP_2   0.518708  [0.7223]
     LDRP_3       1.70743 [0.1624]       LDRP_4   1.63946   [0.1783]
      LM3_1      13.7886  [0.0000] **    LM3_2    0.379729  [0.8221]
      LM3_3       1.98945 [0.1098]       LM3_4    2.59448   [0.0470] *
   Constant       2.35168 [0.0661]

correlation of actual and fitted
                    LEX           LDRT          LDRP          LM3
                 0.96992       0.98674       0.99661       0.99821
```

Lag Reduction

Lag 3 and 4 are not significant and hence are reduced.

Procedure: Go to model in PcFiml, formulate system, select lag 3 and 4 and click on delete and accept.

Table 4.26: Estimation of unrestricted form by OLS for LEX

```
Estimating the unrestricted reduced form by OLS(using KENYA EX.xls)
The present sample is:1993 (7) to 2000 (5)

URF Equation 1 for LEX
```

Variable	Coefficient	Std.Error	t-value	t-prob
LEX_1	1.1458	0.12076	9.489	0.0000
LEX_2	-0.17830	0.13098	-1.361	0.1783
LDRT_1	-0.074999	0.044667	-1.679	0.0981
LDRT_2	0.067819	0.042919	1.580	0.1191
LDRP_1	0.16903	0.38916	0.434	0.6655
LDRP_2	-0.29697	0.34370	-0.864	0.3908
LM3_1	-0.35421	0.29067	-1.219	0.2275
LM3_2	0.43623	0.29278	1.490	0.1412
Constant	-0.66647	0.73085	-0.912	0.3653
Seasonal_3	0.0082180	0.025015	0.329	0.7436
Seasonal_2	-0.0074936	0.024340	-0.308	0.7592
Seasonal_4	0.027567	0.024014	1.148	0.2553
Seasonal_1	-0.00064434	0.024847	-0.026	0.9794
Seasonal_5	-0.00061087	0.024571	-0.025	0.9802
Seasonal_8	-0.011075	0.022891	-0.484	0.6302
Seasonal_9	-0.0067694	0.024580	-0.275	0.7839
Seasonal_6	0.025809	0.024097	1.071	0.2882
Seasonal_7	0.022813	0.023589	0.967	0.3372
Seasonal_10	0.024743	0.023010	1.075	0.2863
Seasonal_11	0.0079442	0.023250	0.342	0.7337

```
\sigma = 0.0422307RSS = 0.1123560964
```

Table 4.27: Unrestricted equation for LDRT

```
URF Equation 2 for LDRT
```

Variable	Coefficient	Std.Error	t-value	t-prob
LEX_1	0.85419	0.31518	2.710	0.0087
LEX_2	-0.85615	0.34185	-2.504	0.0149
LDRT_1	1.2314	0.11658	10.563	0.0000
LDRT_2	-0.31754	0.11202	-2.835	0.0062
LDRP_1	0.92891	1.0157	0.915	0.3639
LDRP_2	-1.1197	0.89704	-1.248	0.2166
LM3_1	-0.11273	0.75865	-0.149	0.8824
LM3_2	0.15655	0.76415	0.205	0.8383
Constant	-0.15115	1.9075	-0.079	0.9371
Seasonal_3	0.028405	0.065289	0.435	0.6650
Seasonal_2	0.012547	0.063526	0.198	0.8441
Seasonal_4	-0.0093608	0.062676	-0.149	0.8818
Seasonal_1	-0.058189	0.064850	-0.897	0.3730
Seasonal_5	0.064319	0.064129	1.003	0.3197
Seasonal_8	0.11617	0.059744	1.944	0.0563
Seasonal_9	0.0090913	0.064153	0.142	0.8878
Seasonal_6	0.059024	0.062892	0.939	0.3516
Seasonal_7	0.017631	0.061567	0.286	0.7755
Seasonal_10	0.016605	0.060056	0.276	0.7831
Seasonal_11	0.044502	0.060681	0.733	0.4660

```
\sigma = 0.11022RSS = 0.7653533857
```

Table 4.28:   Estimated unrestricted reduced form model for LDRP

```
URF Equation 3 for LDRP
Variable      Coefficient    Std.Error      t-value      t-prob
LEX_1          0.034342      0.038496        0.892       0.3757
LEX_2          0.0060303     0.041753        0.144       0.8856
LDRT_1         0.015840      0.014239        1.112       0.2702
LDRT_2        -0.0079332     0.013682       -0.580       0.5641
LDRP_1         0.91250       0.12406         7.356       0.0000
LDRP_2        -0.054208      0.10956        -0.495       0.6225
LM3_1          0.10610       0.092660        1.145       0.2565
LM3_2         -0.047105      0.093332       -0.505       0.6155
Constant      -0.66847       0.23298        -2.869       0.0056
Seasonal_3     0.0027773     0.0079743       0.348       0.7288
Seasonal_2     0.016260      0.0077590       2.096       0.0401
Seasonal_4     0.0025790     0.0076552       0.337       0.7373
Seasonal_1     0.010335      0.0079207       1.305       0.1967
Seasonal_5     0.0014261     0.0078326       0.182       0.8561
Seasonal_8     0.0051571     0.0072970       0.707       0.4823
Seasonal_9    -0.0082305     0.0078356      -1.050       0.2975
Seasonal_6    -0.0025891     0.0076815      -0.337       0.7372
Seasonal_7    -0.013116      0.0075197      -1.744       0.0860
Seasonal_10   -0.0087565     0.0073352      -1.194       0.2370
Seasonal_11    0.013148      0.0074115       1.774       0.0809

\sigma = 0.0134621RSS = 0.01141744475
```

Table 4.29:   Estimated unrestricted reduced form model for LM3

```
URF Equation 4 for LM3
Variable      Coefficient    Std.Error      t-value      t-prob
LEX_1          0.012042      0.050760        0.237       0.8132
LEX_2         -0.00020889    0.055056       -0.004       0.9970
LDRT_1        -0.038701      0.018775       -2.061       0.0434
LDRT_2         0.044117      0.018040        2.445       0.0173
LDRP_1        -0.22665       0.16358        -1.386       0.1708
LDRP_2         0.16498       0.14447         1.142       0.2578
LM3_1          0.96103       0.12218         7.866       0.0000
LM3_2          0.046605      0.12307         0.379       0.7062
Constant      -0.021483      0.30720        -0.070       0.9445
Seasonal_3    -0.020108      0.010515       -1.912       0.0604
Seasonal_2    -0.014387      0.010231       -1.406       0.1646
Seasonal_4    -0.019781      0.010094       -1.960       0.0545
Seasonal_1    -0.016201      0.010444       -1.551       0.1259
Seasonal_5    -0.018394      0.010328       -1.781       0.0797
Seasonal_8    -0.031678      0.0096219      -3.292       0.0016
Seasonal_9    -0.012005      0.010332       -1.162       0.2496
Seasonal_6    -0.020364      0.010129       -2.011       0.0487
Seasonal_7    -0.013721      0.0099155      -1.384       0.1713
Seasonal_10   -0.0099736     0.0096721      -1.031       0.3064
Seasonal_11   -0.024910      0.0097728      -2.549       0.0133

\sigma = 0.0177512RSS = 0.01985153031
```

Table 4.30: Correlation of URF residuals

```
correlation of URF residuals
                    LEX           LDRT           LDRP            LM3
  LEX            1.0000
  LDRT           0.012316       1.0000
  LDRP          -0.096307       0.0043409      1.0000
  LM3            0.016330      -0.072689       0.083768        1.0000

standard deviations of URF residuals
                    LEX           LDRT           LDRP            LM3
                 0.042231       0.11022        0.013462        0.017751

loglik = 1184.5568log|\Omega| = -28.5435|\Omega| = 4.01513e-013    T
= 83
log|Y'Y/T| = -8.18231
R^2(LR) = 1R^2(LM) = 0.946128

F-test on all regressors except unrestricted, F(36,226) = 1434.5
[0.0000] **
variables entered unrestricted:
Seasonal_3 Seasonal_2 Seasonal_4 Seasonal_1 Seasonal_5 Seasonal_8
Seasonal_9 Seasonal_6 Seasonal_7 Seasonal_10 Seasonal

F-tests on retained regressors, F(4, 60)
      LEX_1      23.8125 [0.0000] **    LEX_2    1.92168 [0.1185]
      LDRT_1     27.9674 [0.0000] **    LDRT_2   3.79348 [0.0081] **
      LDRP_1     14.3078 [0.0000] **    LDRP_2   0.920914 [0.4578]
      LM3_1      15.2388 [0.0000] **    LM3_2    0.606852 [0.6592]
   Constant2.30931 [0.0682]

correlation of actual and fitted
                    LEX           LDRT           LDRP            LM3
                 0.96479        0.98564        0.99556         0.99790
```

Illustration 4.11: Testing the progress

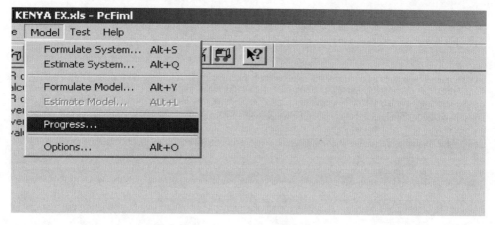

Table 4.31:   Model progress

```
Progress result
Progress to date
system     T    p              log-likelihood        SC        HQ       AIC
    2     83   80   OLS             1184.5568    -24.284   -25.679   -27.544
    1     83  112   OLS             1212.1317    -23.245   -25.198   -27.208


Tests of system reduction
System 1 --> System 2: F(32, 193) =1.1930 [0.2327]
```

The reduction from 4 lag to 2 lag is not rejected. We tested for a further reduction of our VAR and the result rejected the restriction on the second lag. Therefore, we concluded that lag length of 2 is a congruent representation of the data.

```
Progress to date
system     T    p              log-likelihood        SC        HQ       AIC
   40     83   64   COINT           1166.4928    -24.701   -25.817   -27.108
   39     83   80   COINT           1184.5568    -24.284   -25.679   -27.544
   37     83  112   OLS             1212.1317    -23.245   -25.198   -27.208


Tests of system reduction
System 39 --> System 40: F(16, 183) =1.7604 [0.0395] *
System 37 --> System 40: F(48, 202) =1.3929 [0.0604]

System 37 --> System 39: F(32, 193) =1.1930 [0.2327]
```

After determining the lag length which is congruent with the data, we can proceed to the next procedure-i.e. testing for cointegration.

Testing for Cointegration

In PcFiml, go to model and select estimate system[11] to get the following dialogue. Select cointegration analysis and accept.

Illustration 4.12: Estimating cointegrated VAR

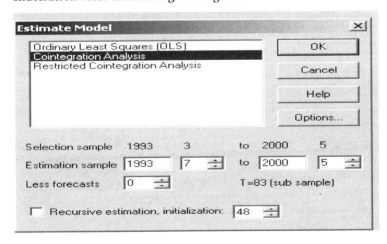

---

[11] Make sure that the lag length of the system is 2.

Table 4.32:   Cointegration and normality tests

```
Result of cointegration test
Cointegration analysis 1993 (4) to 2000 (5)
        eigenvalue      loglik for rank
          1175.82              0
         0.405512            1198.19          1
         0.165759            1205.98          2
        0.0573519           1208.52          3
         0.022054           1209.48          4

Ho:rank=   -Tlog(1-\mu)   using T-nm   95%   -T\Sum log(.)   using T-nm   95%
 p ==  0      44.72**      40.56**    23.8      67.31**       61.05**     39.9
 p <=  1      15.59        14.14      17.9      22.58         20.48       24.3
 p <=  2       5.079        4.607     11.4       6.997         6.346      12.5
 p <=  3       1.918        1.739      3.8       1.918         1.739       3.8

Number of lags used in the analysis: 2
Variables entered unrestricted:
Seasonal Seasonal_1 Seasonal_2 Seasonal_3 Seasonal_4 Seasonal_5
Seasonal_6 Seasonal_7 Seasonal_8 Seasonal_9 Seasonal_10 Seasonal_11

Vector AR 1-6F(96,157)    =  1.4399 [0.0215] *
Vector normality Chi^2( 8)=  12.711 [0.1222]
```

The result shows that the null hypothesis of no cointegration is rejected and we maintained the alternative hypothesis that there is one cointegrating relationship. A very important issue to note at this juncture is that the Johansen test for cointegration relies heavily on the Gaussian nature of the residuals. As can be read from Table 4.32, the vector normality test doesn't reject the null hypothesis of normality of the residuals, while the vector autocorrelation test rejects the null hypothesis of no autocorrelation at 5% level of significance but not at 1% level of significance. We can add the lag length to clear the problem of autocorrelation though this is at the cost of loss in degrees of freedom. Since the problem of autocorrelation can be ignored at least at 1% level of significance, we went along with the above results.

Our result differs significantly from that of Were *et al.* (2001) though we used the same data. Were *et al.* (2001) found two cointegrating relationships while our result showed that there is only one cointegrating vector. As the cointegration test depends on the order of the VAR and the variables entered unrestricted in the cointegration analysis, it is not surprising to get a different result. With this in mind, we changed the order of the VAR in order to obtain somehow similar result. Now we re-specify the VAR to be of order one with seasonal dummies and performed the cointegration test. The result showed that there exist two cointegrating relationships. As can be seen from the result shown in Table 4.33, this result suffers from serious problems of vector autocorrelation and non-normality. With these problems, as noted above, the Johansen cointegration test is not reliable and not valid.

Table 4.33: Cointegration test on Kenyan data

```
Cointegration analysis 1993 (4) to 2000 (5)

eigenvalueloglik for rank
1127.74                    0
0.572956          1164.33        1
0.284875          1178.75        2
0.0753704         1182.12        3
0.013863          1182.72        4


Ho:rank=p   -Tlog(1-\mu   using T-nm    95%  -T\Sum log(.)   using T-nm   95%
  p ==0      73.17**       69.77**     23.8     110**          104.8**    39.9
  p <=1      28.84**       27.49**     17.9    36.78**          35.06**   24.3
  p <=2       6.739         6.426      11.4      7.94            7.57     12.5
  p <=3       1.201         1.145       3.8      1.201           1.145     3.8


Number of lags used in the analysis: 1
Variables entered unrestricted:
Seasonal Seasonal_1 Seasonal_2 Seasonal_3 Seasonal_4 Seasonal_5
Seasonal_6 Seasonal_7 Seasonal_8 Seasonal_9 Seasonal_10 Seasonal_11
```

Vector AR 1-6F(96,172) =1.5183 [0.0089] **
Vector normality Chi^2(8)=21.292 [0.0064] **

```
standardized \beta' eigenvectors
  LEX          LDRT    LDRP  LM3
1.0000       0.10653 -4.76322.0488
0.018902       1.0000  7.8437-3.8645
-0.74182     -0.45220  1.0000-2.1762
-1.7006       0.43894 0.108741.0000


standardized \alpha coefficients
  LEX       0.043805   -0.019573      0.010970      0.020088
  LDRT      0.18461    -0.082260      0.010211     -0.031997
  LDRP      0.041338    0.0047752    -0.00045037   -0.00026245
  LM3       0.0016975   0.0055658      0.014446     0.00016994
```

An important conclusion from this exercise is that:

1.   The order of the VAR matters for the cointegration test.

2.   Gaussian error terms are very important building blocks for the Johansen cointegration test. Thus diagnostic tests, specifically tests for autocorrelation and normality, must be performed before proceeding to the cointegration test.

3.   Even if two researchers used the same data and method of estimation, the results differ markedly based on the particular specification and reduction process followed.

Thus, the Were *et al.* (2001) work has a problem because they have used a VAR of order one that suffers from the problem of vector autocorrelation and non-normality, as we noted above. We, however, followed their specification of the

VAR in order to illustrate, just for pedagogical purpose, how to model the short run dynamics when we have two cointegrating relationships.

Consider our "result" with two cointegrating vectors. The first two standardized beta vectors report the estimated cointegration space. Note that, in such a case, the ordering of the variables matter. To uniquely determine the cointegration vectors relevant to our analysis and hence order our variables at the initial stage, the theoretical knowledge of the subject matter that we are handling is essential. In our case, the cointegrating relationships can be interpreted as the exchange rate and interest rate differential relationships. Motivating our analysis in such a way we can impose rank restriction and uniquely identify the two relationships.

The procedure of imposing rank restriction is similar to the one illustrated previously. In PcFiml, go to model, estimate system as shown in Illustration 4.13.

Illustration 4.13: Imposing rank restrictions in PcFiml

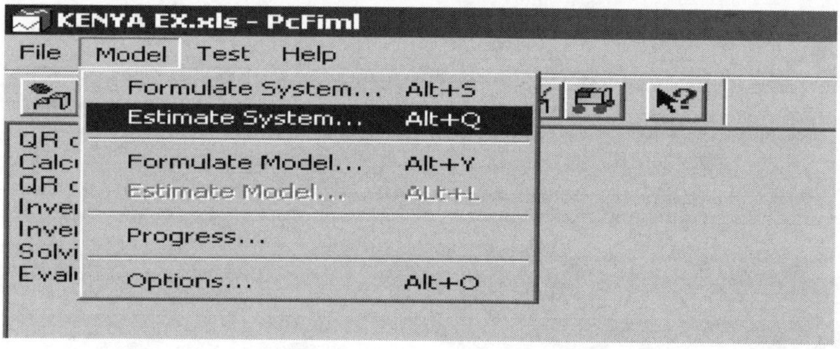

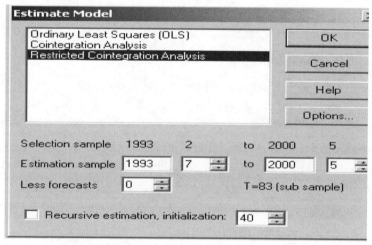

This procedure would take you to the following window in illustration 4.14.

Illustration 4.14: Imposing rank restrictions in PcFiml

Select restricted cointegration analysis and accept. The program would prompt you to supply the rank order to be imposed. Select two as the cointegration rank and accept. This would produce the window in Illustration 4.15.

Illustration 4.15: Imposing rank restrictions in PcFiml

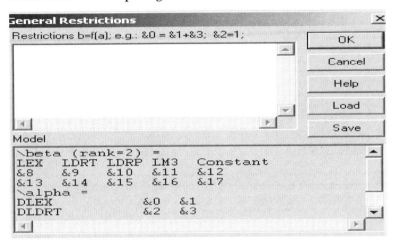

Without writing any restriction, select OK to obtain the following result.

Table 4.34: General cointegration restrictions

```
General cointegration restrictions:
unrestricted
Analysis of restrictions on \alpha and \beta:
- \alpha is unrestricted
- \betais unrestricted
- the restrictions do not identify all cointegrating vectors
SYS(46) General cointegration test 1993 (4) to 2000 (5)

\beta'
                    LEX         LDRT         LDRP          LM3      Constant
                 1.0000      0.10940      -4.7381       2.0292      -21.570
               -0.46156       1.0000       10.832      -6.1255       60.921

\alpha
   LEX          0.042956    -0.010363
   LDRT         0.17852     -0.053763
   LDRP         0.041539     0.0029670
   LM3          0.0032317    0.0082689

Standard errors of alpha
   LEX          0.017073     0.0046516
   LDRT         0.045854     0.012493
   LDRP         0.0046953    0.0012792
   LM3          0.0074130    0.0020196
```

```
Restricted long-run matrix Po=\alpha*\beta', rank 2
                   LEX          LDRT          LDRP          LM3      Constant
    LEX        0.047739    -0.0056641     -0.31578       0.15065     -1.5579
    LDRT        0.20334     -0.034233      -1.4282       0.69158     -7.1259
    LDRP       0.040170     0.0075114     -0.16468      0.066117    -0.71523
    LM3     -0.00058491     0.0086224     0.074255     -0.044093     0.43404

Reduced form \beta'
                   LDRP           LM3      Constant
    LEX          5.6384       -2.5696       26.877
    LDRT        -8.2294        4.9395      -48.515

Standard errors of long-run matrix
    LEX        0.017208     0.0050126     0.095303     0.044857      0.46467
    LDRT       0.046215      0.013462      0.25596      0.12047       1.2480
    LDRP      0.0047322     0.0013785     0.026209     0.012336      0.12779
    LM3       0.0074713     0.0021764     0.041379     0.019476      0.20175

Long-run matrix of first differences \Gamma
               1.0000       0.00000       0.00000      0.00000
               0.00000       1.0000       0.00000      0.00000
               0.00000      0.00000        1.0000      0.00000
               0.00000      0.00000       0.00000       1.0000

Moving average impact matrix
    LEX        0.85990      -0.13598      -0.32908      0.31166
    LDRT      -0.92386       0.31097      -0.46117       1.0295
    LDRP       0.27943      0.019002      -0.41919      0.62417
    LM3        0.27851      0.094614      -0.79174       1.2483

The restrictions do not identify all cointegrating vectors.
loglik = 1174.6137-log|\Omega| = 27.316597unrestr. loglik = 1174.6137
Zero degrees of freedom in LR-test, no binding restrictions imposed.

The two sensible relationships (ordering matters) are
                   LEX          LDRT          LDRP          LM3      Constant
               1.0000       0.10940       -4.7381       2.0292      -21.570
              -0.46156       1.0000        10.832      -6.1255       60.921
```

Once the cointegrating relationships are identified, we can test some restrictions to identify the variables that constitute the cointegration relationships. To do so, in PcFiml, go to model, estimate a system and select restricted cointegration analysis. This would prompt you to supply the rank. Select 2 as cointegration rank and the program would take you to this dialogue box.

Illustration 4.16: Imposing rank testrictions in PcFiml

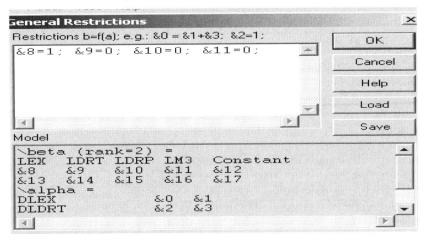

Put the restriction on the editor box as we did previously and accept. This would give you the results in Table 4.35.

Table 4.35:   General cointegration restrictions

```
General cointegration test 1993 (2) to 2000 (5)
\beta'
                LEX           LDRT          LDRP           LM3      Constant
             1.0000       0.00000       0.00000       0.00000       -6.2026
           -0.092318    -0.0064175      0.33838      -0.14599        1.6873

\alpha
 LEX        -0.020095     -0.80023
 LDRT       -0.034070     -2.8261
 LDRP       -0.014851     -0.56475
 LM3        -0.015833     -0.030369

Standard errors of alpha
 LEX         0.010455      0.23965
 LDRT        0.028206      0.64654
 LDRP        0.0027889     0.063926
 LM3         0.0040955     0.093876

Restricted long-run matrix Po=\alpha*\beta', rank 2
                LEX           LDRT          LDRP           LM3      Constant
 LEX         0.053780      0.0051355    -0.27079      0.11682       -1.2255
 LDRT        0.22683       0.018137     -0.95631      0.41257       -4.5570
 LDRP        0.037286      0.0036243    -0.19110      0.082446      -0.86077
 LM3        -0.013029      0.00019490   -0.010277     0.0044335      0.046964

Standard errors of long-run matrix
 LEX         0.019500      0.0015380     0.081094     0.034986       0.37806
 LDRT        0.052607      0.0041492     0.21878      0.094386       1.0200
 LDRP        0.0052015     0.00041025    0.021632     0.0093324      0.10085
 LM3         0.0076385     0.00060245    0.031766     0.013705       0.14809
```

```
Long-run matrix of first differences \Gamma
              1.0000       0.00000    0.00000     0.00000
              0.00000      1.0000     0.00000     0.00000
              0.00000      0.00000    1.0000      0.00000
              0.00000      0.00000    0.00000     1.0000

Moving average impact matrix
  LEX       0.00000       0.00000    0.00000     0.00000
  LDRT      0.94214       1.1363     -7.1881     3.1011
  LDRP      -0.78679      -0.0024698 1.1302      -0.056184
  LM3       -1.8651       -0.055677  2.9358      -0.26655

Linear Switching (scaled analytical); result: Strong convergence
(eps1=0.0001, eps2=0.005)

The restrictions do not identify all cointegrating vectors.
loglik = 1187.0767  -log|\Omega| = 26.979016  unrestr. loglik = 1195.8401
LR-test, rank=2: Chi^2(2) = 17.527 [0.0002] **
```

The result shows that the restrictions are rejected implying that the variables constitute the cointegrating relationship. Similarly, we can also test alternative theories. As an example, we can test whether the PPP condition would hold or not. To do so, we can impose a restriction that LDRP =1 in the vector that is normalized by LEX. Using the same procedure as above, we found out that the PPP theory is rejected. The result is shown below.

```
loglik = 1147.656  -log|\Omega| = 26.689675  unrestr. loglik = 1164.3292
LR-test, rank=1: Chi^2(1) = 33.346 [0.0000] **
```

We can proceed to the estimation of the short run dynamics. Before proceeding to the estimation of the short run dynamics, we need to save the cointegrating relationships. To do so, in PcFiml, go to **test, store in data base** and select **cointegrating vectors**. This would prompt you to name the cointegrating vectors. Name them as CvecL11, CvecL12, CvecL13 and CvecL14, though CvecL13 and CvecL14 are not relevant for our discussion.

Modelling the Short Run Dynamics: The Vector Error Correction Model

In modelling the short run dynamics, Were *et al.* (2001) proceed estimating only the first cointegrating relationship. Once they have found that there exist cointegrating relationships among the variables of their interest, they detour from the system estimation to a single equation ECM upon representing the long run relationship as an autoregressive distributive lag (ADL) process. From this ADL form, they solved for the long run static equation and obtained the error correction (EC) term. This can be easily done using PCGIVE. We, however, will not follow this route. We will rather directly obtain our EC term from our Johansen procedure. In fact, the CvecL11 and CvecL12 variables that we have saved earlier will be used to derive the EC terms. Now, with this note we proceed to estimating the short run dynamics.

In PcFiml, go to model and select formulate system. Press the new model button to clear the existing system. Select one lag, mark DLEX, DLDRT, DLDRP, DLM3, CvecL11 and CvecL12. We also added impulse dummies. Switch to the model column and mark constant then clear its status. Next mark CvecL11 and CvecL12 and change their status to identity.

Illustration 4.17: Data selection for VECM

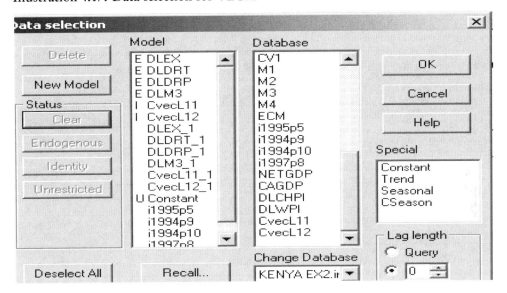

Table 4.36:   **VECM model for DLEX**

Result

```
Estimating the unrestricted reduced form by OLS(using KENYA EX2.in7)
The present sample is: 1993 (5) to 2000 (5)

URF Equation 1 for DLEX
```

Variable	Coefficient	Std.Error	t-value	t-prob
DLEX_1	-0.039787	0.080801	-0.492	0.6239
DLDRT_1	-0.011416	0.026401	-0.432	0.6667
DLDRP_1	0.19108	0.19632	0.973	0.3336
DLM3_1	-0.13099	0.16687	-0.785	0.4350
CvecL11_1	0.0078892	0.014554	0.542	0.5894
CvecL12_1	-0.010515	0.0050502	-2.082	0.0408
i1995p5	0.15887	0.030367	5.232	0.0000
i1994p9	-0.12457	0.030711	-4.056	0.0001
i1994p10	-0.15103	0.031778	-4.753	0.0000
i1997p8	0.11222	0.030687	3.657	0.0005
Constant	-0.51955	0.36803	-1.412	0.1622

```
\sigma = 0.0295046RSS = 0.06441840049

URF Equation 2 for DLDRT
```

Variable	Coefficient	Std.Error	t-value	t-prob
DLEX_1	0.59979	0.28929	2.073	0.0416
DLDRT_1	0.35736	0.094524	3.781	0.0003
DLDRP_1	0.21516	0.70289	0.306	0.7604
DLM3_1	0.011176	0.59742	0.019	0.9851
CvecL11_1	-0.017955	0.052107	-0.345	0.7314
CvecL12_1	-0.046794	0.018081	-2.588	0.0116
i1995p5	0.0068011	0.10872	0.063	0.9503
i1994p9	0.090541	0.10996	0.823	0.4129
i1994p10	-0.29930	0.11377	-2.631	0.0104
i1997p8	0.046123	0.10987	0.420	0.6758
Constant	-1.1937	1.3177	-0.906	0.3679

σ = 0.105634RSS = 0.8257389485

URF Equation 3 for DLDRP

Variable	Coefficient	Std.Error	t-value	t-prob
DLEX_1	-0.013400	0.042363	-0.316	0.7527
DLDRT_1	-0.015904	0.013842	-1.149	0.2543
DLDRP_1	0.14461	0.10293	1.405	0.1642
DLM3_1	-0.025516	0.087486	-0.292	0.7714
CvecL11_1	0.040537	0.0076305	5.312	0.0000
CvecL12_1	0.0013161	0.0026478	0.497	0.6206
i1995p5	0.0095172	0.015921	0.598	0.5518
i1994p9	-0.0062623	0.016102	-0.389	0.6985
i1994p10	0.0052651	0.016661	0.316	0.7529
i1997p8	-0.010864	0.016089	-0.675	0.5016
Constant	-0.83168	0.19296	-4.310	0.0000

σ = 0.015469RSS = 0.01770735753

URF Equation 4 for DLM3

Variable	Coefficient	Std.Error	t-value	t-prob
DLEX_1	-0.045625	0.051348	-0.889	0.3771
DLDRT_1	-0.068021	0.016777	-4.054	0.0001
DLDRP_1	-0.18286	0.12476	-1.466	0.1470
DLM3_1	-0.10037	0.10604	-0.947	0.3470
CvecL11_1	0.021655	0.0092487	2.341	0.0219
CvecL12_1	0.0060268	0.0032093	1.878	0.0643
i1995p5	0.0038380	0.019297	0.199	0.8429
i1994p9	0.0011479	0.019516	0.059	0.9533
i1994p10	0.033649	0.020194	1.666	0.0999
i1997p8	0.013155	0.019501	0.675	0.5021
Constant	-0.26021	0.23388	-1.113	0.2695

σ = 0.0187495RSS = 0.02601430947
correlation of URF residuals

	DLEX	DLDRT	DLDRP	DLM3
DLEX	1.0000			
DLDRT	-0.16493	1.0000		
DLDRP	-0.25320	0.069871	1.0000	
DLM3	0.073905	-0.088051	-0.033427	1.0000

```
standard deviations of URF residuals
                     DLEX        DLDRT       DLDRP           DLM3
                 0.029505     0.10563    0.015469        0.018750


loglik = 1210.9796log|\Omega| = -28.4936|\Omega| = 4.22056e-013 T=85
log|Y'Y/T| = -26.1916
R^2(LR) = 0.899943R^2(LM) = 0.395793


F-test on all regressors except unrestricted, F(40,271) = 5.6593
[0.0000] **
variables entered unrestricted:
  Constant


F-tests on retained regressors, F(4, 71)
     DLEX_1   1.22051 [0.3098]        DLDRT_1    7.33073 [0.0001] **
    DLDRP_1   1.50009 [0.2114]          DLM3_1   0.409897 [0.8009]
  CvecL11_1   9.07093 [0.0000] **   CvecL12_1    3.94914 [0.0060] **
     i1995p5  7.70051 [0.0000] **     i1994p9    4.49968 [0.0027] **
    i1994p10  9.18759 [0.0000] **     i1997p8    3.53607 [0.0109] *


correlation of actual and fitted
                     DLEX        DLDRT       DLDRP           DLM3
                 0.75276     0.68150     0.64634         0.57282
```

From the system estimation of our VECM in Table 4.36, we can see that the correlation of the residuals of the unrestricted reduced form is very low (all are below 0.25 in absolute value). This suggests that we have not encountered the problem of simultaneity. Hence, we can resort to single equation error correction model and OLS will be efficient estimator. But if we had encountered the simultaneity problem, we would have resorted to system estimation of the VECM either using two-stage least square or full information maximum likelihood. (See Box 4.2 for illustration)

Box 4.2:   Model formulation when simultaneity problem exists

Once the VECM is estimated as in Table 4.36, in PcFiml go to model, formulate model to see:

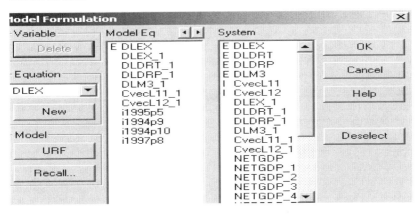

The left most column lists the options and which endogenous variable is under analysis; the middle column shows the current model of that endogenous variable; and the next right column the system currently under analysis. In the leftmost column click on the pull down menu and select the identity CvecL11. From the rightmost column supply the information about the identity. That is, select DLEX, DLDRT, DLDRP, DLM3 and CvecL11_1 and click add. Repeat this procedure for CvecL12. Select DLEX, DLDRT, DLDRP, DLM3 and CvecL12_1 and click add. Now click ok and the estimation dialog appears.

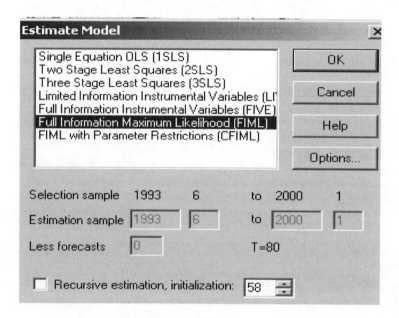

Thusm the VECM can be estimated in any of the above methods depending on the problem at hand. Finally, it is worth noting that the VAR approach discussed so far has recently developed to an approach where economic theory is imposed on the co-integrating vector for identification of the model leading to the approaches named as "Structural VARs and Structural Cointegrating VARs" (see Box 4.3).

Box 4.3: **A brief guide to the structural VAR (SVAR) and structural co-integration VAR (SCVAR) approach to macro modelling**

In his 1980 article, Sims (1980) criticized the dominant macro modelling approach - large scale simultaneous economic models [SEM]. Such models are referred to as a structural simultaneous econometric models too. Sims noted that these SEMs have "incredible" restriction, thus proposing the alternative strategy of estimating unrestricted reduced forms, treating all variables as endogenous. This is the model termed vector autoregressive (VAR). This approach basically says that we don't need to worry about the theory of the SEMs; instead we just model each variable as a function of its lagged series, having a lag as much as our data allows. This has two advantages, especially compared to the traditional theory-inspired simultaneous equation based modeling and its estimation. First, since each of the variable in the traditional SEMs (say the Keynesian IS-LM model equations) are now modeled as a function of their own lagged values, you really do not need a theory because whatever theory you can think of, say any of the consumption theories, that particular theory should motivate also its lagged value and hence, is effectively incorporated. Second, because the current level of each variable in that simultaneous equation model is now specified as a function of its own lagged values, effectively it is modeled as a functional pre-determined (or exogenous) variable. The latter in turn means that OLS estimation on each equation (vector) is efficient as the endogenous variable is specified as a function of predetermined variables. (Pesaran and Pesaran; 1997; McCoy, 1997; Jacobs and Wallis 2003).

Sims' approach was great but has the problem of having a number of lagged variables which limit the degree of freedom in estimation. Its second problem is that since anything goes in such a model you may not know what you are really getting once the estimation is successfully completed. This leads to a need for some kind of guidance about the interpretation of the result. These two major problems in the use of Sims VAR approach are addressed first by resorting to the approach called "Structural VAR" (SVAR). Still another alternative approach is what is called the "Structural Cointegration VAR" (SCVAR) approach which is credited to the works of Pesaran and his colleagues (Pesaran and Pesaran; 1997; Garratt *et al*, 1999).

The SVAR Approach: as noted by McCoy (1997), the SVAR is an extension of traditional VAR analysis but differ in that within a SVAR an attempt is made to identify a set of independent disturbances by means of restrictions provided by economic theory rather than by the (so-called) atheoretic restrictions used in traditional VARs (McCoy, 1997). Following the critics on the unrestricted VAR framework of Sims (1980), the development of the SVAR approach came from the seminal contributions of Sims (1986), Bernanke (1986) and Blanchard and Watson (1986) who made use of economic theory to impose restrictions on the observed values of the estimated residuals (e_t) to recover the underlying structural disturbances (μ_t). In addition to recovering the structure of the disturbances, it is necessary to preserve the assumed error structure to ensure independence between the shocks. Instead of the arbitrary method of restriction imposition used in traditional VARs, the SVAR approach, as advocated by these authors, also estimates the structural parameters by imposing contemporaneous structural restrictions based on economic theory. These can be considered as short-run restrictions in that the shocks are considered to have temporary effects (McCoy, 1997). The main advantage of the SVAR analysis, as McCoy (1997) noted, is that the necessary restrictions on the estimated reduced form model, required for identification of the underlying structural model, can be provided by economic theory. These restrictions can be either contemporaneous or long-run in nature depending on whether the underlying disturbances are considered to be temporary or permanent in nature from a theoretical perspective. Once the identification is achieved, it is possible to recover the structural parameters and shocks, as noted above. These shocks can then be used to generate impulse response and variance decomposition functions to assess the dynamic impacts on different economic variables. In addition, these functions can be used to test whether such shocks affect the economic variables as economic theory would predict or not so providing a check on the theory (McCoy, 1997).

A popular method of restriction is to orthogonalize reduced form errors by Choleski's decomposition as originally applied by Sims. Buckel *et al* (2000), however, argue that this approach to identification requires the assumption that the system of equations follows a recursive structure, that is, a Wold-causal chain. In some circumstances, Choleski's decomposition may coincide with the prior theoretical view of the appropriate model structure. This procedure can therefore be viewed as a special case of a more general approach. There are, however, many circumstances where restrictions resulting from Choleski's decomposition will be unreasonable. It would not be appropriate, for example, if there were contemporaneous interaction between variables. A more general method for imposing restrictions was suggested by Blanchard and Watson (1986), Bernanke (1986) and Sims (1986), as noted by Buckel *et al* (2000), while still giving restrictions on only contemporaneous structural parameters. This method, permits non-recursive structures and the specification of restrictions based on prior theoretical and empirical information about private sector behavior and policy reaction functions (Buckel *et al*, 2002) – this is the essence of SVAR.

The procedure for operating a straightforward SVAR involves a number of discrete steps. The user must determine whether the variables to be included are stationary I(0) or non-stationary I(1). This will determine whether a reduced form representation in levels or in first differences is required. Once the variables have been made stationary the next step involves estimating the reduced form VAR using OLS, ensuring that enough lags are incorporated to ensure no serial correlation from the residuals. Tests are needed to select the appropriate lag length given that VAR analysis, in trying to avoid exclusion restrictions, can quickly become over parameterized losing important degrees of freedom for estimation purposes (McCosy, 1997). When the reduced form VAR is estimated it is then essential to impose sufficient restrictions to identify the structural parameters of the model. In some cases economic theory can suggest more than the necessary restrictions, such that the model is over identified. In the case where the shocks are assumed to have temporary effects on the variables the restrictions are imposed on the contemporaneous element. In contrast, where the shocks are assumed to have permanent effects, the restrictions are imposed on the long-run multipliers in the impulse response functions (McCoy, 1997).

The SCVAR Approach: The SVAR approach noted above offers a VAR framework with structural content obtained through the imposition of restrictions on the covariance structure of different types of shocks. The basis of SVAR is the distinction made between shocks with temporary (transient) effects from those with permanent effects which then relate to economic theory in a rather loose manner by viewing the two types of shocks as demand and supply type shocks (Garratt *et al*, 1999). According to Garratt *et al* (1999), this approach does not attempt to model the structure of the economy in terms of the behavioral relations of economic agents. Its application, moreover, is also limited to relatively small models where the distinction between the two types of shocks is sufficient to deliver identification (Garratt *et al*, 2006). The structural cointegration VAR (SCVAR) approach is based on the desire to develop a macroeconometric model which has transparent theoretical foundation, provide insight on behavioral relationships, and, where economic theory is believed to be most informative about the long-run relationships compared to short run restrictions that are more contentious (Garratt *et al*, 2006).

In the SCVAR approach, as had been noted by Jacobs and Wallis (2002), identifying restrictions drawn from economic theory on the cointegrating relationships rather than on the error-covariances are imposed (see Pesaran and Pesaran, 1997). This "long-run structural modeling" approach has recently been applied in a number of studies conducted by Pesaran and his co-authors. The recognition that, for policy analysis, VAR models still require identifying assumptions (Cooley and LeRoy, 1985) resulted in a variety of ways of formulating such "structural VAR" (SVAR) models, starting from Bernanke (1986), Blanchard and Watson (1986) and Sims (1986) initial attempt that we noted above. In the meantime, the cointegration literature that followed from Granger (1981) saw the VAR transformed into the vector error correction model (VECM), and an alternative proposal is to place identifying restrictions drawn from economic theory on the cointegrating relationships rather than the error covariances used in the SVAR approach (see Pesaran and Pesaran, 1997). This "Long-run structural modelling" approach is what is referred to as the 'structural co-integrated VAR' (SCVAR) approach (Garratt *et al.*, 1999, 2000, 2001; Jacobs and Wallis, 2003).

As has been given rather in detail in Garratt *et al* (2006), the approach is based on log-linear VARX (VARX is where the normal VAR is augmented by weakly exogenous variable such as the world price of oil). Assuming the macro variable in question has a unit root, each of the long run variable relationships derived from theory is associated with cointegrating relationships between the variables. The existence of these conitegrating relationships imposes restrictions on a VARX model of the variables (Garratt *et al*, 2006). Thus, the SCVAR approach provides an estimated structural model of the macroeconomy in which the only restriction on the short run dynamics of the model are those which are imposed through the decision to limit attention to the log-linear VARX models with a specified maximum lag length.

The SCVAR approach, as has been given by Garratt *et al* (2006), begins with an explicit statement of a set of long-run relationships derived from macroeconomic theory. These long-run relationships are then embedded within an otherwise unrestricted VARX model.

107

The VARX model is then estimated to get the augmented cointegrating VAR model which incorporates the structural long-run relationships. This procedure also yields theory-consistent restriction on the intercepts and/or the trend coefficient in the VAR, which play an important role in testing for cointegation and co-trending, as well as for testing restriction on the long run relations. This approach differs from the usual cointegration analysis which normally begins with unrestricted VAR and imposes restriction on cointegrating relations at a later stage without a clear *apriori* view of the macroeconomy. In the best of circumstances the latter approach works when you have just one co-integrating vector and is generally difficult when the cointegrated vectors are greater than one. In contrast, the SCVAR approach begins with an explicit statement of the underlying macreconomic theory and hence places the macroeconomic theory center-stage in the development of the macroeconometric model by handling any number of cointegrated VARs (Garratt *et al*, 2006).

Extracted and compiled from Garratt *et al* (2006) Garratt *et al* (1999); Jacobs and Wallis (2000), McCoy (1997), Buckel *et al*, 2002

Further Readings

Buckle, Robert A, Kunhong Kim, Heather Kirkham, Nathan McLellan and Jared Sharma (2002). "A Structural VAR Model of the New Zealand Business Cycle", New Zealand Treasury, Working Paper 02/26 December 2002.

Graatt, Anthony, Kevin Lee and Yongcheol Shin (1999). "A Structural Cointegrating VAR Approach to Macroecometeric Modelling". Paper presented at ESRC Conference on Macro Modelling, NIESR, London.

Graatt, Anthony, Kevin Lee, H. Peasaran and Yongcheol Shin (2006). *Global and National Macroeconometric Modelling.* Oxford: Oxford University Press.

Jacobs, Jan and Kenneth F. Wallis (2000). "Comparing SVARs and SEMs: More Shocking Stories". Paper prepared for the European Meeting of the Econometric Society, Venice, August 2002 and the Money, Macro and Finance Research Group Conference, Warwick, September, 2002.

McCoy, Daniel (1997). "How useful is Structural VAR Analysis for Irish economics?" Paper presented at an internal seminar of the Central Bank of Ireland, February 6th 1997 and at the Eleventh Annual Conference of the Irish Economic Association in Athlone, April 4–6, 1997.

Pesaran, M.H. and Pesaran, B. (1997). *Working with Microfit 4.0.* Oxford: Oxford University Press.

Pesaran, M.H. and Shin, Y. (1998). "Generalized Impulse Response Analysis in Linear Multivariate Models". *Economics Letters*, 58, 17–29.

Pesaran, M.H. and Smith, R.P. (1998). "Structural Analysis of Cointegrating VARs". *Journal of Economic Surveys*, 12, 471–505.

Pesaran, M.H., Shin, Y. and Smith, R.J. (2000). "Structural Analysis Of Vector Error Correction Models With Exogenous *I*(1) Variables". *Journal of Econometrics*, 97, 293–343.

Sims, C.A. (1980). "Macroeconomics and Reality". *Econometrica*, 48, 1–48.

Problems of Cointegration with I(2) Variables

Introduction

Applied researchers may encounter some of their variables showing an I(2) process. Running a cointegration analysis with variables at different levels of integration, such as I(2) and I(1) variables in one model, is not a legitimate procedure as their linear combination is invariably not stationary. This problems is in particular common in the estimation of production functions. In this chapter, we shall explore how to handle such problems, illustrating it with estimation of a production function. Specification and estimation of production function had been the workhouse of most economic theories. In a macroeconomics context, the growth literature *a la* the Solow Model extensively employs aggregate production function and its parameters to come up with important conclusions. Among others, Mankiw *et al* (1992) used a Cobb-Douglas production function to test the implications of the Solow Model while Easterly and Levin (2001) used it for their growth accounting analysis on the relative importance of total factor productivity *vis-à-vis* total factor accumulation.

In cross country growth analysis, estimation of the Cobb-Douglas production function is fairly straight forward. Most of the empirical studies proxy capital by investment (scaled by GDP) and labor force by the economically active population and proceed to estimation either in cross section or panel framework. The problem of estimation, however, would crop-up when estimating a production function for a single country in the presence of stochastic trend in the time series variables. The problem would be serious as capital is a stock variable which invariably contains double unit roots. In fact, many applied macroeconomists in Africa do confront this problem when they attempt to formulate simple macro model for use in budget formulation and short run forecasting, say for use in the Medium Term Expenditure Framework (MTEF) which is being widely employed in many ministries of finance in Africa. This is at least our experience in Kenya and Ethiopia. The nature of the data in other African countries is not different and hence the problem could be found across countries in the continent (and elsewhere). In this chapter, we have attempted to address this applied problem.

In the presence of I(2) variable, the usual approach is to difference the I(2) series and employ the I(1) analysis on the differenced and the other I(1) variables. This, restricts, however, the possibility of having multi-cointcgration relationships among the variables and hence imposes *a priori* restriction that there are only linear cointegrating relationships. Allowing for multi-cointegration or polynomial cointegration is a less restrictive description of the data that lets us treat different theoretically plausible relationships.

The theory of I(2) modelling was developed by Johansen (1997), Boswijk(2000), Paruolo and Rahbek (1999) and Rahbek, Kongsted and Jogensen (1999). The main message is that the cointegrated I(2) model is well designed to study highly persistent I(2), persistent I(1) and transitory I(0) behavior in a model.

The subsequent illustration employs an I(2) framework to address the issue of I(2)-ness in estimating aggregate production function or similar other models. The method is illustrated using the Ethiopian data for the period 1960/61 to 2001/02.

The Production Function and Data

Following the growth literature we considered a simple Cobb-Douglas (CD) production function[12] given as in equation (4.40) and log-linearized in equation (4.41).

$$Y = AK^{\alpha}L^{1-\alpha} \qquad [4.40]$$

$$\ln Y = \beta + \alpha \ln K + 1 - \alpha \ln L \qquad [4.41]$$

Where Y is total output; A is technological progress, K is total physical capital, L is the total labor force and β is logarithm of A.

Estimating the production function in [4.41] using time series data requires addressing the stochastic trends in the variables. If all the variables are integrated of order one- I(1)-, estimation can be proceeded by testing for the existence of a common trend among the variables. When it is the case that one or more of the variables are integrated of higher order, our cointegration test in I(1) framework may give a misleading result.

Figure 4.1 presents the levels and growth rates of GDP, capital and labor series used for our analysis. As can be read from the figure, the smooth trend of capital stock and its trending growth rate suggest its I(2)-ness. The smooth trend of labor force also suggests that it may be an I(2) series. The growth rate of the labor force, as shown in the figure, does not show a strong trend reverting behavior which also imply that the labor force series might border I(2)-ness. On the other hand, the GDP series shows an I(1) behavior with its growth rate being trend reverting. The univariate unit root tests conducted using the Pantula principle could not reject that capital is an I(2) series and output is I(1). The case for the labor force is not conclusive. The DF statistic shows that labor force is an I(1) series while the ADF statistics could not reject the I(2) null. We also tested for trend stationarity and found that the de-trended series are nonstationary suggesting that the variables contain stochastic trend rather than deterministic one.

---

[12] It should be noted that the preference for a CD production function doesn't imply that it is the best though it is a workhorse in the Solow Model and the growth literature in general. Practioners can experiment with other practical functions such as the Constant Elasticity of Substitution (CES) and translog formulation.

110

At this juncture, it may be necessary to say something about the nature of the data. We obtained GDP and gross capital formation from the national accounts compiled by Ministry of Finance and Economic Development. As frequent revision of the national accounts is prevalent in the Ministry, however , it is difficult to get reliable data that spans for the whole of the four decades. Specifically, the national accounts data from 1960/61 to 79/80 (referred as the old series) and from 1980/81 to 2000/01 (referred as the new series) are generated using different definitions. One way of addressing this problem of change in definitions of our dependent variable (GDP) is to introduce an impulse dummy in our regression. The alternative is to address the change in definition explicitly by looking at how it affected the series. Following the later method and comparing the old and new series of GDP reveals that the change in the definition seems to have a level effect, leaving the growth rate somehow unaffected. In such a case, we can fairly impose the growth rate of the old series on the level series of the new series and extrapolate the GDP series backward from 1980/81. We thus used the later procedure to adjust the GDP and gross capital formation series of the national accounts.

Regarding capital stock, there is no estimate of the capital stock in the country. This is a common problem in many African countries. We generated the data for capital stock using the capital accumulation equation (where K_t is current capital stock and K_{t-1} lagged level of capital stock): $K_t = K_{t-1} + Investment - Depreciation$. As we did not have the initial value of capital stock (K_{t-1}) we used an estimated incremental capital output ratio (ICRO) and generated K_{t-1} as:

$$K_{t-1} = ICRO * Output_{t-1}$$

The data for labor force is extracted from the World Bank's African Development Indicator CD ROM (2005). This database compiles data from 1965, and hence, we extrapolated the labor force series backward using exponential smoothing technique as our sample period goes back to 1960/61. The labor force series exhibited some unexpected trend. We could not explain the abrupt fall in the growth rate of labor force in 1970, 1977, 1993 and 1997. The retrenchment of labor force following the economic liberalization program and the HIV/AIDS epidemic, however, could be plausible conjectures in explaining the sharp decline in the growth rate of labor force.

Figure 4.1: Graphs of variables in levels and differences

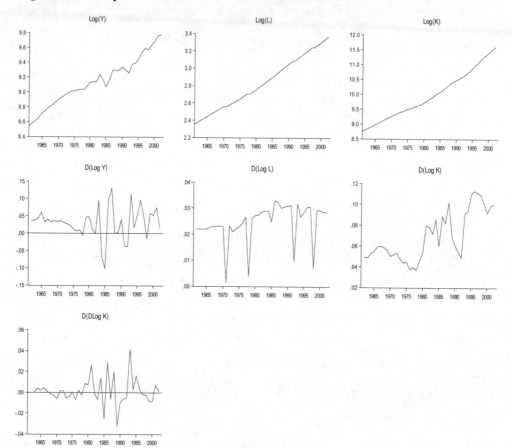

Empirical Results: Capital Stock and Production Function for Ethiopia

The cointegration analysis is preceded by determining the data congruency of the VAR. Using the data from 1960/61–2001/02, VAR (2) appears to be a valid specification based on the Akaike Information Criterion. The restriction that "lags higher than 2 are all zero" cannot also be rejected using F-statistics, confirming the validity of VAR (2) specification.

We first conducted an I(1) cointegration analysis using our VAR (2) specification. The result shows that output, capital and labor are not cointegrated, implying that the variables do not have a stable relationship that leads to an I(0) relationship. That is, the I(2) variables might cointegrate among themselves as C(2,1) but they do not cointegrate with the I(1) variable leading to an I(1) residual[13]. We proceeded to an I(2) analysis to test for a possible polynomial cointegration.

Table 4.37: Testing cointegration in I(1) framework

		Trace test	[Prob]
	0	[0.111]	26.721
	1	10.987	[0.216]
H_0: Rank$\leq$	2	0.43605	

To identify the rank indices of the I(2) model, r and s, we used the trace statistics test, $S_{r,s}$ reported in Table 4.38. The test starts from the most restrictive model, $H_{0,0}$ in the upper left hand side and proceeds down the columns, from top left to bottom right, stopping at the first acceptance *a la* Pantula principle.

Table 4.38: I(2) test for the rank order

r	$S_{r,s}$ S=0	S=1	S=2	Q_r
0	92.308 (0.0003)	58.883 (0.0229)	44.007 (0.0404)	44.005 (0.0036)
1		36.813 (0.0495)	**18.363** **0.3405**	18.341 (0.0897)
2			6.5354 (0.4273)	6.5152 (0.1594)
p-r-s	3	2	1	0

† The (italics) figures are probabilities associated with the trace statistics

Our result shows that our first acceptance is when the number of I(2) trends in the system, *p-r-s=1* and *r=1*. Contrary to our I(1) analysis, we obtained one stable cointegrating relationship with one I(2) trend. The lack of cointegration in our I(1) analysis vis-a-vis the presence of it in the I(2) analysis may suggest the presence of polynomial cointegration. That is, the I(2) variables may cointegrate as C(2,1) which would further cointegrate with the change in the I(2) variable and the remaining I(1) variables. As the number of polynomial cointegration cannot exceed the number of I(2) trends = 1, the cointegrating relationship that we obtained would be due to the polynomial term in our I(2) cointegration analysis.

We first adopted the usual approach that tests cointegration among the differenced I(2) variable and the other I(1) variables. We used VAR (2) specification and tested cointegration among output, labor and change in capital (investment). Our result shows that the null hypothesis of zero cointegration relationship is rejected in favor

---

[13] If the I(2) variables which are integrated among themselves with C(2,1) are also cointegrated with the rest of I(1) variables with C(1,0), then we would have proceeded as the previous section, and hence no need for this section.

of one cointegration relationship. The moduli of the companion matrix are all within the unit circle as shown in Figure 4.2. The existence of large roots close to 1, however, may indicate that there may be some unaccounted trend close to I(2).

Table 4.39: Trace test statistics

		Trace Statistics	[Prob]
	0	65.674	[0.000]**
	1	21.302	[0.169]
H_0: Rank≤	2	8.2542	[0.238]

Figure 4.2: Roots of companion matrix

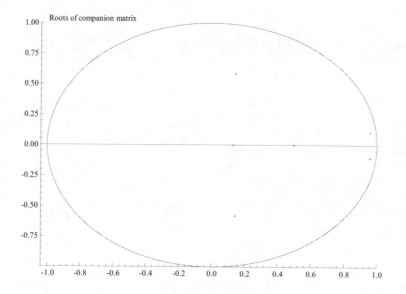

Given the problem of unaccounted I(2) trend and to allow for other type of relationship, we tried to identify the polynomial cointegration relationship. We tried to motivate the polynomial cointegration that the data exhibited theoretically. That is, the polynomial cointegration may indicate that output depends on the common trend of capital and labor (for instance capital labor ratio) and the new investment made. The I(2) capital stock may cointegrate with the near I(2) labor force- C(2,1) which may further cointegrate with the change in the I(2) variables- capital, which is investment as $\Delta K=I$. Change in capital stock can be a theoretically valid candidate in forcing this relationship to cointegrate and hence, it can be used as the polynomial cointegrating term.

To test the polynomial cointegration, we created a variable that captures the common trend of capital and labor as capital labor ratio-i.e. $\ln K - \ln L$. Using this variable, along with output and change in capital stock, we run a cointegration test in I(1) framework and obtained one cointegrating relationship with the roots of the companion matrix being all within a unit circle. This is an interesting result in supporting the hypothesized polynomial cointegration relationship. It also underscores the importance of I(2) analysis in motivating different theoretical relationships. Table 4.40 reports this result.

Table 4.40: Trace test results

		Trace Statistics	[Prob]
	0	63.990	[0.000] **
	1	25.398	[0.055]
H_0: Rank $\leq$	2	8.3336	[0.232]

Once the cointegration relationship is established, the analysis can proceed using the I(1) framework. The long run relationships can be identified using the β vector with the adjustment coefficients contained in the α vector discussed in the previous Chapter. Hypothesis testing can also be conducted in the I(1) framework using the LR test.

At this juncture, it is important to notice that the I(2) analysis is an important framework in detecting a polynomial cointegration relationship though the final analysis is based on an I(1) approach. As opposed to adopting the I(1) framework with the differenced I(2) variables, this approach is more flexible in allowing different types of relationships such as the role of K/L ratio which are filtered out in the earlier approach.

Conclusion

We estimated a simple production function allowing for the presence of I(2) variables. We showed that, in the presence of I(2) capital stock for instance, the I(1) cointegration analysis rejected the presence of cointegration among the variables. The I(2) analysis, however, showed the presence of one I(2) trend with a possible cointegration as the rank *r*=1. This can be attributed to the polynomial cointegration allowed in the I(2) analysis.

We also showed that the polynomial cointegration found in the data could also be motivated theoretically. Capital and labor may cointegrate as C(2,1) forming an I(1) capital labor ratio which, along with investment (i.e. change in capital stock which is also the polynomial integration term), may give a stable relationship. This shows the importance of putting the problem in an I(2) framework to address the higher order integration and their relationship with the lower integration order.

Chapter 5

THE ECONOMETRICS OF FORECASTING: THEORY AND APPLICATION

Introduction

Forecasting economic variables is an important element in policy design and analysis. In this chapter, our interest is to forecast a single variable (as opposed to forecasting in macro model framework) such as growth rate, inflation or exchange rate and learn how the variable behaves in the subsequent periods. For instance, one may be interested to forecast exchange rate that would prevail in the next budget year in order to estimate the local currency value of capital goods that will be imported and form components of the government capital expenditure yet she/he doesn't have a macro model for the purpose. Alternatively, we may be interested to forecast the values of some set of variables either to assess the impact of policy change or to evaluate the likely impact of policies. As an example, consider an increase in government expenditure to achieve the so called Millennium Development Goals, (MDGs). The change in the expenditure affects a range of variables such as budget deficit, money supply, price levels and output. To trace the impact of the shock in the expenditure on major and important economic variables, we need to forecast the variables of interest using a structural model and carry shock simulations.

The starting point either for a univariate or multivariate forecast is to understand the behaviour of the variable/s of interest. Economic variables are mostly composed of trend, seasonal and cyclical components. The trend component shows the long run behaviour of the variable while the seasonal component tells us about the impacts of different seasons or calendar periods on the variable. The variation in the variable that is not explained by the trend and seasonal components constitutes the cyclical component of the variable. Once we have a good grasp of the behaviour of the variable, we can fit a statistical model to forecast the future values of the variable. There are various methods to do that. In the next section, we will see how graphs can be used in studying the behaviour of an economic variable.

Graphics for Forecasting

Time series graphics are important tools in learning the behaviour of variables in a quite straightforward fashion. Figure 5.1 shows Kenya's monthly exchange rate data during the period of 1993 – 2000. The graph shows that the exchange rate depreciated sharply during 1993 and started appreciating until late 1994. It depreciated again and continued to depreciate with some episodes of appreciation in between. The sharp depreciation in 1993 corresponds to the abolition of the pegged exchange rate regime (and general liberalization that followed the 1992 multi-party election) while the appreciation through 1994 was due to the impact of fall in excess liquidity. These regime shift and structural changes are clearly observed in our graph. For our forecasts to be robust, such deterministic shifts have to be accounted for.

Figure 5.1: Kenya's monthly exchange rate 1993–2000

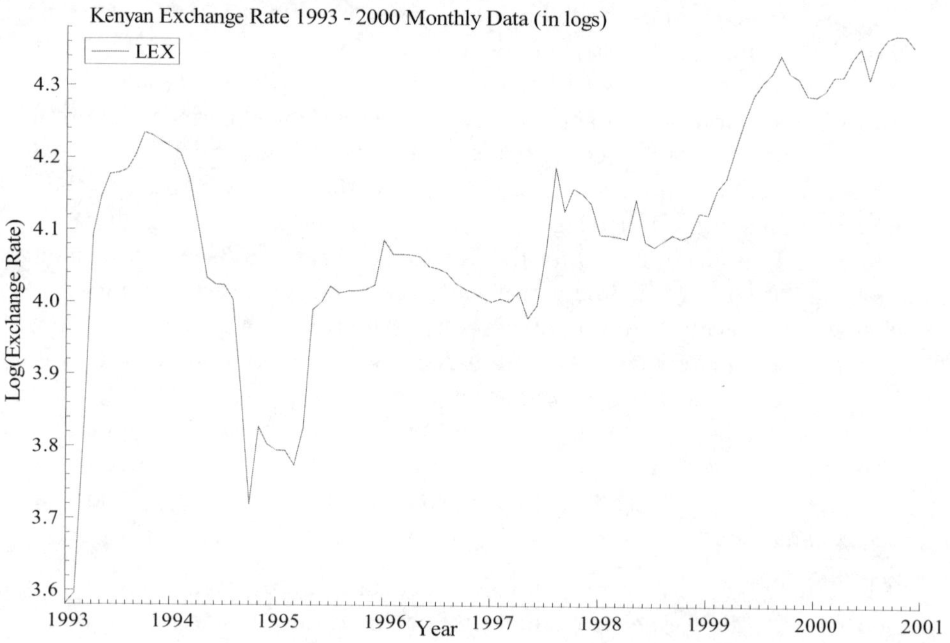

The general message that one can get from this graph is that (i) there is a major regime shift or structural change (in 1993); and (ii) the exchange rate has shown an upward trend showing a continuously depreciating tendency.

Figure 5.2 shows Mozambique's price level during the period December 1990 to December 2001. As can be seen from the figure, the domestic price level was increasing continuously until 1996 and stabilized after then. Figure 5.3 shows the volatility in the price levels. The episode of high inflation until 1996 was followed by the relatively stable inflation rate. The stability may be attributed to the reform programs that the country underwent. These graphs also show that prices show an upward trend and are also subjected to structural changes.

Figure 5.2:   Mozambique price level: Monthly data for 1990–2001

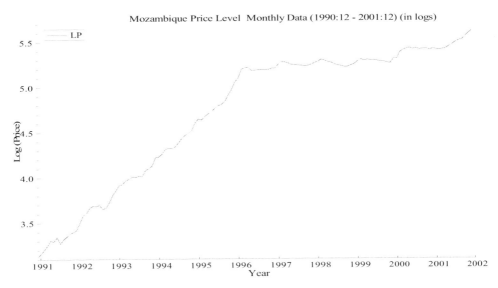

The important point that emerged from our graphical analysis is that our forecasting model should deal with the trends and deterministic shifts. The next section will address these issues.

Figure 5.3:   Growth in prices for Mozambique during 1990:12–2001:12

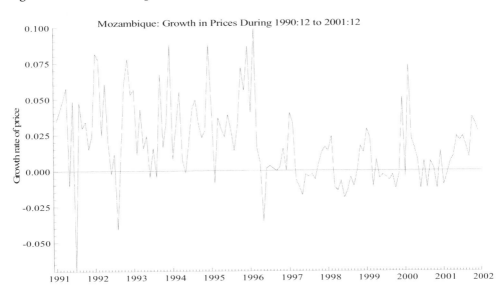

119

Modelling Trends, Deterministic Shifts, Seasonalities and Cycles

Our graphic analysis underscores the importance of trends and deterministic shifts in both the Kenyan and Mozambique data. In this section, we would deal with modelling deterministic shifts, trends and cycles using the above data set. We would also introduce the concept of seasonality and how to account for it. Finally, we will use all the components of the variable for our forecasting purpose.

Modelling Trends and Deterministic Shifts

We can model trends in a simple fashion by running a simple regression of the form;

$$y_t = \beta_0 + \beta_1 T + \varepsilon_t \tag{5.1}$$

Where T is time 1, 2, 3,... and ε_t is the random error term.

We can either model a simple linear trend as in equation [5.1] or an exponential trend in the form of $y = \beta_0 e^{\beta_1 T}$. The exponential trend is useful when we model a trend showing constant growth rate. For estimation purpose it can be log-linearized as

$$\ln y_t = \ln \beta_t + \beta_t T + \varepsilon_t \tag{5.2}$$

In this case, ε_t is the constant growth rate of y_t.

We estimated the trend in the Kenyan exchange rate in the form of equation [5.2] and the result is presented in Table 6.1 below. The result shows that the exchange rate exhibits a positive trend as β_1 is positive and statistically significant.

Table 5.1: **Modelling linear trend in the Kenyan exchange rate**

```
Dependent Variable: LEX
Method:  Least Squares
Date: 09/28/05   Time: 19:45
Sample: 1993:01 2000:12
Included observations: 96
```

Variable	Coefficient	Std. Error	t-Statistic	Prob.
C	3.919436	0.026616	147.2585	0.0000
@TREND	0.003821	0.000484	7.895337	0.0000
R-squared	0.398732	Mean dependent var		4.100948
Adjusted R-squared	0.392336	S.D. dependent var		0.168578
S.E. of regression	0.131411	Akaike info criterion		-1.200355
Sum squared resid	1.623281	Schwarz criterion		-1.146931
Log likelihood	59.61704	F-statistic		62.33635
Durbin-Watson stat	0.168747	Prob(F-statistic)		0.000000

Figure 5.4:   Actual and fitted trend values for LEX

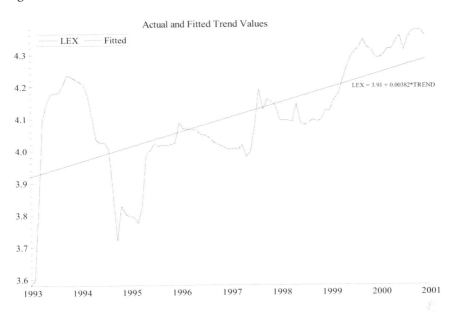

As can be seen from actual and fitted values in Figure 5.4 and the low R^2 in Table 5.1, the linear trend does not fit the exchange rate data quite well. A look at the graph also suggests that the trend looks non-linear. To better fit the data, we can introduce nonlinear trends such as quadratic trend in the form of equation [5.3].

$$\log EX_t = \beta_0 + \beta_1 T + \beta_2 T^2 + \varepsilon_t \qquad [5.3]$$

Table 5.2:   Modelling quadratic trend in the Kenyan exchange rate

```
Dependent Variable: LEX
Method: Least Squares
Date: 09/28/05   Time: 20:32
Sample: 1993:01 2000:12
Included observations: 96
```

Variable	Coefficient	Std. Error	t-Statistic	Prob.
C	4.044631	0.035499	113.9355	0.0000
TREND	-0.004170	0.001727	-2.414386	0.0177
TREND^2	8.41E-05	1.76E-05	4.781788	0.0000

R-squared	0.517390	Mean dependent var	4.100948
Adjusted R-squared	0.507011	S.D. dependent var	0.168578
S.E. of regression	0.118364	Akaike info criterion	-1.399352
Sum squared resid	1.302935	Schwarz criterion	-1.319216
Log likelihood	70.16890	F-statistic	49.85101
Durbin-Watson stat	0.215053	Prob(F-statistic)	0.000000

The quadratic trend picked the U shaped trend as $\beta_1 < 0$ and $\beta_2 > 0$ (see Figure 5.5). The quadratic trend fits the data better as the adjusted R^2 is much higher (although it could be higher by mere addition of a new variable) than the model with linear trend (0.507 compared to 0.392). The Schwarz and Akaike criterion are also lower in the quadratic trend model implying that the quadratic trend is the preferred specification.

To account for the deterministic shifts, we introduced two dummy variables. DMY 1993 takes the value of 1 during the pegged exchange rate regime (before October, 1993) and 0 otherwise; and it is introduced to capture the regime shift. DMY 9410 is an impulse dummy taking a value of 1 in 1994:10 and 0 otherwise. It captures the break in the series due to the appreciation of the currency. The result shows that the impulse DMY9410 is statistically significant while DMY1993 is insignificant and hence dropped. The Schwarz criterion is also lower without the insignificant variable DMY1993. The results are given in tables 5.3 and 5.4.

Table 5.3:   Regression of LEX with impulse dummies

Dependent Variable: LEX				
Method: Least Squares				
Date: 09/28/05 Time: 21:01				
Sample: 1993:01 2000:12				
Included observations: 96				
Variable	Coefficient	Std. Error	t-Statistic	Prob.
C	4.036232	0.059309	68.05464	0.0000
TREND	-0.003641	0.002493	-1.460665	0.1476
TREND^2	7.88E-05	2.30E-05	3.427631	0.0009
DMY1993	0.019310	0.059788	0.322972	0.7475
DMY9410	-0.274387	0.118317	-2.319082	0.0226
R-squared	0.546292	Mean dependent var		4.100948
Adjusted R-squared	0.526348	S.D. dependent var		0.168578
S.E. of regression	0.116019	Akaike info criterion		-1.419440
Sum squared resid	1.224906	Schwarz criterion		-1.285881
Log likelihood	73.13314	F-statistic		27.39233
Durbin-Watson stat	0.235512	Prob(F-statistic)		0.000000

Table 5.4:   Regression of LEX without 1993 step dummy

Dependent Variable: LEX				
Method: Least Squares				
Date: 09/28/05 Time: 21:08				
Sample: 1993:01 2000:12				
Included observations: 96				
Variable	Coefficient	Std. Error	t-Statistic	Prob.
C	4.051714	0.034752	116.5889	0.0000
TREND	-0.004232	0.001685	-2.511756	0.0138
TREND^2	8.37E-05	1.72E-05	4.878471	0.0000
DMY9410	-0.279627	0.116628	-2.397602	0.0185
R-squared	0.545771	Mean dependent var		4.100948
Adjusted R-squared	0.530960	S.D. dependent var		0.168578
S.E. of regression	0.115453	Akaike info criterion		-1.439128
Sum squared resid	1.226310	Schwarz criterion		-1.332280
Log likelihood	73.07815	F-statistic		36.84707
Durbin-Watson stat	0.238150	Prob(F-statistic)		0.000000

The graph of the fitted and actual values (Figure 5.5) also shows that the quadratic trend, with the impulse dummy, fits the data better.

Figure 5.5:   Actual and fitted values with quadratic trend for LEX (Model in Table 5.4)

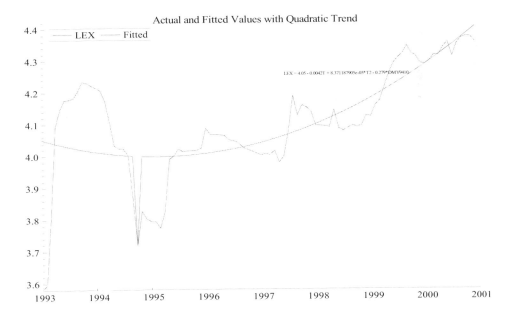

Apart from the fit of the model, there are also some summary statistics to evaluate the forecasting ability of a model. Root mean squared error, mean absolute error, mean absolute percentage error and Theil's inequality coefficient are among the most commonly used statistics for such purpose. The first two forecast error statistics are dependent on the scale of the dependent variables; while the rest are scale invariant (i.e. unit free). In most instances unit-free measures are preferable (Challen and Hagger, 1983). As a result, Theil's inequality coefficient is used in this book.

Theil's inequality coefficient is given as

$$T = \frac{\sqrt{\dfrac{1}{h+1} \sum_{t=s}^{s+h} (\hat{Y}_t - Y_t)^2}}{\sqrt{\dfrac{1}{h+1} \sum \hat{Y}_t^2} + \sqrt{\dfrac{1}{h+1} \sum_{t=s}^{s+h} Y_t^2}} \qquad [5.4]$$

Where Y and $\hat{Y}$ are actual and forecasted values, respectively. S is forecast sample and h is the length of forecast sample.

Theil's inequality coefficient can be decomposed into bias, variance and covariance proportions.

$$\text{Bias proportion} \quad = \frac{(\bar{\hat{Y}}_t - \bar{Y})^2}{\sum (Y_t - \hat{Y}_t)^2 \Big/ h} \qquad [5.5a]$$

$$\text{Variance proportion} \quad = \frac{(S_{\hat{Y}} - S_Y)^2}{\sum (Y_t - \hat{Y}_t) \Big/ h} \qquad [5.5b]$$

$$\text{Covariance proportion} \quad = \frac{2(1-r)S_{\hat{Y}} S_y}{\sum (Y_t - \hat{Y}_t)^2 \Big/ h} \qquad [5.5c]$$

Where $\bar{\hat{Y}}, \bar{Y}, S_{\hat{Y}}, S_Y$ are means and standard deviations of $\hat{Y}$ and Y, respectively; and r is correlation between $\hat{Y}$ and Y.

The bias and variance proportions show how far the mean of the forecast is from the mean of the actual series and how far the variation of the forecast is from the

124

variation of the actual series, respectively. The covariance proportion measures the remaining unsystematic forecast errors. The sum of these three measures would be unity. If the forecast is good, the bias and variance proportions should be small and thus most of the bias would be unsystematic.

These summary statistics are presented for our quadratic trend model. The result shows that our forecast is reasonably well, given that around 85% of the variation is accounted by the covariance proportion.

Figure 5.6: Forecast of LEX with evaluation statistics

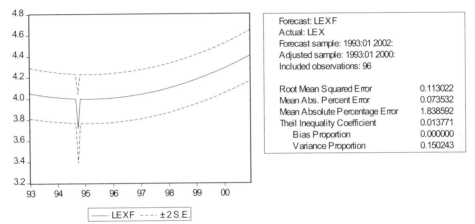

Trend Forecasting

After modelling the trend, the trend model can be used for trend forecasting purpose. Upon substituting the trend values into the estimated equation, the forecasted values of the variable can be found. A statistical distribution for the accuracy of the forecast could also be derived. Using our estimated model, the forecasted values of the exchange rate for 24 months ahead is presented in Figure 6.7 below. The bars accompanying the forecast show that the forecast errors are contained within ± 2 standard deviations suggesting that our model forecasts the trend quite well.

Figure 5.7: **Forecasted values of the Kenyan exchange rate**

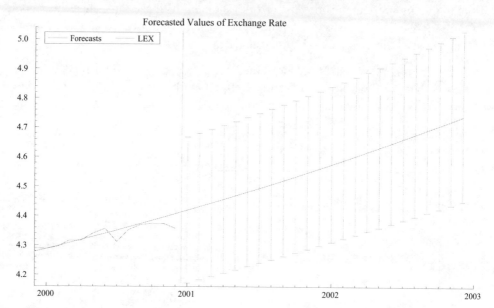

Modelling Cycles

So far, we tried to model only the long run component of the variable using trend. In the process, we filtered out the short run variations. In this section, we will address how to model short run variations- the cycles. Before we proceed to the estimation of the cycles, we introduce the concept of covariance stationarity.

Covariance stationarity: if (y_t) is a stationary series (i.e. time invariant variable), it would have a finite mean, variance, and the covariance between any two consecutive periods which are time invariant or constant. That is,

$$E(y_t) = \mu \text{ and } Var(y_t) = \sigma_y^2$$

$$Cov(y_t, y_{t-s}) = Cov(y_{t-j}, y_{t-s-j}) = \gamma_s \qquad [5.6]$$

Where μ, σ_y^2 and γ_s are all constants. μ is the mean, σ_y^2 is the variance and γ_s is the covariance.

In simple words, a stationary variable is mean reverting while a non-stationary one diverts from its mean with time. A nonstationary variable is said to contain unit root in the autoregressive process. That is,

$$y_t = \phi y_{t-1} + \varepsilon_t \qquad \text{and} \qquad \phi \geq |1| \qquad [5.7]$$

126

In such a case, it is easy to show that $E(y_t) = y_0$ and $Var(y_t) = t\sigma_\varepsilon^2$. Where y_0 is the initial value.

This can easily be done by solving the stochastic difference equation in equation [5.7] by backward substitution method. Assume that $\phi = 1$ so that equation [5.7] becomes

$$y_t = y_{t-1} + \varepsilon_t, \quad \varepsilon_t \qquad Niid(0, \sigma_\varepsilon^2) \tag{5.8}$$

Taking first lag of the equation yields equation [5.9];

$$y_{t-1} = y_{t-2} + \varepsilon_{t-1} \tag{5.9}$$

Substituting equation [5.9] in equation [5.8] yields equation [5.10];

$$y_t = y_{t-2} + \varepsilon_{t-1} + \varepsilon_t \tag{5.10}$$

But, we need to find the value for y_{t-2}. We can find this by lagging equation [5.9] by one period to yield equation [5.11];

$$y_{t-2} = y_{t-3} + \varepsilon_{t-2} \tag{5.11}$$

Substituting equation [5.11] in equation [5.10] yields equation [5.12];

$$y_t = y_{t-3} + \varepsilon_{t-2} + \varepsilon_{t-1} + \varepsilon_t \tag{5.12}$$

If this process is repeated many times, we find that

$$y_t = y_0 + \sum_t \varepsilon_t \tag{5.13}$$

Equation [5.13] is the solution of the first-order stochastic difference equation in equation [5.8]. Taking expectations of equation [5.13]

$$E(y_t) = E(y_0) + E\left[\sum_t \varepsilon_t\right] \tag{5.14}$$

But $E(y_0) = y_0$ i.e. expectation of a constant equals the constant

$$E\left[\sum_t \varepsilon_t\right] = \sum_t E(\varepsilon_t) = 0 \quad \text{since} \quad \varepsilon_t \sim Niid(0, \sigma_\varepsilon^2)$$

Therefore $\quad E(y_t) = y_0 \tag{5.15}$

To compute the variance

$$\left[y_t - E(y_t) \right]\left[y_t - E(y_t) \right]' = \left[\varepsilon_1 + \varepsilon_2 + .. \right]\left[\varepsilon_1 + \varepsilon_2 + .. \right]' \qquad [5.16]$$

Assuming there is no serial correlation so that correlation of cross-terms is zero,

$$Var(y_t) = \left[y_t - E(y_t) \right]\left[y_t - E(y_t) \right]' = \sigma_{\varepsilon 1}^2 + \sigma_{\varepsilon 2}^3 + ... + \sigma_{\varepsilon t}^2 = t\sigma_{\varepsilon}^2 \quad [5.17]$$

Thus, a pure random walk in equation [5.8] does not violate the mean condition but rather the variance conditions for covariance stationarity.

If we now have a random walk with drift,

$$y_t = \mu + y_{t-1} + \varepsilon_t \qquad [5.18]$$

Applying the same procedure as we have done for the pure random walk, we find that

$$y_t = y_0 + t\mu + \sum_t \varepsilon_t \qquad [5.19]$$

Taking expectations of equation [5.19], we find that

$$E(y_t) = y_0 + t\mu \qquad [5.20]$$

This raises an important point that a drift term can generate a time trend. Applying the same approach as for the pure random walk, we can find that

$$Var(y_t) = \sigma_{\varepsilon 1}^2 + \sigma_{\varepsilon 2}^3 + ... + \sigma_{\varepsilon t}^2 = t\sigma_{\varepsilon}^2 \qquad [5.21]$$

Thus, a random walk with drift violates all the three conditions for covariance stationarity. The same applies to a random walk with drift and time trend;

$$y_t = \mu + y_{t-1} + \lambda t + \varepsilon_t \qquad [5.22]$$

Moving Average (MA) and Autoregressive (AR) Modelling

One method of modelling cycle is to model it as a moving average of the innovations. The simple MA process is given as MA(1)

$$y_t = \varepsilon_t - \theta\varepsilon_{t-1} \qquad [5.23]$$

This can be reparameterized as

$$\varepsilon_t = y_t + \theta\varepsilon_{t-1}$$

$$\varepsilon_{t-1} = y_{t-1} + \theta\varepsilon_{t-2}$$

$$\varepsilon_{t-2} = y_{t-2} + \theta\varepsilon_{t-3}$$

$$\varepsilon_{t-3} = y_{t-3} + \theta\varepsilon_{t-4}$$

$$y_t = \varepsilon_t - \theta y_{t-1} - \theta^2 y_{t-2} - \theta^3 y_{t-3} - \theta^4 y_{t-3} - \cdots \qquad \text{[by substituting in 5.23] [5.24]}$$

If $|\theta| < 1$, the above system will become convergent and can be written using lag operator (L) as,

$$\frac{1}{1-\theta L} y_t = \varepsilon_t \qquad\qquad\qquad\qquad\qquad [5.25]$$

When the restriction that $|\theta| < 1$ is fulfilled, the system is referred to as invertible and can be estimated as a finite order AR process. Thus, the stationarity restriction becomes an important element to apply the MA modelling. The stationarity restriction is also necessary for AR models as shown below.

Consider AR(1) model as

$$y_t = \phi y_{t-1} + \varepsilon_t$$

$$y_t(1-\phi L) = \varepsilon_t \Rightarrow y_t = \frac{\varepsilon_t}{(1-\phi L)} \qquad\qquad\qquad [5.26]$$

For convergence, the stationarity restriction that $|\phi| < 1$ will be required.

With the stationarity restrictions, the cycles can also be represented as MA(q), AR(p) or ARMA(p, q) process. The orders (p and q) of the MA and AR terms can be determined using the Schwartz or Akaike information criterion. When the stationarity restriction fails to hold, the variable should first be transformed to guarantee stationarity. In most of the cases, the appropriate transformation is differencing the series until stationarity is achieved. The AR, MA and ARMA models can be, then, fitted on the transformed variable. This type of model is referred as the ARIMA model and the additional letter 'I' implies that the series is integrated process-i.e. stationarity is achieved after differencing. The ARIMA process is specified as (p, d, q) where d refers to the order of (the number of times one need, to do) differencing to achieve stationarity.

We found out that our Kenyan exchange rate data is nonstationary and stationarity is achieved after first differencing. We first estimated an MA model of order 12.

Next, we dropped the insignificant MA terms and calculated the Schwartz criterion (SIC). The SIC statistics is minimized at MA(8) suggesting that the MA(8) is a reasonable specification. The results are displayed below.

Table 5.5:   MA(8) model of the Kenyan exchange rate

Dependent Variable: D(LEX)
Method: Least Squares
Date: 09/29/05   Time: 00:01
Sample(adjusted): 1993:02 2000:12
Included observations: 95 after adjusting endpoints
Convergence achieved after 38 iterations
Backcast: 1992:06 1993:01

Variable	Coefficient	Std. Error	t-Statistic	Prob.
C	0.003684	0.001272	2.895444	0.0048
MA(1)	0.182258	0.083264	2.188929	0.0313
MA(2)	-0.143909	0.076366	-1.884462	0.0629
MA(3)	-0.076961	0.058478	-1.316063	0.1917
MA(4)	0.131488	0.071650	1.835130	0.0699
MA(5)	0.015807	0.062646	0.252328	0.8014
MA(6)	-0.007088	0.075543	-0.093824	0.9255
MA(7)	-0.525076	0.061257	-8.571657	0.0000
MA(8)	-0.494484	0.075920	-6.513253	0.0000

R-squared	0.455361	Mean dependent var		0.008168
Adjusted R-squared	0.404697	S.D. dependent var		0.053805
S.E. of regression	0.041514	Akaike info criterion		-3.435635
Sum squared resid	0.148212	Schwarz criterion		-3.193689
Log likelihood	172.1927	F-statistic		8.987845
Durbin-Watson stat	2.038666	Prob(F-statistic)		0.000000

Inverted MA Roots	.99	.67 +.72i	.67 -.72i	-.14+.90i
	-.14 -.90i	-.74 -.53i	-.74+.53i	-.75

For the AR process, AR(3) is found to be the best fit as suggested by the SIC.

Table 5.6:   AR(3) Model of the Kenyan exchange rate

```
Dependent Variable: D(LEX)
Method: Least Squares
Date: 09/29/05   Time: 00:17
Sample(adjusted): 1993:05 2000:12
Included observations: 92 after adjusting endpoints
Convergence achieved after 3 iterations
```

Variable	Coefficient	Std. Error	t-Statistic	Prob.
C	0.001957	0.005402	0.362275	0.7180
AR(1)	0.168717	0.093395	1.806500	0.0743
AR(2)	-0.007047	0.090819	-0.077589	0.9383
AR(3)	0.042722	0.083969	0.508782	0.6122
R-squared	0.045217	Mean dependent var		0.002881
Adjusted R-squared	0.012668	S.D. dependent var		0.041010
S.E. of regression	0.040749	Akaike info criterion		-3.520249
Sum squared resid	0.146125	Schwarz criterion		-3.410606
Log likelihood	165.9315	F-statistic		1.389191
Durbin-Watson stat	2.026387	Prob(F-statistic)		0.251404
Inverted AR Roots	.41	-.12+.30i	-.12 -.30i	

Following the same procedure, we found ARIMA (2,1,2) to be the data congruent representation. The result is shown in Table 5.7.

Table 5.7:   ARIMA (2, 1, 2) of Kenyan exchange rate

```
Dependent Variable: D(LEX)
Method: Least Squares
Date: 09/29/05   Time: 00:25
Sample(adjusted): 1993:04 2000:12
Included observations: 93 after adjusting endpoints
Convergence achieved after 27 iterations
Backcast: 1993:02 1993:03
```

Variable	Coefficient	Std. Error	t-Statistic	Prob.
C	0.002374	0.004970	0.477699	0.6340
AR(1)	0.744228	0.148032	5.027500	0.0000
AR(2)	-0.260180	0.123664	-2.103924	0.0382
MA(1)	-0.684796	0.158885	-4.310009	0.0000
MA(2)	0.264785	0.140545	1.883986	0.0629
R-squared	0.317466	Mean dependent var		0.005794
Adjusted R-squared	0.286442	S.D. dependent var		0.049525
S.E. of regression	0.041835	Akaike info criterion		-3.457886
Sum squared resid	0.154017	Schwarz criterion		-3.321724
Log likelihood	165.7917	F-statistic		10.23283
Durbin-Watson stat	1.828482	Prob(F-statistic)		0.000001
Inverted AR Roots	.37 -.35i	.37+.35i		
Inverted MA Roots	.34+.38i	.34 -.38i		

Figure 5.8:   MA (8) actual and fitted values

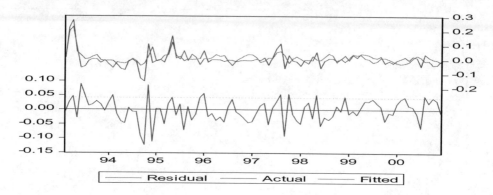

Figure 5.9:   AR (3) actual and fitted values

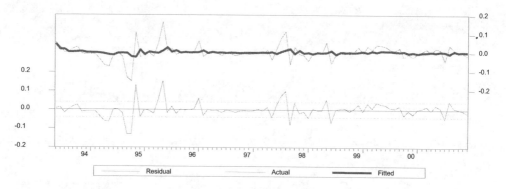

Figure 5.10: ARIMA (2, 1, 2) actual and fitted values

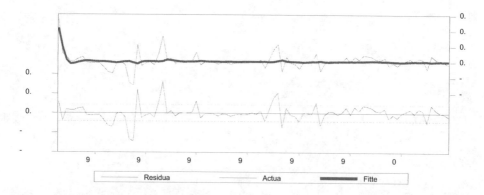

The results and the graphs suggest that the MA (8) fits the data better than both the AR and ARIMA processes presented are forecasts and forecast evaluation results from the above models. In terms of the Theil's inequality coefficients disaggregation, the ARIMA (2,1,2) is the preferred forecasting model as more than 50% of the variation is accounted by the non-systematic component.

Figure 5.11a: MA (8) forecast

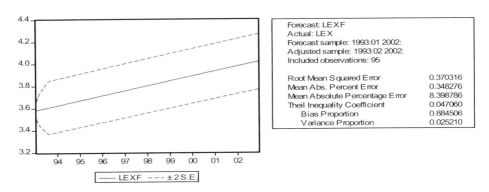

Figure 5.11b: ARIMA (2,1,2)

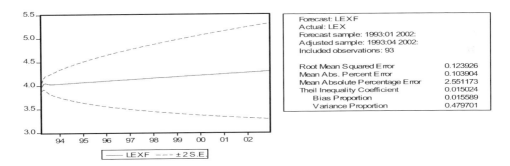

Figure 5.12: AR (3) model forecast

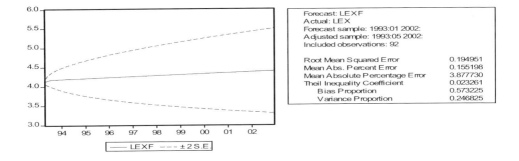

When the stationarity assumption is violated, rather than differencing the series once or twice until stationarity is achieved, the exact level of integration can be estimated along with the ARMA process. This method is referred as the fractional integration process- ARFIMA. Using this method, we found ARFIMA (0, d,8) to be the congruent model. The estimated fractional integration term is 0.34 and significant. The Akaike information criterion is also minimized with this specification. The graph of the actual and fitted values shown below reveals the fit of this model. We left out the issue of fractional integration from this book for your advanced reading.

Figure 5.13: ARFIMA (0,d,8) model of the Kenyan exchange rate

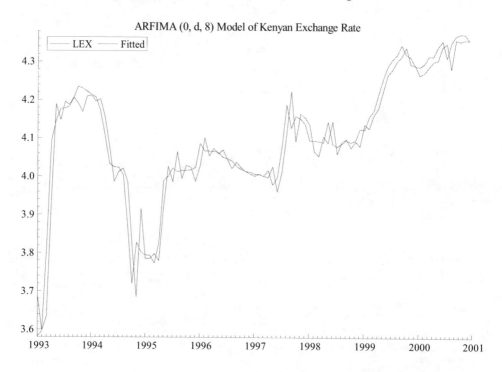

To evaluate the forecasting behaviour of our model, the model is estimated for the period from 1993 to the first month of 2000 withholding the data for 11 months for comparison purpose. We, then, forecasted the exchange rate for the next 11 months outside our estimated sample period. Then, the forecasted results are compared with the actual values. A statistical distribution for the significance of the forecast errors is also computed[14]. In Figure 5.14, this distribution with $\pm\,2$ sd band is indicated by a vertical line with whiskers.

The model forecasts pretty well for the first three months and the forecast quality deteriorates continuously as the forecast horizon expands. Forecasts beyond the eighth month are outside the $\pm\,2$ sd error bands. This result is consistent with other empirical forecasting models that show similar forecast deterioration.

---

[14]   Most standard statistical softwares such as PcGive derive this distribution.

Figure 5.14: Actual and forecasted exchange rate

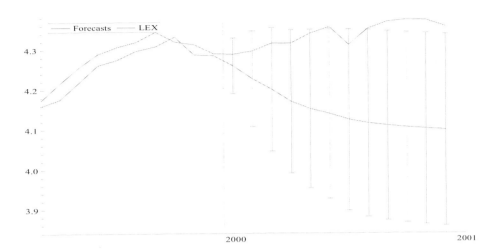

The Box-Jenkins Approach to Forecasting

What we have just done is basically the four steps of the Box-Jenkins forecasting approach. The Box-Jenkins approach has four iterative steps:

(i)   Identification of the "Data Generating Process" of the series (DGP)-Autoregressive (AR), moving average (MA), ARMA, ARIMA, ARFIMA, etc. using the patterns of the autocorrelation function (ACF) and partial autocorrelation function (PACF);

(ii)   Estimate the model using maximum likelihood;

(iii)   Perform diagnostic statistics to ensure that we have modeled the patterns of behaviour and the residual is white noise-You could use Box-Jenkins test;

(iv)   Forecast using the estimated model.

Schematically, this can be shown in Figure 5.15.

Figure 5.15: The four iterative steps of Box-Jenkins modelling approach

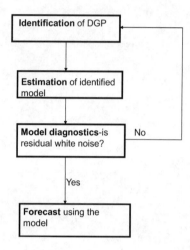

It is important to note two weaknesses of the Box-Jenkins approach. First, the model can only be used for forecasting. It cannot be used for policy simulation (what if analysis). Second, the approach requires a large sample size (at least 50 observations).

Forecasting with Regression

Apart from the univariate forecasting, forecasting with regression is the other popular method of forecasting. The regression can take a single equation or multi equation format. The choice of the regression framework depends on the problem at hand and the feasibility for forecasting. In this section, we will discuss how the single equation and multi equation forecasting models can be formulated and used for forecasting. We will also briefly show the estimation issues involved in relation with the multi equation models.

Single Equation Forecasting Models

The single equation model is the very basic forecasting framework. The model can be given as

$$y_t = \alpha + \beta x_t + \varepsilon_t$$

[6.27]

Where y is the endogenous variable, x is exogenous variable and ε_t is the random error term.

This simple model can be estimated by OLS or two stage least squares if we have an endogenous regressor. The equation can also be reformulated into an error correction format if there is nonstationarity in the variables. Once the coefficients of the model are obtained, the future values of the endogenous variable (y) can be forecasted. The problem in this approach is that in order to obtain the forecasted value of the endogenous variable, we have to supply the future values of the exogenous variable (x) which in turn necessitates forecasting the x values. In such a case the exogenous variables can be forecasted in a univariate framework like ARIMA model as discussed in the previous sections. The forecasted values of the exogenous variable from the univariate model can then be used, along with the estimated coefficients, to compute the forecasted values of the endogenous variable.

The task of forecasting the exogenous variable in a univariate framework in order to forecast the values of the endogenous variable can be avoided if our interest is to forecast only one period ahead. In this case, we can re-specify equation [5.27] by using the lagged value of the exogenous variable as a regressor, and given as equation [5.28].

$$y_t = \alpha + \beta x_{t-1} + \varepsilon_t \qquad\qquad [5.28]$$

In this formulation, a one period ahead value of the endogenous variable can be forecasted using the current value of the exogenous variable. We showed the performance of this approach using the Kenyan exchange rate data. We regressed the growth in exchange rate on growth in the domestic price level for the period 1993:03 to 2000:10. Using this we can forecast the growth in exchange rate for 2000:11. According to our forecast, the exchange rate for November 2000 is expected to grow by -0.0009%. The forecast accuracy is satisfactory as the forecast error is statistically insignificant having a t-value of 0.003.

Table 5.8:   Single equation model

```
Dependent Variable: D(LEX)
Method: Least Squares
Date: 10/17/05   Time: 14:41
Sample(adjusted): 1993:03 2000:10
Included observations: 92 after adjusting endpoints
```

Variable	Coefficient	Std. Error	t-Statistic	Prob.
C	0.003635	0.006088	0.597112	0.5519
DLDRP(-1)	0.555226	0.274894	2.019780	0.0464
C	0.003635	0.006088	0.597112	0.5519
R-squared	0.043362	Mean dependent var		0.008457
Adjusted R-squared	0.032733	S.D. dependent var		0.054613
S.E. of regression	0.053712	Akaike info criterion		-2.988869
Sum squared resid	0.259646	Schwarz criterion		-2.934048
Log likelihood	139.4880	F-statistic		4.079511
Durbin-Watson stat	1.241066	Prob(F-statistic)		0.046380

Table 5.9: 1-Step forecast results from the single equation model

Horizon	Forecast	SE	Actual	Error	t-value
2000-11	-0.000891306	0.05371	-0.000756	0.00013	0.003

Multiple Equation Forecasting Models

Multiple equation forecasting models can take two forms—structural equations forecasting model and vector autoregression models. In the first case, we can have a set of individual structural equations that describe some behavioral relationships. These individual equations can be estimated using single equation information estimation technique (SEIE), limited information relating to the whole system (LISE), and full information estimation relating to the whole system technique (FISE) (Challen and Hagger, 1983). OLS, distributive lag class of models and ARIMA models can be classified as the single equation information technique, while 2SLS, instrumental variable estimation and limited information maximum likelihood (LIML) methods are classified as limited information relating to the whole system; and 3SLS and full information maximum likelihood (FIML) estimation techniques can be categorized as full information relating to the whole system. As their name indicates, the main difference among these techniques is on the information content of the estimator. The other important distinction of these methods is that single equation and limited information estimation techniques involve estimation of the stochastic equations one at a time while in the full information estimation all the stochastic equations are estimated simultaneously.

Once the individual equations are estimated, the next step is to solve the model—i.e. solving for the values of the endogenous variables given the values of exogenous variables. This enables us to examine the fit of the model to the historical data since the fit of the individual equations does not guarantee a good fit in the system or in the complete model. According to Challen and Hagger (1983:164) "It is possible that every stochastic equation of the system performs adequately on the basis of the individual equation evaluation procedures but that the system as a whole gives a poor representation of the real economy in which the historical time paths of the endogenous variables were generated." This may be the result of a more complex dynamic structure in the model as a whole than any of the individual equation it is composed of (Oshikoya, 1990). Thus, with-in-sample tracking performance of the whole system should be examined based on the standard statistical tools such as MSE, RMSE and Theil's index discussed in the previous section. This method requires a sound theoretical specification, consistent accounting framework and closure rules. We leave that for your further reading and proceed to VAR modelling in the rest of this section. We focus on vector autoregression (VAR) method of forecasting.

VAR is the multivariate counterpart of the univariate autoregression framework. As opposed to the univariate model, VAR allows for cross variable dynamics. The VAR model is also important when we are not sure about the endogenous-exogenous classifications (i.e., the theoretical relationships) of the variables (see Sims, 1982). In this approach, all the variables are treated as endogenous. Consider the reduced-form VAR model below:

$$y_t = b_{10} + b_{11}y_{t-1} + b_{11}z_{t-1} + \varepsilon_{yt}$$
$$z_t = b_{20} + b_{21}y_{t-1} + b_{22}z_{t-1} + \varepsilon_{zt}$$

[5.29]

As can be seen from the above formulation, in a VAR model each variable is regressed on its lag and the lag of all other variables. The VAR model above is referred as VAR(1) or VAR order 1 as the longest lag length is one. As in the univariate autoregression model, the lag length is selected using the AIC and SIC. Once the data congruent VAR is determined, we can handle our forecasts easily. As all our right hand side variables are lagged values, we can have the 1-period ahead forecast easily. Using the 1-period forecast, we can forecast the subsequent period forecasts. We used this approach to forecast the Kenyan exchange rate.

The first task is determining the appropriate lag length. Given the available data, we started with VAR(4) and dropped the insignificant lag length while observing the change in the AIC and SIC in the process. Both the AIC and SIC are minimized at lag length of two and our F-test does not reject the null hypothesis that third and forth lags are jointly insignificant while the null hypothesis that all the higher order lags except the first one are zero is rejected. Thus, we selected VAR(2) as a congruent model describing the data properly.

Table 5.10: Lag length selection

LAG	SIC	HQ	AIC
4	-8.2292	-8.5296	-8.7325
3	-8.3952	-8.6288	-8.7866
2	**-8.5724**	**-8.7393**	**-8.852**
1	-8.6239	-8.724	-8.7917

Table 5.11: 1-Step ahead forecast result from VAR (2)

Horizon	Forecast	SE	Actual	Error	t-value
2000-11	0.00292011	0.04123	-0.000756	-0.0037	-0.089

We estimated the model for the period 1993:03 to 2000:10 (October, 2000). Then, we forecasted the growth in exchange rate for the month of November, 2000. The forecasted growth rate of the exchange rate for November 2000 is 0.003% with the forecast error being insignificant having a *t*-value of -0.089 as shown in Table 5.11. Overall, the VAR(2) model forecasts reasonably well though the performance of the single equation based model seems better (the forecast error being -0.0037 as opposed to 0.00013 in the case of the single equation based model).

Impulse Response Analysis Using VAR Model: An Application with Kenyan and Ethiopian Data

Impulse response is a method of assessing the interaction among the variables in the VAR. It can be used either to assess the dynamic behavior of the VAR or to investigate the policy impact of the variables that constitute the VAR. For instance, you may have a macroeconometric model using a VAR approach that contains "key" macroeconomic variables. The impulse response exercise could be employed to examine, say, the conventional stabilization policies such as monetary and fiscal policy shocks on these key macroeconomic variables.

Impulse response analysis is carried out by looking at the impact of a unit innovation in the random error term in the overall system (see below). The impulse response function can easily be derived by reparameterizing our VAR model in [5.30] as in the same way equation [5.23] was reparameterized into [5.24] and [5.25]. That is,

$$y_t = \varepsilon_{yt} + b_{11}\varepsilon_{yt-1} + b_{12}\varepsilon_{zt-1} + \ldots$$
$$z_t = \varepsilon_{zt} + b_{21}\varepsilon_{yt-1} + b_{22}\varepsilon_{zt-1} + \ldots$$

[5.30]

By normalizing the MA representation by the standard deviation σ (this is referred as Cholesky normalization factor), our impulse response function can be given as equation [5.31].

$$y_t = \beta_{11}^0\varepsilon_{yt} + \beta_{11}^1\varepsilon_{yt-1} + \beta_{12}^1\varepsilon_{zt-1} + \ldots$$
$$z_t = \beta_{21}^0\varepsilon_{yt} + \beta_{22}^0\varepsilon_{zt} + \beta_{21}^1\varepsilon_{yt-1} + \beta_{22}^1\varepsilon_{zt-1} + \ldots$$

[5.31]

The first equation contains only current innovation ε_{yt} while the second equation contains two innovations ε_{yt} and ε_{zt} implying that the ordering of the variables matter for our result. In practice, however, ordering does not mostly matter. The β coefficients in equation [5.31] are referred as impulse multipliers.

Figure 5.16: Forecast and actual changes in exchange rate

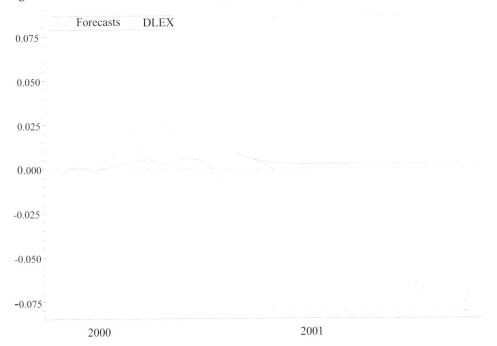

To show the importance of the impulse response analysis, we used the Kenyan exchange rate and Ethiopian GDP/output data. For the Kenyan exchange rate, we estimated VAR(1) containing exchange rate, prices, interest rate, money supply, trade balance and debt to GDP ratio. Since the data contained unit root, we estimated the VAR in first difference except for trade balance and debt to GDP ratio. It is, however, important to note that in using these variables in difference form, we are implicitly assuming that they are I(1) but not cointegrated (i.e. the rank of the Π matrix used in chapter 4 is zero). Our impulse response result in Figure 5.16 shows that one standard deviation shock to the innovation of the exchange rate equation leads to increase in the growth of interest rate, domestic prices and money supply while trade balance has fallen. Our result may suggest that in an open economy, exchange rate depreciation may promote export and also lead to a fall in import. As a result, improvement in the trade balance may be observed (given what is called the Marshall-Learner condition which states that the sum of the elasticities of imports and exports should be greater than 1, holds). As the demand for the local currency increases with the rise in export, the domestic currency may appreciate with time implying that the improvement in the trade balance is only temporary. The depreciation of the currency has also a bearing on the domestic price level depending on the weight of the import prices on the overall price level. As Figure 5.17 shows, there is a hike in the price level following the depreciation of the exchange rate which may propagate the rise in money supply to maintain the real money balance constant.

The impulse response analysis is an important and popular method of understanding how policies or shocks affect the variable that we are interested in. This method, however, should be used cautiously as its result would significantly be affected if there exists a deterministic shift that is not observed and hence not modelled.

Figure 5.17: Impulse-responses of variables

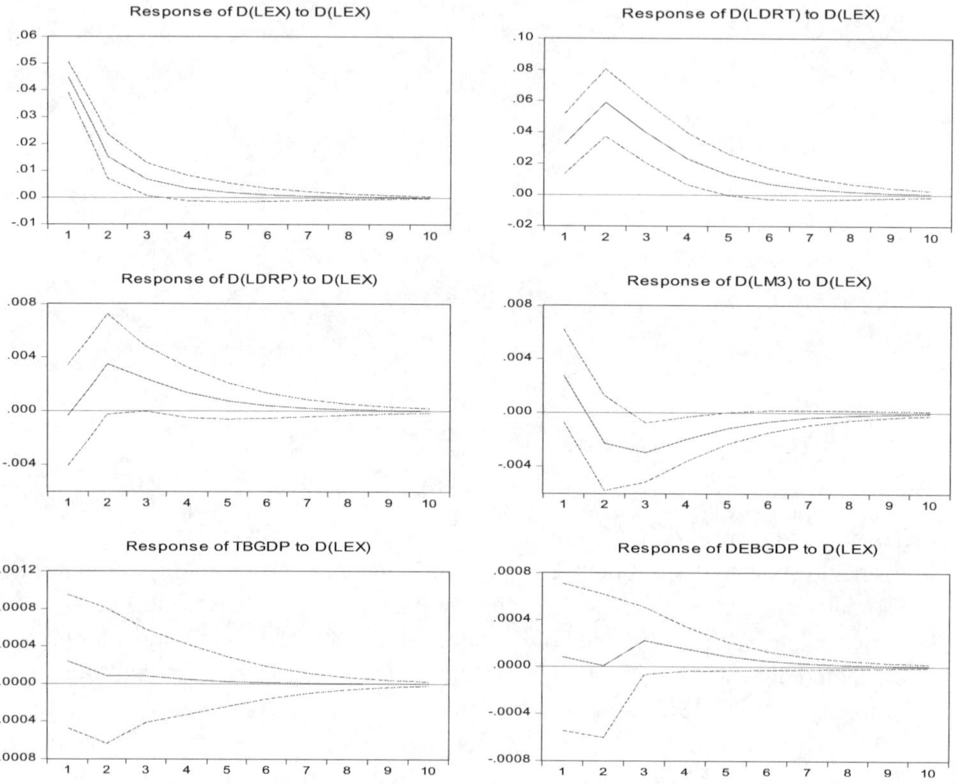

Note: Response to Cholesky One S.D. Innovations ± 2 S.E.

We also used the same approach to examine the impact of rainfall shocks on output using Ethiopian annual data. We specified our production function to be composed of output, labor, capital and rainfall. As the data contain unit root, we estimated the VAR in first difference. Our SIC and AIC statistics suggested that VAR(1) is an appropriate specification. In estimating the VAR model, we faced a problem of "wrongly" treating a purely exogenous variable – rainfall – as endogenous in our VAR model. To address this problem, we used a constrained full information maximum likelihood estimation method by constraining the coefficients of all other variables to zero in the rainfall equation. This method enables us to run our impulse response analysis that is not possible had rainfall were treated as endogenous in our VAR.

142

The result of our impulse response analysis is presented in Figure 5.18. The result shows that a one standard deviation shock in rainfall leads to a fall in the growth in output. The effect of this fall in output is observed in the period following the decline in rainfall. The impact of this shock is observed only in one period suggesting that the shock is not persistent as it might be expected. The impact of the shock in capital, however, is much more persistent. The fall in capital may be explained by the consumption smoothing behaviour of agents that may involve in sales of capital (such as oxen) in the face of drought to maintain the habitual (which is invariably subsistent) level of consumption.

Figure 5.18: Responses to shock in rainfall in Ethiopia

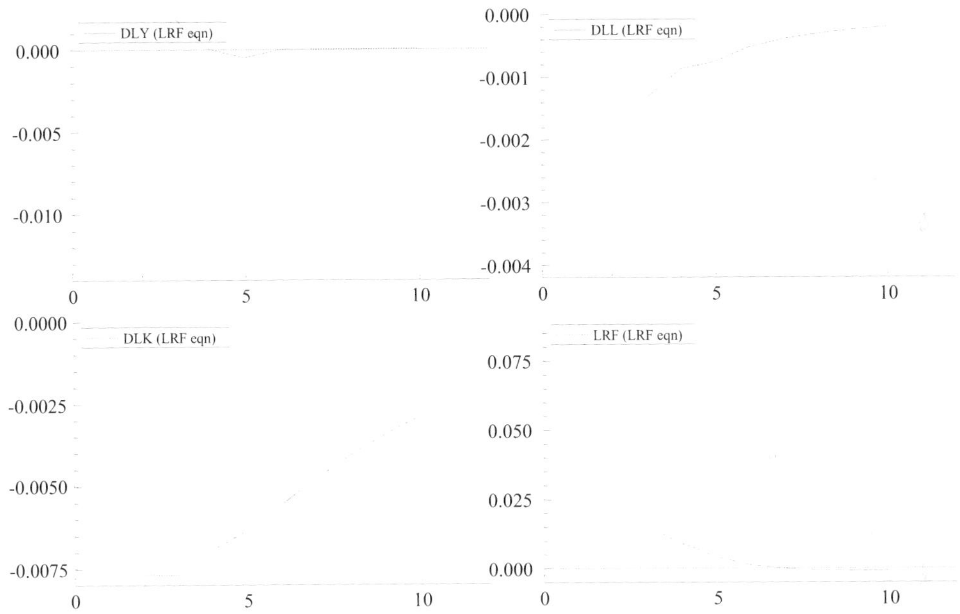

In sum, this section shows the techniques of forecasting in a univariate and multivariate framework. Both approaches are important in forecasting economic variables and could be used in different circumstances. However, one should be aware of the caveats of this approach—that forecasting is handled in a partial equilibrium framework. Important feedback effects coming from the rest of the economy are disregarded. One way of dealing with this issues is by building economy wide model for forecasting and policy analysis purpose.

Chapter 6

AN INTRODUCTION TO PANEL UNIT ROOTS AND COINTEGRATION

Introduction

As Arellano and Honore (2000) noted, panel data analysis is the watershed of timeseries and cross-section analysis. Unlike our analysis thus far, in this chapter we add one dimension to the time series dimension which we have been discussing. This dimension is – the cross section dimension which could be firms, countries or any other units. By combining the cross-section and time-series dimensions, panel data set enriches the set of identification arrangements such as exogenous instrumental variables and hence the importance of working on them (see Arellano and Honore, 2000).

African applied macroeconometric researchers might be interested to work with Africa-wide data. At times, it could be important to investigate the evidence across the continent or across the developing world. This is in particular true when the time span of data of a particular country such as Zimbabwe is limited. Such cross-country analysis is useful when an issue is ambiguous and we want to know the evidence elsewhere in the continent or in a particular region. In addition, sometimes we may have a data set with sufficient cross section units as well as its evolution over time. The two dimenstion can be simultaneously used – in a panel form – to shed more light on the issue at hand. A good example is data on "Survey of Manufacturing Firms" which is common in many African countries and usually has limited time dimension but sufficient cross-section units. This leads us to the use of time series and cross-section evidence.

It is now widely accepted that the commonly used unit root tests in the previous chapters like the Dickey Fuller (DF), Augmented Dickey Fuller (ADF) and Phillips Perron (PP) tests lack power in distinguishing the unit root null from stationary alternatives. Using panel data unit root tests is one way of increasing the power of unit root tests based on a single time series (Maddala and Wu, 1999: 631). In a panel data setting, we have time-series observations on multiple entities, for example firms or countries. We denote the cross-section sample size by N, and have $t=1, \ldots T$ time-series observations covering the same calendar period. This is called a balanced panel. In practice, it often happens that some cross sections start earlier, or finish later and hence the panel can be unbalanced.

Panel data solves the low power of the unit roots and cointegration tests especially in environments in which the time series for the data may not be very long but very similar data may be available across a cross section of units such as countries, regions, firms or industries (Banerge, 1999). Panel data can provide more degrees of freedom for testing unit roots and cointegration more reliably. This section discusses the available methods of testing for unit roots and cointegration in panel data. There is a recent advance in this area and we have attempted below to present that. We have used EVIEWS software (version 6) which handles panel-unit root test and panel cointegration.

Panel Unit Root Tests

The panel unit root test is the first step in the "panel cointegration based" estimation technique. Conceptually, it is similar to the single country time series model based "unit root test" that we have discussed so far. One advantage of panel unit root tests over time series counter parts is, however, that the power of the tests increases as the cross section component, *N*, increases. Moreover, it is shown that unlike time series unit root test statistics, which have no standard distribution, the panel data based unit root test statistics are asymptotically normally distributed (Hadri, 2000; Baltagi and Kao, 2000; Hall and Mairesse, 2002; Baltagi, 2005). There are a number of tests suggested by different authors. The EVIEWS software (version 5 and above) does easily handle these tests. We will first look at the two most important tests, the Levin and Lin (the LL test); and Im, Pesaran and Shin test (the IPS test) as well as modifications and extension made on them by Harris and Tzavalis (1999), Maddala and Wu (1999), Breitung (2000) and Choi (2001). This class of tests basically does test for the null of unit root (non-stationarity). We will also look at the Hadri test (Hadri, 2000) that tests for the null of no-unit root (stationarity).

There are two natural assumptions that we can make about the ρ_i given in equation [6.1] and subsequent equation. First, one can assume that the persistence parameters, ρ_i are common across cross-sections so that $\rho_i = \rho$ for all *i*. The Levin and Lin (LL), The Levin, Lin, and Chu (LLC), Breitung, and Hadri tests all employ this assumption. These are discussed in section 6.2.1. Alternatively, one can allow ρ to vary freely across cross-sections and thus have ρ_i. The Im, Pesaran, and Shin (IPS), and Fisher-type ADF and Fisher-PP tests are of this form. These are discussed in section 6.2.2.

Tests with Common Unit Root Process

a) The Levin and Lin (1992, 1993) test – the LL test

Levin and Lin (1992, 1993) used the following variants of equation [6.1] to test for the null that each individual series contains a unit root.

$$y_{it} = \rho_i y_{i,t-1} + z_{it}'\gamma + \varepsilon_{it} \qquad\qquad [6.1]$$

With $i(=1,...N)$ denoting individuals, countries, firms etc and $t(=1...T)$ denoting time. Y and x are the model variables with dimension $(T\mathrm{x}1)$ and $(T\mathrm{x}N)$, respectively; z_{it} is the deterministic component in the model.

In all cases, the disturbance terms ε_{it} are assumed independently and identically distributed with mean 0 and variance σ^2, $\varepsilon_{it} \sim$IID $(0, \sigma^2)$, thus individual process for each i are cross-sectionally independent and there is no serial correlation (i.e. $\rho_i = \rho$ for all i). We note here that the latter assumption imposes what is called *homogeneity assumption* by assuming that each individual-specific process is the same across all cross-sectional units of the panel. There are various forms of the LL tests that differ based on their hypothesis about the value of ρ and the drift term z_{it} that could take different terms including zero, one, simple time trends, a fixed effect α_i and a mixture of fixed effect and heterogeneous time effect. This is shown in Table 6.1 with the LL test given by LL_1 to LL_6. The bench mark LL test equation is derived by taking the difference of equation [6.1] and given as equation [6.2] below. Note here that the null-hypothesis of $\rho=1$ in equation [6.1] needs to be changed to $\rho^*(=[\rho-1])=0$ in equation [6.2] (see Chapter 3 for this basic notion).

$$\Delta y_{it} = \rho_i^* y_{i,t-1} + \sum_{L=1}^{p_i} \theta_{iL}\Delta y_{i,t-L} + z_{it}'\gamma + \varepsilon_{it} \qquad \text{where} \quad \rho_i^* = \rho-1 \qquad [6.2]$$

147

Table 6.1:   Different variants of the LL panel unit root test

$LL\_1 \cdots \Delta y_{it} = \rho y_{it-1} + \varepsilon_{it};$ $\qquad\qquad H_0 : \rho = 0; H_1 : \rho < 0$

$LL\_2 \cdots \Delta y_{it} = \rho y_{it-1} + \delta_0 + \varepsilon_{it};$ $\qquad\qquad H_0 : \rho = 0; H_1 : \rho < 0$

$LL\_3 \cdots \Delta y_{it} = \rho y_{it-1} + \delta_0 + \delta_1 t + \varepsilon_{it};$ $\qquad H_0 : \rho = \delta = 0; H_1 : \rho < 0; \delta \in R$

$LL\_4 \cdots \Delta y_{it} = \rho y_{it-1} + \alpha_t + \varepsilon_{it};$ $\qquad\qquad H_0 : \rho = \alpha_t = 0; H_1 : \rho < 0; \alpha_t \in R$

$LL\_5 \cdots \Delta y_{it} = \rho y_{it-1} + v_t + \varepsilon_{it};$ $\qquad\qquad H_0 : \rho = 0; H_1 : \rho < 0$

$LL\_6 \cdots \Delta y_{it} = \rho y_{it-1} + \alpha_i + \eta_i t + \varepsilon_{it};$ $\qquad H_0 : \rho = \eta_i = 0; H_1 : \rho < 0; \eta_i \in R \ \text{for all} \ i$

$LL\_7 \cdots \Delta y_{it} = \rho y_{it-1} + \varepsilon_{it};$ with serial correlation $\qquad H_0 : \rho = 0; H_1 : \rho < 0$

$LL\_8 \cdots \Delta y_{it} = \rho y_{it-1} + \sum_{L=1}^{P_i} \theta_{iL} \Delta y_{i,t-L} + \varepsilon_{it};$ $\qquad H_0 : \rho = 0; H_1 : \rho < 0$

$LL\_9 \cdots \Delta y_{it} = \rho y_{it-1} + \sum_{L=1}^{P_i} \theta_{iL} \Delta y_{i,t-L} + \alpha_i + \varepsilon_{it};$ $\qquad H_0 : \rho = \alpha_i = 0; H_1 : \rho < 0; \alpha_i \in R \ \text{for all} \ i$

$LL\_10 \cdots \Delta y_{it} = \rho y_{it-1} + \sum_{L=1}^{P_i} \theta_{iL} \Delta y_{i,t-L} + \alpha_i + \eta_i t + \varepsilon_{it};$ $\quad H_0 : \rho = \eta_i = 0; H_1 : \rho < 0; \eta_i \in R \ \text{for all} \ i$

Source: *Harris and Sollis (2003).*

The last three models in Table 6.1 are three versions of the LL test derived from the generic form given as equation [6.2] with assumption of $z_{it} = 0$; $z_{it} = \alpha_i$; and $z_{it} = \alpha_i + \eta_i t$, respectively. In all the above cases, the equations are estimated by OLS as a pooled regression model, and ρ and ρ_i are then obtained for testing the panel unit root test.

According to Harris and Sollis (2003), Harris and Tzavalis (1999) conducted a Monte Carlo experiment to look at the power of the LL tests above. They found that the test is poor when the time dimension is small (such as T<50). This is important because it is difficult to find T of above 50 in most African macro data. Thus, in a situation where T is small and n is relatively large Harris and Tzavalis have suggested their version of test which we could refer as HT test. The HT test is basically a panel unit root test of the LL type with the additional assumption that T is fixed instead of the LL test assumption of T→∞. They found this version of their test to have better power properties when T is small. The HT tests are available for a model based on equation [6.1] with homogeneity assumption imposed ($\rho_i = \rho$) and $z_{it} = 0$ $z_{it} = \alpha_i$ or $z_{it} = \{(\alpha_{it}, t)'\}$. If these tests are labelled as HT_1, HT_2 and HT_3, they are equivalent to the LL tests given as LL_1, LL_4 and LL_6, respectively, in Table 6.1 above (See Harris and Sollis, 2003).

An extension of the LL test is made by Levin, Lin, and Chu (LLC), Breitung, and Hadri. In all these cases, for purposes of testing, it is assumed that the persistence parameters are common across cross-sections so that for all ρ_i, $\rho_i = \rho$. The Levin,

Lin, and Chu (LLC), Breitung, and Hadri tests all employ this common unit root process assumption and hence could be categorized as such and briefly outlined below.

Levin, Lin, and Chu (LLC), Breitung, and Hadri tests all assume that there is a common unit root process so that ρ_i is identical across cross-sections. The first two tests employ a null hypothesis of a unit root while the Hadri test uses a null of no unit root. LLC and Breitung both consider the following basic ADF specification

$$\Delta y_{it} = \alpha y_{it-1} + \sum_{j=1}^{p_i} \lambda_i \Delta y_{it-j} + X_{it}' \delta + \varepsilon_{it} \qquad [6.3]$$

where we assume a common $\alpha = (\rho - 1)$, but allow the lag order for the difference terms, ρ_i, to vary across cross-sections. The null and alternative hypotheses for the tests may be written as: $H_0 : \alpha = 0$ and $H_1 : \alpha < 0$, respectively. Under the null hypothesis, there is a unit root, while under the alternative, there is no unit root.

The method described in LLC derives estimates of α from proxies for Δy_{it} and y_{it} and that are standardized and free of autocorrelations and deterministic components.

LLC show that under the null, a modified t-statistic for the resulting $\hat{\alpha}_i$ is asymptotically normally distributed. The LLC method requires a specification of the number of lags used in each cross-section ADF regression, ρ_i. In addition, you must specify the exogenous variables used in the test equations. You may chose to include no exogenous regressors, or to include individual constant terms (fixed effects), or to employ individual constants and trends (see EVIEWS version 5 for details). The Breitung method differs from LLC in two distinct ways. First, only the autoregressive portion (and not the exogenous components) is removed when constructing the standardized proxies; second, the proxies are transformed and detrended, then the persistence parameter is estimated from the pooled proxy equation. Breitung shows that under the null, the resulting estimator is asymptotically distributed as a standard normal. The Breitung method requires only a specification of the number of lags used in each cross-section ADF regression, ρ_i, and the exogenous regressors. As with the LLC test, you may chose to include no exogenous regressors, or to include individual constant terms (fixed effects), or individual constants and trends. Note that in contrast with LLC, no kernel computations are required for Bretung (See EVIEWS manual version 5).

The Hadri panel unit root test (Hadri, 2000) is in the class of common unit root test and has a null hypothesis of no unit root in any of the series in the panel. It is based on the residuals from the individual OLS regressions of y_{it} on a constant, or on a constant and a trend. Hadri (2000) considers the following model

$$y_{it} = r_{it} + \beta_{it} + \varepsilon_{it}$$ [6.4]

Where $r_{it} = r_{i,t-1} + u_{it}$ is a random walk process and ε_{it} is a stationary process. u_{it} and ε_{it} are mutually independent normal and IID across i and over t. The initial values r_{i0} are treated as fixed unknowns and play the role of heterogeneous intercepts.

Given the residuals from the individual regressions $\hat{\varepsilon}_{it}$, we form the LM statistic as:

$$LM_1 = \frac{1}{N} \left[\sum_{i=1}^{N} \left(\sum_t S_i(t)^2 \middle/ T^2 \right) \middle/ \bar{f}_0 \right]$$ [6.5]

Where $S_i(t)$ is the cumulative sum of the residuals as, $S_i(t) = \sum_{j=1}^{t} \hat{\varepsilon}_{ij}$ and $\bar{f}_0$ is the average of the individual estimators of the residual spectrum at frequency zero: $\bar{f}_0 = \sum_{i=1}^{t} f_{i0} \middle/ N$.

EVIEWS, version 5, provides several methods for estimating the $\bar{f}_{i0}$ and S. An alternative form of the LM statistic allows for heteroskedasticity across i and could be given by

$$LM_2 = \frac{1}{N} \left[\sum_{i=1}^{N} \left(\sum_t S_i(t)^2 \middle/ T^2 \right) \middle/ \bar{f}_{i0} \right]$$ [6.6]

The Hadri panel unit root tests require only the specification of the form of the OLS regressions: whether to include only individual specific constant terms, or whether to include both constant and trend terms. EVIEWS reports two Z-statistic values, one based on LM_1 with the associated homoskedasticity assumption, and the other using LM_2 that is heteroskedasticity consistent (Hadri, 2000 and Eviews, version 5 for details).

Tests with Individual Unit Root Process

a)   The Im, Pesaran and Shin (1995, 1997, 2003) Test – the IPS test

The most commonly cited limitation of the Levin-Lin tests is what is called the *homogeneity assumption* that ρ is the same for all individuals ($\rho_i = \rho$), which is very restrictive (see Madalla and Wu, 1999; Banerjee, 1999). In the context of the LL test, thus (see equation 6.1), the alternative hypothesis is (H_1: $\rho_i < 1$) which says that *all* i cross sections are stationary. The IPS test basically relaxes this homogeneity constraint by estimating equation [6.1] with ρ_i free to vary across the i individual series or cross sections in the panel. Their test also allows for different lags for the i cross section in the model, using the model given by equation [6.1] which we reproduced below for your convenience (see Im *et al*, 1995, 1997, 2003; Harris and Sollis, 2003).

$$\Delta y_{it} = \rho_i^* y_{i,t-1} + \sum_{L=1}^{p_i} \theta_{iL} \Delta y_{i,t-L} + z_{it}' \gamma + \varepsilon_{it} \quad \text{where} \quad \rho_i^* = \rho - 1 \quad \quad [6.7]$$

Where the null hypothesis is $\left(H_0 : \rho^* = [\rho - 1] = 0\right)$ is that each series in the panel contains a unit root for all i, and the alternative being $\left(H_1 : \rho^* = [\rho - 1] < 0\right)$ for at least one i) that at least one of the individual series in the panel is stationary. Except with this major departure, the IPS test is very simple and similar to an ADF test of the type that we did for individual time series analysis in chapter 3. In fact the IPS test averages the ADF individual unit root test statistics that are obtained from estimating equation [6.2] for each i, allowing each series to have different lag length, L, if needed, which could be given by equation [6.8] and sometimes referred as t-bar test,

$$\bar{t} = \frac{1}{N} \sum_{i=1}^{N} t_{p^*} \quad \quad [6.8]$$

As $T \to \infty$ (for fixed value of N) followed by $N \to \infty$ sequentially, they showed that their test statistics for panel unit root (let us call it IPS_97) is standard normally distributed. They have also proposed an LM bar test (let us call it IPS_LM) which is based on Lagrange multiplier test rather than t-statistics, although they advised the former to be a better one (Harris and Sollis, 2003). As aptly noted by Harris and Sollis (2003), the IPS test is a generalization of the LL tests that relaxes the form of the alternative hypothesis in LL.

Like that of the LL test, the IPS test has a number of problems. One important limitations relates to its assumption that each i is cross-sectionally independent. In practical terms and in the context of macro and international economics, this assumption contradicts issue of globalization where each country is assumed to affect and be affected by another county. Second, even though IPS test considers the case where T_i differs across groups, the statistics and moment calculations are based on the implicit assumption of the same number of time series for all groups – i.e. it is relevant for balanced, as opposed to unbalanced data. This is considered to be one serious criticism of the IPS test. Finally, the IPS test is also found to be sensitive of the critical values to the choices of lag lengths in the ADF regression (see Maddala and Wu, 1999; Choi, 2001; Breitung, 2000).

b)   The Maddala and Wu (MW) or Fischer-type tests

The MW test is proposed as a means to overcome some of the limitations of the previous tests. Maddala and Wu (1999) proposed a χ^2 test that combines the observed significance levels (*p*-values) for rejecting the null obtained when conducting a unit root test (the ADF test for each cross section *i* separately, following Fischer (1932)) (see Maddala and Wu, 1999). Thus, the MW test will have the following form

$$P = -2\sum_{i=1}^{N} \ln p_i \qquad [6.9]$$

Equation [6.9] has a χ^2-distribution with 2N degree of freedom. This approach is similar to the IPS test that averages the ADF individual unit root test statistics for rejecting the null of a unit root than the *t*-test values. The MW test has a number of advantages. First, it can be done for any type of unit root test. Second, it does not require a balanced data or the same lag length. Finally, it is not only very easy to compute but is found by Maddala and Wu (1999) to be superior to the IPS test (see Harris and Sollis 2003). When N is large, Choi (1999) proposed a modified *P*-test (Fisher or MW test) in such a way that it will have a non-degenerate limiting distribution and could be given by equation [6.10]

$$P_m = \frac{1}{2\sqrt{N}}\sum_{i=1}^{N}\left(-2\ln(p_i)-2\right) = -\frac{1}{\sqrt{N}}\sum_{i=1}^{N}\left(\ln(p_i)+1\right) \qquad [6.10]$$

Where P_m is shown to have a standard normal distribution of the form $P_m \Rightarrow N(0,1)$. The rejection criteria is a condition where $P_m > C_{p\alpha}$, where $C_{p\alpha}$ is from the upper tail of the standard normal distribution.

In sum, The Im, Pesaran, and Shin (IPS), and Fisher-type ADF tests (such as the MW test) that we discussed above do allow the persistence parameters, ρ to vary freely across cross-sections (i.e. ρ is assumed to vary across cross section units and thus) be ρ_i.

Table 6.2: Summary of available unit root tests in EVIEWS (version 5)

Test	Null	Alternative	Possible Deterministic Component	Autocorrelation Correction Method
Levin, Lin and Chu	Unit root	No Unit Root	None, F, T	Lags
Breitung	Unit root	No Unit Root	None, F, T	Lags
IPS	Unit Root	Some cross-sections without UR	F, T	Lags
Fisher-ADF	Unit Root	Some cross-sections without UR	None, F, T	Lags
Fisher-PP	Unit Root	Some cross-sections without UR	None, F, T	Kernel
Hadri	No Unit Root	Unit Root	F, T	Kernel

Note: None - no exogenous variables; F - fixed effect; and T - individual effect and individual trend.

Source: *EVIEWS Manual, Version 5.*

Hands on Panel Unit Root Test

We apply the panel unit root procedure to test for the existence of the poverty trap in the sub-Saharan African countries for the period of 1950–2004 using data from Penn Table 6.2. This procedure is used by Easterly (2006) to test the poverty trap hypothesis for the period of 1950 to 2001 for 137 countries. "If the poverty trap hypothesis holds, then the poorest countries' log per capita incomes should be stationary (assuming zero trends). Income will fluctuate randomly around this level, but will always tend to return to it" (Easterly, 2006:299). Similar to Easterly's finding, the panel unit root tests could not reject the non- stationarity of SSA countries log per capita income.

Table 6.3: Unit root tests results for log per capita income in EVIEWS (version 5)

```
Panel unit root test: Summary
Sample: 1950 2004
Exogenous variables: None
Automatic selection of maximum lags
Automatic selection of lags based on SIC: 0 to 5
Newey-West bandwidth selection using Bartlett kernel
```

Method	Statistic	Prob.**	Cross-sections	Obs
Null: Unit root (assumes common unit root process)				
Levin, Lin & Chu t*	4.31612	1.0000	39	1666
Null: Unit root (assumes individual unit root process)				
ADF-Fisher Chi-square	40.3101	0.9999	39	1666
PP-Fisher Chi-square	48.6503	0.9963	39	1684
** Probabilities for Fisher tests are computed using an asympotic Chi -square distribution. All other tests assume asymptotic normality				

We further run the panel unit root test with individual effects and with both individual effects and individual linear trends. When individual unit root process is assumed with only individual effects, the ADF-Fisher Chi-square test supports the stationarity of per capita income only at 10% level of significance and PP-Fisher Chi-square test at 11.5%. The Im, Pesaran and Shin W-stat test could not reject the unit root hypothesis, though. With both individual effects and linear trends, the Levin & Lin and ADF tests reject the unit root hypothesis while the other results support the hypothesis.

Table 6.4: Unit root tests with individual effects

```
Panel unit root test: Summary
Sample: 1950 2004
Exogenous variables: Individual effects
Automatic selection of maximum lags
Automatic selection of lags based on SIC: 0 to 3
Newey-West bandwidth selection using Bartlett kernel
```

Method	Statistic	Prob.**	Cross-sections	Obs
Null: Unit root (assumes common unit root process)				
Levin, Lin & Chu t*	-1.00903	0.1565	39	1669
Null: Unit root (assumes individual unit root process)				
Im, Pesaran and Shin W-stat	0.05508	0.522	39	1669
ADF - Fisher Chi-square	94.1023	0.1034	39	1669
PP - Fisher Chi-square	93.247	0.1147	39	1684
Null: No unit root (assumes common unit root process)				
Hadri Z-stat	17.6622	0	39	1723
** Probabilities for Fisher tests are computed using an asympotic Chi -square distribution. All other tests assume asymptotic normality.				

Table 6.5: Unit root tests with individual effects and individual linear trends

```
Panel unit root test: Summary
Sample: 1950 2004
Exogenous variables: Individual effects, individual linear trends
Automatic selection of maximum lags
Automatic selection of lags based on SIC: 0 to 7
Newey-West bandwidth selection using Bartlett kernel
```

Method	Statistic	Prob.**	Cross-sections	Obs
Null: Unit root (assumes common unit root process)				
Levin, Lin & Chu t*	-1.42318	0.0773	39	1658
Breitung t-stat	1.01764	0.8456	39	1619
Null: Unit root (assumes individual unit root process)				
Im, Pesaran and Shin W-stat	-0.92797	0.1767	39	1658
ADF - Fisher Chi-square	99.1618	0.0533	39	1658
PP - Fisher Chi-square	85.1936	0.2702	39	1684
Null: No unit root (assumes common unit root process)				
Hadri Z-stat	17.6622	0	39	1723

```
** Probabilities for Fisher tests are computed using an asympotic Chi
      -square distribution. All other tests assume asymptotic normality.
```

Testing for Cointegration in Panel Data

The literature about cointegration in panel data could be divided into those which test for the null of no cointegration between the variables in the panel, against the alternative of at lease one cointegration relationship; and those which provide estimation of the cointegration vector. Like that of the time series cointegration tests, the former are generally single equation based tests (Kao, 1999; Pedroni, 1995, 1999; McCoskey and Kao, 1998) while the latter are multi-equation based tests (see for instance Larsson *et al*, 2001; Groen and Kleibergen, 2001). In this section, we will briefly describe these two types of tests with a focus on their application in the African context.

Single Equation Based Tests

Some of the single equation based models test the null of no cointegration (Kao, 1999; and Pedroni, 1999a), while others test the null of cointegration (MCckoskey and Kao, 1998). There is no fundamental difference in these as both are based on single equation based estimated parameters.

Kao (1999) proposed a Dickey-Fuller (DF) and an Augmented Dickey-Fuller (ADF) tests to test the null of no-cointegration in the panel data. This procedure is similar to the Engle-Granger two step approach that we have discussed in chapter 4. Consider the panel regression equation given by equation [6.11]

$$y_{it} = \alpha_i + \beta x_{it} + e_{it} \,, \, i = 1, \, ..., \, N; \, t = 1, \, ..., \, T \qquad\qquad [6.11]$$

The DF test can be applied to the residual using

$$\hat{e}_{it} = \rho \hat{e}_{it-1} + v_{it} \qquad\qquad [6.12]$$

where $\hat{e}_{it} \left(\equiv yit - x'_{it}\hat{\beta} - z'_{it}\hat{\gamma} \right)$ is the estimate of e_{it} from equation [6.11].The null hypothesis that H_0: $\rho = 1$ against the alternative that y and x are cointegrated (H_1: $\rho < 1$) can be tested using the *DF* and *ADF* statistics. Kao has developed four DF type tests with z_{it} in equation [6.11] limited to the fixed effect case (i.e. $z_{it} = c$). Two of these tests assume strong exogeneity of the regressors and the errors in [6.11] and are denoted as DF_p and DF_t, while the other tests make (non-parametric correction for any endogenous relationship are denoted DF_p^* and DF_t^*. Alternatively, Kao also proposed extension of [6.12] to include lagged change in the residuals which is equivalent to the *ADF* version of test that we discussed in Chapter 3. All the tests are asymptotically normally distributed and are one-sided left tailed tests so that you will reject the null if the test statistics is a large enough negative number. It is interesting to note that all the Kao tests noted imposed homogeneity assumption in that the slope coefficient β is not allowed to vary across the i individual members of the panel (Harris and Sollis, 2003).

The assumption of homogeneity in Kao's test is relaxed by Pedroni (1995, 1999). Moreover, Pedroni's test allows for a possibility of multiple regressors. Pedroni used the residuals from the following regression equation:

$$y_{i,t} = \alpha_i + \delta_i t + \beta_{1i} x_{1i,t} + \beta_{2i} x_{2i,t} + ... + \beta_{mi} x_{mi,t} + e_{it} \qquad\qquad [6.13]$$

With test for the null of no cointegration being based on the residuals $\hat{e}_{it}$ using,

$$\hat{e}_{it} = \rho_i \hat{e}_{i,t-1} + v_{it} \qquad\qquad [6.14]$$

Since in the formulation of equation [6.13] the α_i and β_i's are allowed to vary across the i individuals of the panel, Pedroni's approach allows for short and long run heterogeneity and, thus, the cointegration vector could differ across members under the alternative hypothesis (Harris and Sollis, 2003).

The heterogeneities are introduced as individual specific intercepts (α_i), individual specific time trends (δ_{it}) and member specific slope coefficients. Based on [6.13], Pedroni developed seven different statistics for testing the null of no cointegration. Four of these statistics, which are termed as panel cointegration statistics, are based on pooling along the within dimension. And three of them, which are referred to as group mean panel cointegration statistics, are based on pooling along the between dimension[15]. Pedroni (1999) has also shown that each of these statistics have an asymptotic standard normal distribution (See Pedroni 1995, 1999 for detail).

A similar single equation and residual based cointegration test is also provided by McCoskey and Kao (1998). Their test is based on the null of cointegration, however, it used LM based test similar to Hadri (1999) that we discussed in section 6.1.1 above.

For I(1) process (y_{it}, x_{it}) McCoskey and Kao (1998) considered the following model:

$$y_{it} = \alpha_i + x'_{it}\beta_i + v_{it}, i = 1,2,...,N; t = 1,2,...,T \qquad [6.14]$$

where

$$x_{it} = x_{it-1} + \varepsilon_{it} \qquad [6.15]$$

$$v_{it} = \gamma_{it} + u_{it} \qquad [6.16]$$

$$\gamma_{it} = \gamma_{it-1} + \theta u_{it} \qquad [6.17]$$

where μ_{it} are IID(0, $\sigma^2 u$).

The null hypothesis of cointegration is H_0: $\theta = 0$ against H_1: $|\theta| \neq 0$. Through backward substitution of [6.16] in to [6.14] we will have:

$$y_{it} = \alpha_i + x'_{it}\beta_i + e_{it} \qquad [6.18]$$

Where $e_{it} = \theta \sum_{j=1}^{t} u_{ij} + u_{it}$, E(e_{it}) = 0.

If $\theta = 0$, then $e_{it} = u_{it}$ and is stationary, where as if $\theta \neq 0$ then e_{it} will be non-stationary. McCoskey and Kao (1999) proposed an LM test statistics that is asymptotically normally distributed. Harris and Sollis (2003), however, noted that this statistics and its distribution is dependent on a complex mean and variance terms that are provided through Monte Carlo simulation that in turn depends on the number of regressors in the model (see Harris and Sollis 2003; and Mcoskey and Kao, 1999, for details). McCoskey and Kao (1998) also noted that in the presence of serial correlation and endogenous x_{it}, OLS estimation of their LM statistics will be biased.

---

[15] The former terminology refers to estimators that effectively pool the autoregressive coefficients across different members for the unit root tests on the estimated residuals. While the latter refers to estimators that simply average the individually estimated coefficients for each member i (Pedroni, 1999: 657).

Thus, in such cases they advised to use fully modified (FM) OLS estimator or Dynamic OLS (DOLS) estimator to correct the problem.

Multiple Equation (Multivariate) Based Tests

The panel data cointegration tests that we discussed so far are basically an extension of the single unit (individual) univariate based unit root test to panel data where the residual from the first step regression is tested for cointegration akin to the two-step Engle Granger approach that we discussed in chapter 4.

In contrast to this approach, a second strand of the literature tests for cointegration using multivariate model in the spirit of the Johansen test for cointegration that we have discussed in Chapter 4. We refer to such test here as multivariate based panel cointegration test. Larsson *et al* (2001) developed one such likelihood ratio (LR) based panel cointegration test. Their test is based on the average of the individual rank trace statistics generated using the Johansen (1988, 1995) method noted. Their test is thus similar to IPS *t*-bar statistics used to test for the unit root in the panel data.

Larsson *et al* (2001) considered a VAR (ki) model with the following data generating process (dgp) for each individual as:

$$Y_{it} = \sum \Pi_{ik} Y_{i,t-k} + \varepsilon_{it}, i = 1,2,...,N \qquad [6.19]$$

Where for each group i the values $Y_{i,k+1}, \cdots, Y_{i,0}$ are considered fixed and the errors ε_{it} are IID as $\varepsilon_{it} \sim N_p(0,\Omega_i)$ $\varepsilon_{it} \ \Box \ N_P(0,\Omega_i)$. Then the heterogeneous error correction representation of equation [6.19] is given by equation [6.20]:

$$\Delta Y_{it} = \Pi_i Y_{i,t-1} + \sum \Gamma_{ik} \Delta Y_{i,t-k} + \varepsilon_{it}, i = 1,2,...,N \qquad [6.20]$$

Where Πi is of order p×p and is of reduced rank, with $\Pi i = \alpha i \beta i$'. αi and βi are of order p×ri and of full column rank. The panel cointegration test then amounts to testing, $H_0 = rank(\Pi_i) = r_i \leq r$ for all $i = 1,...,$ N against $H_p = rank(\Pi_i) = P$, which basically says that the N groups in the panel have at most r cointegrating relationships among the *p*-variables under the null. Larsson *et al* (2001) defined the standardized LR-bar statistic for testing the null hypothesis as the average of the N individual trace statistics. As N and T approach infinity (i.e.; N and T →∞), this standardized (using the mean and variance of the underlining trace statistics defining the model that are obtained using Monte Carlo simulation) panel trace statistic is shown to be asymptotically distributed as Standard Normal. Groen and Kleibergen (2001), however, noted that the Larsson *et al* (2001) test can only be valid if one assumes that the individual model parameters and test statistics are determined independently of each other. They argued that one should allow for interdependencies between the different individuals in cointegration test so as to enhance the power of the test (see also Harris and Sollis, 2003).

Estimation and Inferences in Panel Cointegration Models

The literature has established that OLS estimation of panel data based models is problematic. There are at least three reasons for this. First, it is highly likely that almost all macro variables, which are of our interest in this book, will be non-stationary. If so, they need to be estimated using a method such as an Error-Correction Model that tackles the spurious regression problem. Second, given the possible link among macro variables, which is the focus of this book again, you will have problem of endogeneity (i.e. contemporaneity and failure of weak exogeneity) in your panel based models. These are akin to what we call problems of "simultaneous equation bias" in classical econometrics. Third, the t-statistics from a simple OLS can not be used for inference in the case of panel data. These and related problems call for use of two new approaches for estimation of panel based time series model equations: the Fully Modified OLS (FMOLS) or the Dynamic OLS (DOLS) (see Box 4.1 for detail).

For estimation of long-run cointegration parameters, Pesaran and Smith (1995) proposed what is known as the group mean estimator obtained by averaging the coefficients for each group. Pedroni (1999b) also employed another estimator called the Fully Modified OLS (FMOLS)[16] to handle heterogeneous panels.

The latter approach can only be valid if one assumes that the individual model parameters and test statistics are determined independent of each other—the cross-sectional independence assumption (Groen and Kleibergen, 2001; Banerjee, 1999; Phillips and Moon, 1999). This condition is too restrictive in particular for a multi-country analysis where by many economic variables (such as GDP, exchange rates, interest rates, prices, etc.) are cross-sectionally dependent through global economic shocks and complicated interdependence among themselves (Banerjee, 1999; Phillips and Moon, 1999).

Hence, an optimal approach that tries to address both issues: cross-sectional dependence and heterogeneity effects, is sought. While the research in this regard is at infancy, few attempts have already been made. One of such efforts is Groen and Kleibergen (2001). According to these authors, their study adds three major novel features to panel data cointegration analysis. The first feature is that the method allows for an unrestricted disturbance covariance matrix within the panel. This in turn allows for instantaneous feedbacks between the different individuals in the panel— allowing for cross-sectional dependence. Second, their method allows the

---

[16] Readers are advised to refer to the author for full exposition of the issue.

researcher to test the number of cointegrating vectors within the panel. The only effort in this regard was by Larsson *et al* (2001). Finally, the framework can enable us to test the possibility of homogeneous long-run parameters combined with heterogeneous short run dynamics.

The framework was developed by stacking individual vector error correction (VEC) models into a joint panel VEC model. Then, cointegration rank tests on all the individual VEC models are simultaneously tested based on a common cointegration rank value. The corresponding likelihood ratio tests are found to have limiting distributions based on a summation of the limiting behavior of Johansen's trace statistics across the individual models.

Following the foot steps of Johansen (1995), Groen and Kleibergen (2001) showed that the likelihood ratio tests of the restrictions have χ2 limiting distribution.

For estimation of the cointegrating vectors, the authors developed an iterated GMM framework, which is highly sophisticated to be presented at this stage.

Finally, simulation analysis shows that the Larsson *et al* (2001) framework for panel cointegration analyses is found to be equivalent with Groen and Keibergen (2001) framework only under certain circumstances, i.e., when we have cross-sectional independence. Hence, in addition to the flexibility in treating any number of cointegrating vectors the Groen and Kleibergen (2001) method allows for cross-sectional dependence, which is a remarkable development in the area.

Again, which one is preferable is not established in the literature. Thus, your choice could be informed by your specific condition.

Illustration: Panel Cointegration Tests of an Oil Consumption Equation in 11 African Countries

Using the oil consumption equation, for a typical African country, specification of the recent UNECA (2008) Global Macroeconomic model, we illustrate the tests of panel cointegration. The oil consumption equation is specified as

$$LogC_{it} = f\left(\log GDP_{it}, \log P_{it}\right)$$ [6.21]

where C_{it} is real consumption of oil, GDP is real gross domestic product and P_{it} is oil price.

We used data from 11 West and Central African countries for the period of 1970 to 2003 and tested for panel cointegration using Pedroni (1995, 1999), Kao (1999) and Larsson *et al* (2001) cointegration tests. All of these tests are available in EVIEWS 6.0.

While the Pedroni test results are mixed, the Kao and Larsson *et al* Johansen-Fisher tests reject the null of no cointegration. Pedroni's test results reject the null of no cointegration in four of the seven tests. In the case of Pedroni cointegration test, it is not easy to decide whether to use the within-group or between-group test, or to use parametric or non-parametric tests as each test has its own strengths and weaknesses. The between-group tests are less restrictive in terms of allowing for potential heterogeneity across individual members in the panel; non-parametric tests are better in the face of significant outliers though they tend to over-reject the null when it is true in cases where the residual term has large negative moving average components; and a parametric test has greater power in handling data with AR errors (Harris and Sollis, 2003). The between-group tests have also lower small sample distortion as compared to the within-group tests. If we prefer the between-group tests, the null of cointegration is rejected in two of the three tests.

The Kao ADF based test, that assumes homogeneity in the slope coefficients, rejects the null of no cointegration. The Larsson et al Johansen-Fisher multivariate based test rejects the null of no cointegration and the alternative hypothesis of one cointegrating relationship cannot be rejected. The overall evaluation of the results suggests for the rejection of the null hypothesis of no cointegration. We have reported these results in Table 6.6. It is instructive to note that there is no hard and fast rule as such in doing econometrics. You need to examine from different angles as we just did them above. Moreover, we want to inform the reader that this "panel co-integration test" is fairly new research and not consolidated yet.

Table 6.6: Cointegration tests of the oil equation in ECA's global micro model

Pedroni Residual Cointegration Test				
Series: $\log C_{it}, \log GDP_{it}, \log P_{it},$				
Sample: 1970 2003				
Included observations: 374				
Cross-sections included: 11				
Null Hypothesis: No cointegration				
Trend assumption: Deterministic intercept and trend				
Lag selection: fixed at 1				
Newey-West bandwidth selection with Bartlett kernel				
Alternative hypothesis: common AR coefs. (within-dimension)				
	Statistic	Prob.	Weighted Statistic	Prob.
Panel v-Statistic	-1.224139	0.1886	-2.012721	0.0526
Panel rho-Statistic	1.229024	0.1875	0.831299	0.2824
Panel PP-Statistic	-3.581028	0.0007	-4.896007	0.0000
Panel ADF-Statistic	-3.111049	0.0032	-2.278938	0.0297

Alternative hypothesis: individual AR coefs. (between-dimension)		
	Statistic	Prob.
Group rho-Statistic	1.589103	0.1129
Group PP-Statistic	-5.996431	0.0000
Group ADF-Statistic	-2.800224	0.0079

Kao Residual Cointegration Test

Series: $\log C_{it}, \log GDP_{it}, \log P_{it},$

Sample: 1970 2003
Included observations: 374
Null Hypothesis: No cointegration
Trend assumption: No deterministic intercept and trend
Lag selection: fixed at 1
Newey-West bandwidth selection with Bartlett kernel

	t-Statistic	Prob.
ADF	-2.117982	0.0171
Residual variance	0.546775	
HAC variance	0.265445	

Johansen Fisher Panel Cointegration Test

Series: $\log C_{it}, \log GDP_{it}, \log P_{it},$

Sample: 1970 2003
Included observations: 374
Trend assumption: Linear deterministic trend
Lags interval (in first differences): 1
Unrestricted Cointegration Rank Test (Trace and Maximum Eigen value)

Hypothesized No. of CE(s)	Fisher Stat.* (from trace test)	Prob.	Fisher Stat.* (from max-eigen test)	Prob.
None	70.71	0.0000	65.02	0.0000
At most 1	27.79	0.1826	20.84	0.5306
At most 2	34.18	0.0471	34.18	0.0471
* Probabilities are computed using asymptotic Chi-square distribution.				

Conclusion

The chapter, attempted to introduce the readers to the current development in panel unit root and cointegration tests. We noted that one advantage of panel unit root tests over its time series counter part is that the powers of the tests increase as the cross section component, N, increases. It is shown that unlike time series unit root test statistics, which have no standard distribution, the panel data unit root test statistics are asymptotically normally distributed (Hadri, 2000; Baltagi and Kao, 2000; Hall and Mairesse, 2002). We have classified the existing literature on panel unit root tests as those, which test for unit root assuming common unit root process or allowing its variation across cross section units. In the first group, we have the studies by Levin and Lin (LL), Levin, Lin, and Chu (LLC), Breitung, and Hadri and in the second group we have Im, Pesaran, and Shin (IPS), and Fisher-type ADF and Fisher-PP tests such as that of Maddala and Wu (1999). The review of each is provided in the chapter. Version 5 of EVIEWS offers the possibility to test most of these tests. We suggest you carry out all the tests because any one test may not yield conclusive results, at least at the current level of knowledge about panel unit root and panel cointegration process.

We also noted in this chapter that once we are done with the unit root test, the next step is to carry out a Panel Co-integration test. Here we have two approaches of conducting a panel co-integration test that are reported in the literature. The first group is an extension of the single unit time series Engle-Granger residual based test for co-integration. Thus, we have Single Equation based Tests (Kao, 1999; Pedroni, 1999a; McCoskey and Kao, 1998). The second approach is the use of "multi equation based tests" which are again similar to the Johansen based multivariate co-integration test (Larsson *et al*, 2001; Groen and Kleibergen, 2001; Kao, 1999; and Pedroni, 1999a; MCckoskey and Kao, 1998). We again suggest you explore all tests, given the level of knowledge that we currently have which is not conclusive.

The final issue that we addressed in the chapter relates to estimation and inference in panel data. The literature has established that OLS estimation of panel data based model is problematic because of three major problems. First, it is highly likely that almost all macro variables will be non-stationary. If so, they need to be estimated using a method such as an Error-Correction Model that tackles the spurious regression problem. Second, given the possible link among macro variables, which is the focus of this book, you will have a problem of endogeneity (i.e. contemporaneity and failure of weak exogeneity assumption). These are akin to what we call problems of "simultaneous equation bias" in standard econometrics. Third, the t-statistics from a simple OLS can not be used for inference. This call, for use of two new approaches for estimation of panel based time series model equations: the Fully Modified OLS (FMOLS) or the Dynamic OLS (DOLS). Again which one is preferable is not established in the literature. Thus, your choice could be informed by your specific condition.

163

APPENDICIES

Appendix: Review of Basic Statistics for Time Series Econometrics

A.   *Conditional Expectations*

The conditional expectation plays a crucial role in modern econometric analysis. Although it is not always explicitly stated, the goal of most applied econometric studies is to estimate or test hypotheses about the expectation of one variable—called the explained variable, the dependent variable. This variable, call it Y is given being conditional on a set of explanatory variables, independent variables, regressors, usually denoted X. In economic research, thus, we attempt to find ways to estimate conditional expectations that arise in economic applications that allow us to infer causality from one or more explanatory variables to the response variable. If we can collect data on Y, and give X a random sample from the underlying population of interest, then it is fairly straightforward to estimate Y if we are willing to make an assumption about its functional form. As Weeldrige (2005) noted, unfortunately, complications often arise in the collection and analysis of economic data because of the nonexperimental nature of economics which may have measurement error, or they are sometimes the outcome of a simultaneous process. Sometimes we cannot obtain a random sample from the population, which may not allow us to estimate Y given X. The most prevalent problem is that some variables we would like to control for (elements of c) cannot be observed. In each of these cases there is a conditional expectation (CE) of interest, but it generally involves variables for which the econometrician cannot collect data or requires an experiment that cannot be carried out. Under additional assumptions—generally called identification assumptions—we can sometimes recover the structural conditional expectation originally of interest, even if we cannot observe all of the desired explanrotory variables, or if we only observe equilibrium outcomes of variables. The notion of conditional expectation is fundamental in this process. In addition to providing a unified setting for interpreting economic models, the CE operator is useful as a tool for manipulating structural equations into estimable equations. In a simplified manner, the expected value could be defined as follows.

Let $g()$ be a function, then the *expected value* of $g(.X)$, denoted $E[g(X)]$, for random variable X with sample space $f\{x_1; x_2; x_3; : : : ; x_N \}$, is defined by:

$$E[g(X)] = \sum_{i=1}^{N} g(x_i) p(x_i)$$

Where: $p(x_i)$ is the probability of the realization x_i. Note also small letters (say, x) are used for realization while capital letters (say X) for random number.

If X is a continuous random variable (provided $E[g(X) < \infty$, it is given by,

$$E[g(X)] = \int_{-\infty}^{\infty} g(x)p(x)dx$$

This formulation has the important special cases that:

- The mean, $\mu = E(X)$,

- The variance, $\sigma = \text{var}(X) = E[X–E(X)]^2 = E(X^2) - \mu^2$

- The r th moment, $E(X^r)$, and

- The r th moment about the mean, $E[.X - \mu^r]$.

Notes: the mean and variance are common measures of the location (central tendency or average) and dispersion, respectively, of a random variable. The third and fourth moments about the mean are common measures of skewness and kurtosis (i.e. fatness of tails of the probability density function, p.d.f., see next), respectively, of a random variable. The standard deviation is the square root of the variance (see Koop, 2003 for details).

B.   The Concept of Probability Distribution

Probability is a mechanism by which one may study random or chance occurrences as compared to deterministic phenomena. For example, no one is expected to predict with certainty a simple experiment as the toss of fair coin. Probability plays a crucial role in the application of statistical inference because a decision based on the information contained in a random sample may be wrong. Without a basic understanding of probability theory, it is difficult to utilize statistical methods effectively. A complete description of any population is contained in its probability distribution, and the process of sampling and estimation could be characterized as the attempt to derive an approximation to this probability distribution.

The *probability function* associated with a discrete random variable X with sample space f$\{x_1; x_2; x_3; x_N\}$, is denoted by $p(.x)$, where,

$$p(x) = \begin{cases} pr(X = x_i) & \text{if} \quad x = x_i \\ 0 \quad otherwise \end{cases}$$

p.x/ D

For $i = 1; 2; \dots N$. The *distribution function*, denoted by $P(x)$, is defined as

$$P(X) = \Pr(X \leq x) = \sum_{i=j} \Pr(x_j)$$

Where J is the set of j's with the property that $x_j < x$. Probability and distribution functions satisfy the following conditions:

$P(x_i) > 0$ for $i = \{1; 2;. \dots N, \}$ and

$$\sum_{i=1}^{N} = p(x_i) = P(x_N) = 1$$

We note from the foregoing that a probability function simply gives the probability of each event occurring and the distribution function gives the cumulative probability of all events up to some point occurring. In relation to this, the distribution function of a continuous random variable, X, is $P(x) = \Pr(X \leq x) = \int_{-\infty}^{x} p(t)dt$ where $p()$ is the probability density function or *p.d.f.* Probability density and distribution functions satisfy the following conditions:

$p(x) \geq 0$, for all x

$$\int_{-\infty}^{x} p(t)dt = P(\infty) = 1 \qquad \text{and}$$

$$p(x) = \frac{dp(x)}{dx}$$

It has to be noted that with discrete random variables the definition of a probability function is clear, it is simply the probability of each event in the sample space occurring. With continuous random variables, such a definition is not possible since there are an infinite number of events. For instance, there is an infinite number of real numbers in the interval [0; 1] and, hence, if this is the sample space in an experiment we cannot simply attach a probability to each point in the interval. With continuous random variables, probabilities are thus defined only for intervals, and represented as areas under (i.e. integrals of) p.d.f.s. Given the discussion thus far we can define the probability density function.

Definition The function $f(x)$ whose graph is the limiting curve obtained for an extremely large number of observations and an extremely small interval width is the probability density function of the continuous variable x, provided that the vertical scale is chosen so that the total area under the curve equals one. The probability density function of a continuous variable x is: defined as:

If there exists a function $f(x)$ such that: $f(x) \geq 0$, where $-\infty < x < \infty$

$$\int_{-\infty}^{\infty} f(x)dx = 1, \quad \text{and}$$

$$P(a \le x \le b) = \int_{a}^{b} f(x)dx$$

for any a and b, then f(x) is the probability density function of the continuous random variable x. Since the total area under *f(x)* is one, the probability of the interval $a \le x \le b$ is the area bounded by the density function.

B1   The Normal Distribution

In econometrics the normal distribution plays a central role. The density function for a normal distribution with mean μ and variance σ^2 is given by the following mathematical form

$$f(x) = \frac{1}{\sqrt{2\pi\sigma^2}} \exp\left\{ \frac{1}{2} \frac{-(x-\mu)^2}{\delta^2} \right\} \quad \text{where} \quad -\infty < x < \infty$$

Where: both π and e are constants (approximately equal to 3.1415 and 2.71828, respectively). Note that, given the formula for *f(x)* and given values of μ and σ^2 we can trace out a smooth curve enclosing an area of one square unit. This distribution encloses an area of a curve which must equal one square unit. We can denote this function *f(x)*, which is referred to as the probability density function (P.d.f) of x. This function describes a curve which encloses an area of one, such that the various component areas equal the probabilities of the corresponding ranges of x occurring. The general properties of the normal distribution are that it is a continuous, bell-shaped, symmetrical distribution, with approximately 68% of the distribution contained within one standard deviation of the mean, approximately 95% of the distribution contained within two standard deviations of the mean, and 99.7% of the distribution contained within 3 s.d. of the mean. The normal distribution is sometimes called the Gaussian distribution after the famous statistician C.F. Gauss.

One special case of the normal distribution occurs when the mean is zero and the variance (and, therefore, the standard deviation) is unity. If a random variable Z has a Normal (0,1) distribution, then we say it has a standard normal distribution. The pdf of a standard normal random variable is denoted $\varphi(z)$; using the formula of the normal distribution above), with $\mu=0$ and $\sigma^2=1$, it is defined by

$$\emptyset(x) = \frac{1}{\sqrt{2\pi}} \exp\left\{ \frac{-z^2}{2} \right\}$$

The standard normal cumulative distribution function is denoted $\Phi(z)$ and is obtained as the area under φ, to the left of z; since Z is continuous, $\varphi(z) = P(Z < z)$.

There is no simple formula that can be used to obtain the values of $\Phi(z)$ because $\Phi(z)$ is the integral of the function given above), and this integral has no closed form sometimes referred as the Z-distribution and its values are tabulated in standard textbooks and standard econometrics software's.

Using basic facts from probability concerning cdfs we can use the standard normal cdf for computing the probability of any event involving a standard normal random variable. The most important formulas are

$$P(Z > z) = 1 - \Phi(z)$$

$$P(Z > -z) = P(Z > z), \quad \text{and}$$

$$P(a \leq z \leq b) = \Phi(b) - \Phi(b)$$

Because Z is a continuous random variable, all three formulas hold whether or not the inequalities are strict. Some examples include $P(Z > 44) = 1 - 0.67 = 0.33$; $P(Z < -0.92) = P(Z > 0.92) = 1 - 0.821 = 0.179$, and $P(-1 < Z \leq 0.5) = 0.692 - 0.159 = 0.533$.

There are also several other distributions with accompanying density functions. They help us in hypothesis formulation and testing. We will briefly describe the most important ones below.

The Chi-Square Distribution

The chi-square distribution is obtained directly from independent, standard normal random variables. Let Z_i, $i \_ 1, 2, \ldots, n$, be independent random variables, each distributed as standard normal. Define a new random variable as the sum of the squares of the Z_i:

$$X = \sum_{i=1}^{n} Z_i^2$$

Then, X has what is known as a **chi-square distribution** with n **degrees of freedom** (or df for short). We write this as $X \sim \chi_n^2$. The df in a chi-square distribution corresponds to the number of terms in the sum given in its formula above. The concept of degrees of freedom will play an important role in our statistical and econometric analyses. The pdf for chi-square distributions with varying degrees of freedom could vary from a concave curve that asymptotically approach both the X and Y axis with a smaller degrees of freedom such as 2 to a curve that resembles a normal distribution as the degree of freedom increasers say to 10. We also note that a chi-square random variable is always non negative, and that, unlike the normal distribution, the chi-square distribution is not symmetric about any point. It can be shown that if $X \sim \chi_n^2$, then the expected value of X is n [the number of terms in formula above, and the variance of X is $2n$.

The t Distribution

The t distribution is the workhorse in classical statistics and multiple regression analysis. We obtain a t distribution from a standard normal and a chi-square random variable. Let Z have a standard normal distribution and let X have a chi-square distribution with n degrees of freedom. Further, assume that Z and X are independent. Then, the random variable

$$T = \frac{z}{\sqrt{\dfrac{X}{n}}}$$

has a t-distribution with n degrees of freedom. We will denote this by $T \sim t_n$. The t distribution gets its degrees of freedom from the chi-square random variable in the denominator of its formula above.

The pdf of the t distribution has a shape similar to that of the standard normal distribution, except that it is more spread out and therefore has more area in the tails. The expected value of a t distributed random variable is zero (strictly speaking, the expected value exists only for $n > 1$), and the variance is $n/(n - 2)$ for $n > 2$. (The variance does not exist for $n < 2$ because the distribution is so spread out.). As the degrees of freedom gets large, the t distribution approaches the standard normal distribution.

The F Distribution

Another important distribution for statistics and econometrics is the F distribution. In particular, the F distribution will be used for testing hypotheses in the context of multiple regression analysis. To define an F random variable, let $X_1 \sim \chi_{k1}^2$ and $X_2 \sim \chi_{k2}^2$ and assume that X_1 and X_2 are independent. Then, the random variable F,

$$F = \frac{X_1 / k_1}{X_2 / k_2}$$

has an F distribution with (k_1, k_2) degrees of freedom. We denote this as $F \sim F_{k1, k2}$.

C.   *Distributions, Estimation and Hypothesis Testing*

The whole idea of having this appendix is to underscore that our estimated results using time series econometrics is about hypothesise testing, and identification of the likely value of population parameters, say the level of investment in a certain period in a certain county (the population parameter). This requires an idea about probability distribution, estimation, hypothesis testing and/or inference. To understand the essence of statistical inference, it is necessary to understand sampling distribution or the essence of both a population and a sample. A complete description of any population is contained in its probability distribution, and the process of sampling and estimation could be characterized as the attempt to derive an approximation to this probability distribution. We have looked at some examples of distribution thus far. The next stage is to look at estimation as a prelude to hypothesis testing.

The process of sampling and estimation could be characterized as an attempt to derive an approximation to the population probability distribution. Typically, the population distribution will be unknown, and all that we realistically hope to achieve is an approximation to some of the broader characteristics of this population, e.g. estimates of mean and variance.

Thus, the basic sampling and estimation problem can be expressed as: We are interested in a population which has an unknown probability distribution, with an unknown mean (μ) and an unknown variance (s^2). A sample is randomly selected from this population, and we wish to derive a method of estimating these unknown parameters from the sample data. Additionally, we also require some indication as to the occurrence of the estimation method we have used, and hence the confidence which can be placed in the derived estimates.

C1 Estimations

Two types of estimates:

(a) *Point estimates*: That is the sample is used to produce a single number which can be interpreted, in some sense, as the most likely value of the population parameter.

(b) *Interval estimate*: That is, the sample is used to produce a range or interval of values which is considered likely to contain the true value of the population parameter.

A point estimate provides a definitive statement and provides an unambiguous basis for taking decisions about the population. It says, however, nothing about how accurately the parameter is being estimated and hence the risk involved in any decisions which are taken. A point estimate obtained from a particular sample does not, by itself, provide enough information for testing economic theories or for informing policy discussions. A point estimate may be the researcher's best guess at the population value, but, by its nature, it provides no information about how close the estimate is "likely" to be to the population parameter.

One way of assessing the uncertainty in an estimator is to find its sampling standard deviation. Reporting the standard deviation of the estimator, along with the point estimate, provides some information on the accuracy of our estimate. Reporting, however, the standard deviation along with the point estimate makes no direct statement about where the population value is likely to lie in relation to the estimate. This limitation is overcome by constructing a confidence interval. Suppose the population has a Normal (μ,1) distribution and let $\{Y_1,..., Y_n\}$ be a random sample from this population. (We assume that the variance of the population is known and equal to unity for the sake of illustration; we then show what to do in the more realistic case that the variance is unknown.) The sample average $\bar{Y}$, has a normal distribution with mean μ and variance $1/n$: $\bar{Y} \sim$ Normal (μ ,$1/n$). From this, we can standardize $\bar{Y}$, and since the standardized version of $\bar{Y}$ has a standard normal distribution, we have

$$P\left(-1.96 < \frac{(\bar{Y} - \mu)}{1/\sqrt{n}} < 1.96\right) = 0.95 \equiv P\left(\bar{Y} - 1.96/\sqrt{n} < \mu < \bar{Y} + 1.96/\sqrt{n}\right) = 0.95$$

The formulation above tells us that the probability that the random interval $\left[\bar{Y} - 1.96/\sqrt{n}, \; \bar{Y} + 1.96/\sqrt{n}\right]$ contains the population mean μ is .95, or 95%. This information allows us to construct an *interval estimate* of μ, which is obtained by plugging in the sample outcome of the average, $\bar{Y}$. Thus, $\left[Y - 1.96/\sqrt{n}, \; \bar{Y} + 1.96/\sqrt{n}\right]$ is an example of an interval estimate of μ. It is also called a 95% confidence interval.A shorthand notation for this interval is: $\bar{Y}$ $\pm 1.96/\sqrt{n}$. The confidence interval in equation such as this is easy to compute, once the sample data $\{y_1, y_2,..., y_n\}$ are observed. When we say that the formulation above is a 95% confidence interval for μ, we mean that the *random* interval contains μ with probability .95. In other words, *before* the random sample is drawn, there is a 95% chance that interval above contains μ. The formulation above is thus is an example of an interval estimator. It is a random interval, since the endpoints change with different samples. A confidence interval is often interpreted as follows: "The probability that μ is in the interval noted above is .95%. This is incorrect. Probability plays no role, once the confidence interval is computed for the particular data at hand. The probabilistic interpretation comes from the fact that for 95% of all random samples, the constructed confidence interval will contain μ.

Methods of Point estimation

How does one obtain estimators that generally have good properties: We have two methods: The method of maximum likelihood and the method of moments.

The starting point of maximum likelihood estimation is the assumption that the (conditional) distribution of an observed phenomenon (the endogenous variable) is known, except for a finite number of unknown parameters. These parameters will be estimated by taking those values for them that give the observed values the highest probability, the highest likelihood. The maximum likelihood method thus provides a means of estimating a set of parameters characterizing a distribution, if we know, or assume we know, the form of this distribution. For example, we could characterize the distribution of some variable Y_i (for given X_i) as normal with mean $\beta_1 + \beta_2 X_i$ and variance σ^2. This would represent the simple linear regression model with normal error terms. In what follows, we have illustrated the principle of maximum likelihood taken from Verbbek (2004) in a discrete setting where Y_i only has a finite number of outcomes. Consider a large pool, filled with red and yellow balls. We are interested in the fraction p of red balls in this pool. To obtain information on p, we take a random sample of N balls (and do not look at all the other balls). Let us denote $Y_i = 1$ if ball i is red and $Y_i = 0$ if it is not. Then it holds by assumption1 that $P\{Y_i = 1\} = p$. Suppose our sample contains $N_1 = \Sigma_i y_i$ red and ($N - N_1$) yellow balls. The probability of obtaining such a sample (in a given order) is given by

$$P\{N_1 \; red \; balls, \; N - N_1 \; yellow \; balls\} = p^{N_1}(1 - p_1)^{N - N_1}$$

The formulation above, interpreted as a function of the unknown parameter p, is referred to as the likelihood function. Maximum likelihood estimation for p implies that we choose a value for p such that the above function is maximal. This gives the maximum likelihood estimator $\hat{p}$. For computational purposes it is often more convenient to maximize the (natural) logarithm of the equation above, which is a monotone transformation. This gives the loglikelihood function

$$L(p) = N_1 \log(p) + (N - N_1) \log(1 - p_1)$$

Maximizing this loglikelihood function gives as first order condition $d \log L(p)$

$$\frac{d \log L(p)}{dp} = \frac{N_1}{p} - \frac{(N - N_1)}{(1 - p)} = 0$$

Solving this equation for p, gives the maximum likelihood (ML) estimator,

$$\hat{p} = \frac{N_1}{N}$$

The ML estimator thus corresponds with the sample proportion of red balls. In principle, we also need to check the second order condition to make sure that the solution we have corresponds to a maximum, as

$$\frac{d^2 \log L(p)}{dp^2} = -\frac{N_1}{p_2} - \frac{(N - N_1)}{(1 - p^2)} < 0$$

This shows, indeed, that we have found a maximum. To sum up, the intuition of the maximum likelihood principle is as follows. From the (assumed) distribution of the data (e.g. y_i), we determine the likelihood of observing the sample that we happen to observe as a function of the unknown parameters that characterize the distribution. Next, we choose as our maximum likelihood estimates those values for the unknown parameters that give us the highest likelihood. In other words, the method of ML consists of finding as an estimate the value of a parameter that maximizes the likelihood function [Try to derive the OLS estimators using ML estimation technique, having the normal distribution discussed above and substituting the OLS regression estimator in that formula: See Varbeek, 2004: 164; after your own trial].

Method of Moments: This method consists of equating appropriate moments of the population distribution with the corresponding sample moments to estimate an unknown parameter of the distribution. For example, let X_1, X_2, ... X_n be a random sample from a distribution with probability (density) function f(x; θ). The rth sample moment about zero is defined to be:

$$M_r^1 = \frac{1}{n}\sum_{i=1}^{n} X_i^r$$

C2.   Testing Statistical Hypotheses

A statistical hypothesis is a claim about some unknown feature of a population of interest. The essence of testing a statistical hypothesis is to decide whether the claim is supported by the experimental evidence obtained through a random sample. Usually, the claim involves either some unknown parameter or an unknown functional form of the underlying distribution from which we are sampling. The decision on whether the sample data statistically support the claim is based on probability. Simply put, the claim will be rejected if its chance of being correct is small in the face of the observed.

Basic concepts for testing statistical Hypotheses: Suppose we are interested in the average time it takes for units to be assembled in an assembly line operation. Under standard operating conditions, the target average time to assemble units is 10 minutes. The plant manager would like to allow the process to continue unless substantial evidence is found that the average time is not 10 minutes. The evidence will be in form of a random sample of size n obtained from the underlying distribution for a unit's assembly time. *How should one approach the problem of deciding whether to allow the process to continue operating?* Here we are interested in estimating the unknown meantime μ. We want to determine whether μ = 10. We would like to find the sample whether μ is statistically different from 10 to support the manager's claim. This in turn mean we now have a null hypothesis μ = 10, commonly written as

$H_0 : \mu = 10$

A null hypothesis should be regarded as true unless sufficient evidence to the contrary is presented. In other words, we will reject the null hypothesis that the mean assembly time is 10 minutes only if the experimental evidence is strongly against it. We have the following possibilities in the course of doing this,

$$\text{Reject } H_0 \quad \begin{cases} \textit{When in fact } H_0 \textit{ is true} \\ \textit{When in fact } H_0 \textit{ is false} \end{cases}$$

$$\text{Fail to Reject } H_0 \quad \begin{cases} \textit{When in fact } H_0 \textit{ is true} \\ \textit{When in fact } H_0 \textit{ is false} \end{cases}$$

When a decision is made about a null hypothesis, two of the possible consequences relative to the true state of nature may lead to inferential errors. The rejection of the hypothesis H_0 when in reality H_0 is true constitutes what is called type I error. Failure to reject H_0 when in reality H_0 is false constitutes type II error.

Be that as it may, a *test* of a statistical hypothesis concerning some unknown feature of a population of interest is any rule for deciding whether to reject the null hypothesis based on a random sample from the population. The decision is based on some test statistic. For certain values of the test statistic, the decision will be to reject the null hypothesis. These values constitute what is known as the critical region of the test. To construct a suitable decision rule for testing a statistical hypothesis, it is also necessary to state an alternative hypothesis that reflects the possible value or range of values of the parameter of interest if the null hypothesis is false. That is, the alternative hypothesis represents some form of negation of the null hypothesis, this is normally given as:

H_0: $\mu = 10$

H_1: $\mu > 10$

General case: Let $X_1, X_2, \ldots\ldots X_n$ be a random sample from a normal distribution with unknown mean μ. Of interests is to test one of the following sets of hypotheses with regard to μ:

H_0: $\mu = \mu_0$	H_0: $\mu = \mu_0$	H_0: $\mu = \mu_0$
H_1: $\mu \neq \mu_0$	H_1: $\mu > \mu_0$	H_1: $\mu < \mu_0$

Assume further that the population variance σ^2 is known. Then the test statistic is the sample mean X, which under the null hypothesis is normally distributed with mean μ_0 and standard deviation δ/n. For the two-sided hypotheses the critical region of the size X is of the form

175

$$\text{Reject } H_0 \text{ if } \begin{cases} \text{mean } X \geq X_{(1-\frac{\alpha}{2})} \\ \text{mean } X \leq X_{(\frac{\alpha}{2})} \end{cases}$$

Where $X_{(1-\alpha/2)}$ and $X_{(\alpha/2)}$ are the critical quintile values of X such that:

$$P(\text{mean } X \leq X_{(1-\alpha/2)}) = \alpha/2$$

and,

$$P(\text{mean } X \leq X_{(\alpha/2)}) = \alpha/2$$

Since under H_0, mean $X \sim N(\mu_0, \sigma/n)$, then equivalently;

$$P\left(Z \leq \frac{X_{1-\alpha/2} - \mu_0}{\delta/\sqrt{n}}\right) = \alpha/2 \quad \text{and}$$

.

$$P\left(Z \leq \frac{X_{\alpha/2} - \mu_0}{\delta/\sqrt{n}}\right) = \alpha/2$$

Or

$$Z_{1-\alpha/2} = \frac{X_{1-\alpha/2} - \mu_0}{\delta\sqrt{n}} \quad \text{and} \quad Z_{1-\alpha/2} = \frac{X_{\alpha/2} - \mu_0}{\delta\sqrt{n}}$$

Where $Z_{1-\alpha/2}$ and $Z_{\alpha/2}$ are the corresponding quintile values of Z. It follows, therefore, that H_0 is rejected when a value X of the sample Mean X is such that:

$$X \geq \frac{\delta Z_{1-\alpha/2}}{\sqrt{n}} + \mu_0 \quad \text{and} \quad X \leq \frac{\delta Z_{\alpha/2}}{\sqrt{n}} + \mu_0$$

Equivalently, H_0 is rejected whenever,

$$Z \geq Z_{1-\alpha/2} \quad \text{or} \quad Z \leq Z_{\alpha/2}$$

Where $Z = (\text{mean } X - \mu_0)/(\sigma/\sqrt{n})$ is the value of the standard normal corresponding to the value mean X of X.

For one sided alterative hypothesis, $H_1: \mu > 0$, the critical region of the size α of X; it is of the form:

$$\text{Reject } H_0 \text{ if mean } X \geq X_{(1-\alpha)}$$

Where mean $X_{(1-\alpha)}$ is the quintile value of mean X such that P(mean $X \geq X_{(1-\alpha)} = \alpha$. Similarly, for the alternative hypothesis, H_i: $\mu < \mu_0$, the critical regional is of the form:

Reject H_0 if mean $X \leq X_\alpha$

Where the value X_α is such that $P(X \leq X_\alpha) = \alpha$.

We have illustrated so far the issue of testing a hypothesis using normal distribution. The procedure is similar when similar distributions, such as the *t*-distribution, are used. The key in choosing what distribution to use when testing a hypothesis lies in the theoretical formulation of the distribution of the parameters of interest. The theoretical formulators of the estimable parameters of a model normally offer us how the particular parameter in question is distributed. For instance, the error term in OLS is normally distributed as that condition assumed in the formulation and use of OLS (while the estimated parameters of such OLS models are assumed to have a *t*-distribution, etc.). Similarly, the RESET test for normality (the Ramsey test) is Chi-square distributed as the parameters is computed as a combination (product) of measure of Kurtosis and skewness, each of which are normally and independently distributed. We know from the definition of Chi-square distribution that the product/combination/ of such statistics will have a Chi-square distribution.

Reference and Further Readings

Bierens, Herman J. (2005). *Introduction to the Mathematical and Statistical Foundations of Econometrics*. Cambridge: Cambridge University Press.

Koop, Gary (2003). *Bayesian Econometrics*. Sussex: John Wiley & Sons.

Salvatore, Dominick and Derrick Reagle (2002). *Theory and Problems of Statistics and Econometrics, second edition*. New York: McGraw-Hill.

Varbeek, Marno (2004). A Guide to Modern Econometrics. Sussex: John Wiley & Sons.

Wooldridge, J.M. (2002). *Econometric Analysis of Cross-Section and Panel Data*. Cambridge, MA: MIT Press, Cambridge, MA.

Wooldridge, J.M. (2003). *Introductory Econometrics: A Modern Approach*, 2nd edition., Mason, OH: Thomson South-Western.

A GUIDE FOR FURTHER READINGS

General Readings

Alemayehu. Geda. and N.S. Ndung'u (2001). "Specifying and Estimating Partial Equilibrium Models for Use in Macro Models: A Road Map for the KIPPRA-Treasury Model", *KIPPRA Discussion Paper* No. DP/08/2001, Nairobi, Kenya.

Engle, R.F. and C.W.J. Granger (1987). "Co-integration and error-correction: representation, estimation and testing". *Econometrica,* 55:251–276.

Getenet Alemu (2008). "Lecture Notes on Quantitative Analysis for Development Research", Institute of Development Research, Addis Ababa University, Memo).

Greene, William H. (1993). *Econometric Analysis.* New York: Macmillan.

Griffith, W., C. Hill and G. Judge (1993). *Learning and Practicing Econometrics.* New York: John Wiley and Sons.

Hamilton, James (1994). *Time Series Analysis.* Princeton: Princeton University Press.

Herman, G. (1965). "The Inference to the Best Explanation", pp. 323–327 in Brody, B.A. and Grandy, R.E. (1989). *Reading in the Philosophy of Science,* Prentice Hall, New Jersey.

Kennedy, P. (1992). *A Guide to Econometrics.* Oxford: Blackwell.

Lipton, P. (1991). *Inference to the Best Explanation.* London and New York: Routledge.

Mukherjee, C. and M. Wuyts (1991). "Data Analysis in Development Research: An Argument", *ISS Working Paper No. 103.* The Hague: Institute of Social Studies.

Mukherjee, C., H. White and M. Wuyts (1998). *Econometrics and Data Analysis for Developing Countries.* London: Routledge.

Thomas, R.L. (1993). *Introductory Econometrics: Theory and Application.* London: Longman.

Tukey, J.W. (1977). *Exploratory Data Analysis.* London: Addison-Wisley.

Wuyts, M. (1992b). "Thinking with Data", Unit 5', in School of Oriental and African Studies (SOAS). *Research Methods in Financial Economics.* London: University of London.

On Mathematical Background

Chiang, A.C. (1984). *Fundamentals of Mathematical Economics*. London: McMillan.

Sydsaeter, K. and P. Hammond (1994). *Mathematics for Economics*. Harare: Academic Books.

On Unit Roots and Cointegration

Banerjee, Anindya, J. Dolado, J.W. Galbraith and D.F. Hendry (1993). *Co-Integration, Error-correction and the Econometric Analysis of Non-Stationary Data*. Oxford: Oxford University Press.

BAUM, C.F. (2001). "Stata: The Language of Choice for Time Series Analysis?" *The Stata Journal*, 1, 1–16.

Boswijk, P. (2000). "Mixed Normality and Ancillarity in I(2) Systems". *Econometric Theory*, 16:878–904.

Charemza, W.W. and D.F. Deadman (1992). *New Directions in Econometric Practice: General to Specific Modelling, Cointegration and Vector Autoregression*. Aldershot: Edward Elgar Publishing.

Clemente, J., A. Montañés and M. Reyes (1998). "Testing for a Unit Root in Variables with a Double Change in the Mean". *Economic Letters*, Vol.59, 175–182.

Dickey, D.A. and W.A. Fuller (1981). "Likelihood Ratio Statistics for Autoregressive Time Series with a Unit Root", *Econometrica*, Vol. 49, 1057–1072.

Enders, W. (2004). *Applied Econometrics Time Series*. 2nd Edition. New York: John Wiley.

Engle, R.F. and C.W.J. Granger (1987). "Co-integration and Error-Correction: Representation, Estimation and Testing", *Econometrica*, 55: 251–76.

Engle, R.F. and C.W.J. Granger (eds.) (1991). *Long run Economic Relationships: Readings in Co-integration*. Oxford: Oxford University Press.

Engle, R.F. and C.W.J. Granger, eds. (1991). *Long-run Econometric Relationships: Readings in Co-integration*. Oxford: Oxford University Press.

Granger, C.W.J. and P. Newbold (1974). "Spurious Regressions in Econometrics", *Journal of Econometrics*, Vol.2, 111–120.

Hendry, D.F. (1995). *Dynamic Econometrics*, Oxford: Oxford University Press.

Johansen, S. and K. Juselius (1990). "Maximum Likelihood Estimation and Inference on Cointegration: With Applications to the Demand for Money". *Oxford Bulletin of Economics and Statistics*, 52(2): 169–210.

Johansen, S. (1988). "Statistical Analysis of Cointegration Vectors". *Journal of Economic Dynamics and Control*, 12: 231–54. (Also in Engle and Granger (eds) (1991), Chapter 7).

Johansen, S. (1991). "Estimation and Hypothesis Testing of Cointegration Vectors in Gaussian Vector Autoregressive Models". *Econometrica*, 59(6): 1551–1580.

Johansen, S. and K. Juselius (1992). *Identification of the Long-run and the Short-run Structure: An Application of the ISLM Model*. Discussion Paper. Copenhagen: Institute of Economics, University of Copenhagen.

Johansen, S. (1997). "Likelihood Analysis of the I(2) Model". *Scandinavian Journal of Statistics*, 24: 433–462.

Johansen, S. (2002). "Small Sample Correction for the test of Cointegration Rank in the Vector Autoregressive Model, *Econometrica*, Vol. 70, 1929–1961.

Juselius, K. (1991). *Domestic and Foreign Effects on Prices in an Open Economy: The Case of Denmark*. Copenhagen: Institute of Economics, University of Copenhagen.

Juselius, K. (2006). *The Cointegrated VAR Model: Methodology and Applications*. New York: University of Copenhagen.

Kwiatkowski, D., P.C.B. Pillips, P. Schmidt, and Y. Shin (1992). "Testing the Null of Stationarity Against the Alternative of a Unit Root". *Journal of Econometrics*, Vol. 54, 159–178.

Paruolo, P. and A.C. Rahbek (1999). "Weak Exogeneity in I(2) VAR Systems". *Journal of Econometrics*, 93:281–308.

Phillips, P.C.B. (1987). "Time Series Regression with a Unit Root". *Econometrica*, 55, 277–301.

Phillips, P.C.B. and P. Perron (1988). "Testing for a Unit Root in Time Series Regression". *Biometrica*, 75, 355–446.

Rahbek, A.C., Kongsted H.C. and C. Jogensen (1999). "Trend-Stationarity in the I(?) Cointegration Model". *Journal of Econometrics*, 90: 265–289.

Stock, J.H. (1987). "Asymptotic Properties of Least Square Estimators of Co-integrating Vectors". *Econometrica*, 55: 1035–56.

Wickens, M.R. and T.S. Breusch (1988). "Dynamic Specification, The Long-run and The Estimation of Transformed Regression Model", *The Economic Journal*, 98 (conference, Supplement): 189–205.

Osterwald-Lenum, M. (1992). "A Note with Quantiles of the Asymptotic Distribution of Maximum Likelihood Cointegration Rank Test Statistics" *Oxford Bulletin of Economics and Statistics* 51: 219–239.

Palm, F. C. (2004). Structural econometric modeling and time series analysis: an integrated approach. In A. Zellner & F. C. Palm (Eds.), *The Structural Econometric Time Series Analysis Approach* (pp. 96–174). Cambridge: Cambridge University Press.

Patterson, Kerry (2000). *An Introduction to Applied Econometrics: A Time Series Approach.* Basingstock: Pallgrave-Macmillan.

Phillips, P.C.B. and Hansen, B.E. (1990). Statistical Inference in Instrumental Variables Regression with I(1) Processes. *The Review of Economic Studies,* 57(1), 99–125.

Rao, B. Bhaskara, ed. (1994). *Cointegration for the Applied Economist.* London: Macmillan.

Were, M., Alemayehu Geda, S.N. Karingi and N.S. Ndung'u (2001). "Kenya's Exchange Rate Movement in a Liberalised Environment: An Empirical Analysis". The Kenya Institute for Public Policy Research and Analysis Discussion Paper No. DP/10/2001.

Sims, C. (1980). "Macroeconomics and Reality", *Econometrica*, Vol. 48, 1–48.

Stock, J.H., and Watson, M.W. (1993). A Simple Estimator of Cointegrating Vectors in Higher Order Integrated Systems. *Econometrica*, 61(4), 783–820.

Zivot, E. and D.W.K. Andrews (1992). "Further Evidence on Great Crash, the Oil Price Shock and the Unit Root Hypothesis", *Journal of Business and Economic Statistics*, Vol.10, 251–270.

On Modelling an I(2) Variable and Production Functions

Easterly, Williams and Ross Levin. (2001). "It is not Factor Accumulation: Stylized Facts and Growth Models." *The World Bank Economic Review*, 15:2, pp. 177–219.

Haldrup, Niels (1998). "An Econometric Analysis of I(2) Variables", *Journal of Economic Survey.* 12(5): 595–650.

Johansen, Soren (1988). "Statistical Analysis of Cointegration Vectors", *Journal of Economic Dynamics and Control*, 12:231–54. (Also in Engle and Granger (eds) (1991), Chapter 7).

Johansen, Soren (1991) "Estimation and Hypothesis Testing of Cointegration Vectors in Gaussian Vector Autoregressive Models", *Econometrica*, 59(6): 1551–1580.

Johansen, Soren. (1995). "A Statistical Analysis of Cointegration for I(2) Variables." *Economic Theory*, 11, pp. 25–59.

Johansen, Soren. (1997). "Likelihood Analysis of the I(2) Model." *Scandinavian Journal of Statistics*, 24, pp. 433–62.

Mankiw, Gregory N., David Romer and David N. Weil. (1992). "A Contribution to the Empirics of Economic Growth." *The Quarterly Journal of Economics*, 107:2, pp. 407–37.

On Forecasting

Bischoff, Charles W. (2000). *Bayesian VAR Forecasts Fail to Live Up to Their Promise.* http://www.looksmartsavings.com/p/articles/mi_m1094/ is_3_35/ ai_64396570/pg_2?pi=monsav.

Bodart, V. And Le Dem, J. (1996) "Labour Market Representation in Quantitative Macroeconomic Models for Developing Countries: An Application to Côte d'Ivoire," *IMF Staff Papers* 43:2, 419–451.

Challen, D.W and Hagger, A.J (1983) *Macroeconometric Systems: Construction, Validation and Applications*, London: Macmillan Press.

Litterman, Robert B. (1986). "Forecasting with Bayesian Vector Autoregressions: Five Years of Experience." *Journal of Business and Economic Statistics*, 4:1, pp. 25–38.

Ramos, Francisco Fernando Ribeiro (2003). "Forecasts of Market Shares from VAR and BVAR Models: A Comparison of Their Accuracy." *International Journal of Forecasting*, 19, pp. 95–110.

Reifschneider, David L., Stockton, David J. and Wilcox, David W. (1997). "Econometric Models and the Monetary Policy Process." *Carneige-Rochester Conference Series on Public Policy*, 47, pp. 1–37.

Robalino, David A., Voetberg, Albertus and Picazo, Oscar (2002). "The Macroeconomic Impact of AIDS in Kenya Estimating Optimal Reduction Targes for the HIV/AIDS Incidence Rate." *Journal of Policy Modeling*, 24, pp. 195–218.

On Panel Cointegration

Arellano, Manuel and Bo Honore (2000). "Panel Data Methods: Some Recent Development". Princeton University, Working Paper 0016, Princeton University.

Baltagi, B.H. and C., Kao (2000). *Non-Stationary Panels, Cointegration in Panels and Dynamic Panels: A Survey*, Centre for Policy Research, Working Paper No. 16, Syracuse University.

Baltagi B.H. (2005). *Econometrics of Panel Data*, John Wiley & Sons, Chichester, UK.

Banerjee, A. (1999). "Panel Data Unit Root Tests and Cointegration: An Overview", *Oxford Bulletin of Economics and Statistics,* Special Issue, 607–629.

Breitung, J. (2000). "The Local Power of the Some Unit Root Tests for Panel Data, in B.H. Baltagi, T.B.Fomby and R.C.Hill(eds). *Nonstationary Panels, Panel Cointegration and Dynamic Panels, Advances in Econometrics*, Vol.15, Elsevier Science, Amsterdam.

Choi, I. (2001). "Unit root tests for panel data", *Journal of International Money and Banking*, Vol. 20, 249–272.

Groen, J.J.J. and F., Keibergen (2001). *Likelihood-Based Cointegration Analysis in Panels of Vector Error Correction Models,* Econometrics Research and Special studies department, De Nederlandsche Bank, http://www.tinbergen. nl/discussionpapers/99055.pdf.

Hadri, K. (2000). "Testing for Stationarity in Heterogeneous Panel Data", *Econometric Journal*, Vol. 3, 148–161.

Hall, B.H. and J., Mairesse (2002). *Testing for Unit Roots in Panel Data: An Exploration using Real and Simulated Data,* http://www.emlab.berkeley.edu/ users/bhhall/papers/ HallMairesseJan03% 20unitroot.pdf.

Hall, S.G. and G., Urga (online). *New Developments in the Analysis of Panel Data Sets,* http://www.ms.ic.ac.uk/sghall/icms6.pdf.

Harris, R.I.D. and R., Sollis (2003). *Applied Time Series Modeling and Forecasting*, West Sussex: John Wiley & Sons Ltd.

Harris, R.I.D. and E.Tzavalis (1999). "Inference for Unit Roots in Dynamic Panels Where the Time Dimension is Fixed". *Journal of Econometrics*, 91: 201–226.

Im, K.S., Pesaran, M.H. and Shin, Y. (2003, previously 1997). "Testing for Unit Roots in Heterogeneous Panels", *Journal of Econometrics,* Vol.115 , 53–74.

Johansen, S. (1995). *Likelihood-Based Inference in Cointegrated Vector Autoregressive Models*, New York: Oxford University Press.

Kao, C. (1999). "Spurious Regression and Residual-Based Tests for Cointegration in Panel Data", *Journal of Econometrics*, 90, 1–44.

Larsson, R., J. Lyhagen and M. Lothergen (2001). "Likelihood-Based Cointegration Tests in Heterogeneous Panels", *Econometrics Journal*, Vol. 4, 109–142.

Levin, A. and Lin C.F. (1992). *Unit Root Tests in Panel Data: Asymptotic and Finite-Sample Properties*, Discussion Paper 92–93, University of California, San Diego.

Levin, A. and Lin C.F. (1993). *Unit Root Tests in Panel Data: New Results*, Discussion Paper No. 93–56, Department of Economics, University of California at San Diego.

Maddala, G.S. and Wu S. (1999). "A comparative study of unit root tests with panel data and a new simple test", *Oxford Bulletin of Economics and Statistics,* Special Issue, 631–652.

McCoskey, S. and C. Kao (1998). "A Residual-Based Tests of the Null of Cointegration in Panel Data, *Econometric Review*, Vol. 17, 57–84.

McCoskey, S. and C. Kao (1997) "A Residual-based test of the Null of Cointegration in Panel Data", memo (University of Syracuse and United States Naval Academy).

Njuguna, Angelica E. (1999). *Growth and Convergence in A Disequilibrium Solow-Swan Model: The Case of ASEAN Countries 1960–1995,* (Ph.D. Dissertation, University of New England, Australia).

Pesaran, M.H. and R. Smith (1995). "Estimating Long-run Relationship from dynamic heterogeneous Panels", *Journal of Econometrics*, Vol. 4, 79–113.

Pedroni, P. (1995). "Panel Cointegration: Asymptotic and Fine Sample Properties of Pooled Time Series Test with an Application to the PPP Hypothesis", memo, Department of Economics, Indiana University.

Pedroni, P. (1999a). "Critical Values for Cointegration Tests in Heterogeneous Panels with Multiple Regressors", *Oxford Bulletin of Economics and Statistics,* Special Issue, 653–670.

Pedroni, P. (1999b). *Fully Modified OLS for Heterogeneous Cointegrated Panels*, www.arts.cornell.edu/econ/cae/panel-fm.pdf.

Pedroni, P. (2004). "Panel Cointegration: Asymptotic and Finite Sample Properties of Pooled Time Series Tests With an Application to the PPP Hypothesis", *Econometric Theory,* Vol. 20; 597–625.

Pesaran, M. Hashem and Ron Smith (1995). "Estimating Long-run Relationships form Dynamic Heterogeneous Panels", *Journal of Econometrics*, 68: 79 113.

Phillips, P.C.B. and H. Moon (1999). "Linear Regression Limit Theory for Non-Stationary Panel Data", *Econometric*, Vol. 67, No. 5, 1057–1111.

INDEX

The Impact of Open Data in Developing Economies across Sectors

The preceding section has described a logic framework that examines the different components that determine how open data could create an impact. It identifies both enabling and disabling factors for open data initiatives that seek to create four different types of impacts, and expands on them in a practitioner-focused Periodic Table of Open Data Elements. This in effect allows us to create more particular or fine-grained theories of change for each sector and area of impact. In this section, we consider the emerging (and again, variable) evidence of open data's impact on specific sectors that are relevant to the development context. We focus on six sectors: Health, Humanitarian Aid, Agriculture and Nutrition, Poverty Alleviation and Livelihoods, Energy, and Education.

For each sector, we describe illustrative examples of open data's use in developing economies. The cases described here are provided to offer a glimpse into the current field of practice. Some sectors have seen more notable (and novel) applications of open data than others, and some of the examples described here have had little impact to date, or represent instructive failures. But even these lower impact initiatives can aid in identifying testable premises to guide future practice and experimentation. Considered together, these over-arching and sector-specific theories of change build a more complete and detailed matrix of how and under what conditions open data impacts development, providing a set of hypotheses for further research and experimentation.

Health

Improving Governance	Empowering Citizens	Innovation & Creating Opportunity	Solving Public Problems
The health sector is a major recipient of public funds and international aid, particularly in developing countries.[61] Increasing the transparency of this large area of government expenditure in turn increases accountability, helping ensure resources efficiently and adequately target public health needs.	Accessing quality-of-care information for different health care providers can bolster citizens' ability to make informed choices regarding their service providers.[62] Data on corruption or malpractice in the health care system can particularly enable evidence-based advocacy efforts for patients.	As the health sector becomes increasingly data-driven, open data can help spur job creation and the establishment of new service models as a result of both making more information available on the supply side, and using newly accessible health data on the demand side. Though concerns regarding the potential for technology and automation to negatively impact employment also exist.	Especially in the wake of health crises (such as the Ebola outbreak in West Africa or mosquito-borne epidemics in India, for example[63]), access to data across institutions on the availability and location of health resources and on emergent health outcomes can play an important role in addressing major epidemics or ingrained public health concerns.

Predicting Dengue Outbreaks in Paraguay with Open Data

Logic Framework Components:

- Input: Open health, climate, and water data
- Actors: Researchers and academia
- Activity: Data analysis
- Output: Process improvements, alerts
- Users: Government officials, researchers
- Indicators: Accuracy of data-driven predictions
- Intended Impact: Solving public problems

Description: Since 2009, dengue fever has been endemic in Paraguay. Recognizing the clear problem at hand, and the lack of a strong system for communicating dengue-related dangers to the public, the National Health

---

61 Organization for Economic Cooperation and Development, "Aid at a Glance Charts," http://www.oecd.org/dac/stats/aid-at-a-glance.htm.

62 Tawnya Bosko and Matthew Briskin, "Transparency in Healthcare: Where does it stand?" *Management in Healthcare* 1, no. 1 (2016): 83–96.

63 Like similar efforts in Paraguay and Singapore, researchers in India demonstrated how open data can be analyzed using statistical modeling and machine learning to determine how transmission of dengue (or other mosquito-borne illnesses like Zika) could be minimized through increased citizen awareness and/or more strategic allocation of resources. Vandana Srivastava and Biplave Srivastava, "Towards Timely Public Health Decisions to Tackle Seasonal Diseases with Open Government Data," *World Wide Web and Public Health Intelligence: Papers from the AAAI-14 Workshop*, June 18, 2015, http://www.aaai.org/ocs/index.php/WS/AAAIW14/paper/view/8728/8221.

Surveillance Department of Paraguay opened data related to dengue morbidity. Leveraging this data, researchers created an early warning system that can detect outbreaks of dengue fever a week in advance. The data-driven model can predict dengue outbreaks at the city-level in every city in Paraguay. Importantly, the system can be deployed in any region as long as data on morbidity, climate, and water are available.

Code for South Africa Cheaper Medicines for Consumers

Logic Framework Components:

- Input: Open medicine data
- Actors: NGO
- Activity: Dissemination
- Output: Searchable database
- Users: Citizens, health service providers
- Indicators: Money saved by individuals
- Intended Impact: Empowering citizens

Description: In 2014, Code for South Africa, a South Africa-based nonprofit organization active in the open data space, took a little known dataset from the national Department of Health website and created the Medicine Price Registry Application (MPRApp), an online tool allowing patients (and their doctors) to make sure that they aren't being overcharged by their pharmacies. With no marketing or promotions to speak of, MPRApp has had an impact on the lives of a few South Africans; with a more sustainable model and increased awareness of MPRApp, particularly among trusted intermediaries in the health sector, it could provide more patients access to cheaper medicines.

Open Health Data in Uganda

Logic Framework Components:

- Input: Open health data
- Actors: NGO, media
- Activity: Aggregation and commingling, dissemination
- Output: Apps and platforms, dashboards
- Users: Citizens
- Indicators: Improved health service delivery, increased public participation
- Intended Impact: Empowering citizens

Description: In Uganda, open data initiatives are being used in an attempt to improve health outcomes and revolutionize a health care industry marred by staff shortages, lack of resources and corruption. The Kampala-based organization CIPESA has collaborated with a local media organization, Numec, to create the iParticipate project (http://cipesa.org/tag/iparticipate/), which analyzes open government data, and trains citizens and intermediaries to use that data toward empowering citizens to play a bigger role in health governance. Similarly, the Women of Uganda Network (http://wougnet.org), which trains women to use information technology, created an online platform to collect and document information relating to poor health care services. Both these initiatives allow citizens to scrutinize and lobby the public health care sector, aiming to improve its efficiency and ensure that services respond to the needs of citizens in a robust manner.

Open Health Data in Namibia

Logic Framework Components:

- Input: Open health and climate data, private data
- Actors: Researchers and academia
- Activity: Aggregation and commingling, dissemination
- Output: Maps
- Users: Government officials
- Indicators: Distribution of mosquito nets
- Intended Impact: Solving public problems

Description: An effort by the government of Namibia to eradicate malaria in the country was bolstered by the use of satellite and cell phone data. Researchers were able to draw "maps of environmental factors like vegetation density, population, and rainfall that affect mosquito and parasite populations and the likelihood of transmission" and identify areas where citizens were at high-risk.[64] Cell phone data provided by Namibia's largest telecommunications provider assisted researchers to track human movement—and thus the spread of malaria. As a result, the Ministry of Health distributed 1.2 million bed nets to the communities that needed them most.

---

64 Open Data Watch, "Data Impacts Case Studies: Using satellite and cell phone data to eliminate malaria in Namibia," http://dataimpacts.org/project/malaria/.

Open Results and Performance Based Financing

Logic Framework Components:

- Input: Open results-based financing data
- Actors: NGOs, government officials
- Activity: Dissemination
- Output: Process improvements, searchable databases
- Users: NGOs, government officials
- Indicators: Decreased instances of corruption
- Intended Impact: Improving governance

Description: As part of efforts to improve health outcomes and health system functioning, Burundi was one of the first African countries to introduce RBF. RBF is an instrument that links development financing with pre-determined results. Payment is made only when the agreed-upon results are shown to have been achieved. Open RBF—a platform for opening data related to RBF initiatives—was first delivered in Burundi in response to the Burundian Ministry of Health's efforts to improve health care functioning at the national level and strengthen accountability mechanisms. By opening RBF data, it was believed that increased accessibility and scrutiny of the data could lead to improvements in data quality and engender more accountable data practices. Early returns appear to be positive—Ministry of Health staffers played a role in pushing their peers toward making information on results accessible, for example—though not transformational, and Open RBF engaged in a longer-term partnership with the government. Open RBF was concurrently applied to the education and AIDS awareness programs in Burundi; as another sign of impact and scalability, since its launch in Burundi, Open RBF has scaled across 15 countries.

Open Data and Open Contracting for Nigerian Health Care Centres

Logic Framework Components:

- Input: Open budget and contracting data
- Actors: NGO
- Activity: Dissemination
- Output: Apps and platforms, dashboards
- Users: Citizens, NGOs and interest groups
- Indicators: Decreased instances of corruption
- Intended Impact: Improving governance

47

Description: In Nigeria, primary health care centers (PHCs) are often located far away from the people who need them most—namely the greater than 50 percent of Nigerians living in poverty. As a result of open data and open contracting efforts, the platform Budeshi enables citizens and watchdogs to actively monitor and unearth financial discrepancies and inefficiencies in the construction of badly needed PHCs around the country. In addition to increasing the transparency of these health care providers, Budeshi positions itself as an advocacy tool, aiming to push the Nigerian government to make a fuller-scale commitment to open contracting principles.[65]

Humanitarian Aid

Improving Governance	Empowering Citizens	Innovation & Creating Opportunity	Solving Public Problems
The misuse of international aid has a long history, with money targeted for specific development efforts failing to be put to use in the expected way. For developing countries that receive a significant amount of aid funding from international organizations, tracking how that money is being used can help root out corruption and catalyze better spending practices in government.	When funnelled through institutional bureaucracies, humanitarian aid can often overlook the micro-level needs of citizens and their communities. By opening aid allocation data to the public, citizens can provide valuable feedback to governments on how aid is being used, and become active co-partners, rather than mere recipients, of the aid industry.[66]	In a field commonly disabled by inaccurate data, where guess-work is rife,[67] open data in humanitarian aid allows NGOs and other civil society organizations to create innovative strategies based on new and accurate information, for example, to help communities in conflict areas or recovering from natural disasters.	Open data initiatives, when built on high-quality, accurate data, can help organizations better identify where and how to invest humanitarian aid to most effectively solve social problems, allowing governments and humanitarian actors to better coordinate relief efforts[68] (for example, through the Humanitarian Data Exchange[69]) and identify sectors that most urgently require humanitarian assistance.

Open Development Data in Cambodia

Logic Framework Components:

- Input: Open government data and open NGO data

---

65 Seember Nyager, "Can Data Help Us Attain Healthier Lives?" Budeshi, May 15, 2016, http://www. budeshi.org/2016/05/can-data-help-us-attain-healthier-lives/.

66 Regarding the discursive attributes related to the terms "participation," "empowerment" and "citizenship" in aid, see Andrea Cornwall, *Beneficiary, Consumer, Citizen: Perspectives on participation for poverty reduction*, Stockholm: Sida, 2000, http://www.alnap.org/resource/10271.

67 Vanessa Humphries, "Improving Humanitarian Coordination: Common challenges and lessons learned from the cluster approach," *The Journal of Humanitarian Assistance* 30 (2013).

68 Eleanor Goldbert, "Open Data Platform Lets Aid Groups Respond More Efficiently to Crises," *Huffington Post*, May 31, 2016, http://www.huffingtonpost.com/entry/open-data-platform-enables-aid-groups-to-respond-more-efficiently-to-crises_us_574876fee4b03ede4414a6a4.

69 The Humanitarian Data Exchange, https://data.humdata.org/.

- Actors: Researchers, NGOs
- Activity: Data analysis, presentation, aggregation and commingling, dissemination
- Output: Infographics, maps, apps, and platforms
- Users: Government officials, citizens, researchers, NGOs, media
- Indicators: Decreased instances of corruption
- Intended Impact: Improving governance

Description: Developed by the East-West Management Institute, and part of the broader Open Development Initiative, Open Development Cambodia (ODC) seeks to improve public awareness and information-sharing around development data. ODC uses data aggregated from a diversity of governmental and nongovernmental sources to provide visualizations, maps and other data-driven products and tools to provide the public sector, private sector, civil society, data-driven journalists, and the general public with a view into the workings and impacts of development efforts, with news reports drawn from its information offerings representing its most apparent benefit to date.

AidData in Africa

Logic Framework Components:

- Input: Open development funding data
- Actors: NGOs
- Activity: Dissemination
- Output: Searchable databases
- Users: Media, NGOs, and interest groups
- Indicators: Decreased instances of corruption, improved allocation of aid money
- Intended Impact: Improving governance

Description: The open data initiative AidData (http://aiddata.org) tracks international development funding and can be used by developing countries to track and scrutinize their government's foreign aid spending. The project is housed at the College of William & Mary in Virginia; its database has already revealed that China appears to provide more foreign aid to African countries that support their vote in the United Nations General Assembly.[70] Information made available through AidData has also allowed journalists in Africa to chart

---

70 "Diplomacy and Aid in Africa," *The Economist*, April 14, 2016, http://www.economist.com/blogs/graphicdetail/2016/04/daily-chart-10.

levels of foreign investment to their countries, owing to the discovery that China has become Tanzania's single largest trading partner, and that Chinese firms receive the lion's share of Tanzanian engineering contracts.[71] The project makes clear that access to aid data can transform the way aid is targeted, and provides citizens and watchdogs with information needed to monitor and give feedback on development projects in their communities.

Response to Nepalese Earthquake

Logic Framework Components:

- Input: Open geospatial data, crowdsourced data
- Actors: NGOs, private sector
- Activity: Presentation, dissemination
- Output: Maps, process improvements
- Users: Government officials, citizens
- Indicators: Lives saved
- Intended Impact: Solving public problems

Description: In the wake of the devastating earthquake that struck Nepal in 2015, so-called "digital humanitarians"—both local and international volunteers—took it upon themselves to create detailed maps in the most affected areas.[72] One such platform, Quakemap.org, allowed citizens to report needs to organizations that provide relief—with 434 of 551 actionable reports acted upon.[73] This response built upon an already robust mapping project in Nepal and demonstrates how open data efforts can work in collaboration with humanitarian relief efforts at both the local and international level.

Open Aid and Budget Data in Nepal

Logic Framework Components:

- Input: Open aid and budget data
- Actors: NGOs
- Activity: Data analysis, dissemination

---

71 Mzwandile Jacks, "China Emerges as Tanzania's Major Investor," *Ventures Africa*, January 29, 2014, http://venturesafrica.com/china-emerges-as-tanzanias-major-investor/.

72 "Open Data's Role in Nepal's Earthquake," ICT.govt.nz, 2015, https://www.ict.govt.nz/assets/Uploads/Case-Study-Nepal-Earthquake2.pdf.

73 Nirab Pudasaini, "Open Source and Open Data's Role in Nepal Earthquake Relief," OpenSource.com, June 8, 2016, https://opensource.com/life/16/6/open-source-open-data-nepal-earthquake.

- Output: Searchable databases
- Users: Citizens, NGOs and interest groups
- Intended Impact: Improving government

Description: The early impact of a project in Nepal to open aid and budgetary data held by the government has shown limited impact to date, likely due to the political and economic reality of the nation, which is rebuilding from decades of civil unrest and governance breakdown. Political, legal, and technical realities present significant challenges to advocates of greater digital transparency, key stakeholders interviewed demonstrated widely-varying perceptions of what "open data' meant, stakeholders viewed themselves more as facilitators than end-users, and government data quality was called into question by several experts.[74]

Agriculture and Nutrition[75]

Improving Governance	Empowering Citizens	Innovation & Creating Opportunity	Solving Public Problems
Open data can make agricultural agencies and implementing organizations more accountable, by making information accessible on whether or not financial resources provided were used according to contractual obligations; and whether they serve people and farmers they are supposed to be supporting.	A major problem in developing countries is the different levels of food access across populations, with research pointing to the emergence of "food deserts" in Africa's urban centers.[75] Open data that pertains to regional food access can allow citizens to identify these disparities in nutrition and food access, empowering citizen groups to lobby government institutions for more equitable food policy. In addition, smallholder farmers could be full participants in defining, implementing, and evaluating projects intended to improve their farms and lives when provided access to data.	An increased awareness of weather trends, models of crop yields and other relevant datasets can help inform more strategic, evidence-based agricultural decision making and increase the viability of individual farms.	On a micro level, open data can play a role in both predicting potentially damaging conditions for crops, and informing more strategic planting choices following, for example, a catastrophic weather event. At the macro level, the increased availability of usable data on climate change can help governments to advance a forward-looking sectoral approach to the end of ensuring food security in the future.

74 Krishna Sapkota, "Exploring the Impacts of Open Aid and Budget Data in Nepal," *Freedom Forum*, August 2014, http://www.opendataresearch.org/sites/default/files/publications/Open%20Aid%20and%20Budget%20Data%20in%20Nepal%20-%2015th%20Sept-print.pdf.

75 See also the Agriculture Open Data Package developed by GODAN, http://AgPack.info.

76 Jane Battersby and Jonathan Crush, "Africa's Urban Food Deserts," *Urban Forum* 25, no. 2, Springer Netherlands, 2014.

Uganda's Banana Bacterial Wilt Solution

Logic Framework Components:

- Input: Open international organization data, crowdsourced data
- Actors: Government officials, international organization
- Activity: Aggregation and commingling dissemination
- Output: Apps and platforms, data-driven journalism
- Users: Citizens, media
- Indicators: Crops and money saved
- Intended Impact: Solving public problems

Description: Faced with a crisis caused by the spread of banana bacterial wilt (BBW), the Ugandan government turned to open data included in U-Report (http://ureport.ug), UNICEF's community polling project. U-Report helped spread awareness of the disease, mobilized a network of nearly 300,000 volunteers across the country, and also provided vital information to the government about the disease and its pattern of spreading. Using U-Report, the government was able to disseminate information (via SMS) about treatment options and actionable crop-protection strategies to some 190,000 citizens.

Colombia and the Cultivation of Rice

Logic Framework Components:

- Input: Open climate and agricultural data, semi-public agricultural data
- Actors: NGOs and researchers
- Activity: Data analysis
- Output: Decision trees, apps and platforms, searchable databases
- Users: Citizens, Industry groups
- Indicators: Money saved by smallholder farmers
- Intended Impact: Creating opportunity

Description: The production of rice is in a state of continual decline, adversely affecting local farmers. These trends are often blamed on the shifting climate. Researchers analyzed climate and meteorological data alongside measures of rice production and found that the most commonly planted rice in the region, Cimarron Barinas, is highly sensitive to changes in temperature. As a result, farmers adjusted when they planted the crop. Farmers were thus able

to improve their yield and protect themselves from the environment. It is estimated that $3.5 million in potential losses were avoided as a result.[77]

Improving the Global Farming Knowledge Base

Logic Framework Components:

- Input: Open agriculture data, open science data, open international organization data
- Actors: NGOs
- Activity: Data analysis, aggregation and commingling, dissemination
- Output: Apps and platforms, advocacy
- Users: Citizens, industry groups
- Indicators: Crops and money saved
- Intended Impact: Empowering citizens

Description: To combat the pests and diseases responsible for killing 40 percent of the world's planted crops each year, Plantwise (https://www.plantwise. org) combines a diversity of relevant global and local databases, government data, and research publications in an openly accessible platform to improve decision making related to pests and disease. This tool has been accessed by over 600,000 farmers from 198 countries, who have contributed to over 900,000 factsheets on crop pest prevalence and best practices to help manage and prevent potential crop loss from pests and diseases.[78]

Empowering Smallholder Farmers in Ghana

Logic Framework Components:

- Input: Open agriculture data, crowdsourced data
- Actors: Private sector
- Activity: Data analysis, dissemination
- Output: Decision trees, process improvements
- Indicators: Crops and money saved by smallholder farmers
- Intended Impact: Creating opportunity

---

77 "Big Data, Big Prospects: Crunching data for farmers' climate adaptation," *CCAFS Annual Report 2015*, https://ccafs.cgiar.org/blog/big-data-big-prospects-crunching-data-farmers-climate-adaptation#. WFBRtKOZORu.

78 CABI, "Plantwise Knowledge Bank Wins Open Data Award for Social Impact," *Plantwise Blog*, November 5, 2014, https://blog.plantwise.org/2014/11/05/plantwise-knowledge-bank-wins-open-data-award-for-social-impact/.

Description: Esoko is a for-profit company, with close relationships with the public sector, offering a simple communication tool for businesses, government, NGOs, and others to connect with farmers. Managed from its main office in the capital city of Accra, Esoko is principally directed at businesses, while individual farmers only constitute its secondary group of interest. Nevertheless, the information that Esoko provides to farmers by repackaging data from different sources (including government and crowdsourced data) and disseminating the information via mobile phones with call-center support in local languages gives smallholder farmers a new addition to their toolkit— that is, if they are made aware of the opportunity to the extent needed for a meaningful impact. In addition, Farmerline, a mobile communications organization, offers similarly data-driven offerings to smallholder farms in Ghana.[79]

Poverty Alleviation

Improving Governance	Empowering Citizens	Innovation & Creating Opportunity	Solving Public Problems
Identifying and addressing corruption through open data can lead to resources being reallocated toward public services that are better suited for addressing systemic poverty.	An improved understanding of how government allocates resources can enable public mobilization around issues that are being under-addressed according to official datasets, including issues related to poverty.	Whether enabling job creation, frugal innovation efforts, or more systemic economic growth, as developing economies begin to leverage data as an economic asset, poverty alleviation can accelerate as a result.	Open data can improve intervention programs that seek to alleviate poverty and improve quality of life by enhancing the understanding of cities, organizations, and donors as to where the needs are the biggest, and why, as well as evaluating what intervention is most appropriate.

Code for Africa

Logic Framework Components:

- Input: Open budget data
- Actors: NGOs
- Activity: Data analysis, presentation, dissemination
- Output: Apps and platforms, process improvements
- Users: Media, researchers
- Indicators: Decreased corruption in extractives industry
- Intended Impact: Improving government, empowering citizens

79 Business Call to Action, "Empowering Farmers Through Mobile Communication in West Africa," *The Guardian*, October 15, 2014, https://www.theguardian.com/sustainable-business/2014/oct/22/empowering-farmers-through-mobile-communication-in-west-africa.

Description: Unlike North America and Europe, countries in Africa often have limited access to open government data, and are consequently also limited in their ability to harness technology and use it as a driver of growth. Code for Africa (https://codeforafrica.org) aims to nurture skills in technology and coding from within communities to create opportunities for citizens to act as watchdogs for governments, corporations and public institutions. Fundamental to this is seeing civic technology and open data as potential public assets, and Code for Africa has developed a Data Fellowship program that embeds people trained in data skills to work on projects in a variety of media and nonprofit organizations. School of Data offers a similar fellowship program aimed at increasing data skills and literacy and putting them to use in local partner organizations around the world.[80] By nurturing this burgeoning field, Code for Africa's projects have in turn interrogated public expenditure, as seen in the platform 'Where My Money Dey?'[81] which tracks open data on public revenues received from mining companies. This effort is aimed at providing citizens, NGOs, and watchdogs with information that can help ensure communities benefit from large industrial projects on their land.

Bhoomi Project

Logic Framework Components:

- Input: Open land record data
- Actors: NGO
- Activity: Dissemination
- Output: Searchable database
- Users: Citizens
- Indicators: Increased use of land record information by the poor
- Intended Impact: Empowering citizens

Description: This project in Karnataka, India, was intended to install kiosks in local communities that would provide access to newly digitized land records and democratize the flow of information, reduce inequality, and empower the poor. The system, however, was widely exploited by richer members of society, which weakened the social standing of poorer citizens, exactly the opposite of the goal of the project. Despite its good intentions, the project largely resulted

---

80 "Fellowship Programme," School of Data, http://schoolofdata.org/fellowship-programme/.

81 http://wmmd.codeforafrica.org.

in the transfer of wealth from poor to rich in those communities due to pre-existing inequalities in access to information.[82]

Energy

Improving Governance	Empowering Citizens	Innovation & Creating Opportunity	Solving Public Problems
Like the health sector, energy is the subject of significant public money expenditures, and government sponsorship and procurement (especially in the extractives field). Improving the transparency of a country's energy budget could potentially identify and prevent corruption. In addition, open datasets such as open address data, can improve service delivery by providing energy companies and government with a better understanding of current conditions.	By providing more information to citizens about energy consumption—including perhaps individualized information about their own habits, as offered by GreenButton in the United States[83]— citizens can make more informed decisions regarding usage and, as a result, decrease their energy spending. Open data on utility services and pricing can also be used to identify the best-priced service.	The use of open energy data to bolster predictive capabilities and reel in energy expenditures could have wide-ranging economic impacts for both the public and private sectors.	An improved understanding of energy consumption patterns (at the aggregate and/or individual level) can help individuals, organizations, and policymakers take concrete steps toward decreasing consumption and addressing climate change's impacts. Open data from various sources can help decision makers prioritize investments in energy production and delivery.

India's Electricity Supply Monitoring Initiative

Logic Framework Components:

- Input: Energy provider data
- Actors: NGO
- Activity: Data analysis
- Output: Dashboards, searchable databases
- Users: Citizens, corporations, researchers, government officials
- Indicators: Improved power supply, increased citizen advocacy around energy

---

82 Michael Gurstein, "Open Data: Empowering the empowered or effective data use for everyone," *First Monday,* February 2011, http://journals.uic.edu/ojs/index.php/fm/article/view/3316/2764; Kevin Donovan, "Seeing Like a Slum: Towards open, deliberative development," *Georgetown Journal of International Affairs* 13, no. 1, April 26, 2012, https://papers.ssrn.com/sol3/papers.cfm?abstract_id=2045556.

83 http://www.greenbuttondata.org.

- Intended Impact: Empowering citizens

Description: The poor quality of energy infrastructure in India results in frequent shortages, blackouts, and interruptions. The Indian government does not consistently provide open data on these energy issues. In response to this, the Electricity Supply Monitoring Initiative (ESMI) was launched in 2014 by the Pune-based non-profit Prayas Energy Group. ESMI collects information from cities across 200 locations in India through electricity supply monitors (ESMs)—devices installed in key sites to record voltage data, which log this information with a central server. This data is then made publicly available through the website watchyourpower.org, where users can monitor their power supply and compare this with other regions. ESMI has collected one million location-hours of data, and already found that rural areas experience four to five times more power disruptions than cities or districts. ESMI has already surfaced important evidence about the Indian power supply, but whether and how the capture of this evidence will create meaningful change remains an open question, dependent on an institutional willingness to act upon insights generated—a willingness that has not yet surfaced.

Azerbaijan's Extractive Industries Transparency Initiative Efforts

Logic Framework Components:

- Input: Open extractive industry data
- Actors: NGO
- Activity: Dissemination
- Output: Searchable databases
- Users: NGOs and interest groups, researchers, government officials
- Indicators: Reduced discrepancies between government and contracting business receipts
- Intended Impact: Improving governance

Description: The Extractive Industries Transparency Initiative (EITI) is a global partnership that requires member countries to provide open data and information on the governance of oil, gas, mining, and other extractives. Though questions remain about the line between true impact and positive public relations (see "open washing" discussion above), Azerbaijan, one of the earliest compliers to the EITI standards, saw its "double-digit discrepancies between corporate receipts and government intakes"—an indicator of corruption—essentially disappear between 2003 and 2009. The World Bank

Independent Evaluation Group went on to rate the country's EITI efforts as "highly effective."[84] This example, however, also points to the frequency of backsliding in open initiatives, and the challenges created by the political contexts in which open data initiatives are launched. In 2015, Azerbaijan's EITI membership status was downgraded due to crackdowns on civil society, political opponents, and the media. In 2017, the country's membership was suspended entirely.[85]

Education

Improving Governance	Empowering Citizens	Innovation & Creating Opportunity	Solving Public Problems
Low quality in public education can often point to corruption or more ingrained problems in public expenditure. By opening education data and allowing this data to be scrutinized by the public, governments are encouraged to weed out vested interests that may overdraw the public educational fund.	More information on the expenditures and performance of schools can help parents make more informed decisions about school choice, and mobilize citizens to demand changes to any identified deficiencies.	Like other sectors, the world of education is increasingly data- and technology-driven. More accessible data on schools and on the subjects taught in schools can spur the creation of a data-driven "ed-tech" industry.	Analyzing open data through learning analytics can improve the often poor quality of the education sector in developing countries by, for instance, sharing insights on how teaching can be improved or how the education environment can be designed to support both teachers and students.

Tanzania's Education Dashboards

Logic Framework Components:

- Input: Open education performance data
- Actors: NGO, private sector entrepreneurs, donor organizations
- Activity: Aggregation and commingling, dissemination

---

84 Benjamin Sovacool and Nathan Andrews, "Does Transparency Matter? Evaluating the governance impacts of the Extractive Industries Transparency Initiative in Azerbaijan and Liberia," *Resources Policy* 45 (2015), https://eiti.org/sites/default/files/documents/Sovacool%20%26%20Andrews%20 %5B2015%5D%20-%20Does%20transparency%20matter%20-%20%20Evaluating%20the%20 governance%20impacts%20of%20the%20Extractive%20Industries%20Transparency%20Initiative%20 %28EITI%29%20in%20Azerbaijan%20and%20Liberia.pdf.

85 "Azerbaijan Suspended from the EITI – a Bankwatch and Counter Balance statement," *Bankwatch*, March 9, 2017, http://bankwatch.org/news-media/for-journalists/press-releases/azerbaijan-suspended-eiti-%E2%80%93-bankwatch-and-counter-balance-.

- Output: Dashboards
- Users: Citizens, media
- Indicators: Education advocacy efforts
- Intended Impact: Empowering citizens

Description: Two recently established portals in Tanzania tried to improve low national examination pass rates, providing the public with more data on education and Tanzania's schools. The first, the Education Open Data Dashboard (educationdashboard.org), is a project established by the Tanzania Open Data Initiative, a government program supported by the World Bank and the United Kingdom Department for International Development (DFID) to support open data publication, accessibility and use. The second, Shule (shule.info), was spearheaded by a lone programmer, entrepreneur, and open data enthusiast who has developed a number of technologies and businesses focused on catalyzing social change in Tanzania. Although these projects initially encouraged citizens to demand greater accountability from their school system and public officials, both are in a state of near abandonment resulting from the lack of a clear sustainability and long-term management strategy.

Mexico's Mejora Tu Escuela

Logic Framework Components:

- Input: Open education performance and budget data
- Actors: NGO
- Activity: Data analysis, aggregation and commingling, dissemination
- Output: Dashboards, research report
- Users: Citizens, media, NGOs and interest groups, government officials
- Indicators: Reductions in education corruption, education advocacy efforts
- Intended Impact: Empowering citizens

Description: Founded by the Mexican Institute for Competitiveness (IMCO), with support from Omidyar Network and others, Mejora Tu Escuela (http://mejoratuescuela.org) is an online platform that provides citizens with information about school performance. It helps parents choose the best option for their children, empowers them to demand higher quality education, and gives them tools to get involved in their children's schooling. It also provides school administrators, policymakers, and NGOs with data to identify areas that require improvement and hotbeds of corruption, in the process raising the

overall quality of education in Mexico. Some of the data used to create the Mejora Tu Escuela platform was also instrumental in identifying widespread corruption in the education sector and targeting public outrage regarding "phantom" teachers on school payrolls, unchecked teacher absenteeism, and misappropriated funds, among other issues.[86]

Brazil and Education Monitoring

Logic Framework Components

- Input: Open education performance and budget data, census data
- Actors: NGOs, researchers
- Activity: Aggregation and commingling, dissemination
- Output: Searchable databases
- Users: Citizens, NGOs and interest groups, government officials
- Indicators: Money saved in education, education advocacy efforts
- Intended Impact: Empowering citizens and improving government

Description: The development of QEdu[87] in Brazil highlights the link between improved educational standards and open data initiatives. The database—which monitors state, county, and school performance based on metrics like test scores, census data, and educational spending—is easily searched and freely accessible. Reliable data can allow school managers to implement more targeted reforms and allow parents to understand the system that is educating their children. Similar projects have been undertaken in Mexico, Kenya, Tanzania, and the Philippines and appear to be meeting with success.

---

86 Andrew Young and Stefaan Verhulst, "Mexico's Mejora Tu Escuela: Empowering citizens to make data-driven decisions about education," GovLab, http://odimpact.org/case-mexicos-mejora-tu-escuela.html.

87 http://www.qedu.org.br.

PART 2
Case Studies

Open Data's Impact on Improving Government

Burundi's Open RBF

Making health spending and performance transparent

Auralice Graft, Andrew Young and Stefaan Verhulst

Summary

As part of efforts to improve health outcomes and the functioning of health systems, Burundi was one of the first African countries to introduce results based financing (RBF) in the health care sector. RBF is an instrument that links development financing with pre-determined results. Payment is made only when the agreed-upon results are shown to have been achieved. Open RBF, a platform for opening data related to RBF initiatives, has been central to the Burundian Ministry of Health's efforts to introduce RBF methodology and more generally strengthen accountability in health care. Open RBF was first introduced in 2014. Early returns were positive and Open RBF entered into a longer-term partnership with the government. Open RBF has also been applied to education and AIDS awareness programs in Burundi.

Context and Background

Problem Focus/Country Context

Burundi is a low-income nation with a population of 10.5 million. It is one of the world's poorest countries, with development and economic indicators that are among the weakest. Burundi ranks 166th out of 169 countries on

the United Nations 2010 Human Development Index,[88] and the national GDP per capita was under USD 210 in 2015.[89] Health outcomes are poor, with a heavy disease burden characterized by infectious and communicable diseases, primarily HIV/AIDS, malaria and diarrhea. Life expectancy in 2016 was just 50 years (for both men and women). [90,91] National healthcare expenditures are estimated at 9 percent of GDP.[92] In addition to low public health expenditures, Burundi's national healthcare system faces significant challenges, including a scarcity of health professionals, poor quality of health services, poor access to essential medicines throughout the country, and a weak health information system.[93]

Results Based Financing (RBF)

Results based financing (RBF) is a method that links development financing with pre-determined results.[94] Payment is made only when the agreed-upon results are shown to have been achieved, an approach that seeks to shift the focus from inputs to results. According to one report that outlines the benefits of RBF: "By only paying for results once they have been achieved, we partly avoid the risk that the donor contribution is not used effectively."[95]

RBF is used across developing countries in cooperation with the private sector, the public sector, and civil society organizations. It is used in a range of sectors, including health care, education, security, and energy. RBF is emerging as a particularly important mechanism in efforts to scale up provision of essential health care services, including child and maternal health care, for example in countries like Cambodia and Rwanda. The OECD has designated

---

88 U.S. Global Health Initiative, "Burundi Global Health Initiative Strategy: 2011–2015," September 2011, https://www.ghi.gov/wherewework/docs/BurundiStrategy.pdf.

89 Trading Economics, "Burundi GDP Per Capita: 1960–2017," http://www.tradingeconomics.com/burundi/gdp-per-capita.

90 U.S. Global Health Initiative, "Burundi Global Health Initiative Strategy: 2011–2015," September 2011, https://www.ghi.gov/wherewework/docs/BurundiStrategy.pdf.

91 *BBC News*, "Burundi Country Profile," December 14, 2016, http://www.bbc.com/news/world-africa-13085064.

92 Soeters Bonfrer, Presentation, Erasmus University, Rotterdam, 2015, http://rghi.nl/wp-content/uploads/2015/06/5.-Presentation-Igna-Bonfrer-PBF-in-Burundi-Bonfrer-et-al-Symposium-11062015.pdf.

93 U.S. Global Health Initiative, "Burundi Global Health Initiative Strategy: 2011–2015," September 2011, https://www.ghi.gov/wherewework/docs/BurundiStrategy.pdf.

94 RBF is sometimes also referred to as performance based financing (PBF) or output based aid (OPA). In some contexts, PBF refers specifically to RBF in the health care sector. See Jurien Toonen, et al., *Learning Lessons on Implementing Performance Based Financing, from a Multicountry Evaluation*, Royal Tropical Institute, Cordaid and WHO, May 2009, http://www.who.int/contracting/PBF.pdf.

95 Swedish International Development Cooperation Agency, *Results Based Financing Approaches: What are they?* SIDA, 2015, http://www.sida.se/contentassets/1869345299754bddbf58857e2d92c726/110557c1-7b5e-4a0d-97b0-cbeae5258533.pdf.

RBF as a key tool for achieving WHO Universal Health Coverage goals.[96] Studies also show that RBF increases health care provider performance, with important differences identified "before and after" the introduction of RBF. RBF was further shown to strongly influence health system development at the operational level in RBF projects in some countries.[97]

Burundi was one of the first African countries to introduce results based financing (RBF). Second on the African continent only after Rwanda, it began implementing RBF in its health care systems in 2010. In 2015, Burundi also began using RBF in the education sector.[98]

Technology and RBF

The key to a successful RBF program is effective daily management, and information management tools are essential for this. Large amounts of data have to be entered, verified, and validated for RBF programs to function, and that data must then be processed against pre-set criteria to calculate and disperse subsidy payments. Technology plays a vital role in ensuring that this is all done effectively and accurately.

While many RBF programs use Microsoft Excel for this purpose, an increasing number use Open RBF, a customizable financing management tool designed specifically for RBF projects. Because this tool easily makes data open and machine readable, it has the added benefit of making RBF data accessible for public consumption and analysis.

KEY ACTORS

Key Data Providers

The key data providers are Burundian health service providers who participate in RBF programs that use the Open RBF tool. These service providers generate qualitative and quantitative data relating to the services provided, and the Open RBF tool manages and processes that data and the different stages it passes through. These stages include recording, verification, processing, and calculation and dispersal of payments. Outcomes are also shared in the public domain.

---

96 György Bèla Fritsche, Robert Soeters and Bruno Meessen, *Performance-Based Financing Toolkit*, Washington, DC: World Bank, 2014, http://www.oecd.org/dac/peer-reviews/PBF-%20toolkit.pdf.

97 See Jurien Toonen, et al., *Learning Lessons on Implementing Performance Based Financing, from a Multicountry Evaluation*, Royal Tropical Institute, Cordaid and WHO, May 2009, http://www.who.int/contracting/PBF.pdf.

98 "RBF IT system for Education sector in Burundi." OpenRBF, http://www.openrbf.org/project/rbf-it-system-for-education-sector-in-burundi/Ve_9qR8AABUBfdDj.

Key Data Users and Intermediaries

Several entities make use of the data. Primarily, participating RBF programs use it to ensure accurate and timely recording, verification, processing, and publication of data, as well as payments dispersal. Also, funding organizations use the data to oversee program progress and to determine allocations. In addition, Burundi's Ministry of Public Health and the Fight Against AIDS uses the data to coordinate their nation-wide health sector improvement efforts. Medical practitioners and policymakers also use the data. Finally, citizens have access to the data (although, as explained elsewhere in this case study, citizen uptake seems somewhat limited).

The key data intermediaries are Burundi's Ministry of Public Health and the Fight Against AIDS, which together spearhead Burundi's national health system improvement efforts. In addition, Cordaid, a Netherlands-based organization that works to create "opportunities for the world's poorest, most vulnerable and excluded people,"[99] has implemented community health and education sector RBF programs in Burundi using the Open RBF tool.

Key Beneficiaries

Entities working directly and indirectly with RBF programs benefit from the technological functions Open RBF provides. Also, governments, policymakers, funding organizations, students, and citizens benefit from the publicly-available data and data comparisons. Most broadly, all citizens of Burundi benefit from any health and education sector improvements that have been achieved as a result of Open RBF platforms.

Project Description

Initiation

Open RBF's origins are in Belgium, where Nicolas de Borman, the founder and current CEO of BlueSquare, a company that works to harness technology for the public good, sought a way to promote RBF in developing nations. Borman correctly identified high demand for a tool that would help collect, analyze, and disseminate RBF data. As a result, Borman and a team of five partners created such a tool and named it Open RBF.[100] The tool is deployed and administered around the world by BlueSquare.

RBF pilot projects began in Burundi in 2006 across six provinces, with such pilots covering the entire country by 2010. The Open RBF platform was first

---

99 See: https://www.cordaid.org/en/.

100 GovLab interview with Antoine Legrand and Elena Ignatova, Program Managers at BlueSquare, August 9, 2016.

delivered in Burundi in 2010, in response to a request from the Burundian government and coinciding with the national-level embrace of results-based financing.[101] The Burundian Ministry of Health was seeking ways to improve health care functioning at the national level and strengthen accountability mechanisms.[102,103] Early returns were positive and Open RBF then entered into a longer-term partnership with the government. Open RBF has also been applied to both the health and education sectors in Burundi. [104,105]

Open RBF in Burundi operates in a similar way to Open RBF around the world. Its broad aims are to improve the openness of data to enable its access by a range of stakeholders in healthcare, thereby promoting the overall RBF goals of efficiency, transparency, accountability, and good governance.[106] The platform is built as an open-source, web-based solution, using a combination of technologies, including Php, Mysql, Jquery, Bootstrap, Highcharts, and Dompdf. The tool also integrates with Google Maps.[107]

To access the Open RBF tool, users visit a portal that has both a private and a public interface. The private area contains dashboards that display project data from the field—data that has been recorded and verified by different parties, and only then published on the platform. Data in this area includes information relating to project progress, including quality, quantity, and performance indicators.

The public, front-end interface (image shown below) includes slightly more data than the private interface. The public area allows users to view information at a province or national level, for example, information related to vaccination rates, reproductive health, preventative health, and HIV/AIDS. In the representative image included here, the interface shows that 100 percent of children attending participating clinics were verified as having been fully vaccinated in March 2015, while 80.36 percent were fully vaccinated in November of that year. It also shows that, in September 2015, almost 50

---

101 GovLab interview with Elena Ignatova, Program Manager at BlueSquare, January 19, 2017.

102 Christel Jansen and Jurrien Toonen, "Learning from Experiential Performance Based Financing Knowledge in Burundi and Cameroon," KIT Health Blog, June 21, 2016, https://www.rbfhealth.org/blog/learning-experiential-performance-based-financing-knowledge-burundi-and-cameroon.

103 György Bèla Fritsche, Robert Soeters and Bruno Meessen, *Performance-Based Financing Toolkit*, Washington, DC: World Bank, 2014, http://www.oecd.org/dac/peer-reviews/PBF-%20toolkit.pdf.

104 Aléa Kagoyire, "Inspiring Change in Burundi's Education System with OpenRBF, BlueSquare.org, March 17, 2016, https://medium.com/@BlueSquare.org/inspiring-change-in-burundi-s-education-system-with-openrbf-by-al%C3%A9a-kagoyire-project-manager-af1fbb6d31d9#.ac8i9w7es.

105 See: http://www.bluesquare.org/technologies.

106 Alice Irakoze, "An OpenRBF portal for the Community PBF in Makamba, Burundi: verified data, transparent management and budget monitoring!" BlueSquare.org, July 17, 2015, https://medium.com/@BlueSquare.org/an-openrbf-portal-for-the-community-pbf-in-makamba-burundi-verified-data-transparent-management-8afc0610fd99#.tyefjelsl.

107 See: http://www.openrbf.org/faq.

percent of patients were screened for TB.[108] Each key indicator is compared with regional and global figures.

All the information contained within the portal (especially the private area) is used to determine the progress of projects, and whether they are eligible for performance-based subsidies. Once subsidies have been calculated and paid, this information is displayed on the public interface, which includes provider performance indicators that allow citizens and policy makers (and anyone else interested) to gauge progress of particular projects or groups and see how public funds are being allocated. One goal of the public interface is to open up data to encourage greater civic ownership and participation.[109]

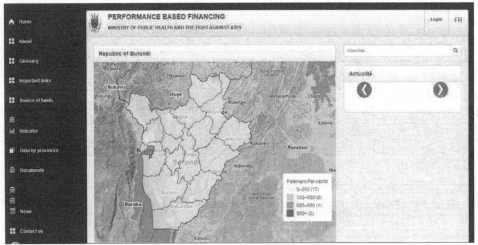

Image from http://www.fbpsanteburundi.bi/ which displays health data for Burundi as generated by Open RBF.

Demand and Data Use

As mentioned above, demand for Open RBF comes primarily from within RBF programs. Such programs could be managed by non-profit organizations, civil society groups, or government departments. In Burundi, additional demand comes from Burundi's Ministry of Public Health and the Fight Against AIDS. All these organizations use the data available on the portal not only to track the progress of their own projects, but also of other projects throughout the country. Civil society actors and journalists also draw on Open RBF data to

---

108 Ministere de la Sante Publique et de la Lutte Contre Le SIDA, Performance Based Financing, 2013, http://www.fbpsanteburundi.bi/data/indicators.html#dataelt11.

109 Cordaid, "Open RBF," https://www.cordaid.org/en/topics/healthcare/result-based-financing/open-rbf/.

inform their work, but neither group represents a prime target audience for the platform.[110]

Impact

Measuring the impact of open data projects is never easy, especially as some projects may have indirect effects that are harder to capture. Nonetheless, a range of indicators suggest that Open RBF has not only had a positive impact Burundi, offering important lessons for the potentially transformative role of data in improving healthcare and more generally solving complex public problems in the developing world.

Improving Health

Overall, as noted, the state of healthcare in Burundi remains poor. But there are encouraging signs of improvement within RBF programs in particular that suggest the positive impact of Open RBF. One example can be found in Cordaid's work with community health workers in Makamba province, which has resulted in a significant reduction in cases of severe malaria.[111] In addition, Cordaid's work in 81 Burundi preschools, which includes 27 local organizations verifying community education indicators and a network of 12 regulatory boards, has been found to correlate with improved educational access for students of all ages, a better gender balance in programs, better teaching methods, and improved academic performance scores among students.[112]

These improvements are of course the result of many factors, but people familiar with the results cite the important role played by Open RBF. For example, Dr. Etienne Nkeshimana, RBF and health system strengthening expert in Burundi who currently coordinates a Cordaid community RBF project, says: "I cannot scientifically say that Open RBF has led to some of the positive results we see in RBF programs. However, I can say that without Open RBF, we would not have achieved these positive results."[113]

---

110 GovLab interview with Elena Ignatova, Program Manager at BlueSquare, January 19, 2017.

111 Republic of Burundi, Ministry of Public Health and the Fight Against AIDS, "Evaluation Final de Projet Pilote FBP Communautaire au Burundi," December 2015.

112 GovLab interview with Simone Soeters, Cordaid Program Manager and Vincent Kamenyero, Cordaid, September 22, 2016.

113 GovLab interview with Dr. Etienne Nkeshimana, Cordaid Community RBF Coordinator, and Simone Soeters, Cordaid Program Manager, September 13, 2016.

Better Project Management and Cost Savings

A significant benefit of Open RBF is its role in improving project management, which in turn enhances the services that use it and introduces greater cost efficiencies. Open RBF achieves better project management by allowing stakeholders to regularly and rigorously follow project results in virtual real-time, including through sophisticated visualizations. Such monitoring not only improves the outcomes of the projects but also leads to financial savings, helping organizations manage scarce development resources more efficiently. As Vincent Kamenyero, Data and Portal Manager at Cordaid, puts it: "The Open RBF portal has allowed for greater transparency in finance management, cost reduction of organizational functioning, and is a considerable time saver for our verifiers."[114] Rigorous project management is particularly important in the early or pilot stages of a program, when donors may be monitoring to determine the effectiveness of a method and whether or not to scale up funding.

Open RBF also helps aid agencies and governments monitor projects remotely, a factor that is of great help to foreign funding groups. The benefits of remote project management were apparent during the recent political upheaval in Burundi, when foreign agencies were more comfortable monitoring their projects from the relative safety of their host countries.[115] Similarly, Cordaid's work with community health workers in the remote Makamba province is significantly facilitated by its ability to follow projects from the national capital of Bujumbara. For instance, if there is a problem with health worker data collection methods on the ground, program experts can quickly identify it and attempt to solve the issue on their dashboards in the capital.[116]

The Inherent Value of Data

Open RBF Burundi is also a good example of the powerful role that data can play in solving public problems in the developing world. Increasingly, it is becoming clear that the data generated by specific RBF programs can be used in other situations as well; the data has *inherent* value. For example, in its current efforts to expand community health efforts (known as the Kira program), the Ministry of Health is making extensive use of publicly available Open RBF

---

114 Cordaid, "Open Development Movement: Co-creation leads to transformation," Position Paper, May 2014, https://www.cordaid.org/en/wp-content/uploads/sites/3/2014/05/OpenDevPaper-MAY2014-LR_5.pdf.

115 GovLab interview with Antoine Legrand and Elena Ignatova, Program Managers at BlueSquare, August 9, 2016.

116 GovLab interview with Dr. Etienne Nkeshimana, Cordaid Community RBF Coordinator, and Simone Soeters, Cordaid Program Manager, September 13, 2016.

data generated by previous programs. The data includes various qualitative and quantitative costing indicators, as well as information pertaining to patient numbers and vaccine rates that had been used to assess earlier interventions.[117] In this way, publicly available Open RBF data can serve as an important reference point and guide for developing future programs.

Several donor organizations and student groups similarly rely on publicly available Open RBF data. For example, the World Bank, which will help fund the above-mentioned Kira project, has relied on earlier existing Open RBF healthcare sector data to determine its funding packages. Likewise, students researching Burundi health or other sector outcomes regularly access Open RBF public-facing pages for their research.[118]

Empowering Citizens

As indicated by the example of students, Open RBF data can play a powerful role beyond the development community, empowering citizens at large with information and insights. The Open RBF tool in Burundi provided the public with its first opportunity to review and potentially comment on healthcare (and other) projects across the country. Through community groups and other advocacy channels, citizens can contribute to healthcare planning, verify performance, track government spending, and generally ensure greater accountability. "It puts communities in the driver's seat," said Dr. Rose Kamariza, Cordaid Program Officer, Burundi.[119]

It is of course important to mention that many citizens lack Internet access and thus direct access to the data generated by Open RBF. But organizations like Cordaid play an important role in overcoming such barriers, suggesting the important role of intermediaries in spreading the benefits of open data. For example, Cordaid organizes bi-annual feedback workshops where it shares data with citizens and allows them to engage with RBF findings and Open RBF results.[120]

---

117 Ibid.

118 Ibid.

119 Cordaid, "Open Development Movement: Co-creation leads to transformation," Position Paper, May 2014, https://www.cordaid.org/en/wp-content/uploads/sites/3/2014/05/OpenDevPaper-MAY2014-LR_5.pdf.

120 GovLab interview with Dr. Etienne Nkeshimana, Cordaid Community RBF Coordinator, and Simone Soeters, Cordaid Program Manager, September 13, 2016.

Risks

Burundi's Open RBF initiative is not intended to make any personally identifiable information accessible to the public. Some level of privacy risk does remain, however, when open data projects are active in sectors like health care. There has been no evidence to date that Open RBF has introduced any privacy issues, but it will be important to maintain vigilance when redacting personal information from data releases or anonymizing datasets going forward.

Lessons Learned

Several important lessons with wider applicability emerge from this particular case study. These can broadly be categorized by considering the key enablers of the project, as well as the most important barriers or challenges to its success.

Enablers

Government support

Burundi's Ministry of Public Health and the Fight Against AIDS were significant enablers in Open RBF's success. They incorporated RBF into the government's national health program, using the Open RBF tool in delivering that program. The ultimate impact and success of that tool has, to a large degree, flowed from the support received by the national government, which helped fund its implementation, adapt it to a range of health sector categories, and generally propagated it throughout the country. In this respect, Open RBF in Burundi is a good example of how strong institutional support and political and administrative buy-in are instrumental to the success of open data projects. Many of the projects discussed in this series lack such support.

It is worth mentioning that the current political climate in Burundi may prove to be a challenge in the months and years ahead. Although this project is both beneficial and useful for the nation, the possibility of further political strife may limit the ability to monitor the efficacy of programs within the health care sector.

International development organizations

International development organizations also played a key enabling role in Open RBF's success. Cordaid, which adopted the tool for its community health, education and security sector programs, was among the most important

73

supporters. The World Bank has helped too, especially by using and thus validating the usefulness of publicly-available Open RBF data.

Barriers

Regional and Sectoral Specificity

Open RBF's use in a variety of countries is testament to technology's cross-border potential. However, it is also true that the first version of the Open RBF software used in Burundi was not entirely adapted to local conditions and the different needs of various RBF programs. Not all such programs are alike. Each has a different set of pre-determined criteria. Some may receive funds from one donor while others from several donors. [121] This first version of the platform was tweaked and a second unveiled in 2014. This second version allows for the possibility of multi-management funding, includes new data visualizations, and also includes an alert system to allow auditors to update the data.[122]

Technical Expertise

According to the International Telecommunication Union (ITU), the percentage of Burundian citizens who use the Internet more than tripled from 2014 to 2015. Nonetheless, fewer than 5 percent of Burundians regularly use the Internet—a low rate even by the typical standards of less developed economies. To an extent, the negative consequences can be mitigated by the use of intermediaries who share information with citizens that are not connected. But overall, the country's poor state of Internet readiness curtails citizens' and users' ability to access Open RBF-generated data.

Even among those who are connected to the Internet and generally technically proficient, a lack of data knowledge and expertise often limits the potential of Open RBF projects. Open RBF teams find that many statisticians they work with are not trained to work with data in a manner that Open RBF requires. This complicates and slows training missions. For example, statisticians at the province level in some countries are not always versed with data management beyond the use of Microsoft Excel.

---

121 Ibid.

122 Alice Irakoze, "Un portail OpenRBF pour le FBP communautaire à Makamba, Burundi : des donnéees verifiées, une gestion et un suivi budgétaire transparents!" BlueSquare.org, https://medium.com/@BlueSquare.org/un-portail-openrbf-pour-le-fbp-communautaire-%C3%A0-makamba-burundi-des-donn%C3%A9ees-verifi%C3%A9es-une-f419eb6b6ebc#.ptx0n29b4.

Design Flexibility

Building reliable and truly useful software requires adapting it to local conditions and needs. Software is often designed from the top-down, but in order to be useful across a variety of contexts, it must also adapt to new information from the field and from users. Software design is an iterative process. This has proven to be a challenge not only in Burundi, where, as mentioned above, users struggled early on to adapt the software to local conditions, but virtually everywhere where Open RBF has been implemented. For example, program managers Antoine Legrand and Elena Ignatova estimate that up to 80 percent of Open RBF clients come back to the BlueSquare team requesting changes, and as a result the RBF program itself changes over time. Enabling this level of flexibility based on the initial Open RBF design continues to present challenges, but is essential to the success of open data projects—and more generally technical interventions, especially in the developing world.[123]

Replicability

Open RBF has been replicated repeatedly, within and beyond the healthcare sector—suggesting the value of the model and its tool to a wide variety of stakeholders. Since its inception in the health and education sectors within Burundi, Open RBF has also been used in the security sector.[124] And, of course, the dissemination of Open RBF has also extended far beyond Burundi. A total of 15 countries now use Open RBF to facilitate RBF program management, including Benin, Cameroon, DRC, Haiti, Kyrgiztan, Laos, and Nigeria.[125] The cases of DRC and Nigeria are particularly interesting because of their sheer size: 1,000 facilities are included in Nigeria's program and 2,000 in DRC's.[126] So while Open RBF efforts require some level of customization for specific contexts, the platform and general approach rolled out in Burundi has proven flexible enough to scale geographically and across sectors.

---

123 GovLab interview with Antoine Legrand and Elena Ignatova, Program Managers at BlueSquare, August 9, 2016.

124 Cordaid, "Open Development Movement: Co-creation leads to transformation," Position Paper, May 2014, https://www.cordaid.org/en/wp-content/uploads/sites/3/2014/05/OpenDevPaper-MAY2014-LR_5.pdf.

125 GovLab interview with Antoine Legrand and Elena Ignatova, Program Managers at BlueSquare, August 9, 2016.

126 Ibid.

Looking Forward

The organizers of Open RBF are working on several initiatives to improve their software and programs across implementation areas.

Mobile Platform Updates

Expanding functionalities and improving the responsiveness of the mobile elements of Open RBF are clear focus areas going forward. For health care implementations of Open RBF, like in Burundi, BlueSquare is testing a new patient feedback mechanism to collect information directly from those receiving health care. Additionally, a mobile data collection tool was introduced in July 2015 to allow for data to be uploaded onto the Open RBF platform. Developed by BlueSquare specifically for RBF efforts to improve Burundi's education system, the tool was designed to improve data collection and verification. It includes a simple interface and allows for data storage until the tool is connected to the internet and data can be uploaded to the system. The tool saves time for data verifiers and enhances the quality of data collected.[127] Both cell phones and tablets are being tested, keeping cost requirements in mind.

A More Stable, User Friendly Platform

Open RBF working to solve connectivity issues by establishing interoperability between information systems. The goal here is to better correlate collected and validated data analysis which in turn will enable better and more complete reading of the performance of each RBF approach.[128] Teams are working to improve interoperability layers between support tools using DHIS2 systems and integrating them with Open RBF.[129]

Open RBF is also taking steps to improve data visualization on their dashboards. They aim to improve the way that results are displayed to make the platform more user friendly, especially at a glance.

---

127 *Aléa Kagoyire*, "A New Mobile Data Collection Tool Is Out!" BlueSquare.org, July 17, 2015, https://medium.com/@BlueSquare.org/a-new-mobile-data-collection-tool-is-out-c3746ae4233d#.alv6gelpm.

128 Alice Irakoze, "Un portail OpenRBF pour le FBP communautaire à Makamba, Burundi : des donnéees verifiées, une gestion et un suivi budgétaire transparents!" BlueSquare.org, https://medium.com/@BlueSquare.org/un-portail-openrbf-pour-le-fbp-communautaire-%C3%A0-makamba-burundi-des-donn%C3%A9ees-verifi%C3%A9es-une-f419eb6b6ebc#.akspjkv9h.

129 Nicolas de Borman, "How Can New Technologies Enhance Efficiency and Good Governance of Results-based Financing," RBFHealth Blog, July 16, 2014, https://www.rbfhealth.org/blog/how-can-new-technologies-enhance-efficiency-and-good-governance-results-based-financing.

Integrations and Plug-Ins

Finally, the next stage of Open RBF will feature a number of new plug ins and integrations to bring new functionalities to the platform, and to better connect it with other platforms users are likely to frequent. Likely the most important new integration will be improved geolocation capabilities and mapping features. Organizers are also pushing forward more social media integration, with Facebook and Twitter functionalities representing first priorities.[130] Beyond the specific integrations under development, the plug-in and integration focus exhibited by Open RBF makes clear that a key part of the plan for evolving the platform over time involves finding ways to bring existing platform features to bear for Open RBF users.

Conclusion

The results-based financing approach is growing in momentum, especially across developing countries. The rapid expansion and scaling of the Open RBF platform shows how quickly successful open data projects can be replicated across regions and sectors when a clear value proposition can be articulated and early positive impacts can be demonstrated. Perhaps even more importantly, the Open RBF platform itself is helping to make it easier for governments to quickly roll out open data-driven RBF efforts, with the key out-of-the-box features and functionalities ready to implement once a clear problem area is identified and political will and buy-in is present.

---

130 Alfred Antoine U., "Efficient Health Financing: Transparency, accountability and benchmarking in health systems," Open RBF Initiative, October 22, 2013, http://www.health4africa.net/wp-content/uploads/local_health_systems_future_technology_impact_OPENRBF_Data.pdf.

India's ESMI

Civil society complementing
government data in an open manner

Michael P. Canares, Anirudh Dinesh, Andrew Young and Stefaan Verhulst

Summary

Across the developing world, roughly 1.2 billion people[131] do not have access to electricity. Of this number, at least 30 percent live in India. In addition, at least 247 million people in India experience irregular access to electricity, with many receiving only around four hours a day. The government of India, under Prime Minister Narendra Modi, has committed to establishing universal access across the country. However, India's electricity problem is not just about insufficient coverage; it is also about poor power quality, especially in the form of voltage fluctuations.

Poor power quality impacts all segments of consumers; it can damage equipment and cause various other problems, including data loss and other forms of loss or inefficiencies for businesses and other entities. Improving power quality is, however, challenging, and requires real-time access to data. In 2007, The Prayas Energy Group (PEG), an Indian NGO, launched the Electricity Supply Monitoring Initiative (ESMI) to complement existing data sources and collect real-time power quality information by installing Electricity Supply Monitors (ESMs) in various locations. ESMI now works in 200 locations[132] in 18 Indian states. The initiative has made power supply

---

131 Energy Access Database, *World Energy Outlook* http://www.worldenergyoutlook.org/resources/ energydevelopment/energyaccessdatabase/.

132 "Using technology for evidence based feedback to ensure quality electricity access", Electricity Supply Monitoring Initiative (ESMI), *Prayas Energy Group*, https://d2oc0ihd6a5bt.cloudfront.net/wp-content/ uploads/sites/837/2016/04/2-Shantanu-Dixit.pdf.

monitoring data available for different users across the country, in the process increasing awareness of the state of electricity supply, helping to advocate for better service provision, and influencing policy at both the state and country level. Despite certain limitations—and the daunting scale of the problem— ESMI represents an important example of how civil society can address public problems, and fill gaps arising from government data failures, when NGOs take an open approach to data collection and use.

Context and Background

Problem Focus / Country Context

According to conservative estimates, at least 300 million[133] of India's 1.25 billion people do not have access to electricity. The problem is aggravated by the fact that, even for those who do have power, approximately 26 percent get only irregular access, sometimes as little as four hours a day. In 2015, the World Energy Outlook[134], considered the world's most authoritative source of energy market analysis, projected that the country would require 110 billion USD a year to meet its energy requirements.

Prime Minister Narendra Modi, elected in 2015, included universal access to electricity as one of his top priorities. The government has devoted considerable resources to a rural electrification program[135] that aims to electrify 121,225 un-electrified villages, improve power supply to 592,979 partially electrified villages, and provide free electricity to all rural households. As of June 30, 2016, it is estimated that between 50 and 80 percent of these targets have been achieved.

Nonetheless, the quality of electricity service provision remains poor, as emblematized by India's infamous 2012 blackout[136], in which 680 million people were affected. The root causes of the problem are manifold. Distribution on India's antiquated and poorly connected grid is one of the main issues; by some estimates, up to 30 percent of the nation's electricity is lost in grid inefficiencies. But the problem isn't only about distribution. The nation simply doesn't generate enough power. According to a 2015 report from the Institute

---

133 Martin, "India's Energy Crisis", MIT Technology Review, 2015, https://www.technologyreview. com/s/542091/indias-energy-crisis/.

134 "World Energy Outlook 2015 Factsheet", International Energy Agency, 2015.

135 "Rural Electrification: Status of Rural Electrification (RE) under DDUGY, Ministry of Power, Government of India, http://powermin.nic.in/content/rural-electrification.

136 "India's Power Network Breaks Down", The Wall Street Journal", 2012, https://www.wsj.com/articles/ SB10000872396390444405804577560413178678898.

for Policy Research[137], an independent policy research institute, the nation's power deficit stands at 3.6 percent. Even this figure probably underestimates the problem, given that energy statistics calculate demand only on the basis of existing connected consumers, meaning that such power deficit figures fail to take into account the millions who do not have power at all.

One of the biggest, though perhaps least acknowledged, problems concerns the *quality* of India's power supply. Power Quality[138] encompasses voltage variations (sags and swells), voltage reductions, power interruptions, voltage surges and harmonic distortions in the supply. Simply put, poor power quality refers to interruptions in power supply (which might last from a few minutes to a few days) or dangerous spikes in supply that could damage household electronic devices.

Such quality problems are widespread in India and they have major implications for domestic as well as industrial consumers. While it is difficult to quantify the consequences, one study conducted in 2009[139] suggested that businesses had to invest 15.5 billion USD in back-up power generation facilities to avoid the various adverse impacts[140] of poor power quality. These adverse effects include frozen computer screens, data loss, flickering lights and equipment damage, among other issues.

Addressing power quality issues represents a considerable challenge—in some ways, more so than addressing the problem of non-existent supply. To address the issue, real-time data is required, and such data is hard to come by. Regulators, electricity producers and consumers need as much information as possible on when electricity is likely to be cut or spike, and on what factors typically trigger voltage fluctuation. Data that can help to predict power fluctuations and provide forewarnings on voltage dips or spikes are also extremely important.

To make progress toward meaningfully addressing the many current problems in the Indian energy sector, a far more sophisticated data setup is needed. According to a recent study[141], there are different regulations on power quality in India, issued by the Central Electricity Authority (CEA) and also by

---

137 "Vital Stats: Overview of issues in the power sector in India", PRS Legislative Research, 2015, http://www.prsindia.org/administrator/uploads/general/1449060077_Vital%20Stats%20-%20power%20sector.pdf.

138 "Power Quality- What is it?", HSB.com, https://www.hsb.com/TheLocomotive/PowerQualityIsImportantHereisWhatYouCanDo.aspx.

139 Wärtsilä, *The Real Cost of Power*, Wärtsilä, 2009, http://www.wartsila.com/docs/default-source/Power-Plants-documents/downloads/White-papers/asia-australia-middle-east/The-Real-Cost-of-Power.pdf?sfvrsn=2.

140 "Impact of Power Quality on Indian Industries", Asia Power Quality Initiative, http://apqi.org/download/delhi/01-dr-bhuvaneswari.pdf.

141 "White Paper: Power Quality Regulations in India", Forum of Regulators (FOR), India, 2015, http://www.forumofregulators.gov.in/Data/Achievements/apqi.pdf.

the State Electricity Regulatory Commissions. There exist several shortcomings and variations in these regulations, notably when it comes to enforcement, but also in the way data is handled or treated. For example, voltage variation limits[142] for some states is 10 percent but for others it is 12.5 percent. Across states, there exists no reliable voltage monitoring program to provide power quality data. The only way to report low voltages or power outages is to call the local power company and lodge a complaint—a time consuming, manual process, which in any case is unlikely to have any meaningful impact.

Such shortcomings affect policymakers and those who seek to improve power quality. Consumers are also directly affected by a lack of data, for example in lodging complaints against distribution companies regarding problems in power supply. Without data, they have no evidence to back their claims. While there do exist clear standards regarding acceptable variations in supply parameters, defined[143] by the Institute of Electrical and Electronic Engineers (IEEE), citizens or even regulators often have no reliable data to show that those standards are not being adhered to.

Open Data in India

The Government of India approved the National Data Sharing and Accessibility Policy (NDSAP) in early 2012. This policy can be considered the first enabling regulation regarding the proactive disclosure of government data and extends the mandate of the Right to Information Act (RTIA). The act established policies and procedures in the publication of government datasets from different agencies in the central government through a single national portal.

The national open data platform[144] was launched in the same year. Since then, the portal has become the main repository of government data sets, covering 102 departments and involving at least 111 chief information officers. To date, the portal houses 44,174 resources in 4,043 catalogs covering essential sectors, such as health, environment, education, agriculture, commerce, mining, legislation, labor, power and energy, tourism, among others. However, the 2015 Open Data Barometer[145] has shown that despite the increasing number of data sets, there is little evidence of impact on government's accountability, effectiveness, and efficiency and in environmental stability or social inclusion.

---

142 Voltage variation limit, simply put, is the maximum allowable value for voltage value to fluctuate.

143 "IEEE Std 1159-2009- IEEE Recommended Practice for Monitoring Electric Power Quality", IEEE, 2009, http://ieeexplore.ieee.org/document/5154067/.

144 "Open Government Data Platform India", https://data.gov.in.

145 "Open Data Barometer", 2015, http://opendatabarometer.org/data-explorer/?_year=2015&indicator=ODB.

The Open Data Index places India at 55 percent open and ranked the country at number 15 in its 2015 edition.[146]

The power and energy sector database in the national portal consists of at least 137 data catalogs, 47 of which are dedicated to electricity and power. The others include information on areas like the functioning of thermal power stations, efforts to expand the use of renewable energy and the supply of and demand for natural gas. None of the datasets includes information on power quality; they are largely focused on power generation. The data catalogs are also difficult to navigate, as several of the datasets are structured by state and are not linked in any way that would permit a national or otherwise aggregate analysis.

KEY ACTORS

Key Data Providers

Ministry of Power, Government of India

The Ministry of Power of the Government of India governs the three major pillars of the country's power sector: generation, transmission, and distribution. On policy and regulation, at least two agencies have a mandate: the Central Electricity Authority (CEA), in charge of overall power development in the country; and the Central Electricity Regulatory Commission[147] (CERC), in charge of tariffs, inter-state transmission, grid standards, and adjudication of power-related disputes. CERC is also mandated to ensure that stakeholders have access to information related to electricity service provision. These agencies collect various datasets related to their mandate.

Generation, Transmission, and Distribution Companies (GTDs)

Power generation in India is divided into three sectors: central, state, and private. As of June 30, 2016[148], the private sector accounts for at least 41.45 percent of installed capacity, with the central and state sectors generating 22.15 percent and 33.59 percent, respectively.

The PowerGrid Corporation of India[149] is responsible for the inter-state transmission of electricity and the development of the national grid. It is the country's Central Transmission Utility (CTU) responsible for transmitting power of central generating utilities and interstate independent power producers. State Transmission Utilities (STUs) are responsible for wheeling power from state generating companies and

---

146 "India," Global Open Data Index, Open Knowledge International, http://index.okfn.org/place/india/.

147 Central Electricity Regulatory Commission, Government of India, http://opendatabarometer.org/data-explorer/?_year=2015&indicator=ODB.

148 "Power Sector at a glance- All India", Ministry of Power, Government of India, http://powermin.nic.in/content/power-sector-glance-all-india.

149 https://www.powergridindia.com/.

state-level independent power producers. The power grid plays an important role in establishing new transmission systems as well as strengthening existing transmission systems at the central level.

Power distribution is the final and the most important link to the consumer in the electricity value chain. Unfortunately, power distribution is highly inefficient, with an average of 20 percent distribution loss on an annual basis. Distribution at the state level is done either by state companies or private firms (averaging a slightly better 13 percent distribution loss).[150] The efficiency of distribution differs from one state to the other.

Power distribution companies hold vast amounts of data, covering generation, transmission, and distribution. The information contained is quite granular, down to household-level consumption data. Data held by the Ministry of Power, in the Central government, is collated from submissions made by these state-level companies.

Key Data Users and Intermediaries

Prayas Energy Group

Prayas Energy Group is part of Prayas, a non-governmental organization based in Pune, India, that protects and promotes the public interest—more particularly of disadvantaged sectors of the society.[151] It has four working groups: energy, health, resources and livelihoods, and learning and parenthood. The energy group has been one of the strongest and longest-acting advocates for better power service delivery in India, especially among the poor.

Prayas Energy Group is a key user of electricity data for its work. However, because of the lack of official government data devoted to power quality (open or otherwise), Prayas launched the Electricity Supply Monitoring Initiative (ESMI), thus becoming a provider of data as well.

The Energy Resources Institute (TERI)

Based in New Delhi, TERI is one of the leading energy think-tanks in India. It focuses its research on clean energy, water management, pollution management, sustainable agriculture, and climate resilience. TERI's projects in the energy sector includes research studies on renewable energy—including biomass, wind, solar, and hydro power—to explore options for India in the energy sector. Over the past few years, TERI has conducted several analysis papers on the state of power generation in India.

Private Companies and Research Groups

Data on electricity in India is widely used by different private companies and consulting firms to predict future scenarios, influence investing opportunities and inform power

---

150 Lori Aniti, "India Aims to Reduce High Electricity Transmission and Distribution System Losses," *Today in Energy*, October 22, 2015, http://www.eia.gov/todayinenergy/detail.php?id=23452.

151 See the Prayas website, http://www.prayaspune.org/peg/index.php.

stakeholders of opportunities and challenges. McKinsey & Company, KPMG, and AT Kearney, for example, regularly use power sector data for their work in the country.

Key Beneficiaries

Consumer Watch Groups or Organizations

Consumer organizations are generally advocacy groups that promote consumer protection from different types of corporate abuse. In India, there are several consumer groups that also work in the energy sector, such as New Delhi's Consumer VOICE, Chennai's Citizen Consumer and Civic Action Group, Kolkata's Federation of Consumer Association, among others. ESMI was designed partly with these groups in mind; they were seen as key users that could help strengthen advocacy for power quality monitoring at local levels by using existing consumer grievance redressal channels.

State regulators

State-level regulatory commissions perform the same functions as the CERC, but they focus on individual states. India has 29 states and seven union territories. These are managed by 27 state-level electricity regulators, and two joint commissions (one of which covers the union territories and the other two states). State regulators can use power quality data to monitor power delivery and enforce standards of quality.

Project Description

Initiation of the Open Data Activity

In 2007, the Prayas Energy Group (PEG), an Indian NGO, launched the Electricity Supply Monitoring Initiative (ESMI)[152] to collect real-time power quality information by installing Electricity Supply Monitors (ESM) in various locations in the city of Pune, India. The initiative was part of an ongoing effort by consumer groups and regulators in the Indian state of Maharashtra to monitor power quality after numerous complaints about frequent interruptions and power outages. Having been involved in evidence-based advocacy in the Indian power sector since the early 1990s, Prayas was aware of these issues and created the ESM initiative in line with its "proactive approach to point out gross inefficiencies"[153] and to bring greater transparency and citizen participation into the power sector. The organization has also carried out numerous regulatory and policy interventions in areas such as capacity

---

152 See the ESMI website, http://www.watchyourpower.org/.

153 "Electricity Generation and Supply", Research Areas, Prayas Energy Group, http://www.prayaspune.org/peg/research-areas/electricity-generation-supply.html.

addition, capital expenditure in electricity transmission and distribution, and service delivery to un-electrified consumers.

Initially, there was some skepticism regarding the viability of a technology-based solution for monitoring electricity supply. Concerns included the possibility of mobile network failures (the ESMs transmitted information via cellular networks), the difficulty of finding field volunteers to host the monitoring devices, and the challenges of developing a low-cost monitoring module. In addition, some questions were posed about the need for such a system in a rapidly developing environment of intelligent hardware (e.g., smart meters) and software tools (e.g., Supervisory Control and Data Acquisition, or SCADA, systems, which provide industrial monitoring and control mechanisms for complicated processes like energy distribution).

Over time, however, it became apparent to all stakeholders that there was indeed a pressing need for a transparent and automated data collection system. As of May 2016, ESMI covered 200 locations in 18 states, with 1.5 million hours of power quality[154] monitoring data available.[155] It has also become apparent that the project can play a powerful developmental role, in particular by helping to address certain inequalities in power distribution and consumption. As Shweta Kulkarni, a Research Associate at Prayas and one of those chairing the ESM project, put it:

Most energy sector policies focus on financial viability and economic growth while good governance and equity remain neglected. This often leads to poor supply quality, especially in marginalized neighborhoods. One of the important avenues to change this situation is to improve the transparency and accountability in the sector by creating a publicly-accessible database on supply quality information to show the variations in supply quality between urban and rural areas, different states, distribution companies and areas of economic importance.[156]

Funding

ESMI was one of six finalists in the 2013 Google Social Impact Challenge awards. Each finalist was awarded ₹15 million (roughly $225,000) in seed funding. With the funding, Prayas was able to install power quality monitors

---

154 "Using technology for evidence based feedback to ensure quality electricity access", Electricity Supply Monitoring Initiative (ESMI), *Prayas Energy Group*, https://d2oc0ihd6a5bt.cloudfront.net/wp-content/uploads/sites/837/2016/04/2-Shantanu-Dixit.pdf.

155 Electricity Supply Monitoring Initiative, "Using Technology for Evidence-based Feedback to Ensure Quality Electricity Access," Presentation at ACEF, June 2016, https://d2oc0ihd6a5bt.cloudfront.net/wp-content/uploads/sites/837/2016/04/2-Shantanu-Dixit.pdf.

156 Interview with Shweta Kulkarni, Research Associate, Prayas Energy Group- Pune.

in 60 locations across eight states, including in at least five megacities.[157] That initial coverage has expanded rapidly in the years following.

Demand and Supply of Data Type(s) and Sources

ESMI has made it clear that good power quality management is impossible without real-time data. This is true not only for consumers, who suffer the most direct impact of poor power quality, but also for electricity producers and distributors, and even for regulators. For producers and distributors, real-time power quality data is important in identifying problems in production, transmission and distribution. Such data helps them identify and potentially address shortcomings in their own processes and management. In addition, regulators can use data to hold private companies to account, potentially assessing fines or other penalties for under-performers; overall, data helps regulators ensure the quality of electricity distribution across the country.

The institutional arrangements, in this case, are complex. Demanding accountability regarding power quality in many ways creates an endless cycle of buck-passing from one stakeholder to the other. While grievance and redress mechanisms are enshrined in India's Electricity Act[158], through a legalistic and layered procedural mechanism, use and impact of this process is hardly visible, and normally ends in frustration and subsequently, consumer apathy. A few organizations, however, focus time and resources into research and advocacy on power issues, among them The Energy and Resources Institute[159], monitoring groups like Andra Pradesh's People's Monitoring Group on Electricity Regulation, and Prayas.

It is important to note that some useful open energy data did exist before the advent of the ESMI project. For example, the Ministry of Power[160] and the Central Electricity Authority[161] (CEA) have released several data sets on the national open data portal (data.gov.in). These are available for free download. However, the bulk of this data relates to power generation, supply and demand, and tariff information. For example, the government publishes the number of electrified villages and other information pertaining to its monthly rural electrification mission on a monthly basis. As of late 2016, there is virtually no

---

157 Prayas (Energy Group), "Electricity Supply Monitoring Initiative (ESMI)," March 2015, http://www.prayaspune.org/peg/publications/item/61-electricity-supply-monitoring-initiative.html.

158 The Electricity Act, 2003, http://www.cercind.gov.in/Act-with-amendment.pdf.

159 The Energy and Resources Institute (TERI), http://www.teriin.org/about-teri.

160 Ministry of Power datasets, data.gov.in, https://data.gov.in/ministrydepartment/ministry-power.

161 Central Electricity Authority datasets, data.gov.in, https://data.gov.in/ministrydepartment/central-electricity-authority.

data available to gauge the quality of power—hence the vital importance of the data being generated by ESMI.

Open Data Use

All the data being used for this project are generated by the ESMs installed by Prayas. ESMs are "smart, connected energy meters" that can accurately measure voltage fluctuations as low as 90V and as high as 320V. The devices use very little power; they simply need to be plugged into a socket and immediately start measuring and transmitting voltage data over 2G/3G networks using an internal SIM card. Currently, three Indian companies supply Prayas with ESMs, each of which also offers a one-year maintenance contract: Syslabs Automation Pvt. Ltd., HelioKraft Technologies Pvt. Ltd, and Altizon Systems.

The data generated by the ESMs is made available for free at a website set up by Prayas[162]. The data is presented in three different forms: (1) minute-by-minute voltage information of all monitored areas; (2) reports that analyze voltage data for each location; and (3) more general analysis of the aggregated data that considers the voltage situation at a regional as well as the national levels. The analysis is often presented in the form of reports, which typically include information about the number and duration of power disruptions (including fluctuating voltages and frequency of supply). A sample report for March 2016 is shown in Figure 1.

Currently, data cannot be downloaded from the portal in bulk, and instead must be downloaded for a single location at a time. Users can view data for a given 31-day period on the website itself, but data for up to 100 days can be downloaded and viewed offline. Downloading of multiple locations or for longer periods is only possible through a user-request made directly to Prayas. Prayas assesses the request and can choose to grant a one-time username and password to access bulk data. Overall, the system requires very little technical knowledge, and the easy availability of data on a digital platform adds a new, automated level of transparency to the industry.

---

162 http://watchyourpower.org.

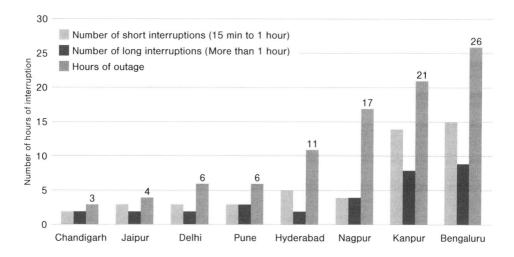

Figure 2. ESMI Sample Analysis of Power Quality

Impact

At the project's inception, Prayas envisioned that several different types of users would be able to use the data and make a positive impact on the power situation in India. Consumer rights groups would be able to implement evidence-based advocacy on power quality. Government regulatory agencies at the country and state levels would be able to use the data to monitor performance of power generation, distribution, and transmission companies, and to identify new policy and legal interventions to improve the power situation. Prayas also expected researchers to use the data to find new mechanisms to improve power quality across the different states, as well as to identify alternative sources and channels for better power service delivery.

While direct evidence of impact is often hard to capture, it is clear that many of these envisioned uses have, to a greater or lesser extent, in fact been borne out. An internal assessment conducted by Shweta Kulkarni, the person within Prayas responsible for the program, claims that ESMI has had an impact in bolstering, consumer satisfaction, improving power quality improvement, and enabling evidence-based advocacy.

However, perhaps no surprise due to the newness of the project and the many stakeholders needed to make meaningful progress action, at this stage we do not yet have documented cases that show the power quality has actually improved as a result of the advocacy mentioned above using ESMI data (outcome-level results) or improved satisfaction of consumers because of improved service (impact level results).

As Dr. Pendse puts it:

"The question is, in the 200 houses that it (ESMs) has been placed in, has the power quality improved? And if it hasn't then at least has someone been made accountable using this evidence? The whole idea is that the use of data should lead to improvement. Otherwise, it isn't working."

Nonetheless, in our assessment of the evidence, through desk research and interviews with key stakeholders, we do identify the following three main areas of impact.

Awareness Raising

ESMI has been used by various individuals and organizations to raise awareness on the serious power quality problem faced by India. One of the most important constituencies for the data are journalists who write on power supply conditions.[163] Several of these journalists have raised the profile of issues related to power quality in India, which are often eclipsed in public discussions by the topic of electricity access.

In addition, Prayas was able to present its project and findings to the CERC's meeting of regulators, also raising their awareness of power quality issues.[164] As a result, some state-level energy regulatory commissions volunteered to use ESMI to monitor the performance levels of utility companies that fell under their jurisdiction. We discuss this issue further below.

Effectiveness of Power Quality Advocacy

There is some clear evidence that data from ESMI has been effective in enhancing the efforts of those advocating for greater power quality. For example, in the Akola Industrial Area, in the state of Maharashtra, data recorded by an ESMI device was presented by a consumer to the local officials of the distribution company. This data proved that the Akola Industrial Area had experienced unplanned interruptions and other power quality problems which caused loss and damage to industrial products and equipment. The local distribution company officials were thus to acknowledge the problem, and to plot out some remedial actions.

---

163 See for example, Manasi Mathkar, "Making Power Supply Data a Tool for Progress," *India Together*, May 6, 2015, http://indiatogether.org/a-easy-to-use-interface-to-view-ones-power-supply-and-consumption-information-via-a-simple-electricity-supply-monitor-esm-environment.

164 "Minutes of the Forty-eighth Meeting of Forum of Regulators (FOR) Held at New Delhi," June 10–11, 2015, http://www.forumofregulators.gov.in/Data/Meetings/Minutes/48.pdf.

The ESM reports available on watchyourpower.org, also helped identify a number of lapses in the system including non-adherence to protocols for load shedding[165] and exposing loopholes in claims of zero power deficit by the government.[166] There has been little evidence that these insights have led to any concrete actions, however. A common challenge across this series of case studies is a lack of institutional responsiveness to act upon insights generated through such data analyses.

Re-emphasizing Power Quality Monitoring at the Regulatory Level

As mentioned, ESMI has helped to raise awareness of power quality problems. While journalists and advocacy groups have been among the most important target groups, ESMI and its data have also succeeded in raising awareness among regulators and more generally putting the issue of power quality back on the regulatory table.

ESMI has been presented at several regulatory meetings, including the Forum of Regulators, the Delhi Electricity Regulatory Commission, and the Joint Electricity Regulatory Commission—each of which plays a different but important role in the national and state-level regulatory framework. In addition, ESMI data has also been presented to private distribution companies and researchers at various forums and seminars. ESMI has also received support from the Joint Electricity Regulatory Commission to install ESMs in the Union Territory of Chandigarh and State of Goa.[167] As of late 2016, Prayas is in dialogue with another regulatory commission and distribution utility which agrees to support deployment of ESMI in their areas of operation.

Risks

As evidenced by the example of ESMI and various other case studies included in this series, open data holds tremendous potential for positive transformation. But as we also see throughout this series, open data also poses certain risks. It is important to understand these risks in order to ensure that open data

---

165 Suggestions and Objections from Prayas regarding the Maharashtra State Electricity Distribution Company Limited's Petition for Multi Year Tariff for FY 2013–14 to FY 201516).

166 Debjoy Sengupta, "Contrary to Government's Claims, Small Towns, Rural Areas Still Suffer from Power Outages," *Economic Times: Energy World*, July 26, 2016, http://energy.economictimes.indiatimes.com/news/power/contrary-to-governments-claims-small-towns-rural-areas-still-suffer-from-power-outages/53393538.

167 "PUNJAB STATE ELECTRICITY REGULATORY COMMISSION SCO NO. 220–221, SECTOR 34-A, CHANDIGARH," Order in Petition No.46 of 2013, http://www.pserc.nic.in/pages/Order%20in%20Petition%20No.46%20of%202013.pdf.

projects are implemented in as safe a manner and in a way that maximizes the potential upside and limits the downside.

The problem of power quality is multifaceted. While power quality data at the consumer level is useful to emphasize a consumer's complaint, as Dr. Priya Jadhav, Associate Professor at the Indian Institute of Technology-Bombay points out, utility companies are often aware that the power they are supplying is low voltage. Data such as ESMI only re-emphasizes what is already known. But because of the poor financial situation that the distribution companies are in, they are in no position to fix the underlying issues that result in poor quality. While identifying the areas where poor quality is persistent is a useful piece of the puzzle, the real solution may lie in understanding why distribution companies suffer losses (electrical as well as financial) and rely repeatedly on government bail-out packages. To cut their losses, distribution companies often do not purchase power from the power generation companies, which explains why many places in power-surplus India suffer so many power outages.

So, the risks of ESMI not succeeding lies at its very strength—that of providing power quality data. Given that there is already a sophisticated way of monitoring power quality and providing the results of this monitoring to the public, the expectation that this will be able to improve power quality supply may not necessarily happen as users will not use the data and advocate for power reform, or that generation, transmission, and distribution companies will not be made to act on the transgressions that the companies committed. Without power supply improvement, ESMI will just become, sadly, a resource useful for researchers and journalists with no real difference to power consumers, especially those at the base of the triangle.

Lessons Learned

The Prayas initiative has brought to the fore why power quality monitoring is important, and it has re-emphasized a problem that has long been ignored by power sector stakeholders. It is now clear that, properly scaled, ESMI has the potential to identify under-performing power companies and regulators, impose a level of accountability in India's power sector, and, most importantly, contribute to better power quality.

This section considers some key lessons learned from the project—lessons that are potentially applicable to other open data projects, in other parts of the world. We split our analysis into a discussion of Enablers (positive lessons) and Barriers (negative lessons); both are equally important to better understanding the impact and implications of a project like ESMI.

Enablers

High level vision

The India Smart Grid Task Force,[168] which was set up in 2011, released a "Vision and Roadmap" document in 2013,[169] recognizing that improving reliability and quality of power to consumers was one of the key drivers of the smart grid.[170] Real-time monitoring, automated outage management, and faster restoration are some of the key targets of the Smart Grids in order to improve overall power supply quality across the country. While this was not achieved, ESMI took hold at a time when political and public will to leverage technology to improve power supply was at a peak. Drivers of the effort at Prayas point to this growing priority among the public and institutional stakeholders helped to clear the way for the ESMI initiative. This background also points to the ways in which open data can be used to evaluate performance, but a set of indicators or expressed expectations are important for guiding efforts and evaluating success.

Collaboration between civil society and the private sector

The success of ESMI is in large part attributable to the vision, commitment and hard work of Prayas. It was Prayas' prior work in the field of electricity that led the organization to look for new ways of monitoring power supply quality and enforcing accountability. The existence of a civil society champion such as this one, with experience and contacts in the field, cannot be under-estimated.

Prayas' vision was critical. But its ability to scale ESMI to more than 200 ESM locations was boosted by an external grant from Google. In addition, the existence of private companies able to manufacture the ESMs at low cost, and with a commitment to service the monitors, also helped ensure the success of the project. Overall, it is clear that ESMI was the beneficiary of an existing (if under-exploited) ecosystem of both private sector companies and civil society organizations. This inter-sectoral collaboration offers a powerful model for other similar projects around the world.

---

168 "India Smart Grid Forum Website Launched", Press Information Bureau, Ministry of Power, Government of India, http://pib.nic.in/newsite/PrintRelease.aspx?relid=71397.

169 "Vision Roadmap" National Smart Grid Mission, Ministry of Power, Government of India, http://www.nsgm.gov.in/upload/files/India-Smart-Grid-Vision-and-Roadmap_DSG.pdf.

170 India Smart Grid Forum, *Smart Grid Vision and Roadmap for India*, August 12, 2013, GOI, Ministry of Power, http://www.nsgm.gov.in/upload/files/India-Smart-Grid-Vision-and-Roadmap_DSG.pdf.

Barriers

ESMI has seen some success, but it has not managed to really turn the tide on power quality issues in India. Its lack of wider impact also offers lessons, specifically:

Lack of use of ESMI data from key power stakeholders

Despite enthusiasm among existing users, ESMI's data has not really found a critical mass of users that could help scale the project and hold power sector stakeholders accountable. In particular, while journalists and advocacy groups have shown interest in the data, there has not been equal interest shown by consumers—citizens or corporates. This can be attributed to several factors, like the need for more awareness building efforts. The apathy may also have something do with a general sense of hopelessness and disempowerment among consumers; given the scale and long-standing nature of India's power problems, consumers may not hold out much hope for a solution such as ESMI's. Addressing such shortcomings may require greater coordination with intermediaries to spread awareness and confidence, as well as a concerted effort to introduce consumers to the very real potential of open data—both within the electricity sector in particular, but also more generally.

Lukewarm reception from state regulators

While Prayas has been relatively successful in presenting ESMI to power regulators, it is not clear that the willingness of regulators to listen and learn about the project is accompanied by the actual will to use it. Indeed, to date, only one state regulatory agency has actually developed a concrete plan to implement ESMI. This lack of regulatory will (if not interest) suggests that the inherent value of a project may not be enough to get it adopted and that Prayas needs to find new forms of leverage on regulators—e.g., through enhanced public or political pressure.

Lack of capacity on GTD companies to solve power quality problems

As earlier stated, power quality is a problem with a myriad of causes. ESMI data is only able to systematize the provision of data on already-known symptoms of the problem. But the deeper causes—why power companies are not able to supply quality power and why regulators are not able to provide penalties as well as incentives—remain unaddressed, and are unlikely to be solved through this type of initiative, regardless of the level of uptake.

93

Looking Forward

For Prayas, the existing 200 monitors deployed in ESMI represent just a starting point. The organization is also in the process of expanding the reach of ESMI through partnerships with the public sector and other stakeholders interested in power supply quality monitoring.

Sustainability

Prayas believes that the sustainability of ESMI will depend in large part on collaboration and partnerships. Initially, Prayas faced significant challenges in developing its technical solution for remote monitoring of supply quality, owing to lack of in-house expertise in hardware and software development. But it initiated a dialogue with other stakeholders and shared information on the type of technology that it wants to develop to the tech community who are also willing to contribute to and support their goal. In this case, India-wide implementation is only possible if state regulators become convinced of ESMI's value. Thus, Prayas is very actively reaching out to regulators and presenting in the regular regulators' forum so that more support in scaling up and adoption can be gathered.

Replicability

India's ESMI has generated considerable global interest. In fact, Prayas is now in discussions with different stakeholders to pilot ESMI in other countries. Discussion with stakeholders from Kenya, Tajikistan and Tanzania are currently ongoing. In addition, the first overseas pilot implementation is already happening in Indonesia, with the Institute for Essential Service Reform based in Jakarta as local partner.

Conclusion

The main goal of ESMI is to make available reliable data on the quality of electricity supply. Consumers, civil society organizations, researchers, regulatory commissions and other concerned actors can use this data to increase the accountability of electric utilities. The actual performance of companies can be compared to the standards of performance prescribed by regulatory commissions. In addition, utilities' capital expenditures on improvements in supply quality can be scrutinized to verify whether supply quality has actually improved as a result of the investments. The openness of the collected data

also enables multiple stakeholders to verify the government's many goals for rural electrification, notably whether villages receive their mandated six hours of daily supply. Overall, the data generated and opened by ESMI can create greater pressure on regulators and utilities to become more transparent, more accountable and more efficient. The project offers great social and developmental potential.

In order for ESMI to truly reach its potential, stakeholders need to know that the data exists and is accessible. This remains a challenge, and a work in progress. For all its initially impressive results, scaling up ESMI will require a concerted effort to raise awareness about the possibilities offered by open data among average citizens, corporate consumers, and government regulators. In addition, ESMI could benefit from greater political support and public will to ensure that regulators actually use its data and take advantage of the many benefits it does potentially offer. The opportunity—for India's electricity sector, and more generally for its social and economic development is real; the coming years will tell whether Prayas and other stakeholders can seize that opportunity.

Open Development Cambodia
Opening information on development efforts

Michael P. Canares, Andrew Young and Stefaan Verhulst

Summary

Cambodia has shown impressive improvements in political, economic, and social conditions over the last 10 years. The country has managed to end long years of civil war, grow the economy by at least 7 percent annually, and improve health and education outcomes, especially for children. Despite this, there are underlying weaknesses in Cambodia's political institutions that constrain its economic, social, and cultural development. These include a growing opacity in decision-making and a lack of information regarding different development efforts sweeping across the country. Open Development Cambodia (ODC) was born out of a desire to address these issues. Its goal is to provide "access to current and historical information about Cambodia's development trends in an online 'open data' platform compiling freely available data from a wide range of public sources." Launched in 2011, ODC's online portal (https://opendevelopmentcambodia.net/data/) has been instrumental in providing information to different users from government, civil society, media, and the public sector.

Context and Background

Problem Focus/Country Context

Cambodia has shown impressive improvements in political, economic, and social conditions over the last 10 years. The country has managed to end

long years of civil war, grow the economy by at least 7 percent annually, and improve health and education outcomes, especially for children. Despite this, there are underlying weaknesses in Cambodia's political institutions that constrain its economic, social, and cultural development. Entrenched patterns of political patronage limit governance reforms; the government's intent to be more transparent is overshadowed by a growing opacity in decision-making in governmental transactions; civil society's ability to question and hold government officials accountable remains constricted; and corruption is still prevalent.

Many of these issues could be addressed by increased public access to governmental information. However, Cambodia does not have a freedom of information law, and many legal provisions restrict information disclosure. For example, in the exploration of natural resources, where corruption is reported to be rampant, a legal provision treats applications, reports, plans and notices as confidential. In addition, civil society organizations have questioned the government's failure to disclose details about the national budget for outside scrutiny.[171] In general, there is limited availability of governance information in Cambodia. Even when information is available, it is stored in formats that prohibit easy sharing and re-use. In addition, the little information that does exist online is disorganized, not linked, and hard to locate.

Open Data in Cambodia

In 2015, Open Knowledge Index rated Cambodia as 12 percent open[172]—a rating that means there is very little data available online and in open format. Key critical datasets such as company registers, land ownership, national maps, government spending, national statistics, and weather forecasts are not available online.

To date, there exists no central government repository for government information in the country, and the government does not implement any comprehensive open data initiative. For example, there exists no national directive to disclose government data on websites (though a few agencies publish some datasets on their own initiative). Some encouraging signs are evident in the birth of a few civil society organizations now advocating for open data in the country. Cambodia is one of many countries studied as part of this series where civil society and international organizations stepped up to drive the open data movement as a result of governmental failure to provide

---

171 Erin Handley and Bun Sengkong, "Civil Society, Opposition Criticise Budget's Opacity," *Phnom Penh Post*, November 4, 2016, http://www.phnompenhpost.com/national/civil-society-opposition-criticise-budgets-opacity.

172 Open Knowledge, "Global Open Data Index: Cambodia," http://index.okfn.org/place/cambodia/.

easy access to important datasets. Some of the increasingly active civil society actors in Cambodia include Open Data Cambodia (ODC), the founder of the project under study here, and discussed further below; Open Knowledge, a global open data non-profit organization; the local offices of the World Bank; and a few transparency organizations and international non-governmental organizations advocating for more inclusive information disclosure practices.

KEY ACTORS

Key Data Providers

ODC gathers data from at least five major sources—government, non-governmental, private sector, academics, and from internal local newsrooms and major Cambodian newspapers. ODC gathers data from these various sources (e.g. from websites or printed documents), and converts them into open formats to be published in the ODC portal.

Key Data Users and Intermediaries

ODC acts as an aggregator of the different data and information obtained from these various sources. Its portal has a broad range of users, with the largest category coming from the academic community and non-governmental organizations. Professors and students, for example, cite ODC's database in their research papers, journal articles, and books. Some international non-governmental organizations use map layers and other related geo-referenced documents to analyze development projects. In addition, members of the media also use the data to analyze development trends, projects and patterns.

Intended Beneficiaries

ODC's intended beneficiaries, besides the researchers and academics who directly use the data, can be grouped into four categories. First, government agencies or policy makers who may use the data analyzed by media or NGOs in crafting their policies or in conducting development planning. Second, the business sector, which benefits from looking at maps and geo-referenced data on natural assets and resources, as well as demographic data that may be useful in business decision-making. Third, civil society and community-based organizations use the datasets on the portal for their for development work or to advocate for greater transparency. Finally, average citizens who may be able to access the data from ODC or from the outputs of intermediaries mentioned above.

Project Description

Initiation of the Open Data Activity

Open Development Cambodia (ODC) was born out of a need felt by local grassroots land and natural resource activists working in Cambodia. Terry Pernell, a long-time American resident in Cambodia who worked with different grassroots organizations, including the East West Management Institute (EWMI), a civil society organization seeking "to build accountable, capable and transparent institutions," found that getting access to useful data in Cambodia was often difficult if not impossible. Accessing government data, in particular, was a challenge, and meant going from one office to another, dealing with bureaucracy at each step.[173] As noted, Cambodia does not have a central repository of government data that one can physically visit or consult online.

ODC was developed with the goal of aggregating information about the country from different sources—not only government, but also international organizations, civil society groups, private sector, universities, academic institutions, and individual researchers who had been studying the country for decades. The vision was to create a central repository, to be hosted online, that would consist of raw data, independently collected, edited, and aggregated. The group that would manage it needed to be independent and without political bias—its main role would be to provide information and let those who seek data and information use it for their own purposes. The site was officially launched in August 2011. After almost four years of being implemented as a project of EWMI, it became registered as a non-governmental organization in August 2015.[174]

The platform now houses data-driven information on three central topic areas: Environment and Land (e.g., disaster and emergency response and extractive industries); Economy (e.g., industry and labor) and People (e.g., aid and development and law and judiciary). As of early 2017, raw data is directly available for download on laws, policies and agreements, while other topics feature detailed Wikipedia-like write-ups aggregating a diversity primary datasets, charts and graphs, policies and other relevant information. ODC also offers a number of interactive maps that allow users to deploy and combine layers built from, for example, agriculture, demographic and infrastructure data. It also provides a mapping toolkit and guide using the Harvard WorldMap interface.

---

173 Kyle James, "Cambodia sets pace with open data," *DW Akademie*, December 20, 2013, http://onmedia. dw-akademie.com/english/?p=16857.

174 Interview with Thy Try, Executive Director, Open Development Cambodia, and Penhleak Chan, Regional Network and Partnership Support Manager of EWMI, November 17, 2016.

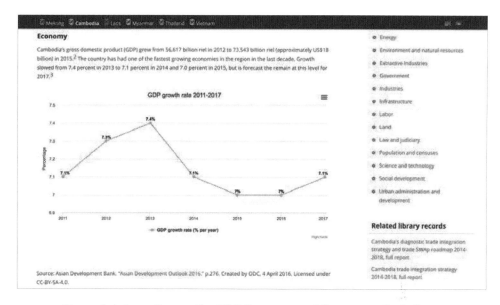

Figure 1. Information on the ODC Economy and Commerce Topic Page

Funding

Initiated by EWMI in 2011 as a part of its USAID-funded Program on Rights and Justice, ODC received its first grant from the Swedish Program for ICT in Developing Regions (SPIDER) in 2012. With a total budget of around 230,000 USD, SPIDER contributed slightly more than 55,000 USD "to develop the existing Proof of Concept site (http://ww.opendevelopmentcambodia.net) into a fully functional open data online platform that will facilitate a network of civil society actors to share, analyze, and publish their data in a coordinated, egalitarian, and secure way."[175] Since then, ODC has received funding support from other USAID-funded projects, American Jewish World Service, Open Society Foundation, and other funders.

Demand and Supply of Data Type(s) and Sources

ODC collects data based on what is already available in the "public domain." By public domain, ODC means data that are generally available for public access and not specifically prohibited by law to be shared widely. Its sources of data include (1) Royal Gazettes, (2) official websites of governmental institutions, (3) published reports from government, (4) Developers/Company websites, (5)

---

175 SPIDER, "Open Development Cambodia: Promoting transparency through open data," http://spidercenter.org/2.31936/project-overview/open-development-cambodia-promoting-transparency-through-open-data-1.149787.

information released to the Media (i.e. news and press releases), (6) published reports from NGOs, and (7) academic research reports and other reports from NGOs. ODC researchers collect the data, submit it to editors for review, and convert this into open formats for publication on its portal.

Open Data Use

While ODC draws information from a variety of sources, open government data is a key driver of the sites offerings. The interactive maps on the site, the raw datasets available for download and the information on topics like the quality of Cambodian governance, environmental policy and construction codes would not be possible without government data being made accessible.

Figure 2. ODC's Open Data Portal

Impact

ODC's mission is to "strengthen public knowledge and analysis of development issues to enable constructive dialogue between public, private, civil society, and international sectors to support development of effective policies and practices bearing on sustainable resource use."[176] The organization has been striving to achieve these goals now for some three years. Although always difficult to clearly measure impact, particularly for relatively young projects, our research

---

176 Interview with Thy Try, Executive Editor, Open Development Cambodia, and Penhleak Chan, Regional Network and Partnership Support Manager of EWMI, November 17, 2016.

indicates at least four ways in which ODC has taken early steps toward having a concrete effect on Cambodian society and development.

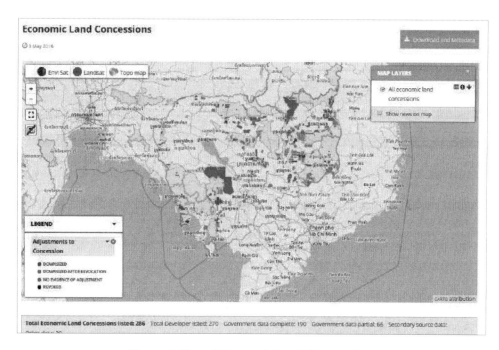

Figure 3. Map of Economic Land Concessions

Seeding Interest Cambodian Open Data

The ODC portal is gaining increasing attention from a number of different kinds of users. As of October 2016, it has an average of 70,000 pageviews per month. Since the launch of the portal, a total of 35,000 users per month, mostly from within Cambodia, have visited the site, with approximately 80 percent being unique visitors. The ODC team based in Phnom Penh has received numerous personal inquiries and interview appointments from journalists and researchers, and the portal has been increasingly quoted as a source in both local and international research publications and media reports.[177]

According to Thy Try, ODC's Executive Director,

"Quite often, maps attract the most attention from media and GIS persons while the database tracking the investment and concessions projects along with references is

---

177 Interview with Thy Try, Executive Director, Open Development Cambodia, and Penhleak Chan, Regional Network and Partnership Support Manager of EWMI, November 17, 2016.

usually used by advocates and workers from NGOs and community-based organization. In this sense, it seems that the tracking database on specific development projects is gradually helping the work of these organizations. However, this requires key persons of the communities to have a better understanding of the development trends and data/ data tools in order to use it with the most impact, either through their own direct work or through their knowledge sharing with their community members."[178]

Journalists from the outlets like *The Guardian*,[179] *Tech President*,[180] and the *New York Times*,[181] among others, have written about ODC's efforts and/or drawn upon the data and information it makes available. They also include agencies such as the United Nations, The Mekong River Commission, and the International Land Coalition. In addition, ODC says that government agencies have also used the site – perhaps not surprising given its focus on bringing together useful datasets from across sectors, not just data already held by the government.

Strengthening Issue Advocacy through Collaboration

ODC has played an important role in strengthening advocacy on issues surrounding open data, a role whose impact has been particularly evident in the way land is granted by the government. Before the emergence of ODC, civil society advocates that monitored the government's grant of land concessions collected their own data and did not coordinate with each other. This fragmentation resulted in inconsistencies in the data presented by these different actors, a weakening of advocacy messages, and a lack of attention from the concerned government agencies. ODC facilitated the process of data sharing, cleaned the data to get rid of inconsistencies, and provided the data on its secure, centralized platform.[182] With a unified basis and voice, coupled with international media coverage and pressure, the government postponed the grant of land concessions to the private sector and hastened the grant of social

---

178 Interview with Thy Try, Executive Director, Open Development Cambodia, November 24, 2016.

179 Naly Pilorge, Virak Yeng, Vuthy Eang, "Think of Cambodia before you add sugar to your coffee," *The Guardian*, July 12, 2013, https://www.theguardian.com/commentisfree/2013/jul/12/cambodia-sugar-eu-policy.

180 Faine Greenwood, "As the Internet Raises Civic Voices in Cambodia, a Struggle Brews Over Net Control," *Tech President*, March 27, 2013, http://techpresident.com/news/wegov/23659/internet-civic-voices-cambodia-struggle-net-control/.

181 Julia Wallace, "Development and Its Discontent," *The New York Times*, April 12, 2013, https://latitude.blogs.nytimes.com/2013/04/12/development-and-its-discontent/?_r=0.

182 Nicolas Mansfield, "Open Development Cambodia: How open data can promote land use transparency," *Devex*, September 20, 2013, https://www.devex.com/news/open-development-cambodia-how-open-data-can-promote-land-use-transparency-81848.

land concessions to the poor. While these results cannot be directly attributed to ODC, it is quite apparent that ODC contributed to the process.

Increasing Access to Important, Previously Inaccessible Data

In Cambodia, Environmental Impact Assessment (EIA) reports are not made publicly available. EIAs are required by law, but several agencies do not seem to place importance on the practice. ODC made available EIA reports on its portal and has made an analysis of currently available EIA data. The resultant increase in public awareness around the topic, particularly among civil society actors, has the potential to push the government to take further action, though there has not been clear evidence that they have done so at this point.

Additionally, natural resource data, including information related to agriculture—one of Cambodia's competitive advantages—is hard to come by. ODC had numerous requests in the past to get data on soil type published on its portal and was able to do so recently. This information was used by the private sector, more particularly by the Cambodian Rice Federation, to determine potential growth areas in crop production. Anecdotal evidence also shows that resource data at the ODC portal has been used by international organizations, such as the World Bank and ANZ.

Risks

Since its inception, ODC has faced numerous challenges, among them lack of support and even resistance from government agencies and certain private sector players. For example, when ODC published forest cover data in 2013, the Forestry Administration, the governmental body under the Ministry of Agriculture, Forestry, and Fisheries, refuted the ODC data that showed a significant decrease in forest cover—from 72 percent in 1973 to 46 percent in 2013—and alleged that the organization did not have a credible applied methodology on forest classification. Attempts to discredit ODC, such as this one, will likely happen again, especially when government is harmed by the narratives that arise from the analysis of sensitive data.

As ODC transitions to a registered civil society organization in Cambodia, it may face several challenges brought about by the adoption of new laws that could potentially impose restrictions on ODC's work. For example, the Law on Association and Non-Governmental Organizations requires all NGOs to report their activities to the government—resulting in additional workloads and restricting freedom of movement via surveillance. Also, the Sub-Decree on Publication of Maps and the use of Produced Maps introduces a new

requirement that any organization which produces maps must get a license from the government. Also, a draft law on Cyber Crime can potentially harm some of the activities of ODC. All of these represent commonly seen risks for an organization seeking to introduce greater transparency and work against vested interests. In a sense, the scale of the risks (and opposition) is also indication of the project's success or at least potential.

Lessons Learned

Several important lessons with wider applicability emerge from this particular case study. These can broadly be categorized by considering the key enablers of the project, as well as the most important barriers or challenges to its success.

Enablers

Trust of different actors in ODC's work and capacity

ODC's ability to tap into an existing ecosystem greatly accelerated its move from idea to implementation. The fact that ODC started as a project under EWMI, and with the support of several international donors, strengthened its reputation as an organization that has the capacity to deliver on its commitments—its vision and mission. The "independent" stance of ODC, presenting the data and factual information it aggregates without necessarily attaching itself to any political agenda or ideology, worked both on the part of government and other actors. In general, government stakeholders do not project animosity against ODC and even use its data, despite initial questions on data integrity. Advocacy groups also view ODC as an independent organization, and not necessarily a mechanism of government.

This increased trust from different actors also made possible ODC's ability to get grants to fund its work and operations.

Volunteerism of different actors in the open data space

Like any new technology that relies on the generosity not only of donors but also of volunteers, ODC benefitted from different individuals who participate in ODC's efforts on proactive disclosure without costs, and from organizations and universities which send interns to ODC to assist them in research and editing processes. ODC has a very lean team—nine people dabbling in work on research, editing, infographics, mapping, writing, finance, among others—and

in order to increase breadth and depth in its work, it has to advertise volunteer opportunities and take in as many volunteers as necessary.

Collaboration among different actors from within Cambodia

As earlier indicated, ODC relied on different data sources to be able to publish quality and comprehensive information in its portal. Non-governmental organizations, advocacy groups, researchers, universities, and government agencies shared data with ODC for it to clean, edit, and publish. Without the collaboration of these actors, data at the ODC portal would be lesser in scope than its current state, and probably less meaningful to the user.

Lack of information fuels the need for this collaboration. Currently, more and more people are interested in data on land, water, and forest governance and have been asking ODC to make these datasets accessible to the public.

ODC also participated in shorter-term collaborations with Columbia University's School of International and Public Affairs (SIPA) toward developing a greater understanding of international development efforts in Cambodia.[183] A partnership with Save Cambodia's Wildlife produced the 2014 Atlas of Cambodia, which provides detailed information and maps on the "changing spatial structures of Cambodia's geography as well as its economic and social development, especially natural resource and environment management"[184] – the elements found in the Atlas are downloadable on ODC and available as layers on its interactive maps.

Barriers

Format and Data Quality

ODC acknowledges that data and information in the public domain are difficult to obtain as sometimes some data have strong restrictions in terms redistribution, reproduction, and reuse. Several of the government data sources are inconsistent, not up to date, and in closed formats (e.g., PDFs). According to Penhleak Chan, Regional Network and Partnership Support Manager of EWMI's Open Development Initiative:

> *"One challenge is that many of the documents released by the government into the public domain are not machine-readable, and so digitizing and analyzing them is*

---

183 "Columbia SIPA," Open Development Cambodia, https://opendevelopmentcambodia.net/about/partnerships/columbia-sipa/.

184 "Save Cambodia's Wildlife," Open Development Cambodia, https://opendevelopmentcambodia.net/about/partnerships/save-cambodias-wildlife-scw/.

very time-consuming. Another challenge is that data and information are not always consistent so there's a need to have a neutral and independent review team that makes sense of the data. For instance, in a project where we looked at reports on rubber production in Cambodia, the numbers provided by two different ministries on the same indicator greatly differed."[185]

These limitations make the work of ODC more difficult and resource-intensive.

Low data literacy on the part of local users

As earlier indicated, the ones that benefitted largely from information availability are organizations that already have the capacity to access and use data—international media outfits and international non-governmental organizations. This is largely because there is low data literacy on the part of local users. To address this, ODC has been doing several capacity building trainings across the country but, given the lack of resources, the ability to cover different sectors across the country is limited.

Looking Forward

ODC believes that its work likely has impacted indirectly on the Cambodian government's recent policies and reforms in the forestry sector and land concessions. This can be observed in the growing number of established natural protected areas, the development of the protected areas management plan, the introduction of eco-tourism, the downsizing of around 1 million hectares of economic land concessions from inactive investors and granting land ownership to the poor through social land concessions. These recent events have inspired ODC to work even harder to make more data more accessible to the public and to those stakeholders in need.[186]

But ODC acknowledges that there are significant challenges to achieving these results—especially with the increasingly limited space for civil society within Cambodian political processes. As ODC wants to maintain its independent stance, it relies largely on other organizations that will take the data that ODC is able to demystify and proactively disclose into processes that influence the way development in Cambodia unfolds. This can be civil society organizations, advocacy groups, or community-based organizations interested

---

185 "DW Global Media Forum: Open Data in Cambodia," DW Akademie, July 3, 2014, http://www.dw.com/en/dw-global-media-forum-open-data-in-cambodia/a-17755220.

186 Interview with Thy Try, Executive Director, Open Development Cambodia, and Penhleak Chan, Regional Network and Partnership Support Manager of EWMI, November 17, 2016.

in particular issues, such as natural resource governance. It can be transparency watch groups that seek to unravel corruption in the public sector. It can even be champions from within government that want to see a more sustainable development model for the country.[187]

Within these processes, ODC has to play at least two roles—that of an advocate for greater openness in public-interest data, and that of a resource institution that builds the capacity of local actors to use data more effectively in decision-making. ODC is committed to ensuring that data-based decision-making processes are institutionalized not only within the halls of government but also in every community in the country.

Conclusion

While Cambodia's open data ecosystem is still in its infancy, Open Development Cambodia is acting as an important leader in pushing the country toward a more transparent, collaborative and data-driven approach to governance. Beyond demonstrating the importance of making important government data available to the public – from open contracts and other legal information to census and demographic data to insight into shifts in forest cover in the country – ODC makes clear the value of taking a broader view of what types of data could be beneficial if made more open and accessible. Rather than relying strictly on government data for its offerings of data and maps, ODC, from the start, sought to aggregate relevant information from across sectors to provide a more multi-faceted view of topics of concern to Cambodians. As the site and Cambodian open data ecosystem continue to mature, we will gain a better sense of whether ODC's still largely aspirational impact will have a larger positive effect on public life in the country.

---

187 Interview with Thy Try, Executive Director, Open Development Cambodia, and Penhleak Chan, Regional Network and Partnership Support Manager of EWMI, November 17, 2016.

Uganda's iParticipate

Open data for achieving better health outcomes

Michael P. Canares, Andrew Young and Stefaan Verhulst

Summary

Uganda has among the worst systems for providing health care in the world, and, as a result, among the poorest health outcomes for its citizens. Several factors contribute significantly to poor health outcomes—a lack of health workers to attend to the needs of a growing population; pervasive corruption in the health service sector; and a lack of data (e.g., related to disease prevalence, health care service delivery indicators, and health outcomes) that could be used for informed judgment and prioritization.

In 2011, the Collaboration on International ICT Policy for East and Southern Africa (CIPESA) began promoting the use of ICT to monitor governance and service delivery in Uganda. The project was funded by the Swedish Program for ICT in Developing Regions (SPIDER).[188] Building on the experience and networks developed by CIPESA through this earlier project, the iParticipate project seeks to leverage the use of open government data to enable citizen participation and more accountable governance. CIPESA used open data available from government portals and sources to analyze service delivery and public investments, especially but not exclusively in the health sector.

The most tangible outcome of this initiative has been better training for civil society organizations and journalists in using data to advance health care advocacy. This has led to increased public awareness about poor public investments in health. Beyond this, however, there is little evidence of tangible improvements in health care service delivery. The initiative has encountered

---

188 Swedish Program for ICT in Developing Regions website, http://spidercenter.org/.

numerous challenges—including those related to technical infrastructure and low ICT capacity—and the future of iParticipate remains somewhat unclear.

Context and Background

Problem Focus / Country Context

According to the World Health Organization (WHO), Uganda has among the worst health service delivery provisions in the world, resulting in poor health outcomes for its citizens. The country has among the lowest life expectancy (54 years in 2015) and highest mortality rates (344 in 2013) in the world.[189] As of 2015, one in every 300 births ends a mother's life, and one of every 30 children born will not be able to survive beyond one year.[190] Communicable diseases, especially tuberculosis, claim the largest portion of lives in the country. HIV prevalence is high, with at least 1.5 million people affected, and the country is among those with the highest new cases of HIV/AIDS globally.[191]

Several factors contribute to such poor health outcomes. First, there is a serious dearth of health workers who can attend to the needs of a growing population. A recent study pointed, for instance, to the very low ratio of health care providers to population in the country, coupled and aggravated by an insufficient budget.[192] Most medical personnel are concentrated in urban areas, to the disadvantage of patients in rural areas. Another problem is pervasive corruption in the health service sector—manifested in a variety of ways, including paid workers failing to arrive at work on time with no fear of repercussion[193] and the misappropriation of public funds for construction of health service facilities.[194]

---

189 African Health Observatory, "Comprehensive Analytical Profile: Uganda," WHO, http://www.aho.afro. who.int/profiles_information/index.php/Uganda:Index.

190 African Health Observatory, "Uganda: Factsheets of health statistics, 2016," http://www.aho.afro.who. int/profiles_information/images/f/fb/Uganda-Statistical_Factsheet.pdf.

191 AVERT, "HIV and AIDS in Uganda," http://www.avert.org/professionals/hiv-around-world/sub-saharan-africa/uganda.

192 Merlin L. Willcox, et al., "Human Resources for Primary Health Care in sub-Saharan Africa: Progress or Stagnation?" *Human Resources for Health*, 13, 2015, https://human-resources-health.biomedcentral.com/articles/10.1186/s12960-015-0073-8.

193 Simon Peter Ogwang, "Fighting Corruption, Empowering People in Uganda's Health Service," Transparency International Blog, July 11, 2012, http://blog.transparency.org/2012/07/11/community-empowerment-in-uganda-using-icts-for-better-health-service-delivery/.

194 Act!onaid, *Corruption and the Service Delivery Tragedy in Uganda: Stories from the eastern leg of the anti-corruption caravan*, Act!onaid, September 2014, http://www.actionaid.org/sites/files/actionaid/anti-corruption_report.pdf.

A lack of data also hampers the quality of service delivery. Studies point in particular to a shortage of data related to disease prevalence,[195] service delivery indicators, and health outcomes.[196] While some forms of health data are collected, these are largely in paper formats and not shared publicly. The Ugandan Ministry of Health Website,[197] which is supposedly the repository of publicly accessible data on health in the country, publishes all information as PDF files. The data is often insufficiently granular to contribute to useful analysis and access to much information, including health human resource data, is often restricted.

Open Data in Uganda

According to the 2015 Open Data Barometer,[198] Uganda ranked 70th out of 92 countries surveyed. The government has made some efforts to use information technology and e-government practices to improve the delivery of public services. In addition, several of its ministries, especially health, environment, and national statistics, have practiced proactive disclosure of data online, though in separate, unlinked websites, and in incompatible formats that make the data difficult to use.

In 2015, the World Bank report on open data readiness in Uganda[199] emphasized that while the country is well-positioned to implement an open data initiative, its ability to actually do so will depend on several issues related to policy, data capacity, and civic engagement. To date, there is no policy which mandates disclosure of government data and protects privacy. In addition, there is a definite lack of technology skills on the part of government employees. Citizens are also limited in their ability to access data by poor broadband access and low data literacy.

A review[200] funded by the Indigo Trust, a funding organization focused on transparency and accountability in Sub-Saharan Africa, found that there exist more than 10 data disclosure mechanisms within the Ugandan

---

195 Jeremy I. Schwartz, et al., "Toward Reframing Health Service Delivery in Uganda: The Uganda initiative for integrated management of non-communicable diseases,"*Global Health Action*, 8, 2015, http://www. globalhealthaction.net/index.php/gha/article/view/26537.

196 African Health Observatory, "Uganda: Health information, research, evidence and knowledge," WHO, http://www.aho.afro.who.int/profiles_information/index.php/Uganda:Health_information,_research,_ evidence_and_knowledge.

197 Ministry of Health, Republic of Uganda website, http://www.health.go.ug/.

198 Open Data Barometer, "Rankings and Data: Uganda," http://opendatabarometer.org/data-explorer/?_ye ar=2015&indicator=ODB&open=UGA.

199 World Bank, *Open Data Readiness Assessment: Uganda*, World Bank, http://opendatatoolkit.worldbank.org/ docs/odra/odra_uganda.pdf.

200 Development Research and Training, *Unlocking the Potential of a More Harnessed Partnership among Open Data Actors in Uganda*, Indigo Trust, November 2015, https://indigotrust.files.wordpress.com/2016/02/ drt-indigo-trust-uganda-final-report.pdf.

government, but that these cover only a few government agencies, namely public finance, water and environment and national statistics. The absence of a centralized open government data portal prompted several actors to publish data relevant to Ugandan governance and public life in different portals like data.ug (supported by UNICEF), uganda.opendataforafrica.org (supported by the African Development Bank) and several other sector-focused initiatives initiated by civil society organizations, international agencies, and academia. The tendency of actors from non-governmental sectors to step up to fill open data gaps left by governments is a common theme across this series of case studies.

Data Collection and Disclosure in the Ugandan Health Care System

Uganda's Ministry of Health is responsible for one of the important sectors in the country. Its primary mandate is to formulate policies related to health, manage partnerships, resource mobilization, capacity building, and quality control on health service delivery, as well as to monitor and evaluate overall health sector performance across the country and at every level of government.

Health care provision in Uganda is undertaken by both public and private actors. Public health service providers have a decentralized structure which consists of national referral hospitals, semi-autonomous regional referral hospitals, and a well-established District Health System under the leadership of the District Directorate of Health Services in each of the country's 111 districts. The intent behind decentralization was to make services reach even the most remote communities, and health centers in the country are broken up into four categories (ranging from the most rudimentary facilities, Health Center 1, to the more advanced, Health Center 4). Health service delivery is based on a referral system, with cases escalated up the categories depending on their level of complexity and facilities required.

Private sector health service provision is offered by a number of actors. These include facility-based private providers, not for profit (PNFP) providers, non-facility based PNFPs, private health practitioners, and traditional medical service providers. Facility-based PNFPs are those who own or operate their own hospitals and clinics; an example of a non-facility based PNFP would be an NGO offering medical services. Private health practitioners refer to those that provide primary and secondary level health services and include a wide range of actors, such as diagnostic centers, private medical and dental clinics, and pharmacies.

The capacity of Ugandans to seek treatment from private sector health service providers, without having to go through the long process of referral in the government system, is affected by their financial capacity and geographic

location. In some areas, especially in rural Uganda, there are no private PNFPs or private health practitioners. For residents of these areas, many of whom also lack the financial capacity to pay for private health care, government health centers are the only option (they may also submit themselves for treatment to traditional herbalists or other "informal" healers without formal training).

The government collects health care data from both the public and private sectors (though it does not collect information from the informal sector). The data collected is largely stored in paper-based formats,[201] based on a set of standardized forms issued by the Ministry of Health (MoH). Aggregation of data is done at the level of MOH, through a Health Management Information System (HMIS[202]) which aims to ensure timely aggregation, storage and retrieval of health information. Data quality is largely (and often negatively) affected by the capacity of lower-level administrative agencies to collect and report data in an effective manner. As a WHO report puts it: "lower administrative levels chronically lack the capacity to capture and report vital events such as community births and deaths."[203] Another study[204] reported that data collected regarding inpatient, outpatient, and health coverage indicators was less than 85 percent complete.

The MOH has made several noteworthy attempts to address these issues. For example, in 2010 the MOH launched the Human Resource for Health Information System (HRHIS),[205] a database platform developed in partnership with USAID that paved the way for comprehensively identifying staffing gaps down to the district level. The MOH has also sought to address data shortcomings by increasing the budget for human resources in public health centers.[206] Despite improvements, however, most of the data collected is not available to the public, and even when available, is difficult for ordinary citizens to understand. HMIS data, for example, requires registration for access and is available only to authorized users through a dashboard. HRHIS data, on the other hand, can be downloaded in spreadsheets format, but needs a trained user for the spreadsheets to be understood.

---

201 African Health Observatory, "Uganda: Health information, research, evidence and knowledge, analytical summary," WHO, http://www.aho.afro.who.int/profiles_information/index.php/Uganda:Health_information,_research,_evidence_and_knowledge#Analytical_summary.

202 Ministry of Health, Republic of Uganda website, http://hmis2.health.go.ug/#/.

203 African Health Observatory, "Uganda: Overview of the Flows of Information," WHO, http://www.aho.afro.who.int/profiles_information/index.php/Uganda:Overview_of_the_flows_of_information.

204 Vincent Michael Kiberu, et al., "Strengthening District-based Health Reporting through the District Health Management Information Software System: The Ugandan experience," *BMC Medical Informatics and Decision Making*, 14, 2014, http://bmcmedinformdecismak.biomedcentral.com/articles/10.1186/1472-6947-14-40.

205 Human Resources for Health Information Systems website, http://hris.health.go.ug/reports/.

206 Jillian Larsen, *Uganda: Winning human resources for health*, International Budget Partnership, December 2015, http://www.internationalbudget.org/wp-content/uploads/case-study-full-uganda-human-resources-for-health-2015.pdf.

KEY ACTORS

Key Data Providers

The Ugandan government, through different portals, makes accessible the majority of data used for iParticipate. In particular, open data provided through the portal by the Ministry of Health plays an important enabling role. The project also leverages some limited data from private sector health providers, demonstrating the potential for more cross-sector data collaborative arrangements.

Key Data Users and Intermediaries

Established under the United Kingdom Department for International Development-funded Catalysing Access to Information and Communications Technologies in Africa (CATIA) initiative, the Collaboration on International ICT Policy in East and Southern Africa (CIPESA) is a civil society organization that "facilitates the use of ICT in support of development and poverty reduction."[207] CIPESA's iParticipate project was established with funding from the Swedish Program for ICT in Developing Regions (SPIDER), a resource center working across sectors to leverage ICTs for development purposes. SPIDER, in particular, seeks to enable "the collaboration and sharing of experience between different actors in the field to reach better development results."[208]

Intended Beneficiaries

The iParticipate initiative aims to catalyze the use of ICT in citizen's engagement and participation in governance.[209] The project intends to build the capacity primarily of journalists and civil society organizations to use ICT tools in increasing public awareness on government issues, especially related to health, as well as potential solutions. iParticipate trains NGOs and journalists to conduct more data-driven analyses of the government information so that they can use these skills to advocate for public service reform, with the view that ordinary Ugandans will enjoy better services in the future.

Project Description

Initiation of the Open Data Activity

In 2011, the Collaboration on International ICT Policy for East and Southern Africa (CIPESA), a technology for development NGO, began promoting the

---

207 Collaboration on International ICT Policy in East and Southern Africa (CIPESA) website, http://cipesa.org/about-us/.

208 Swedish Program for ICT in Developing Regions website, http://spidercenter.org/.

209 "CIPESA," Promoting Human Rights and Democracy Through ICT, http://ict4democracy.org/about/partnerproject-briefs/cipesa/.

use of ICT in monitoring good governance and service delivery in Uganda. The project, called Catalyzing Civic Participation and Democracy Monitoring Using ICTs, was funded by the Swedish Program for ICT in Developing Regions (SPIDER), a development resource center.[210] It established partnerships with three grassroots-based organizations, namely, the Busoga Rural Open Source and Development Initiative (BROSDI) in the Mayuge district (Eastern Uganda); the e-Society Resource Centre (eSRC) in the Kasese district (Western Uganda); and the Northern Uganda Media Club (NUMEC), in Gulu (Northern Uganda). These organizations had been working directly with communities to promote the use of ICTs as tools for citizens to engage with decision-makers and demand accountability. Under their projects, citizens used various tools in engaging with local government officials, including radio (NUMEC), email, blogs, social media (BROSDI), and geo-coded mapping for eSRC.

Informed by the experience and networks developed by CIPESA through these previous efforts, iParticipate, the project under study here, sought to support these existing efforts and to build on them by leveraging open government data (much of it already available in various portals but often in incompatible or inaccessible formats) as an enabler of citizen participation and accountable governance, focusing especially on the health sector. CIPESA's interest in open governance started when it conducted research on open governance network building in Uganda, funded by the International Development Research Center in 2012.[211] Among other results, the research helped identify key datasets that citizen groups would like the government to proactively disclose, as well as the general level of government readiness to implement open governance in the country.

Much of the work undertaken under the iParticipate initiative focused on training intermediaries – particularly media and civil society actors – to enable and promote citizen participation in Ugandan governance. iParticipate also provided support to grassroots citizen-focused ICT centres like eSRC in Kasese. Finally, the project engaged with government officials and policymakers to help communicate the opportunities, tools and tenets of open data and open governance processes to push forward the supply side of open data and ensure that the institutional culture acted as an enabler of greater participation in governance and service delivery.[212] This multi-audience focus helped iParticipate to diversify its offerings, engage relevant stakeholders in a targeted way, and avoid the "if you build it, will they come" question that

---

210 Ibid.

211 "Uganda Open Government Data Readiness Study," CIPESA and Association for Progressive Communications, April 2012, http://cipesa.org/?wpfb_dl=139.

212 "2015 Projects," CIPESA, http://cipesa.org/projects/.

often plagues open data efforts focused solely on citizens with little attention paid to intermediaries or actors on the supply side.

As explained further below, iParticipate provides detailed GIS-maps and visualizations to present mashed up datasets from a number of government data sources, in the process making clear where, how and why health care resources are being used across the country. Much of the project's offerings are real-world rather than digital. iParticipate efforts have included, for example, multi-stakeholder meetings between government officials and educators focused on the challenge of implementing tools to improve community participation.[213] Traditional media outlets are also leveraged – including through the previously mentioned radio broadcasts. The effort also involves the use of a number of training and engagement centers, including the eSRC in Kasese, which "provides ICT training programmes…aimed at enhancing citizens' competence in monitoring government services, promoting accountability, civic participation and good governance."[214]

One specific initiative undertaken in collaboration with NUMEC aimed at making government information more accessible to citizens in the districts of Gulu, Nwoya and Amuru – the regions most affected by Lord's Resistance Army's (LRA) destruction. The project set out to "document service delivery failures as a result of donor aid cuts to the Peace, Recovery and Development Plan (PRDP), and to generate debate by citizens through community debates, radio talk shows and ICT-based engagements on improving service delivery needs of post-conflict communities." The PRDP was launched by the government in 2009 to "revitalise the economy and livelihoods of communities in the post-conflict region" through health service delivery, new infrastructure, clean energy and education initiatives, but widespread allegations of corruption destroyed citizen trust in the effort.[215]

The project's overarching goal was to increase citizen participation in monitoring government service delivery through the use of ICT; advocate for government stakeholders to practice open governance; and document and propagate to the wider public the results of these processes. CIPESA performs the role of an intermediary that gathers government data and translates it into useful, relevant, and meaningful information for citizens. CIPESA's aim is also to increase the capacity and ability of citizen groups and the media to demand

213 Caroline Wamala Larsson, "SPIDER Stories 2013–2014," SPIDER Center, 2015, http://spidercenter.org/wp-content/blogs.dir/362/files/2016/11/spider_stories_2013-2014_for_web.pdf.

214 Ashnah Kalemera, "Citizens' Use of ICTs in Social Accountability in Uganda's Kasese District," CIPESA, January 19, 2015, http://cipesa.org/2015/01/citizens-use-of-icts-in-social-accountability-in-ugandas-kasese-district/.

215 Gladys Oroma, Promoting Community Dialogue on Service Delivery Failures in Northern Uganda," Promoting Human Rights and Democracy through ICT, February 28, 2015, http://ict4democracy.org/promoting-community-dialogue-on-service-delivery-failures-in-northern-uganda/.

better data, and to use this data to exact accountability from governments, especially in the health and education sectors.

Funding

The Swedish Program for ICT in Developing Regions (SPIDER) provided CIPESA with 500,000 SEK (approximately 55,480 USD) for a two-year implementation beginning 2013. The project from which this new initiative was built was also supported by SPIDER at the same funding level. In addition, Indigo Trust also provided 12,000 GBP (14,870 USD) for the initiative.

Demand and Supply of Data Type(s) and Sources

iParticipate's health advocacy was focused on health service delivery and how access to health care, especially by the poor and marginalized in rural areas, is affected by government investments in people and facilities. There were a few primary data sets that were used by CIPESA in this process—those related to health clinics, health centers, and general hospitals, including the location and number of beds for each of these facilities. This existing data originated on the Ministry of Health website and was made accessible through Uganda's Open Data for Africa portal.[216]

The Open Data for Africa portal allowed for online search and query, with the capacity to filter and visualize results (see Figure 1). The platform also allows downloading of data as CSV, XLS, or OData files. Similar datasets are also available at the Electronic Health Management Information System (eHMIS),[217] though this portal requires formal log-on procedures to be able to get access to the data.

To see investments in health per jurisdiction, CIPESA used budget data from the Ministry of Finance Planning and Economic Development available at the ministry's budget portal.[218] The portal has an elaborate query facility and also publishes PDF reports of spending performance for each sector. Access to the data, however, is not fully open, as it requires registration with the data providers, and acceptance of registration is not assured.

---

216 Open Data for Africa, "Uganda Regional Health Statistics Database, 2011," http://uganda. opendataforafrica.org/lhcqofd/uganda-regional-health-statistics-database-2011.

217 Ministry of Health, Republic of Uganda website, http://hmis2.health.go.ug/#/.

218 Ministry of Finance Planning and Economic Development, "Uganda Budget Information," http://budget. go.ug/index.php?p=budget_dashboard.

Source: Uganda Open Data for Africa Portal

Figure 1. Location of hospitals, health clinics in Uganda

Open Data Use

CIPESA used the data available in these portals and from other sources to analyze health service delivery and public investments in health projects. Much of iParticipate's training efforts, for example, focused on providing individuals and journalists with the capacity to access and use geocoded maps made possible by open government data.

CIPESA used data to identify a number of features related to health service delivery. For example, iParticipate's maps could help identify populations with limited access to health care, as well those health facilities that had limited or no beds. This information was cross-

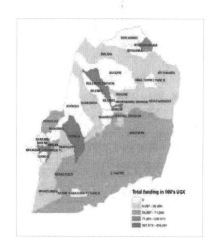

**Figure 2.
Sub-County Health Funding in
Kasese (2012–2013 estimates)**

118

tabulated with funding information. As a result, iParticipate was able to show the need for more data sharing at all levels of the health service delivery infrastructure in Uganda. As Lillian Kisembo, the Assistant Town Clerk in Kasese, put it: "If we can embark upon sharing information at the local level, we can reduce these challenges at District planning."[219]

In addition, CIPESA also made use of open data coming from different sources to build a platform to show how projects implemented through the PRDP, described above, collect reports coming from the field through users with Android phones, and aggregate different reports on health issues and health-related information. Community residents can report information using the Ushahidi[220] crowdsourced mapping application and this, together with different reports and information, are consolidated in a crowd-mapping portal (see Figure 3).[221]

Figure 3. Crowd-mapping Platform developed by CIPESA – PRDP

---

219 "ICT4Democracy in East Africa: A Year in Review 2015," CIPESA, 2016, http://cipesa.org/?wpfb_dl=221.

220 Ushahidi website, https://www.ushahidi.com/.

221 CIPESA, "Promoting Transparency, Civic Agency and the Right to Information in Northern Uganda's Peace Recovery and Development Programme," https://cipesa.crowdmap.com/main.

Impact

The CIPESA project had three main objectives: (a) increasing citizen participation in monitoring government service delivery through the use of ICT; (b) advocating for government stakeholders to practice open governance; and (c) documenting and propagating to the wider public the learning that resulted from these processes. In our analysis, we find that impact is primarily evident only in the area of advocacy, increased engagement of citizens in health governance and information dissemination. In addition, a certain (though limited) impact is evident in the other areas.

Advocacy

Although impact remains relatively limited and difficult to assess, there is some evidence that iParticipate's data offerings and training efforts with civil society and the media have made some impact. By enabling these intermediaries to better understand the conditions of the health sector, highlight issues associated with poor investments in health and publicize the poor's lack of access to quality health care, iParticipate is playing a key role in pushing for improvements to public- and private-sector providers, and also in empowering citizens to demand better service.

Improved Dissemination of Health Information

This advocacy is coupled with wider dissemination of information on health and other health- related issues to different communities using different media—radio, SMS, printed materials, e-resource center, e-library, e-discussion groups, Facebook pages, and web portals. These increased not only information availability, but also user's access to relevant health governance information.

Increasing Citizen Engagement in Health Governance

The advocacy and dissemination activities were done alongside building the capacity of different stakeholders, more particularly journalists, local government officials, civil society organization leaders, and students, on the use of ICT for governance. These trainings increased their capacity to analyze and make use of government data for advocacy, while at the same time monitoring the quality of public health service delivery by government.

Risks

Central to ICT-enabled information dissemination and open data monitoring initiatives is the capacity of these initiatives to actually make a difference in the lives of citizens. For example, data that highlights health spending and inconsistencies in prioritization, as well as those public reporting mechanisms on health governance, will only be useful for citizens if there are actual improvements in government spending and public health service delivery. If positive results are not obtained, citizens will get disillusioned and will likely discontinue availing themselves of these initiatives.

Also, as is the case with many health-focused open data initiatives, the primary risk involves personally identifiable information. While the focus of the government's data provision and iParticipate's data-driven analysis tools are not at all on sharing personal health information, continued vigilance and targeted data responsibility strategies will be essential to ensure that no potentially damaging personal information slips through the cracks.

Lessons Learned

Enablers

Cross-sector collaboration

Without access to resources and expertise from SPIDER, CIPESA's implementation of iParticipate would have been significantly more challenging. While the funding provided by the Sweden-based international organization obviously played a major enabling role, the ability to plug into SPIDER's international network of businesses, universities, NGOs and governments working to leverage ICT for development also helped to shape the approach and offerings of the initiative.

CIPESA's reputation as a development organization

Additionally, CIPESA continues to be a driving force in Uganda's desire to improve transparency and accountability in governance. Just as it was able to tap into an international network of expertise, CIPESA leveraged its own network of development actors, both at the national and sub-national level, to inform the project. Its reputation with donors, government agencies, civil society organizations and other stakeholders is an important element in

CIPESA's ability to influence policy-making as well as government decision-making despite the limitations mentioned below.

Barriers

Lack of demand-side capacity

CIPESA experienced challenges in achieving desired results. First, driving citizen participation is affected by at least two significant barriers—low connectivity and low levels of awareness of ICT use among citizens. While progress has been made in efforts to train citizens in ICT use, the lack of consistent access (especially outside of resource centers) hampered efforts. Also, especially regarding efforts focused on health and budget information, many technical concepts require sophisticated knowledge to enable meaningful participation—highlighting the need for intermediaries who perform the task of making complex information understandable to citizens.

While journalists could have performed this intermediary or explanatory role, CIPESA seems to have found it a challenge to incentivize journalists to spend time learning and educating themselves on the relevant issues. Journalist participation was also limited by geography, as health service delivery generally remains a big problem outside the urban/semi-urban areas where most journalists are based. Citizen groups in these areas were also limited in their ability to participate, primarily by a lack of connectivity and capacity.

Citizen media habits

While CIPESA made use of ICT as a means to disseminate and collect information, a study[222] it conducted in 2015 revealed that newspapers, radio, and television were in fact the most trusted sources of information by Ugandans. The same study indicated that very few Ugandans use ICT as a means to monitor and report on government services. This suggests that the means used by CIPESA to engage citizens with health governance data did not match with the manner in which citizens habitually acquire and share trusted information.

The survey did find that a growing number of people in the country are starting to use the Internet, and especially social networks like Facebook and Twitter, to discuss issues of national and local concern. However, citizen use of such networks was generally limited to information sharing, and not to actually raising concerns to accountable officials (most of whom do not in any

---

222 CIPESA, *ICT in Civic Participation and Democracy in Uganda: Citizens' knowledge, attitudes and practices*, CIPESA ICT Policy Research Series, No. 4/15, 2015, http://www.cipesa.org/?wpfb_dl=196.

case have social media accounts). The main limits on more widespread use of ICTs were illiteracy, and language and cost barriers.

Availability of resources

The capacity of CIPESA to proactively elevate health service delivery concerns to accountable government officials was also hampered by resource constraints. CIPSA tried to surmount fund shortages by using health service delivery reports received by one of its partners, Transparency International Uganda (TIU). But the organization was nonetheless constrained in its outreach and awareness-raising efforts. For example, while CIPESA succeeded in producing potentially useful health service delivery maps, it was often unable to disseminate these widely enough to reach their intended audiences. Funding constraints also affected CIPESA's ability to follow up on adverse findings reported by citizens using its platform.

Looking Forward

CIPESA main goal is to increase the impact that iParticipate will be able to make in using ICT for health service delivery monitoring. Currently, it is trying to find new ways of addressing the challenges identified above through more creative and well-targeted outreach and communication efforts. For example, the previous SPIDER project that was the basis for iParticipate made extensive use of radio programs to increase debate and reaching out to public officials on key concerns of the communities. The radio program implemented with NUMEC was able to reach approximately 1.6 million listeners.

As mentioned above, and as concluded by CIPESA's own research,[223] a number of factors limit the potential of ICT as a tool in monitoring government performance and enforcing accountability. The most important of these factors include poor technological infrastructure, including slow internet speeds and irregular electricity; low levels of ICT capacity among citizens; higher trust and use of traditional media as sources of data and information; and the high cost of internet access. iParticipate's future, and more generally the future of open data as a tool to achieve better health outcomes in Uganda, will be largely dependent on its ability to address and overcome (or at least mitigate) these challenges.

---

223 . Ibid.

Conclusion

Although iParticipate has had relatively little impact on citizen empowerment to date, it has leveraged a number of strategies that have yielded success in other contexts. The initiative's diverse offerings are implemented with a clear understanding of the intended audience – including notably government officials – and efforts are consistently driven through existing intermediaries, like journalists. This focus on empowering intermediaries to act as enablers for greater citizen participation is one reason for optimism regarding the longer-term impacts of iParticipate – including if and when funding is no longer available. Relatedly, the project often seeks to meet its intended audience where they already are – such as at ICT training centers or on popular radio broadcasts – increasing reach and the likelihood that its message is being absorbed by the public. While iParticipate has not yet had a transformative impact on citizen participation in Ugandan health governance, its continued efforts to increase awareness and train potential users of open data have the potential to gradually improve health outcomes by bringing together government actors, intermediaries and citizens to work toward common ends.

Open Data's Impact on Empowering Citizens

GotToVote! Kenya

Improving voter turnout with open data

Auralice Graft, Andrew Young and Stefaan Verhulst

Summary

In the lead up to Kenya's 2013 general election, the country's Independent Electoral and Boundaries Commission (IEBC) released information about polling center locations on its website. The information, however, was difficult to access, indicating the wide gap that separates making data open and actually making it usable. Seeking to bridge that gap, two members of Code for Kenya, a governance innovation initiative, conducted an experiment that aimed to unlock government data and make it more useful to the public. To that end, they scraped the IEBC data and built a simple website where it could be more easily accessed. The result was the initial version of GotToVote! (gottovote. cc), a site that provided citizens with voter registration center information, and also helped them navigate the sometimes complex world of registration procedures. This first version was developed overnight at zero cost.

Context and Background

Problem Focus/Country Context

The Republic of Kenya is a nation of 42.7 million people situated on Africa's eastern coast. Kenya has a sizeable economy, with the highest GDP in East and Central Africa.[224] Despite this, the country is burdened with high unemployment,

---

224 International Monetary Fund, "Data," http://www.imf.org/en/data.

poverty, and crime.[225] Public sector corruption is also a challenge: Transparency International ranked Kenya 139th out of 168 countries in its 2016 Corruption Perception Index (CPI), an index that measures perceived levels of public sector corruption. This ranking places Kenya below countries like Bangladesh and Iran, and even below other Sub-Saharan African countries like Nigeria, Tanzania and Ethiopia.[226]

In December 2007, Kenya held a hotly contested presidential election that ended in a stalemate and protests. Anger over perceived vote rigging and manipulations of the electoral process rapidly metastasized into a national crisis characterized by conflict and violence, including targeted ethnic violence. As many as 1,400 people were killed and 600,000 displaced from their homes during the crisis. A resolution was reached after a few months, following the intervention of former UN Secretary General Kofi Annan; one of the main elements of the resolution was a roadmap toward a series of reforms designed to overcome political divisions and curb electoral manipulation.[227]

Among the most important of the reforms was a redrafting of Kenya's constitution, including a redrawing of constituency boundaries and a provision for a new national Independent Electoral and Boundaries Commission (IEBC). This commission was established in 2011 with a stated mission "to conduct free and fair elections and to institutionalize a sustainable electoral process."[228] One of the IEBC's first tasks was to register all Kenyan voters afresh, according to the new constituency boundaries as designated in the new constitution. Accordingly, a mass voter registration drive was initiated by the IEBC in November 2012 and 19 million people were registered.[229]

In order to achieve its ambitious registration goals, the IEBC released information about polling center locations on its website in late November 2012, a month ahead of the voter registration deadline. This information was considered critical as constituency boundaries had been redrawn, and voters needed to know where to go to register. Yet while the IEBC's release of data represented an important step, the data was actually quite complicated to access: the website itself was almost never available, and the information was provided in PDF format. Moreover, downloading the information was cumbersome because of the file's large size. As Jay Bhalla, executive director of Open Institute, a Kenyan open governance organization, put it: "The file

---

225 BBC News, "Kenya Country Profile," BBC, http://www.bbc.com/news/world-africa-13681341.

226 Mathews Muthai, "Kenya Ranked 139 Out of 168 in Global Corruption Perception Index (CPI)," *Citizen Digital*, January 27, 2016, https://citizentv.co.ke/news/kenya-ranked-139-out-of-168-in-global-corruption-perception-index-cpi-112912/.

227 James Brownsvell, "Kenya: What went wrong in 2007?" *Aljazeera*, March 2013, http://www.aljazeera.com/indepth/features/2013/03/201333123153703492.html.

228 Independent Electoral and Boundaries Commission website, http://www.iebc.or.ke/.

229 GovLab interview with David Lemayian, lead technologist, Code for Africa, November 1, 2016.

was so big it would have taken days for ordinary Kenyans to download. And, once they opened the document all they would have found was complex lists and tables of constituency centers."[230]

It was at this point that a Code for Kenya fellow and the lead developer of the software development team decided to step in and unlock the data with the aim of making it more accessible to the public. Their intervention marked the birth of the GotToVote! website.

KEY ACTORS

Key Data Providers

Two datasets were ultimately used for the GotToVote! Project; both were made publicly available by the IEBC on its website. The first dataset consisted of national polling center location information, and the second visualized a map of registered voters.

Key Data Users and Intermediaries

Kenyan citizens wanting to determine the location of their local polling station in order to register to vote are the main users of the data. Other users included the team of Code for Kenya fellows who scraped the data, built the GotToVote! website, and uploaded the scraped data onto the GotToVote! website. Code for Kenya is a "non-profit civic technology lab and data journalism initiative" that uses digital tools to provide ordinary citizens with "actionable information" and a stronger voice around public interest issues. Code for Kenya opens data, builds tools, and supports progress.[231] Code for Kenya began as a pilot program with funding from the World Bank, with the Africa Media Initiative (AMI) acting as a fiduciary sponsor. The pilot program consisted of four data fellows being embedded into major Kenyan newsrooms and civil society organizations for a period of five months in an effort to kickstart experimentation with data-driven civic engagement tools. The Code for Kenya team also included a four software developers. The above-mentioned Open Institute also provided support by incubating the Code for Kenya fellows.[232] After the initial launch of GotToVote!, Code for Kenya became a founding member of Code for Africa, a "federation of civic technology and data journalism labs," which now manages the initiative.[233]

230 Kenya GotToVote! website, https://kenya.gottovote.cc/about.html.

231 Justin Arenstein, "Finding Voter Registration Centre in Kenya Is Now Just a Click Away," Code for Africa, March 7, 2016, https://medium.com/code-for-africa/finding-voter-registration-centre-is-now-just-a-click-away-102d8206b12c#.gzqcxzzek.

232 Al Kags, "GotToVote! A Way to Bring Open Data to the Ground," Open Institute, November 22, 2012, http://www.openinstitute.com/gotovote/.

233 Justin Arenstein, "Finding Voter Registration Centre in Kenya Is Now Just a Click Away," Code for Africa, March 7, 2016, https://medium.com/code-for-africa/finding-voter-registration-centre-is-now-just-a-click-away-102d8206b12c#.gzqcxzzek.

Key Data Beneficiaries

Kenyan citizens looking to register to vote, to locate their local polling center, or to get answers relating to the registration process benefited from the project. The IEBC, whose voter registration drive was facilitated by the data, was another beneficiary.

Project Description

Initiation

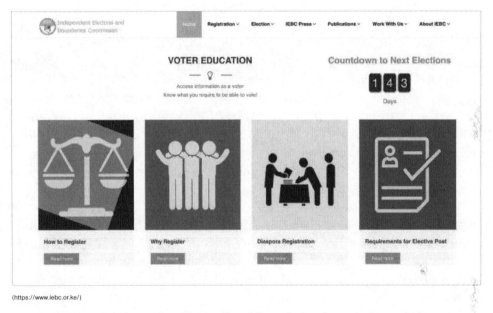

(https://www.iebc.or.ke/)

Figure 1. Independent Electoral and Boundaries Commission website

In late November 2012, Code for Kenya fellow Simeon Oriko logged on to his Twitter account and saw that the IEBC had shared voter polling center information on its website (https://www.iebc.or.ke/). He also saw that the information was difficult to access. He quickly contacted a colleague, David Lemayian, about the information release and the problems with accessibility. According to a third Code for Kenya fellow, Muchiri Nyaggah, who managed the GotToVote! project early on, "they decided to turn the information into a spreadsheet. They had not planned for this; the idea was purely opportunistic."[234]

---

234 GovLab interview with Muchiri Nyaggah, Executive Director, Local Development Research Institute, Kenya, October 20, 2016.

Mr. Oriko and Mr. Lemayian downloaded the polling center data, scraped it, and built a simple website. They spent some time trying to decide on a name, feeling a certain amount of pressure as they needed to purchase a domain name. Finally, they settled on GotToVote! and quickly built an initial version of the site, which made the IEBC data far easier for citizens to access and use. For instance, rather than downloading and scrolling through a cumbersome PDF file, users could select their county or constituency from a drop-down list and find out immediately where to register.

The first version of the site was developed overnight, at no additional cost.[235] "I stayed up all night to build it," says co-creator David Lemayian.[236] The next morning, Mr. Oriko and Mr. Lemayian Tweeted the site out and it immediately got traction. "It did really well during those first days," says Mr. Nyaggah, pointing both to site usage and shares on social media. "People such as Dr. Evans Kidero, the now-Governor, were using and sharing the site," says Mr. Lemayian. "Celebrities were using and talking about it." Overall, GotToVote! received about 6,000 hits during that first week.[237] After this early success, GotToVote! partnered with United States-based Mercy Corps to incorporate a feature that allowed users to spread messages of peace through the GotToVote! website. Users could send free SMS messages that urged constraint at the ballot box. This feature was intended to promote peaceful election and post-election environments, a sorely felt need after the violence of the 2007 elections.

In addition to the peace SMS tool, GotToVote! added a feature to help users find the voter registration center nearest them by mapping data in conjunction with IEBC-released data. Another new feature provided an overview of the registration process, with an explanation of who was eligible to register, and what documents and other material were required.[238,239]

Not all of these efforts were successful. For example, an IEBC map indicating newly changed boundaries could not be incorporated into GotToVote! as was hoped. The map had proprietary issues as a result of a IBEC-Google deal that meant other users were locked out.[240]

While this first GotToVote! iteration focused on helping citizens register, a second iteration, developed after the IEBC's mass registration ended on

---

235 GotToVote! Kenya website, https://kenya.gottovote.cc/about.html.

236 GovLab interview with David Lemayian, lead technologist, Code for Africa, November 1, 2016.

237 GovLab interview with Muchiri Nyaggah, Executive Director, Local Development Research Institute, Kenya, October 20, 2016.

238 GovLab interview with Muchiri Nyaggah, Executive Director, Local Development Research Institute, Kenya, November 22, 2016.

239 Eric Mugendi, "This Website Is Using Publicly Available Data to Help Kenyans Register to Vote," *TechCabal*, March 8, 2016, http://techcabal.com/2016/03/08/got-to-vote-kenya/.

240 GovLab interview with Muchiri Nyaggah, Executive Director, Local Development Research Institute, Kenya, November 22, 2016.

December 19, 2012, aimed to mobilize people to vote in the upcoming March, 2013 elections, and then analyze results after the elections. Here, GotToVote! partnered with Dutch human rights organization Hivos and arranged to access data from the Kenya-based Ushahidi, a non-profit software company that develops free, open-source software. While these partnerships encountered a series of setbacks (see section on barriers below), they did produce a second GotToVote! iteration included a new post-election feature that provided access to official election results in local counties and constituencies, contextualization of those local level results by overlaying them with local level trends and official reports of fraud or irregularities. This feature was implemented to counter some of the hype that tended to prevail over post-election periods when the media focus was almost uniquely on presidential contest outcomes but ordinary citizens also wanted news about local level outcomes.

Figure 2. Image from the GotToVote! homepage

Demand and Data Use

The GotToVote! Kenya database contains a list of all Kenya's 47 counties, 290 constituencies, and 1450 wards, arranged by administrative area, with polling stations in each ward listed alphabetically. All the data used by GotToVote! Kenya is available for free reuse on the openAFRICA portal, another open data

initiative from Code for Africa.[241] Demand for this data comes from would-be voters wanting to register and/or searching for the polling station closest to them. Demand also comes from users looking for basic voter education information.

Impact

As often is the case with relatively recent open data projects, very little data exists to indicate GotToVote!'s impact. The very newness of these projects contributes to the difficulty. As Mr. Nyaggah put it: "It is difficult to assess the impact because we didn't have baseline or anecdotal data to compare outcomes with." Nonetheless, certain forms of impact were evident.

Solving Public Problems through Data-driven Engagement

Given its popularity, GotToVote! appears to have helped many Kenyans register to vote by providing them with accessible information on voter center location. As mentioned, the site received approximately 6,000 hits during the first week after going live. Although neither baseline nor anecdotal data exists to contextualize this information or indicate actual impact on solving public problems, it suggests that the site was perceived as useful and was in fact used.

The apparent success of GotToVote! in helping voters register is indication that open data can be used—rapidly and with minimal cost—to provide citizens with tools that help them solve real public problems. One of the most powerful testimonies to the site's usefulness came from the IEBC itself, which built an almost identical platform soon after the GotToVote! site was unveiled, in the process clearly indicating that policymakers and government leaders recognized the project's tremendous potential. [242] As Code for Africa Director Justin Arenstein puts it: "[GotToVote!] proved that the real power of civic technologies is their ability to quickly and cheaply translate complex data into 'actionable' information, and to then calibrate the information to a citizen's exact location or other circumstances."[243]

---

241 "Voter Registration 2016," openAFRICA, https://africaopendata.org/dataset/voter-registration-2016.

242 GovLab interview with David Lemayian, lead technologist, Code for Africa, November 1, 2016.

243 GotToVote Kenya website, https://kenya.gottovote.cc/about.html.

Cross-Border Dissemination

According to co-founder David Lemayian, many sub-Saharan countries share similar problems (and opportunities for resolution) when it comes to the need for enabling more peaceful and inclusive elections. He believes that a tool like GotToVote! could be useful beyond the Kenyan context. "If we look at ways we can take tools that work in one country and apply them to other countries GotToVote! is clearly one of them," he says.[244]

Since its launch GotToVote! has, in fact, been replicated in several other African countries—a phenomenon that has been made possible by the open source nature of the original site. For example, Hivos, the Dutch organization that partnered with Code for Kenya to launch the original site, also showcased GotToVote! in Zimbabwe ahead of that country's 2013 general elections. "That was really heart-warming," says David Lemayian. "That's when we had a sort of light bulb reaction, realizing this is wanted in different countries in Africa."[245]

The site has also been replicated in Malawi, where a similar platform (http://gottovote.malawivote2014.org/) was implemented by the Malawi Election Information Center, a local NGO, and the Malawi Electoral Commission. The project was adopted by the government as its official voter registration solution and was used to register 7 million citizens. One distinctive trait of the Malawi project distinct was an SMS-to-SMS feature that allowed users to send messages containing their voter identification number, and then to receive a message in reply confirming whether they were registered to vote. Overall, 400,000 people in Malawi accessed registration information by SMS and online. "It was a fantastic roll-out," says David Lemayian.[246]

GotToVote! was also replicated in Ghana, where local organization Odekro and civic technologists Emmanuel Okyere and Nehemiah reached out to Code for Kenya expressing interest in the technology. While Odekro chased down polling station data, Code for Kenya providing technical assistance in this project. Ghana's case offered a particular challenge (and opportunity) because polling station information was maintained separately in each province, with no centralized list. A first step was therefore to create Ghana's first ever national consolidated voters roll, which was handed over to the government electoral commission. This list provided the basis for GotToVote! Ghana, which was built in two days for just $500 and unveiled for the 2016 elections.[247]

---

244 GovLab interview with David Lemayian, lead technologist, Code for Africa, November 1, 2016.
245 Ibid.
246 Ibid.
247 GotToVote! Ghana website, https://ghana.gottovote.cc/about.html.

Risks

Given that the project is primarily built around information provision and peace messaging, risks appear to be somewhat limited. That said, data quality is of paramount importance, due to the potential of providing citizens with incorrect – or biased – information regarding their voting process. Additionally, the two-way nature of the SMS functionality could create risks around the security of any personally identifiable information held by GotToVote!, but such risks appear to be minimal.

Lessons Learned

Several important lessons with wider applicability emerge from this particular case study. These can broadly be categorized by considering the key enablers of the project, as well as the most important barriers or challenges to its success.

Enablers

Engagement

The importance of local partner engagement was clear from the outset. "You can't just fly into a country and solve problems," says David Lemayian. "You have to work with local partners." He adds, however, that national, regional or international partners are important as well. Over the years, the trio of Code for Africa, Code for Kenya and the Open Institute have been able to pull together their diverse yet complimentary areas of expertise, incubating and mobilizing skills among their various fellows. Lemayian also notes that, "Governments and international partners add leverage and credibility, as well as funds." Hivos and Mercy Corps, in particular, helped amplify and expand the site's offerings and visibility.

Agility and MVPs

A further key lesson of this project—once seen in other examples in this series of case studies—is that successful open data projects can be built quickly and without considerable expense. The initial development of GotToVote! incurred no additional cost, and the size of the founding team was very small, basically just two people (Simeon Oriko and David Lemayian), though they were later joined and helped by other colleagues.

Finally, the process of building an open data project does not need to be complicated or cumbersome. As noted, for example, GotToVote! was built in just one night. The data contained on the site was relatively simple, and did not require complicated algorithms to make useful. All told, GotToVote! is a good example of how much can be achieved with very little—at least in the early stages of an open data project (see the discussion of Sustainability in Barriers, below).

Barriers

Sustainability of event-based initiatives

The impact of GotToVote! is clear, but the site's focus on a single, time-bound event (e.g., a given presidential election) does raise questions about long-term sustainability. Questions remain about what to do with the project between elections, and whether the user base can be re-engaged during the next election. This lack of certainty also raises questions about access to further funding, a key consideration for the sustainability of open data initiatives. The site's current status, discussed below, only increases this uncertainty.

Unhelpful partnerships

According to Muchiri Nyaggah, it was assumed that relationships with big media companies would translate into those companies utilizing GotToVote! to disseminate election results. However, as it turned out, these companies had actually invested money creating their own results-dissemination platforms. They ultimately had no use for GotToVote! This was a big blow to GotToVote!'s success, with significantly less dissemination and ultimate use than initially assumed and worked toward.[248]

Data access failures

Another barrier came in the form of failed access to data. In one instance, the IEBC's system crashed while results were being tallied after the March 2013 elections. This was a major failure that ultimately led to a crisis in Kenya that had to be resolved by the national Supreme Court. For GotToVote!, the system crash meant it did not have access to election results data that it hoped to incorporate into the project. In an unrelated challenge, GotToVote!'s

---

248 Skype interview with Muchiri Nyaggah, Executive Director, Local Development Research Institute, Kenya, November 22, 2016.

attempted data access arrangement with Ushahidi did not come to fruition as a result of backend technical issues. GotToVote! and Ushahidi had planned to work to tell a political story of what happened post-2013 elections by merging election results with a diversity of other datasets held by Ushahidi (including geospatial data).[249]

Looking Forward

Current Status

Kenya's GotToVote! website was updated ahead of the 2017 general elections, but no concrete plans are in place for rolling it out. "We are definitely looking for people who can pick it up and run with it," says David Lemayian. "We [at Code for Africa] have been approached by three different organizations to run GotToVote! in Kenya ahead of elections planned for August 2017. But we are hoping civil society will take it up. We've also actively reached out to IEBC and election observation groups on the same." With the next election fast approaching, the identification of an organization with the human capital and funding resources needed to maintain the platform capable of taking it up is becoming urgent.

Replicability

As described above, the potential for replicating GotToVote! has been realized across a number of countries in Sub-Saharan Africa. The simplicity and open source basis of the platform, the general availability of the data required and the clearly defined problem it seeks to solve are key drivers of this replicability.

Early project manager Muchiri Nyaggah believes that GotToVote! needs to be established as a more formalized, cross-border civil society program or mission going forward. "Tech-heavy organizations are not very good at old school NGO language," he says. "This needs to be turned into a program with people thinking about how to capture data on impact and other indicators." Mr. Nyaggah also stated that GotToVote! needs to collaborate with the IEBC if it is to have any value in upcoming elections.[250]

---

249 Skype interview with Muchiri Nyaggah, Executive Director, Local Development Research Institute, Kenya, November 22, 2016.

250 GovLab interview with Muchiri Nyaggah, Executive Director, Local Development Research Institute, Kenya, October 20, 2016.

Conclusion

GotToVote's impact is clear in the way it has improved public awareness of election information, the fact that it has been replicated throughout the continent, and in the messages of harmony and inclusiveness it has helped foster in more recent elections. The project's birth and experience are in several ways indicative of many open data projects created across developing economies. It was created on a non-existent budget on a short timeline; it expanded in scope and usefulness as a result of partnerships across civil society and international organizations. These are all markers of success. At the same time, the lack of a longer-term sustainability strategy has raised questions about whether the initiative will survive going forward. This, too, is characteristic of many projects examined in this series of case studies on open data. The opportunities and obstacles are clear for advocates of open data in developing economies: they need to seize the immediate potential of data while also finding ways to address the longer-term questions and challenges.

Tanzania's Open Education Dashboards

Improving education with open data[251]

Juliet McMurren, Andrew Young and Stefaan Verhulst

Summary

Low national examination pass rates in 2012 caused a public outcry in Tanzania, but the public's understanding of the broader context and ability to demand accountability was limited by a lack of information about the country's education sector. Two portals tried to remedy that situation, providing the public with more data on examination pass rates and other information related to school quality. The first, the Education Open Data Dashboard (educationdashboard.org), was a project established by the Tanzania Open Data Initiative, a government program supported by the World Bank and the United Kingdom Department for International Development (DFID) to support open data publication, accessibility and use. The second, Shule (shule.info), was spearheaded by Arnold Minde, a programmer, entrepreneur, and open data enthusiast who has developed a number of technologies and businesses to catalyze social change in Tanzania. Although both portals show considerable promise – especially as it relates to visualization open data to make it more comprehensible to a wide audience –they have, to date, had limited success in actually changing citizen decision-making about education or generating greater institutional accountability. This is due in part to the challenges posed by Tanzania's low Internet penetration rates and unfamiliarity with open data.

---

251 This case study builds on and updates a previous piece drafted as part of the GovLab and Omidyar Network Open Data's Impact initiative.

Context and Background

Problem Focus / Country Context

In 2012, education in Tanzania became the subject of significant public discontent and controversy. That year, six out of every ten Tanzanian students failed the standardized national secondary-level examination, resulting in a media outcry and demand for reforms.[252] The poor results were the product of recent changes to the Tanzanian education system, in which tuition fees for government primary schools were eliminated in an effort to raise the country's school enrollment and literacy rates. The move triggered a rapid increase in net primary enrollment, from 66 percent in 2001 to 90 percent in 2004.[253] This increase, however, was not matched by a proportional increase in school funding.

As the Tanzanian school system strained under the burden of the additional enrollments, examination pass rates among the 30 percent of secondary-aged children enrolled in school[254] began to decline. After the particularly bad set of results in 2012, the government introduced changes to the grading system[255] that appeared to raise the pass rate in 2013 and 2014.[256] However, the root causes of the nation's education problems remained unaddressed: inadequately funded and supplied schools, a shortage of trained teachers,[257] limited teacher training and professional development, discontent regarding teachers' pay,[258] and stubborn regional, economic, and social inequalities.

At the same time, information about public education was not easy to come by, making it hard for citizens to understand the true state of the education sector and demand accountability from government officials. Although several Access to Information bills have gone before the Tanzanian Parliament, none has yet been enacted, while other legislation, including the country's defamation law, constrains the media's capacity to function critically and

---

252 Frank Kimboy, "High Pass Rate Greeted as Good as Well as Bad News," *The Citizen*, July 23, 2014, http://www.thecitizen.co.tz/magazine/politicalreforms/High-pass-rate-greeted-as-good/1843776-2394162-14jmnxhz/index.html.

253 UNESCO, "World Data on Education,United Republic of Tanzania," 2010, http://www.ibe.unesco.org/fileadmin/user_upload/Publications/WDE/2010/pdf-versions/United_Republic_of_Tanzania.pdf.

254 World Bank, World DataBank, "Tanzania," http://databank.worldbank.org/data//reports.aspx?source=2&country=TZA&series=&period=.

255 Elisha Mangolanga, "No More Div. Zero as Government Guts National Grading System," *The Citizen*, November 1, 2013, http://www.thecitizen.co.tz/News/Govt-in-major-change-of-national-exam-grading/1840340-2055404-n8mhil/index.html.

256 Frank Kimboy, "High Pass Rate Greeted as Good as Well as Bad News," *The Citizen*, July 23, 2014, http://www.thecitizen.co.tz/magazine/political-reforms/High- pass-rate- greeted-as- good/-/1843776/2394162/-/umh9xl/-/index.html.

257 The Citizen Reporter, "Teacher Shortage Hurtiing Tanzania," The Citizen, October 14, 2014, http:/ http://www.thecitizen.co.tz/News/Teachers-shortage-hurting-Tanzania/1840340-2485582-3ktjd2z/index.html.

258 Jacob Kushner, "Tanzanian teachers learning that education doesn't pay," *PRI*, December 20, 2013, https://www.pri.org/stories/2013-12-20/tanzanian-teachers-learning-education-doesnt-pay.

independently. The Tanzanian media is considered only partly free by Freedom House,[259] and the country was ranked 75th out of 180 countries in the 2015 World Press Freedom Index.[260]

In addition, there is a noticeable lack of independent voices in the Tanzanian media. While media ownership is transparent, it remains concentrated among a few proprietors. All four radio stations with national reach are regarded as favoring the ruling party, although the African Media Barometer did report in 2010 that the state-run Radio Tanzania had demonstrated more balanced views. Media outlets favorable to the opposition reportedly have government advertising contracts withheld.[261] Consequently, when stories about the state of education do make it to press, they tend to favor the official version of events, and often lack balance or context.

Citizens were for the most part unable to turn to the Internet or open data as substitutes for the information they needed. Open data use in Tanzania remains in its infancy. The Open Data Barometer places Tanzania in the "capacity constrained" cluster of countries whose open data initiatives are challenged by limits in government, civil society or private sector capacity, Internet penetration, and data collection and management.[262] Tanzania joined the Open Government Partnership Initiative in September 2011. The second phase of its OGP action plan, currently under development, commits the government to establishing an open data portal (opendata.go.tz) that would release key datasets in the education, health, and water sectors in machine-readable form.[263] As of October 2016, the portal has 100 datasets available for download, 65 of which are supplied by the Ministry of Education.

KEY ACTORS

Key Data Providers

Education Open Data Dashboard (educationdashboard.org)

Data was supplied by the National Examinations Council of Tanzania (NECTA), with additional resources from the World Bank integrated to improve the comprehensiveness of datasets.

---

259 Freedom House, "Tanzania," https://freedomhouse.org/country/tanzania#.VaQZFvlViko.

260 Reporters sans Frontieres, "Tanzanie," http://index.rsf.org/#!/index-details/TZA.

261 Freedom House, "Freedom of the Press: Tanzania," 2011, https://freedomhouse.org/report/freedom-press/2011/tanzania#.VaARQ_lVikp.

262 Open Data Barometer, "Data and Analysis: Clusters," Web Foundation, http://www.opendatabarometer.org/report/analysis/index.html.

263 Open Government Partnership, "Tanzania, 2014–15 Action Plan Documents," 2015, http://www.opengovpartnership.org/country/tanzania/action-plan.

Shule.info

Shule.info was built on similar data sources, but they were often manually scraped and collected by project organizers.

Key Data Users and Intermediaries

Education Open Data Dashboard

The project was developed as part of the Tanzania Open Data Initiative, a government program supported by the World Bank and the United Kingdom Department for International Development (DFID).

Shule.info

Shule.info was developed by Arnold Minde, a Tanzanian programmer, with some practical support and assistance from Twaweza.

Key Beneficiaries

Both portals aimed to improve parents' decision-making regarding their children's schools. In addition, they sought to improve journalism, especially regarding education-related issues, and to inform public debate regarding education.

Project Description

Initiation of the Open Data Activity

In 2013, the National Examinations Council of Tanzania (NECTA), a government body, rolled out a pilot education dashboard[264] offering data downloads, searches, and visualizations of primary and secondary examination results by district and school. The dashboard also included statistics on pupil-teacher ratios, annual and average pass rates, national rankings of school performance, and changes in pass rates since 2011. With the help of the World Bank, an updated version of the pilot was launched in 2015 as Education Open Data Dashboard (educationdashboard.org).[265] Despite some challenges and gaps described in more detail below, the data contained on the site represents a significant advance in the context of Tanzania's previous information drought.

---

264 Available at: http://www.necta.go.tz/opendata/, and subsequently updated at: http://www.necta.go.tz/opendata/brn/.

265 Available at: http://educationdashboard.org/#/.

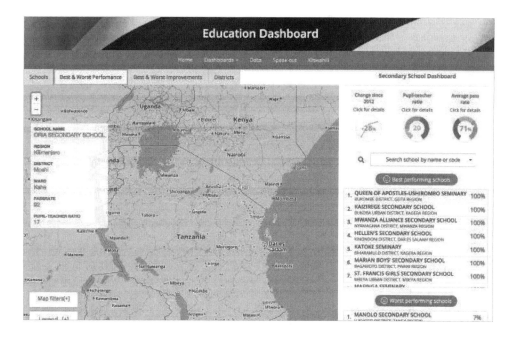

Figure 1. Mapping of school performance on the educationdashboard.org

Shule.info was the brainchild of the Tanzanian programmer Arnold Minde. It was released shortly after NECTA's original dashboard, and was conceived when Minde became aware that NECTA had been publishing individual exam results online since 2004. It wasn't until 2012, however, when poor examination pass rates prompted nationwide soul-searching, that Minde began working on the project in earnest. At that point, he realized the potential value of a single, readily usable, online source of national examination data.[266] Such data needed to be online and presented in a comprehensible format, he concluded, so that citizens could see that the poor results in 2012 were not a new phenomenon, but part of a downward trend over the past six to seven years. Minde had previously been involved in data visualization through his work for the Tanzanian development policy think tank REPOA (formerly Research on Poverty Alleviation); that work convinced him of the power of data visualization to communicate data trends and linkages, and helped shape the development of Shule.[267]

---

266 See: http://www.shule.info/about.
267 GovLab Interview with Arnold Minde, July 9, 2015.

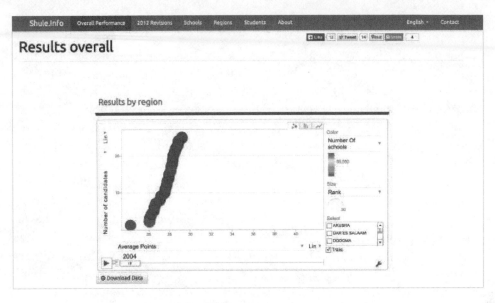

Figure 2. Education results by region on Shule.info

Demand and Supply of Data Type(s) and Sources

Both sites made the data on which they were built open for download by users. In addition, charts and visualizations were available directly on the platforms.

Although the data used to create Shule.info was available in isolated reports and websites, intended for individual students, it had never been made fully open in searchable and machine-readable format for citizens at large. Minde scraped, cleaned, and consolidated the data from the examination results as they were released each year.[268]

Education Open Data Dashboard used the government's own data, much of which is available through the official government open data portal. While there is much useful data available, some gaps do exist, including a dearth of individual examination results, pass rates before 2012, average pass rates over time, and pass rates by gender and region.

Funding

Shule.info was created on Minde's own time and at his expense. Education Open Data Dashboard was funded by the Tanzanian government, with some support from the World Bank.

---

268 Ibid.

143

Open Data Use

Both dashboards rely on government data. The data used to create Shule. info were publicly available but not open, requiring scraping, cleaning and standardization. The data on Education Open Data Dashboard were fully open, having been released on the Tanzanian government's open data portal.

Shule.info presents data for Form 4 examination results from 2004 to 2013 at candidate, school, regional and national levels. It also offers data visualizations of results (broken up by region and gender), which permits users, for example, to track average performance over time, the number of candidates in each grading division over time, and the impact of the government's controversial revision of the 2012 results. All data used to build the site is available for download. Shule therefore offers considerably more, and more granular, data than Education Open Data Dashboard. In addition (and in contrast to NECTA's dashboard), Shule offers commentary on its data visualizations, making it easier for users to understand the significance of the data they are accessing.

Impact

Tanzania is a country with low Internet penetration rates (5.3 percent in 2016, according to ITU, the United Nations specialized agency for information and communication technologies),[269] and is marked by a general lack of technical skills and expertise among the population. As noted, there is very little familiarity with the concept and potential of open data, or data in general. As such, although these projects represent notable advances within the current open data ecology, uptake and usage have generally been limited, making it hard to assess impact.

Nonetheless, a few metrics can be considered to measure the effects— limited though they are–of Shule and Education Open Data Dashboard. Impact can be gauged in three broad ways: engagement and use by both citizens and intermediaries; data quality and diversity; and spillover effects on other open data projects.

---

269 International Telecommunication Union, "ICT Facts and Figures," http://www.itu.int/en/ITU-D/Statistics/Pages/stat/default.aspx.

Engagement and Use

After Shule went live in June 2013, the site averaged around 1,500 visits per month, according to Arnold Minde.[270] Feedback directly on the site and through Twaweza suggests that visitors fell into two categories. The first consists of data sophisticates, typically programmers or employees of civil society organizations, who were already aware of the potential of open data to inform decision-making, and visited the site to research education in Tanzania and better understand the overall educational context. These visitors may have become aware of the site through Twaweza and its civil society partners, or the emerging open data community in Dar-es-Salaam.

The second category of site visitors consisted of former students making use of the site's archive of examination results to look up their scores.[271] These students may not initially have been interested in or even aware of open data, but they are nonetheless exposed to Shule's visualizations on, for example, school performance by region, and other tools when they access the site. Engaging the ordinary Tanzanian families Minde had originally hoped to reach has been more challenging. Low rates of Internet penetration and a lack of experience using the Internet have restricted the amount of casual traffic received through search engines.

Minde says he fears that average Tanzanians don't have much interest yet in looking at data visualizations, preferring to get their information predigested by the media. "I don't see people asking the real questions," says Minde. "I don't see discussions around the issues, even among people I know."[272] Aidan Eyakuze, Executive Director of Twaweza, believes both the public and policymakers are looking for the insight contained in the data, not the data itself. "Data is frightening for many people, so raw data is going to appeal to a vanishing few," he says. "Open data needs to be open plus curated plus chewed plus digested to appeal to most people, including policymakers."[273] Few in the media, however, have the knowledge and skills to digest Shule's data offerings, despite initiatives like the Data Bootcamp, which was designed to introduce members of the Tanzanian media to open data.[274]

Education Open Data Dashboard's use was similarly constrained by Tanzania's low rate of Internet use. Nonetheless, the site's developers point out that Tanzanians don't necessarily need Internet access to benefit from

---

270 GovLab Interview with Arnold Minde, July 9, 2015.

271 Ibid.

272 Ibid.

273 Ibid.

274 Michael Bauer, "The Data Bootcamp in Tanzania," October 25, 2012, Open Knowledge International Blog, http://blog.okfn.org/2012/10/25/the-data-bootcamp-in-tanzania/.

the information stored on the site. Members of civil society organizations, for example, including Tanzania's active parent-teacher organizations, can act as intermediaries, printing out information about school performance to share on a community notice board or at meetings, for example.[275]

Data Quality and Diversity

The combination of Education Open Data Dashboard and Shule increased the diversity and thus the usefulness of available data on education in Tanzania. Taken together, the information they provided is richer and more interesting than either site would have been on its own (or, of course, than the pre-existing lack of data). Education Open Data Dashboard offered indicators such as pupil-teacher ratios, regional and district rankings, and improvement rankings over time, all of which are navigated via a clickable map and drop-down menu of schools. Shule captured a much longer span of data, with examination results going back to 2004. In addition to results by gender, Shule offered average performance over time, instead of Education Open Data Dashboard's simple pass rate, and looked at the breakdown of candidate numbers per grading division over time. It also modeled the effect of the 2012 grading revision to examine how it changed candidate pass rates.

Although based on government data, the dataset used to build Shule is not completely identical to that used for the government dashboard; this is due to differences in methods of data collection. Perhaps as a result, Shule's figures can depart in significant ways from the government version. For example, NECTA traditionally published an annual list of the ten government and secondary schools with the highest examination results. In 2012, Minde reports that NECTA's official list contained a number of government schools, but Shule's analysis showed that all ten of the top performing schools were private.

For the developers of Education Open Data Dashboard, one of the more surprising discoveries was that feeding a dashboard was a potent incentive to compliance with data reporting. Regional officials and head teachers were excited by finding their school or region in the dashboard, and by seeing what the data they submitted was creating, and this excitement appeared to translate to improved reporting, at least in the short term.[276] This suggests that the novelty of open data use and data visualization can be a useful tool in improving data quality.

---

275 GovLab interview with Samhir Vasdev and Verena Luise Knippel, June 30, 2015.
276 Ibid.

Spillover Effects on Other Open Data Projects

As the developers of the latest version of Educationdashboard have indicated, Shule forms part of a nascent data ecosystem of which they were very much aware during the development and refinement of their own site. For government officials involved in creating the dashboard, the existence of such independent projects validated both the demand for the kinds of open data portal they were building, and provided evidence that the local technical and other capacity existed to build it.[277] Their own dashboard was, in turn, a powerful tool in demonstrating the potential and uses of open data to a non-technical audience, particularly among policymakers. In addition, the data visualizations and linkages it made possible ignited interest in, and impetus for, the development of dashboards in other sectors, such as moves by the Department of Justice to map courthouses across the country.[278]

Lessons Learned

Shule and Education Open Data Dashboard were both experimental projects, launched into a society that was just beginning to grasp the potential of open data. If projects like these are to succeed, they will need to overcome significant societal challenges. This section examines some of the most important enablers of and challenges to these projects. Although these enablers and barriers are particular to this project, they offer hints of what may face other open data projects in other developing countries.

Enablers

Leveraging intermediaries

As Internet penetration slowly expands in Tanzania, civil society organizations like parent- teacher organizations or NGOs have an important role to play as intermediaries that can disseminate insights gleaned from open data among citizens who would otherwise not have access to the data. The developers of Educationdashboard note that ultra-low-tech solutions like posting printouts of information drawn from open data dashboards on school or community notice boards can be effective in getting information to the people who can use

---

277 Ibid.

278 Open Data for Africa, "Tanzania Data Portal," November 22, 2013, http://tanzania.opendataforafrica. org/igcpumb/social-justice.

it.[279] The focus on easily comprehensible data visualizations also made such low-tech solutions possible.

Engaging civil society

Even among such intermediary groups, however, awareness of the potential of open data remains nascent at best. Like the public at large, civil society groups also need to be trained to analyze and visualize data. Some efforts have taken place in Tanzania to involve civil society: in 2012, in an effort to encourage interest and build skills among coders and the media, the World Bank Institute and the Africa Media Initiative combined to offer the Data Bootcamp in Dar-es-Salaam.[280] A similar initiative was offered by Twaweza in 2013, and community groups such as the Open Knowledge Foundation Network TZ have attempted to promote open data meetups in Dar-es-Salaam. Thus far the work has been mostly carried forward by local civil society organizations like Twaweza and REPOA, but international development organizations already operating in Tanzania would be well placed to assist them. As is the case across many of the case studies in this series, the existence of a strong ICT4D and D4D ecosystem cleared the way for these new and innovative open data uses.

Barriers

Internet penetration

Perhaps the most important challenge stems from Tanzania's low Internet penetration and usage rates. The two dashboards begin from the premise that providing information to target audiences will improve conditions on the ground. However, given Tanzania's low Internet penetration rates, particularly in rural areas, where Internet penetration is estimated to be about a quarter of that in urban areas,[281] getting information to those target audiences remains a challenge. This clearly limits the reach of education-related data, and open data more broadly. Furthermore, of the 4.7 percent of Tanzanians who used the Internet in 2014, the great majority did so only by mobile phone; only 0.17 percent of Tanzanians had a fixed broadband subscription.[282] In order to appeal

---

279 GovLab Interview with Samhir Vasdev and Verena Luise Knippel, June 30, 2015.

280 Michael Bauer, "The Data Bootcamp in Tanzania," October 25, 2012, Open Knowledge International Blog, http://blog.okfn.org/2012/10/25/the-data-bootcamp-in-tanzania/.

281 Africa Focus, "Tanzania: Old media, new media," *AfricaFocus Bulletin*, April 5, 2011, http://www.africafocus.org/docs11/tan1104.php.

282 International Telecommunication Union, "ICT Facts and Figures," http://www.itu.int/en/ITU-D/Statistics/Pages/stat/default.aspx.

more widely, any open data site clearly needs to consider launching a mobile application to appeal to "the retail user of data sitting in a bus shelter with a mobile phone."[283]

This is a challenge faced by data projects throughout the developing world, and some have dealt with it by developing low-cost, low-bandwidth solutions more accessible to users on slow mobile connections.[284] In some cases, too, sharing information over SMS has proven effective.[285]

Public interest and trust in technology

Although technology remains inherently a challenge in the developing world, the barriers may be even higher when it comes to using technology (and data) as instruments of social change. Minde notes that, in general, the Tanzanian public is deeply unfamiliar with the potential of the Internet, and perhaps not yet inclined to trust it. He adds that Tanzanians have yet to embrace or commit to digital solutions for the problems of everyday life, whether complex or mundane. As an example, he cites the difficulty he experienced in convincing bus operators to adopt an earlier application he developed that allowed passengers to purchase tickets by phone. "It will only take one [company], and then people will see the benefit," he says. "But first you have to convince the one."[286]

Looking Forward

Current Status

Education Open Data Dashboard displays data visualizations for data only from 2012 to 2014. Given that education data for 2016 is now available on the Tanzanian government open data portal, opendata.go.tz, it appears that the site is no longer being actively updated and may have reached the end of its lifespan.

Similarly, Shule.info has not had any results added since 2013. Although Minde says he contemplated further refinements to his project (including

---

283 GovLab Interview with Aidan Eyakuze, July 14, 2015.

284 See, for example: http://www.aptivate.org/webguidelines/Why.html.

285 See, for example: Participedia, "Enabling Youth Participation through Technology: U-report Uganda, June 21, 2016, http://participedia.net/en/cases/enabling-youth-participation-through-technology-u-report-uganda.

286 GovLab Interview with Arnold Minde, July 9, 2015.

adding Form 4 examination results[287] and an increased range of information about schools),[288] the dashboard should probably now be considered dormant.

Although the short lifespans of these projects make clear the difficulty in sustaining open data projects over the long term absent a clear business model or operational strategy for engaging target audiences, their impact has nonetheless been undeniable and both projects offer valuable insights for open data projects across the developing world.

Sustainability

Projects by sole developers, such as Shule.info, are inherently vulnerable as the developer's available time, energy, and interest in the project change. Minde has indicated that the biggest constraint on Shule's growth was his own time.[289] As a government site, Education Open Data Dashboard should have had greater longevity, but even it was unable to sustain itself. The fact that neither was driven by end-user demand could also have made them more vulnerable to abandonment. Indeed, this appears to have been the case: although Minde says that he is still convinced of the usefulness of and need for the data, there were no demands for updates to it, and he was unable to obtain the necessary investment to build Shule into a commercial product to ensure its long-term sustainability.[290]

Moreover, given low Internet penetration rates, the existence of two separate dashboards for education information could also prove confusing to parents, and limit the effectiveness of both platforms. Greater impact could perhaps have come from integrating the two platforms and cooperatively advancing a single project, rather than providing a limited user base with two separate entry points for accessing essentially the same information. It is worth noting that moves toward greater coordination were in fact made, notably including Minde's involvement in development strategy meetings for Education Open Data Dashboard.[291] However, these efforts at coordination do not appear to have yielded the desired results.

Replicability

These dashboards illustrate the power of a deceptively simple tool, that can be built locally in a matter of a few weeks by a single developer (Shule.info) or a

---

287 See: http://www.shule.info/about.
288 GovLab Interview with Arnold Minde, July 9, 2015.
289 GovLab Interview with Arnold Minde, September 20, 2016.
290 Ibid.
291 GovLab Interview with Samhir Vasdev and Verena Luise Knippel, June 30, 2015.

small team (Education Open Data Dashboard), with little or no outside support or funding, then refined through user feedback. As one of the developers of the Education Open Data Dashboard put it: "Get a minimum viable product [MVP] out there. Make some assumptions about the data, get it out there, and provoke a response."[292] So whether or not the specific tools or methods used by the developers of the platforms are replicated, their general approach—drawing on open data to quickly create platforms aimed at bettering the public good—can be seen as inspiration for similarly community-minded innovators across developing countries.

Conclusion

While neither Shule nor Education Open Dashboard was able to achieve longer-term sustainability or the types of transformative impact on education and parent decision-making that they set out to accomplish, they can be seen as clear indications of how dedicated, data-driven efforts to enhance citizen decision-making and benefit the public good can quickly become tangible. Indeed, the projects also make clear the need for a longer-term business model to ensure that initial MVPs grow into "sticky," widely used platforms—a key lesson for the field of open data practice.

---

292 Ibid.

South Africa's Medicine Price Registry

Cheaper medicines for consumers

François van Schalkwyk, Andrew Young and Stefaan Verhulst

Summary

In 2014, Code for South Africa, a South Africa-based non-profit organization active in the open data space, took a little-known dataset from the national Department of Health website and created the Medicine Price Registry Application (MPRApp, https://mpr.code4sa.org/), an online tool that allows patients to compare medicine prices. MPRApp allows patients to compare the costs of doctor-prescribed medicines with those of other (e.g., generic) medicines containing the same ingredients. It also helps patients verify that they aren't being overcharged by their pharmacies, and ensures cost-savings for both patients and society without compromising on efficacy.

It was initially expected that middle- to upper-class patients with better online access would be the primary beneficiaries of MPRApp. However, there is evidence that doctors also use the information provided by MPRApp to save their patients money. Because MPRApp currently relies on the time and skills of its developer to ensure regular updates its continued use and impact remains uncertain unless sustainable funding can be secured. With no marketing or promotions to speak of, MPRApp has had an impact on the lives of a few South Africans; with a sustainable model and increased awareness of MPRApp, particularly among trusted intermediaries in the health sector, it could provide many more patients access to cheaper medicines.

Context and Background

Problem Focus/Country Context

Healthcare in South Africa is provided by public hospitals and clinics, and by private hospitals and doctors. Private general practitioners (GPs), with surgeries across the country, are the first port of call for many middle-class South Africans seeking medical advice and who can afford private consultation fees that range from USD 20 to USD 50. For those who cannot afford private GPs, state medical facilities such as clinics and hospitals provide the only alternative. Many middle to upper class South Africans take out medical insurance (or "medical aid" as it is known in South Africa) to cover the cost of private hospitalization and/or day-to-day medical expenses.

Medical doctors prescribe medicines, and pharmacies dispense medicines. In the case of private doctors, the doctor will prescribe a specific medicine and the patient will purchase the medicine from a private pharmacy. The patient has access to a choice of medicines, and there are likely to be both branded and generic alternatives to medicine prescribed by a doctor. In some cases, if doctors are unfamiliar with the alternatives available for a particular medicine, they may leave it up to the pharmacist to provide the patient with an equivalent alternative (and may request this on the prescription note). However, the possibility of alternatives will depend on the availability of the medicine from the pharmaceutical company or distributor, and on whether the alternative medicines are stocked by the pharmacist. In the case of the public system, there is no or very limited choice available to the patient if the patient elects to obtain their medication from the dispensary at a public hospital. Public hospitals stock only those medicines made available to them through the public procurement system, and will typically only stock one brand for each type of medicine.

Medicine prices in South Africa are regulated by the government,[293] and generic medicines that are cheaper than their brand-name equivalents are approved by the government to provide patients[294] with access to more

---

293 The restructuring of the South African public health sector resulted in the development and implementation of the National Drug Policy in 1996. The primary objective of the Policy was to decrease the cost of medicines in both the private and public sectors. In 1997, the Medicines and Related Substances Control Amendment Act 90 was gazetted. It allowed government to reduce the cost of medicines.

294 Patients in the public healthcare system access prescribed medication via hospital dispensaries. These dispensaries are stocked with publicly procured medicines. Patients do not have a choice as to which medicine they receive and they do not pay for the medicines as they are charged a single fee (determined by their income level) for both the consultation and the medicines prescribed.

affordable alternatives.[295] Moreover, legislation introduced in 2004 prohibits drug firms from giving customers in the private sector discounts or rebates; they are required to sell their products at what is known as the "single exit price" (SEP) to all buyers. The national government's Department of Health is required by law to publish an annual notice of the maximum price hike allowed. In order to make medicine prices transparent, and in keeping with the Regulations Relating to a Transparent Pricing System for Medicines and Scheduled Substances,[296] the Department of Health publishes a publicly-accessible SEP database on the Medicine Price Registry website (http://www.mpr.gov.za/).

Medicine challenges

The problem in the regulated market for pharmaceuticals in South Africa is that doctors do not always prescribe generic medicines, and although pharmacists are obliged by law to offer private patients lower-priced generic medicines, this does not always happen.[297] According to an article in *Health24*, a South African consumer health site, only 56 percent of patients in the South African private health sector use generic medicines while the global norm is closer to 80 percent.[298] Price differentials between branded and generic medicines can be significant, and this affords private patients with greater opportunity to choose cheaper alternatives than those seeking care in the public sector. According to a study conducted by Bangalee and Suleman, of the 346 branded drugs in the study's sample, the median cost differential was 50.4 percent; 75 percent of the generic drugs considered were more than 40 percent cheaper than the branded version.[299] Although public patients encounter the biggest problems (since they are not given a choice of medicines), private patients also suffer from this price differential as they lack access to information allowing them to identify and purchase more affordable alternative to those prescribed.

As noted in the text box, medicine price data is actually published by the Department of Health (DoH) and available online. However, the information

---

295 V. Bangalee and F. Suleman, "Has the Increase in the Availability of Generic Drugs Lowered the Price of Cardiovascular Drugs in South Africa? *Health SA Gesondheid*, 21, No. 1 (2016), pp. 60–66.

296 *Medicines and Related Substances Act, 1965*, Department of Health, South Africa, 2004, http://www.hst.org.za/uploads/files/pricing_system_for_medicines.pdf.

297 M. Deroukakis, "Mandatory Substitution Successful," *South African Medical Journal*, 97, No. 1 (2007), pp. 63–64.

298 Health24, "Cost of Medicine in South Africa Set to Skyrocket," March 30, 2016, http://www.health24.com/Lifestyle/Health-and-your-money/News/the-high-cost-of-medicines-in-south-africa-20160323.

299 Ibid.

is difficult to find, and requires technical skills and some expert knowledge to use.[300]

KEY ACTORS

Key data provider(s)

The South African national government, through its Department of Health (DoH), has regulated medicine prices for the past decade, and is required by law to make medicine pricing transparent. The DoH does so by publishing medicine price data on its Medicine Price Registry site. The DoH is therefore the primary supplier of medicine price data. Mention should also be made of the Minister of Health, Aaron Motsoaledi, who has championed affordable medicines and has gone so far as to clash with multinational pharmaceutical companies operating in South Africa in his efforts to improve access to medicines through the use of affordable generics.[301]

The primary sources for the data are the privately owned and licensed pharmaceutical companies, which are required by law to submit their medicine prices on an annual basis to the DoH.

Key Data Users and Intermediaries

The central actor in the reuse of open government data is Code for South Africa (Code4SA, http://code4sa.org). Code4SA is a non-profit organization based in Cape Town, South Africa. Code4SA works with governments (national, regional and metropolitan), civil society organizations, the media and the tech community to promote the release, use and impact of open government data in South Africa. Adi Eyal, Director of Code4SA, was the prime driver behind the development of the MRPApp.

Other data intermediaries include private doctors who may rely on the MRPApp to advise private patients on alternative and potentially better priced medicines. Additionally, privately owned pharmacies act as both data users and intermediaries, as they may wish to familiarize themselves with the generic equivalents of prescribed branded medicines in order to provide the generic alternatives that they are legally obliged to offer patients. It is also conceivable that journalists, civil society organizations or consumer watchdog organizations may be interested in using the MRPApp to keep tabs on medicine prices and to call government to account if discrepancies appear in the prices listed online and those actually made available to patients.

---

300 The issue of the prices of medicines in South Africa and their affordability relative to international prices is not addressed here partly because there is limited research available on the issue (see, for example, A. Makholwa, "Medicine Pricing: New prescriptions needed," *Financial Mail*, January 30, 2014, http://www.financialmail.co.za/features/2014/01/30/medicine-pricing-new-prescriptions-needed.), partly because there is unevenness in the affordability of medicines across different medicines types in the South African market, and partly because the specific problem here is the lack of information available to support informed medicine purchasing decision-making.

301 A. Makholwa, "Medicine Pricing: New prescriptions needed," *Financial Mail*, January 30, 2014, http://www.financialmail.co.za/features/2014/01/30/medicine-pricing-new-prescriptions-needed.

Private companies that offer free medical advice services (such as websites), may also embed the MRPApp as a useful tool to attract patients to their services. Similarly, private medical aid providers may incorporate the MRPApp as a value added service into their product offerings.

Key Beneficiaries

Patients in the South African private healthcare sector are the primary beneficiaries of the available information on medicine prices. They are able to alter their decisions on which medicines to purchase based on the information provided by MRPApp. Such price-sensitive decisions may also lead to general efficiencies in the healthcare sector, which would benefit the South African economy as a whole.

Project Description and Inception

Initiation of the Open Data Activity

In 2014, Adi Eyal, the director of Code for South Africa, one of Africa's largest data journalism and civic technology initiatives, began wondering if there was a better way to make the information on medicine prices in South Africa available. He believed that if the information on medicine prices was more accessible and easier to understand, it could save private patients money. He soon realized that he could develop a simple application using a little known dataset from the Department of Health website that would help solve the problem confronting him and millions of South African patients. The dataset was the Medicine Price Registry (described further below) and it contained the single price exit data—the government-regulated price of all available medicines in the South African private health sector. Eyal's goal was to use this dataset to present information to patients in an easy-to-use format that would allow them to identify and request equivalent generics, and to make sure they weren't being overcharged by their pharmacies.

Eyal himself takes a number of medications for his own chronic conditions. In a blog post, he describes how the application he developed has benefited him personally, and how a search for a personal, individual solution led to a potential solution for society at large:

Here's a real life example of how this app has benefited me. I take chronic medication A and B. The branded version of A costs R741.27 and B costs R947.78. A generic of A is available at R420.22. Not only that but my medical aid pay for it in full whereas

they only cover around R420.00 for the branded medicine. I only learnt about this by using the app.[302]

Demand and Supply of Data type(s) and Sources

The primary data source used for the Medicine Price Registry application (MPRApp, https://mpr.code4sa.org/) is the database on medicine prices (the Medicine Price Registry), published by the national Department of Health of the Government of South Africa. The database contains prices, product details (e.g. schedule and form), ingredients and available dosages of all government-approved medicines in South Africa. The database is published annually following the publication of single exit price for medicines as required by law. Occasional updates are made by the Department during the course of the year to correct errors or make unforeseen adjustments. An RSS feed is available to notify interested parties of updates and changes made to the database. The database is also available for download in Microsoft Excel format from the Medicine Price Registry website.

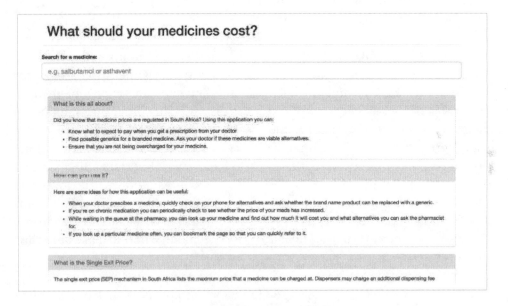

Figure 1. MPRApp Main Page

---

302 Adi Eyal, "Open data FTW!" Code for South Africa, April 2014, http://code4sa.org/2014/04/25/generic-medicines-ftw.html.

Although the data contained on the site is in theory "open," users have to jump through a number of hoops to use it. Here are some of the steps a typical user would have to take in order to compare medicine prices:[303]

1. Know about and locate the Medicine Price Registry website.
2. Locate the page http://www.mpr.gov.za/PublishedDocuments. aspx#DocCatId=21 from the landing page by clicking on "SEP Databases" in the "Frequently Used Links" menu.
3. Download the latest single exit price database, a 40 megabyte Microsoft Excel spreadsheet.
4. Open a large spreadsheet which contains the 14,728 rows of medicines and 22 columns of descriptive data for each medicine listed.
5. Search for the relevant medicine.
6. To find generics, search by ingredient and discard all those alternatives that have a different strength (e.g. 200mg or 400mg) and dosage form (e.g. tablet or suspension).
7. To calculate the over the counter price, add the pharmacist dispensing fees (not provided in the spreadsheet) to the single exit price (provided in the spreadsheet).[304]

Needless to say, this process is complex, cumbersome and well beyond the abilities of most patients. Code4SA's innovation was to simplify the process for the end user to determine the cheapest alternative to a prescribed medicine.

Code4SA's application consists of a single page providing some contextual and instructional information, and a search bar allowing users to search for specific medicines or active ingredients. The results returned contain matching products and/or ingredients. An icon is also displayed, indicating the medicine form (tablet, suspension, etc.). For each matching product, the following information is provided: maximum price, schedule, dosage form, tablets/ml/ doses, number of packs, generic/innovator, and a list of active ingredients (name and amount). Users are able to click on a link labelled "Find Generics" for each result.

The application data is updated on an asynchronous basis. The process involves the director of Code4SA downloading any data updates, cleaning

---

303 These steps are based on the Medicine Price Registry website as of September 14, 2016, and on the Database of Medicine Prices of August 8, 2016.

304 According to the Code for South Africa website, the Medicines and Related Substances Act allows for the following charges (excl. VAT):
- Where the SEP is less than R85.69, the maximum dispensing fee is R7.04 + 46% of the SEP.
- Where the SEP is less than R228.56, the maximum dispensing fee is R18.80 + 33% of the SEP.
- Where the SEP is less than R799.99, the maximum dispensing fee is R59.83 + 15% of the SEP.
- Where the SEP is greater than or equal to R799.99, the maximum dispensing fee is R140.00 + 5% of the SEP.

the data and importing the updated and cleaned data into the application database.[305]

Funding

No external funding was available for this open data initiative, nor is there any intention to generate any income from the MPRApp in order to cover its development or operation. The development of the application was primarily made possible by non-material inputs—in particular, the developers' entrepreneurial spirit, time, energy, and technical skills. Code4SA's existing organizational infrastructure to house and support the application also contributed to its development.

Open Data Use

Initially, the developers of the MPRApp anticipated that it would be used primarily by patients, and possibly to a limited extent by other developers who might feed the data into other personal health applications or platforms.[306] Neither Eyal nor Code4SA did much to promote or market the application, and initial uptake and monitoring appeared to be slow, as evidenced by the fact that the developers were unaware that the website hosting the application went down in mid-2014.[307] As it turned out, the unavailability of the application unintentionally provided evidence of the application's use. This evidence took the form of an email sent to Code4SA, enquiring when the website would be back up, and indicating the application's usefulness to the sender:

It is with sadness that I not [sic] that your medicine price registry website is no longer working. The site was a powerful tool in my medical practice, it really helped me to work out treatments that my patients could afford. I'd like to know if the website will be coming back online anytime soon. Thank you very much for your efforts in general.[308]

Once the online application was restored, the sender followed up with this message:

---

305 At the time of writing, the last update of the MPRApp was on July 19, 2016 while the latest government data available was dated 8 August 2016.

306 Adi Eyal, "How Much Should You Be Paying for Your Medicines?" Code for South Africa, October 2013 http://code4sa.org/2013/10/15/comparing-medicine-prices.html.

307 Adi Eyal, "Open data FTW!" Code for South Africa, April 2014, http://code4sa.org/2014/04/25/generic-medicines-ftw.html.

308 Adi Eyal, "Open data FTW!" Code for South Africa, April 2014, http://code4sa.org/2014/04/25/generic-medicines-ftw.html.

I work in a mixed-income neighbourhood and being able to figure out what works for my patients' budgets is extremely helpful—there's is no point in prescribing medicine that the patient cannot afford to buy. Please keep up the good work.[309]

The emails revealed an unexpected use case for MPRApp. While the application had been created primarily with patients in mind as end-users, and while the MPRApp's creator himself was able to benefit from the application as a patient, in many cases it wasn't patients who accessed the application directly, but rather medical practitioners. These practitioners served as trusted and expert intermediaries for patients, who were unable to understand and benefit from the information contained in the application without guidance. In fact, the situation was even somewhat more complex: it turned out that the medical practitioner who emailed Eyal had not discovered the application directly, but rather through one of his patients. All of this suggests not just the important role of intermediaries (e.g., physicians or pharmacists) in propagating and using such applications, but the symbiotic role intermediaries play with end-users (e.g., patients). Together, intermediaries and end-users are able to maximize the potential of open data.

Impact

Impact is often difficult to measure, especially as many projects included in this series of case studies have been initiated relatively recently. The larger, systemic impact of open data can take many years to be evident, and in most countries is very much a work in progress. Nonetheless, a couple initial forms of impact from the MPRApp project can be identified.

Use Indicators

The above analysis relies heavily on blogs written by Eyal and on the email exchange between Eyal and the appreciative doctor as evidence of use. The reality is that many small-scale open data initiatives simply do not have the time or resources to evaluate the use and impact of their products. In fact, if the MPRApp website had not gone down, Code for South Africa might never even have known that their product was in fact being used.

Eyal confirmed the lack of resources to establish who is using the MPRApp and what they may be using it for. What he could provide were website analytics that show that approximately 2,000 unique visitors per month access

---

309 Ibid.

the application. Most of these visitors are repeat visitors. In addition, Code for South Africa also receives regular requests for the application data to be updated when it is no longer in sync with the latest available government data. All of this suggests that the application is being used, and that users are deriving benefit from it. See Figures 2 and 3 for further web analytics for 2016 providing evidence of frequent and increasing use of the MPRApp to query the prices of medicines (Figure 2) and generic alternatives (Figure 3).

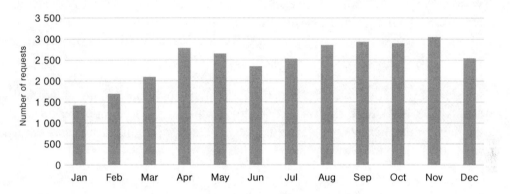

Figure 2. MPRApp Request for Product Details in 2016

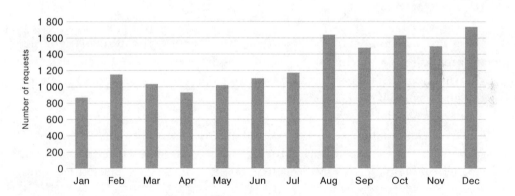

Figure 3. MPRApp Requests for Generic Medicines in 2016

There is also evidence that the MPRApp API is being used by other intermediaries to access medicine price data in their efforts to reach and engage patients

(see, for example, HEALTH-E News, a popular South African health news website).[310]

Changed Outcomes

The immediate problem being addressed is a lack of access to usable information on medicine prices, which results in private patients not being able to make informed purchasing decisions in relation to prescribed medicines. There are various ways to measure impact. Key indicators would be those that provide evidence of change directly attributable to the creation of the MPRApp. Measuring change at a macro level and ascribing a causal connection between the introduction of a new piece of technology and the change observed is, however, tenuous. Ascribing causal connections at the micro level is more feasible (though not without challenges). Evidence of impact at the micro level in this case could, for instance, take the form of private patients or other citizens changing their behavior in relation to the prescription and/or purchasing of medicines in South Africa.

Outcomes and Impacts

Demonstrated Use

From the anecdotal evidence available, it is clear that the availability of new information on medicine pricing, extracted from open government data, has changed how certain patients make decisions (in this case, by proxy) related to the purchasing of medicines.

It is not possible to claim that patients are healthier, and even if additional evidence came to light that showed that a particular community or a group of patients linked to a doctor using the application are in fact healthier, it would still be problematic to draw a causal relationship between better decision-making and healthier citizens.

There is also evidence in the form of web analytics of the same people making repeated use of the MPRApp. While it is not possible to say with certainty what the value or benefits accrued from using MPRApp are, it can be said with some degree of certainty that repeated use and the need for up-to-date data are indicative of some form of positive impact being experienced by users.

---

310 "[Updated] Health-e News, Code4SA launch new medicines pricing app," *Health-E News*, March 2, 2015, https://www.health-e.org.za/2015/03/02/health-e-news-code4sa-launch-new-medicines-pricing-app/.

It is acknowledged that impact is claimed based on an extremely limited number of cases and on shallow web analytics data. It is beyond the scope of this study to conduct a large-scale survey on the awareness, use and impact of the MPRApp. Interviews were conducted with two medical doctors who work in both the public and private sectors to get a better understanding of the medicines market and the prescriptions process. Both did, however, reveal that neither of them knew about the MPRApp although both confirmed its value for private patients. While a lack of numerous sources supporting claims of use and/or impact are frustrating, this should not be seen as overly limiting. Breadth of evidence is less of an issue than firm evidence. Moreover, assuming that a particular number of users is indicative of actual use or impact can be highly problematic. As is evidenced in this case study, a single intermediary user may be reaching tens or hundreds of beneficiaries who will not show up in usage analytics. This may be particularly relevant in environments where low technical skills or limited Internet access prevail.

Nevertheless, further research is clearly required to provide additional supportive evidence of the use and impact of MPRApp.

Risks

As evidenced by the example of MPRApp and various other case studies included in this series, open data holds tremendous potential for positive transformation. But, as we also see throughout this series, open data also poses certain risks. It is important to understand these risks in order to ensure that open data projects are implemented in as safe a manner and in a way that maximizes the potential upsides and limits the downsides.

Two doctors were interviewed for this case study in order to assess the risks inherent in the MPRApp. They raised two broad issues. The first concerned the accuracy of the information contained within the application. One doctor suggested, for instance, that the MPRApp needs to make it clearer to users when alternative medications suggested in the search results do not in fact contain *exactly* the same active ingredients as the queried medication. For example, a search for "Sandoz Atenolol 50" (of which the only active ingredient is adenol) provides a list of 12 alternative medicines, two of which contain additional active ingredients (one contains hydrochlorothiazide while the other contains chlortalidone). Such imperfect matches pose several potential risks, including the possibility of adverse reactions or medical inefficacy. Similar examples were found when Code4SA conducted live testing of the application with doctors prior to its full-scale launch.

In addition, the doctors interviewed queried the comprehensiveness of the data provided. They stated, for instance, that they were aware of alternative (and sometimes cheaper) medicines that were not in fact listed in the MPRApp. The reasons for these gaps in information are unclear, but a number of factors could be at play: errors in the source data provided by the government, outdated data, or confusion introduced due to different procurement mechanisms across different aspects of the South African health sector. Regardless of the reasons, if the database does not correspond with existing knowledge and the actual availability of medications, it could result in less-than-optimal cost savings and, more generally, jeopardize the trust that doctors place in the application.

Lessons Learned

While impact, beyond anecdotal stories of use, remains difficult to define in the case of MPRApp, the project did surface some key lessons regarding enabling conditions and barriers for establishing successful open data initiatives in developing economies.

Enablers

Policy and legislative framework

A key enabler for the MPRApp open data initiative was South Africa's legislative framework that promotes and enacts transparency in medicine pricing. The existence of such a framework compels the Department of Health to collect and publish data on medicine prices in South Africa.

The right policy or legislative framework is not, however, on its own sufficient to enable an application such as this one.[311] For example, government departments may collect data in compliance with existing laws, but fail to publish the data in a manner or format that enables access or reuse (despite such an approach being required in the policy framework). In this particular case, the department in question complies with the regulations and publishes timely, complete data on medicines pricing in machine-readable format, allowing a developer to repackage the data into useful information.

---

311 See for example, F. Van Schalkwyk, M. Willmers and T. Schonwetter, "Embedding Open Data Practice: Developing indicators on the institutionalisation of open data practice in two South African countries," UCT IP Unit, University of Cape Town, 2015, http://webfoundation.org/docs/2015/08/ODDC-2-Embedding-Open-Data-Practice-FINAL.pdf, on the disjuncture between policy and practice in the case of Kenya and South Africa.

Committed and skilled technical community

MPRapp also very much owes its existence to the presence of a skilled and committed developer, who was backed by a wider technical ecology. This personal and institutional commitment was especially important given the lack of available funding, which means that the application depended almost exclusively on personal drive and vision.

Trusted and expert intermediaries

As we have seen, MPRapp's usefulness to patients was often mediated through the expertise and knowledge of doctors, pharmacists and other medical practitioners. Such trusted intermediaries often play a vital role in spreading the benefits of open data and, more generally, technology. They serve as vital go-betweens that allow the benefits of technology to manifest, and that ensure its potential is apparent and seized by even those average citizens who may lack the required technical skills to use applications and platforms on their own.

Barriers

Funding

The lack of funding posed a significant barrier in extending the impact of the MPRApp, even though it was apparent that doctors (and not only patients) were using the application. Shortage of funds for expansion and awareness building limited the uptake and possible impact of the MPRApp. According to Eyal, there was interest from government in taking over the management of the MPRApp but the apparent lack of capacity at the government level to do so means that the application's sustainability remains at risk.

Limited reach

Another barrier stems from the fact that the MPRApp has limited reach—it only benefits patients purchasing medicines from private pharmacies, while those in the public healthcare area are not similarly presented with alternative medicines to purchase. The divide between the private and the public health sector, both of which are regulated by government, is a barrier to the broader application, use and impact of the MPRApp to patients outside of the private health sector. More generally, since those in the private sector tend generally to be better off, the limited reach of the application—especially if it were to be

used more broadly—could reinforce existing socioeconomic inequalities and lead to an all-too-familiar digital divide.

Data problems

The data published by the Department of Health is not interoperable, meaning that it cannot be easily combined with other data sources or processed with existing tools. This places limits on the usefulness of the MRPApp and could jeopardize the trust that users place in the application. Currently, the application data is updated only when the developer has time to do so or when persistent requests from users for updated data are received. Automatic updates of the application data made possible by the government data being interoperable would help mitigate this barrier.

Looking Forward

Current Status

The application is still active, and the director of Code4SA updates the data as and when time permits. These updates are often prompted by users of the MPRApp, and not conducted according to a regular schedule.

Sustainability

The flow of data and information from the government is likely to continue, but the sustainability of the application itself remains in question. There are at least two reasons for this: (1) the application relies on the infrastructure of an organization that itself depends on donor funding for its functioning; and (2) the application depends on the generosity of one individual—i.e., Adi Eyal—to allocate time and energy to the application and maintaining its data. However, according to Eyal, the Department of Health is supportive, and there has been some indication that it may be interested in taking over the management of the MPRApp. To date, this interest has not translated into concrete action.

Replicability

The open data initiative is replicable in other countries, states or provinces where national or subnational governments make data on medicine pricing available, where there is differential pricing for similar medicines, and where patients have a choice in relation to the brand of medicine. Where government

does not collect medicine price data, it is conceivable that data could be collected via crowdsourcing or perhaps even directly from pharmaceutical companies, although a clear incentive (most probably financial) would need to be in place to initiate and sustain data collection.

The open data initiative may also be replicable in other sectors when governments regulate the prices of commodities and consumables. There is not any direct evidence, however, that MPRApp has been replicated in any way to date.

Conclusion

The following points are worth making in terms of how this particular case study could inform a more universal theory of change on the impact of open data in developing countries:

1. It takes a combination of factors and conditions for an open data initiative to have impact. In this case, it was a cocktail of the following: a clear real-world problem; a curious and committed individual with technical skills and a social conscience; a relevant, regular and reliable open data source; an element of luck that allowed the application to be discovered despite no marketing efforts; and, last but not least, genuine usefulness to users who found value in the data (and, in this case, contacted the organizers when the application went down).

2. Relevant, regular and reliable open government data requires effort and resources. The existence of regulations mandating transparency are critical in ensuring that government departments publish open data. It should also be noted that regulations in the absence of compliance is an insufficient condition. What is required is the right regulatory framework combined with a culture of compliance (or tools to ensure compliance).

3. The ultimate beneficiaries of an open data initiative may not necessarily be the best target group in terms of marketing and promoting the use of the application. Trusted intermediaries who possess additional expertise and who have access to beneficiaries may be a better place to start. This is particularly true of data that may require a certain expertise to use and make sense of.

4. Not all open data projects require funding to be initiated. However, external funding does help in spreading the benefits of open data applications, and in particular making them sustainable and enabling them to grow over time.

Open Data's Impact on Creating Opportunity

Aclímate Colombia

Open data to improve agricultural resiliency

Andrew Young and Stefaan Verhulst

Summary

In Colombia, as in many other countries, the effects of climate change are increasingly evident. One sector that has been particularly hard hit is agriculture. In this sector, unanticipated weather shifts and extended drought periods have created major challenges for the country's farms, perhaps especially for small, independently owned farms. The Aclímate Colombia project is a cross-sector partnership led by the International Center for Tropical Agriculture (CIAT), a civil society organization, with private-sector industry groups and government actors. The platform (available at aclimatecolombia.org) leverages a diversity of data sources, including many open government datasets, to help farmers understand how to better navigate shifting weather patterns. Although still relatively young, Aclímate Colombia has already had a tangible impact and received widespread recognition. It is a powerful example of how data-sharing across sectors—along with the use of sector-relevant intermediaries—can take high-level data science insights and translate them into concrete, actionable information, in the process helping farmers increase their livelihoods.

Context and Background

Problem Focus / Country Context

Agriculture is a very important sector in Colombia and in the tropics in general. As Ruben G. Echeverría, Director General of the International Center

for Tropical Agriculture (CIAT) put it: "Parts of the humid tropics have the potential to become future breadbaskets for the world. They are where some 70 percent of the world's poor people now live, and they contain most of the world's biodiversity."[312] Colombia, in particular, holds tremendous possibilities as a provider of crops such as coffee, bananas and rice.

However, in order for countries like Colombia to achieve their potential, they must be able to adapt to the effects of climate change. As traditional growing processes are thrown into upheaval as a result of new weather patterns, global warming presents many challenges to the food-growing potential of Colombia. It represents a particularly serious challenge for small farmers, who constitute a large proportion of the crop growers in the country. As Echeverría notes: "Climate change poses a serious threat for these smallholder farmers, who already face significant challenges from poor soils, volatile rainfall patterns, lack of knowledge on best cultivation practices, and lack of investment in new technologies that can help them."[313]

The example of rice is illustrative. Rice is of particular importance to the agriculture sector in Colombia, representing the primary source of income for small farms and a staple food for much of the population, in particular lower-income communities.[314] The country's agriculture sector produced around 1.7 million tons of paddy rice in 2014 – around 65 percent of which was produced by lowland irrigated rice and 35 percent rainfed rice.[315] Recent years, however, have been hard for the country's rice sector. A decade of increases in irrigated rice yields was wiped out between 2007 and 2012 when yields dropped from 6 to 5 tons per hectare.[316] Though explanations vary, climate change is seen as the likely cause of the decrease. As the global research partnership, Consultative Group on International Agricultural Research (CGIAR) puts it, "subtle shifts in rainfall as well as more extreme weather are forcing rice growers to toss aside old assumptions about when, where and what to plant."[317]

---

312 CIAT Communicaciones, "A Powerful Voice for Climate-smart Agriculture in the Tropics," December 6, 2014, CIAT, https://ciat.cgiar.org/news-2-2/a-powerful-voice-for-climate-smart-agriculture-in-the-tropics.

313 Ibid.

314 Elizabeth Stuart, Emma Samman, William Avis and Tom Berliner, *The Data Revolution: Finding the Missing Millions, Research Report 03*, Development Progress, 2015, https://www.odi.org/sites/odi.org.uk/files/odi-assets/publications-opinion-files/9604.pdf.

315 S. Delerce, et al., Assessing Weather-Yield Relationships in Rice at Local Scale Using Data Mining Approaches," *PLoS ONE*, August 25, 2016, http://journals.plos.org/plosone/article?id=10.1371%2Fjournal.pone.0161620.

316 CTIAR and CCAFS, "Big Data for Climate-smart Agriculture," *Change for the Better: The CCAFS 2015 Annual Report*, https://ccafs.cgiar.org/bigdata#.V6jLT5ODGko.

317 Ibid.

Open Data in Colombia

In some ways, the state of open data in Colombia is quite encouraging. For example, in the 2015 Open Data Index, an assessment of data availability across a number of sectors put together by Open Knowledge International, the country ranked number four, up from 12 in 2014. This ranking is probably a reflection of the general openness of data relating to national statistics, procurement tenders, location datasets, and election results. However, despite the country's good performance on such measurements, our research and interviews with key players suggest several remaining shortcomings. While these shortcomings exist in many (perhaps most) countries that have experimented with open data, they are nonetheless important to understand for assessing the overall open data ecosystem.

One notable problem stems from the fact that Colombia's open data supply is fragmented, with little clarity on where and how to access the most useful datasets. As of August 2016, the government's official open data portal, Datos Abiertos Colombia (datos.gov.co), houses around 2,460 datasets and 70 visualizations. An additional data portal, Ciudatos (ciudatos.com), was established by the Corona Foundation in 2015, in collaboration with other civil society actors and funders across the region. The portal contains city-focused public datasets and data drawn from perception surveys conducted by Red Colombiana de Ciudades Cómo Vamos—"the network of city-level networks in Colombia dedicated to improving urban life."[318]

The existence of these two portals, while signs of a strong open data movement, also leads to a certain fragmentation. For example, users may be unsure where to search for data, and may have trouble combining information stored at the two locations for further analysis. Further complicating matters is the World Bank's Climate Change Knowledge Portal, which also hosts a number of Colombian open datasets, mostly on temperature and rainfall.[319]

Colombia originally expressed interest in joining the Open Government Partnership (OGP) in 2011.[320] Many of its OGP commitments—and, perhaps as a result, much of the country's government innovation and data work more generally—is focused on fighting corruption. This points to a further weakness in the open data space—for all its availability, data has had relatively little impact on issues like economic development or catalyzing entrepreneurship and

---

318 Social Progress Imperative, "Contributing to Novel Open Data Platform in Columbia," March 27, 2016, http://www.socialprogressimperative.org/contributing-to-novel-open-data-platform-in-colombia/.

319 The World Bank Group, "Climate Change Knowledge Portal," 2016, http://sdwebx.worldbank.org/climateportal/index.cfm?page=country_historical_climate&ThisCCode=COL.

320 Open Government Partnership, "Columbia," 2015, http://www.opengovpartnership.org/country/colombia.

business.[321] Overall, the lack of incentives for users in the business community to access and use open data has resulted in minimal demand for open data.[322]

KEY ACTORS

Key Data Providers

Government of Colombia

The primary government actor pushing forward Aclímate Colombia is the Ministry of Agriculture and Rural Development (MARD). MARD's mission is to "formulate, coordinate and evaluate policies that promote competitive, equitable and sustainable development of forestry, fisheries and rural development agricultural processes, criteria of decentralization, consultation and participation, to help improve the level and quality of life of the Colombian population."[323]

CIAT project lead Daniel Jimenez notes that the Colombian government, and MARD in particular, were the central funders for the project, and helped to facilitate communication between CIAT and important actors in the agriculture sector, enabling CIAT to access and analyze datasets held by stakeholders in other sectors.[324]

While MARD is the most important government collaborator on the project, the primary government data provider is the National Institute of Hydrology, Meteorology and Environmental Studies (IDEAM), which collects and—as a result of recent legislation[325]—opens climate data for the country.[326]

Key Data Users and Intermediaries

CIAT

The central actor in the development of Aclímate Colombia is the International Center for Tropical Agriculture (CIAT), "an agricultural research institution, nonprofit, focused on generating scientific solutions to combat hunger in the tropics." Originally established in 1970 as part of the Consultative Group on International Agricultural Research (CGIAR), CIAT plays the central data science and project management role in the initiative as part of its research program on Climate Change, Agriculture and Food Security (CCAFS). CCAFS seeks to "address the challenge of increased global warming and declining food security, agricultural practices, policies and measures.[327]

321 GovLab interview with Oscar Montiel, Open Knowledge International, September 8, 2016.

322 GovLab interview with Daniel Uribe, Fundacion Corona, September 13, 2016.

323 Aclímate Colombia, "Quiénes Somos," http://www.aclimatecolombia.org/quienes-somos-2/.

324 GovLab interview with Daniel Jimenez, International Center for Tropical Agriculture (CIAT), August 23, 2016.

325 "Information Request," IDEAM, http://www.ideam.gov.co/solicitud-de-informacion.

326 . GovLab interview with Daniel Jimenez, International Center for Tropical Agriculture (CIAT), August 23, 2016.

327 Aclímate Colombia, "Quiénes Somos," http://www.aclimatecolombia.org/quienes-somos-2/

CIAT not only conceptualized and developed the data analytics capabilities that enabled the project but also worked closely with growers associations and other stakeholders to gain access to and analyze relevant historical datasets.[328]

Fedearroaz and Crop Growers Associations

Demonstrating the potential of cross-sector collaboration on open data projects, the other key piece of the Aclímate Colombia puzzle is the stable of crop grower associations in the country. The associations, which represent and advocate for farmers, exist in both the private and semi-public sectors. The crop grower associations in many ways act as the intermediary translating the insights and tools provided by CIAT to the individual-level farmers they represent. CIAT armed these associations with the know-how to "analyze information from big data tools and determine the most limiting factors in production for the crops in specific regions."[329]

Given the focus on spurring growth in the rice sector, Fedearroz (i.e., the Rice Growers Association) was CIAT's central collaborator. According to Miryam Patricia Guzmán García, the deputy director of technology for Fedearroz, the organization has three central missions. First, it represents rice farmers at the ministerial level to ensure that their interests are known to government decision-makers. Second, Fedearroz works to transfer technological capabilities with the ability "to better the productivity and cost effectiveness" of farming in Colombia. Finally, the association seeks to provide farmers with the services they need—from identifying sellers of needed supplies to establishing partnerships with relevant industry players to finding (or providing) new funding streams.[330]

Fedearroz was eager to collaborate on the project to help ensure that, as Guzmán García puts it, "the research that normally takes place in the research centers gets down to the level where it is really needed: to the farmers."[331] This involved both providing access to relevant data and insights on the country's rice growers to CIAT, and also transferring the end results and tools provided by Aclímate Colombia to those who can use it in practice.

Key Beneficiaries

Associated Farmers in Colombia

While there are potentially massive public benefits of increased yields and sustainability in the agriculture sector, the most direct beneficiaries targeted by Aclímate Colombia are farmers affiliated with growing associations in the country. The project seeks to provide such farmers with the decision-making capability to consistently make the right planting choices and better react to the shifting impacts of climate change. As

---

328 GovLab interview with Daniel Jimenez, International Center for Tropical Agriculture (CIAT), August 23, 2016.

329 Ibid.

330 GovLab interview with Miryam Patricia Guzmán García, Deputy Director of Technology, Fedearroz, September 5, 2016.

331 Ibid.

described in more detail in the Risks and Challenges sections, unaffiliated farmers, while theoretically an intended beneficiary of the initiative, are largely disengaged from its current iteration.

Project Description

Initiation of the Open Data Activity

The summer of 2013 was a particularly dry season in Colombia. An extended drought in many regions of the country had a major impact on agriculture and crops. In the northwestern department of La Guajira, for instance, the drought led to food and water scarcity, and the death of around 20,000 cattle.[332] Farmers in the southern Casanare region also faced consistently high temperatures, ravaged plantations and exhausted water supplies.[333] In response to these struggles, the Colombian government began exploring options for strengthening growers' associations. With this goal in mind, the Minister of Agriculture signed an agreement with CIAT aimed at "strengthening the capacity of Colombia's agricultural sector to adapt to climate vulnerability action." This agreement includes evaluations of seasonal forecasting and providing specific recommendations for increasing productivity.[334] The result of these recommendations is evident in many ways on the Aclímate Colombia website, for example through regular, targeted newsletters, context-specific information analysis tools, data-driven agriculture strategy reports, and a searchable data portal.

As a first step, CIAT developed a methodology for leveraging data to develop productivity-bolstering recommendations for farmers (i.e., which crops to grow, and when, depending on region). In this effort, CIAT was inspired by a number of previous data-driven agriculture projects initiated by other NGOs around the world; these included "the use of both supervised and unsupervised artificial neural networks to model Andean Blackberry (*Rubus glaucus)* yields, and the use of mixed models to determine optimum growing conditions of Lulo (*Solanum quitoense)*" in the Andes.[335] CIAT representatives

---

332 "Colombia: The Effects of Drought in La Guajira," World Food Programme, August 27, 2014, https://www.wfp.org/stories/colombia-effects-drought-la-guajira.

333 "Drought threat to Colombia's southern farming belt," *World Bulletin*, April 3, 2014, http://www.worldbulletin.net/news/132752/drought-threat-to-colombias-southern-farming-belt.

334 GovLab interview with Daniel Jimenez, International Center for Tropical Agriculture (CIAT), August 23, 2016.

335 Silvain Delerce, et al., "Assessing Weather-Yield Relationships in Rice at Local Scale Using Data Mining Approaches," PLOS One, August 25, 2016, http://journals.plos.org/plosone/article?id=10.1371%2Fjournal.pone.0161620.

then approached Fedearroz, the rice growers association, with the idea of using the association's data as well as existing open government datasets to improve farmers' decision-making capabilities.

Fedearroz readily agreed to share data gathered over the course of over twenty-five years, including an annual rice survey, harvest monitoring records and results from agronomic experiments.[336] As Guzmán García puts it, "we decided to be part of the project to enable better analysis of all the information we had and to improve practices and recommendations for farmers to reduce the risks they face."[337] Fedearroz was in part eager to collaborate on the project to help ensure that, as Guzmán García puts it, "the research that normally takes place in the research centers gets down to the level where it is really needed: to the farmers."[338] This involved both providing access to relevant data and insights on the country's rice growers to CIAT, and also transferring the end results and tools provided by Aclímate Colombia to those who could really use it in practice: small farmers who lack the type of R&D capacity enjoyed by larger corporate farms. At a most fundamental level, Aclímate Colombia uses these diverse open data sources to "identify the most productive rice varieties and planting times for specific sites and seasonal forecasts."[339]

The CIAT effort is just one manifestation of a growing global effort to leverage open data to benefit the agriculture sector. The Global Open Data for Agriculture and Nutrition (GODAN) network brings together nearly 500 cross-sector entities around the concept, and we examine the Esoko agriculture platform in Ghana in another case study from this series.[340]

Funding

As Latin America continues to grow as a hotbed for open data activity and experimentation, international funding sources abound. Colombia, in particular, is seen by those in the field as receiving a notable amount of international funding for its data-driven projects, along with Mexico and Argentina.[341] Yet despite the apparent availability of grants from international organizations like the Inter-American Development Bank and others, the primary funding source

---

336 CTIAR and CCAFS, "Big Data for Climate-smart Agriculture," *Change for the Better: The CCAFS 2015 Annual Report*, https://ccafs.cgiar.org/bigdata#.V6jLT5ODGko.

337 GovLab interview with Miryam Patricia Guzmán García, Deputy Director of Technology, Fedearroz, September 5, 2016.

338 Ibid.

339 . CTIAR and CCAFS, "Big Data for Climate-smart Agriculture," *Change for the Better: The CCAFS 2015 Annual Report*, https://ccafs.cgiar.org/bigdata#.V6jLT5ODGko.

340 François van Schalkwyk, Andrew Young and Stefaan Verhulst, "Esoko – Leveling the Information Playing Field for Smallholder Farmers," Open Data for Developing Economies Case Studies, July 2017, http://odimpact.org/case-ghana-empowering-smallholder-farmers.html.

341 GovLab interview with Mor Rubinstein, Open Knowledge International, September 8, 2016.

for Aclímate Colombia is in fact the Colombian government. These funds are primarily targeted at supporting the continued technical development of tools and communications and training efforts to increase the uptake of data-driven insights. As the project continues to grow and mature, it is likely that more diverse funding options will be tapped.

Demand and Supply of Data Type(s) and Sources

Three types of data are primarily available on the Aclímate Colombia platform. The first is commercial crop data collected by Fedearroz, for example the previously mentioned annual rice surveys and harvest monitoring records. Much of this data was already accessible in anonymized form, but had to be centralized and digitized to be usable for Aclímate Colombia.[342] As Guzman Garcia put it: the data was previously "public at a general level for each farm, without naming the saint" – i.e., free of personally identifiable information.[343]

Second, the platform contains station-level daily weather data from the National Institute of Hydrology, Meteorology and Environmental Studies (IDEAM), as well as from a Fedearroz-led agro-meteorological network. This data helps provide insight on what CIAT considers the five most important climatic variables determining rice growth: minimum temperature, maximum temperature, precipitation, relative humidity and solar radiation.[344]

Finally, perhaps the most important datasets on the platform actually contain a combination of data, and in particular a yield record for specific fields along with a record of "cropping events"—essentially, everything that happened to a yield's crop between being planted and being harvested. Important elements feeding into cropping events include soil conditions and "management practices implemented by the farmer."[345]

All this data can be downloaded in raw form by users of the platform. In addition, the platform itself subjects the data to a range of analytic methods that provide users with region- and crop-specific insights. The platform also subjects the data to more sophisticated, machine-learning driven analyses that, according to Daniel Jimenez, "explore non-linear functional relationships between various factors – temperature, radiation, rainfall and productivity,"

342 Silvain Delerce, et al., "Assessing Weather-Yield Relationships in Rice at Local Scale Using Data Mining Approaches," PLOS One, August 25, 2016, http://journals.plos.org/plosone/article?id=10.1371%2Fjournal.pone.0161620.

343 GovLab interview with Miryam Patricia Guzmán García, Deputy Director of Technology, Fedearroz, September 5, 2016.

344 Silvain Delerce, et al., "Assessing Weather-Yield Relationships in Rice at Local Scale Using Data Mining Approaches," PLOS One, August 25, 2016, http://journals.plos.org/plosone/article?id=10.1371%2Fjournal.pone.0161620.

345 Ibid.

to the end of teasing out the most factors most directly influential to a given farming strategy.[346] The machine-learning algorithms used by CIAT were influenced by similar efforts in biology, robotics and neuroscience.[347]

Open Data Use

Open data feeds into all analyses conducted as part of the Aclímate Colombia suite of tools. So while open data is only one piece of the puzzle for the initiative—along with the industry- and NGO-provided data described above—distinguishing between the use of open data for the initiative and the initiative itself is impossible. In the simplest of terms, Aclímate Colombia could not exist without access to open data.

Aclímate Colombia uses its diversity of datasets to create a number of tools and information products, including newsletters related to farming (Figure 1) that are both informative and easily-digestible (Figure 2). The site also provides research topics, modeling, and information about the Convention agreement that launched the site in the first place. Most helpfully, though, the site offers a searchable data portal (Figure 3) and points visitors toward additional data-driven resources and datasets. The end result is that the project is able to communicate its methods, research, and findings in a clear and accessible manner to those who seek it out and have a positive impact.

Impact

Impact is often difficult to measure, especially as many projects included in this series of case studies have been initiated relatively recently. The larger, systemic impact of open data can take many years to manifest, and in most countries open data is very much a work in progress. Nonetheless, several initial forms of impact from the Aclímate Colombia project can be identified.

346 Elizabeth Stuart, "The Data Revolution: Finding the Missing Millions," *Development Progress, Research Report 03*, 2015, https://www.odi.org/sites/odi.org.uk/files/odi-assets/publications-opinion-files/9604.pdf.

347 CTIAR and CCAFS, "Big Data for Climate-smart Agriculture," *Change for the Better: The CCAFS 2015 Annual Report*, https://ccafs.cgiar.org/bigdata#.V6jLT5ODGko.

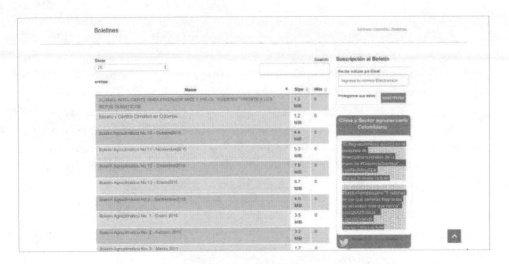

Figure 1. Aclímate Colombia Newsletter Sign Up

Figure 2. Aclímate Colombia Newsletter

One illustrative example of how Aclímate Colombia can work occurred about a year into the initiative. After the site's analysis predicted that a major dry period would disrupt the growing season and necessitate a delay in planting, Fedearroz broadcast a "simple, site-specific message," providing detailed, granular information to 170 farmers in Cordoba on the "ideal windows for planting or the best variety to grow."[348] The combination of highly specific and actionable information broadcast by a trusted and reliable source (i.e., the farmers' growing association) meant that uptake of the recommendation was significant. Many farmers avoided making premature, doomed-to-failure planting decisions, thus escaping significant losses.

Other initial markers of impact are explored in the section below.

New Knowledge and Insights

One of the most impressive aspects of Aclímate Colombia is how quickly it has enabled the transfer of knowledge and research findings from the lab into the field. As CIAT representatives put it in a journal article about the project: "Whilst previous global and continental scale studies have successfully characterized the impact of climate variability on yields, they have limited direct relevance to farm-level decisions."[349] The highly particular and localized nature of the project, as well as its use of intermediaries—i.e., growers associations—and user-friendly tools, helped Aclímate Colombia break that trend and advance new agricultural practice with real-world impact.

According to the previously mentioned article, these are some of the specific ways in which new forms of knowledge and data have changed agriculture in Colombia:[350]

- The type of analysis found on the platform showed that, in the Espinal region, rice yields are primarily influenced by "the average minimum temperature during the ripening stage." Armed with this knowledge, farmers can ensure that crop plantings are sequenced to ensure that ripening occurs when average minimum temperatures are high enough to positively benefit yields.

---

348 Elizabeth Stuart, "The Data Revolution: Finding the Missing Millions," *Development Progress, Research Report 03*, 2015, https://www.odi.org/sites/odi.org.uk/files/odi-assets/publications-opinion-files/9604.pdf.

349 Silvain Delerce, et al., "Assessing Weather-Yield Relationships in Rice at Local Scale Using Data Mining Approaches," PLOS One, August 25, 2016, http://journals.plos.org/plosone/article?id=10.1371%2Fjournal.pone.0161620.

350 Ibid.

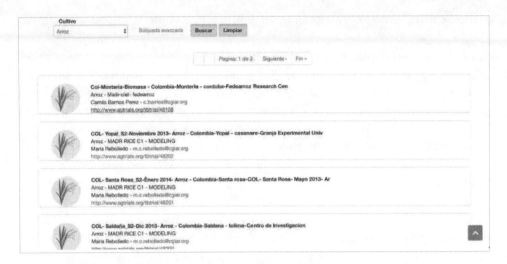

Figure 3. Aclímate Colombia Data Portal

- Analysis has also indicated that hotter regions of the country are not well-suited for planting the Cimarron Barinas rice variety; according to data included on the website, that crop variety is not suitable for growth in regions with temperatures typically exceeding 22°C.

- Farmers in the Saldaña region have also learned that (and why) the level of accumulated solar energy in irrigated rice has probably the largest impact on yield. In particular, the CIAT effort uncovered that the impact of solar radiation is most significant during the ripening stage. As a result, during the El Niño phenomenon, Saldaña faced significant risks because of the dry season. But, as Guzmán García recalls: "Fortunately, the district listened to us, and started rationing water, which, granted, caused less crops to be planted, but minimized the effects compared to another district next door that did not listen to us and had more losses."[351]

- In Villavicencio, the frequency of rainfall of over 10mm during the vegetative stage has the largest impact on yield. The team's findings in this area are particularly important because they show that the *frequency* rather than *total* rainfall is the key to growth. This insight "may foster the development of water harvesting and complementary irrigation infrastructure in that area to adapt to unevenly distributed rainfall."[352]

---

351 GovLab interview with Miryam Patricia Guzmán García, Deputy Director of Technology, Fedearroz, September 5, 2016.

352 Silvain Delerce, et al., "Assessing Weather-Yield Relationships in Rice at Local Scale Using Data Mining Approaches," PLOS One, August 25, 2016, http://journals.plos.org/plosone/article?id=10.1371%2Fjournal.pone.0161620.

One further piece of actionable insight (not included in the article) was indicated by Guzman Garcia. In Montería, an area with an irrigation district, Fedearroz and CIAT encouraged farmers to avoid year-round planting—despite farmers' desire to maximize potential yields surrounding stretches of time when many irrigation pumps were broken. Despite some pushback from farmers, Guzmán García recalls, "I really think we got through to them and people did not plant."[353] Follow on evaluations estimate that losses of around 8 billion Pesos, over USD 300 million, were avoided among 179 farmers.[354]

Considered more broadly, the project points to the potential of open data projects—perhaps especially those combining datasets from across sectors—to uncover highly granular insights. Far from just a tool for large-scale trends analyses and predictions, open data can provide truly useful and entirely different information to two individuals a mere town apart.

Benefits to the Agriculture Research Community

Although practitioners of agriculture have been the most direct beneficiaries of the project, it has also had a considerable impact on the wider agricultural research community. Indeed, the project has shown all those involved in agriculture how new forms of information and knowledge can spur progress in the field. This represents a potentially significant theoretical insight. As the scientists behind Aclímate Colombia put it in an article: "The added value of this effort is that it demonstrates how observational data can be used to efficiently generate actionable and contextualized information for on-farm decision making."[355]

More broadly, one of the aims of the project is to make progress by "accelerating agricultural research, in terms of time taken and money spent."[356] The founders of the project hope that it can serve as a catalyst for the wider community to consider new forms of knowledge, and to think through more carefully the link between research and practice.

---

353 GovLab interview with Miryam Patricia Guzmán García, Deputy Director of Technology, Fedearroz, September 5, 2016.

354 Andrés Bermúdez Liévano, "Los arroceros aprenden a vivir en un mundo con menos agua," *La Silla Nacional*, January 17, 2016, http://lasillavacia.com/historia/los-arroceros-aprenden-vivir-en-un-mundo-con-menos-agua-52478.

355 Silvain Delerce, et al., "Assessing Weather-Yield Relationships in Rice at Local Scale Using Data Mining Approaches," PLOS One, August 25, 2016, http://journals.plos.org/plosone/article?id=10.1371%2Fjournal.pone.0161620.

356 Oluwabunmi Ajilore "Big Data, Big Prospects: Crunching data for farmers' climate adaptation," *Change for the Better: The CCAFS 2015 Annual Report*, September 12, 2014, https://ccafs.cgiar.org/blog/big-data-big-prospects-crunching-data-farmers-climate-adaptation#.V6jLZpODGkp.

Financial Impact

The economic benefits of Aclímate Colombia are already becoming clear, and bear testimony to the success of the project. According to an Open Data Institute study conducted in partnership with CIAT, in the year following the launch of the initiative, improvements to farmers' decision-making led to estimated savings of $3.6m.[357] In addition to these broad, aggregate savings, the various insights described above have of course led to a number of localized cost efficiencies in specific areas of the country, and for specific farmers.

UN Big Data Challenge and the Value of a Model

While not a direct, on-the-ground impact of Aclímate Colombia, it is worth mentioning that the project was recognized as one of the 2014 winners of the United Nations Big Data Challenge.[358] This award represents a validation and recognition of the ingenuity and promise of the platform. In addition, the award and its attendant publicity could also help spur other, similar projects in Latin America and beyond. This is a pattern we see repeatedly in the case studies in this series: success leads to more success, and a single, successful project can open up pathways for many more similar projects that, together, have a much wider regional impact.

As noted, impact is often hard to measure. There have been some regional-level impact assessments and estimates of the types of economic losses avoided as a result of Aclímate Colombia performed. On the whole, though, Jimenez believes that, "we've been very clumsy in measuring impact."[359] An understanding of impact is not only important for iterating on the tools and approach for the initiative, but also, as Jimenez highlights, essential for accessing new and sustained sources of funding. Going forward, CIAT and Fedearroz are looking to build an impact assessment component into the project, gaining better visibility into the number of farmers reached and the number of farmers who increased their productivity.[360]

357 Global Open Data for Agriculture and Nutrition, *How Can We Improve Agriculture, Food and Nutrition with Open Data?* Open Data Institute, 2015, http://www.godan.info/sites/default/files/old/2015/04/ODI-GODAN-paper-27-05-20152.pdf.

358 United Nations Global Pulse, "Big Data Climate Challenge," Press Release, September 2, 2014, https://www3.wider.unu.edu/sites/default/files/News/Documents/Big-Data-Climate-Challenge-press-release-5633.pdf.

359 GovLab interview with Daniel Jimenez, International Center for Tropical Agriculture (CIAT), August 23, 2016.

360 Ibid.

Risks

As evidenced by the example of Aclímate Colombia and various other case studies included in this series, open data holds tremendous potential for positive transformation. But, as we also see throughout this series, open data also poses certain risks. It is important to understand these risks in order to ensure that open data projects are implemented in a way that maximizes the potential upside and limits the downside.

Empowering Only Farmers Connected with Powerful Growers Associations

CIAT is well-positioned to engage farmers affiliated with growers' associations like Fedearroz. It has little capacity, however, to engage those farmers that are not similarly organized. As Jimenez notes, "this approach is totally feasible as long as farmers are well organized and associated."[361] But, of course, the farmers with no affiliations and support from growers' associations likely face the greatest risks as a result of climate change and stand to see the most benefit from gaining access to new tools for improving their decision-making. A move toward more technological and data-driven efforts to benefit the agriculture sector risks leaving behind those who need the most support.

This particular risk is representative of a larger struggle within the Colombian open data and civic technology sectors, and indeed within a number of open data and data projects around the world. While often aimed at eradicating or narrowing the digital divide, technical and governance innovation projects such as this one in fact often graft themselves on to (and can even exacerbate) existing divides. As Daniel Uribe of the Corona Foundation puts it: "We see there is a big gap in citizen engagement, taking into account the population pyramid where the poor are the largest group of population, but we believe that there is the potential in the population and access to ICT platforms to promote and achieve citizen engagement through civic tech in all the population, closing the digital divide."[362]

CIAT is currently exploring pathways for engaging these unaffiliated farmers through, as Jimenez puts it, "some hybrid between development and research."[363] Developing concrete, implementable strategies for such engagement will likely be a key determinant of longer-term sustainability and success for the initiative.

---

361 Ibid.

362 GovLab interview with Daniel Uribe, Fundacion Corona, September 13, 2016.

363 GovLab interview with Daniel Jimenez, International Center for Tropical Agriculture (CIAT), August 23, 2016.

Encouraging Farmers with Little Room for Error to Fundamentally Change Practices

Given the project's focus on arming small-scale farms with recommendations aimed at changing their traditional growing practices, the accuracy and reliability of those recommendations is highly important. If recommendations are not accurate, there is a risk not only of lower crop yields, but also that farmers who already operate near subsistence level may suffer great economic hardship. The organizers recognize this risk, noting that "farmers have different profiles in terms of risk management" and that some are "able to take risks to bet on good weather and outstanding harvest while others need to guarantee a minimum level of productivity to ensure adequate income."[364] Initial signs do point to Aclímate Colombia improving outcomes for farmers, but vigilance in this area is essential.

Lessons Learned

Several important lessons with wider applicability emerge from this particular case study. These can broadly be categorized by considering the key enablers of the project, as well as the most important barriers or challenges to its success.

Enablers

For Jimenez and his team, perhaps the central lesson learned from the project was the realization that "information that is not shared is not information anymore."[365] The data used to create Aclímate Colombia had existed for years, sitting in databases held by different cross-sector stakeholders. Once that data was unlocked in service of a specific objective, it stopped being a series of numbers but instead became actionable information.

Establish credibility, a theory of change and proof of concept

In order to move forward with the data analysis and dissemination of tools and insights that define Aclímate Colombia, CIAT first had to get grower associations like Fedearroz on board—both to gain access to their data and in order to enable them to act as intermediaries between CIAT and the individual farmers.

---

364 Silvain Delerce, et al., "Assessing Weather-Yield Relationships in Rice at Local Scale Using Data Mining Approaches," PLOS One, August 25, 2016, http://journals.plos.org/plosone/article?id=10.1371%2Fjournal.pone.0161620.

365 GovLab interview with Daniel Jimenez, International Center for Tropical Agriculture (CIAT), August 23, 2016.

To make those partnerships a reality, Jimenez argues, "you have to think about the theory of change."[366] The project's theory of change was clear from the start: that data analysis can help farmers make better planting decisions as a result of an improved understanding of how crops react to different weather patterns in different regions. Establishing and articulating this theory of change helped engage data providers and data intermediaries in an effective manner. Pushing for data access without a clear articulation of how that data will be used—and to what ends—can be a losing proposition.

In addition to a clear theory of change, a proof of concept can also help instill confidence in data providers and/or intermediaries. As much as a theory of change can lend conceptual clarity to a project, true confidence and credibility arise when tangible signs of impact and success emerge. Jimenez notes that, at the early stages, growers' associations tended to only share "a small piece of the database," and then as CIAT used the data available to draw meaningful insights, more and more information was made accessible. He adds, "they are skeptical in the beginning, but they start to believe as you demonstrate what you can do to support more informed decision-making."[367]

Know your audience, engage intermediaries and build a common language

As the story of Aclímate Colombia's genesis and implementation makes clear, growers' associations played an essential role in enabling the creation of the initiative. In particular, they played a role through data provision and its use by acting as intermediaries between CIAT and individual farms. As Jimenez describes their role: "We work through them, we empower them and then through them we bridge this gap between scientists and farmers."[368]

Even when working through a data-driven intermediary like Federarroz, CIAT quickly learned that to encourage engagement and use among the intended audience (i.e., individual farmers), it needed to gain a better understanding of that audience and build a common language. Rather than simply running one-off workshops with growers associations and farmers aimed at increasing data literacy, which have questionable impact, CIAT embedded sector-area experts from growers' associations within the organization. During these three-to-four-month engagements, CIAT was able to "empower them properly"—i.e., give them a grounding in how to put into practice the findings of different regional data analyses on optimal planting practices—and plant the notion that data-driven training and tools are truly worth the investment of

---

366 Ibid.
367 Ibid.
368 Ibid.

time and resources.[369] These engagements not only helped to increase buy-in among the intended audience, but also helped increase the skills present in the growers' association, minimizing the resource and time burdens on CIAT and improving the project's potential for sustainability. Jimenez notes that a big driver of success was the identification of the data use and translation processes that CIAT "just needs to supervise because [the associations] can do it by themselves."[370]

Similarly, Jimenez found that demonstrating that Aclímate Colombia's organizers were working toward common goals and willing to build a common language with the user community (i.e., individual farmers) helped encourage greater uptake of their tools and research findings. In an interview with the Overseas Development Institute, he recalled that, "One farmer said to me that they acted on the research because it was based on their own data."[371] As such, Fabrizio Scrollini, chairman of Data Uruguay, labels Aclímate Colombia a clear example of "inclusive innovation."[372]

Barriers

Initial inaccessibility of important datasets

Much of the value and utility of Aclímate Colombia arises from the aggregation and analysis of diverse datasets drawn from diverse sectors and institutions. Given the fact that "open access and data sharing is still in its infancy in many places," gaining access was a relatively slow and difficult process.[373] As described above, the establishment of credibility, proof of concept and a willingness to build a common language with growers' associations and those they represent helped to—gradually—mitigate that challenge.

Immature ecosystem

By working directly with growers' associations that could act as data providers and intermediaries passing its tools and insights onto individual farmers, Aclímate Colombia was able to avoid one of the major challenges faced by open data efforts around the world: the lack of a mature technology and innovation ecosystem.

---

369 Ibid.

370 Ibid.

371 Elizabeth Stuart, "The Data Revolution: Finding the Missing Millions," *Development Progress, Research Report 03*, 2015, https://www.odi.org/sites/odi.org.uk/files/odi-assets/publications-opinion-files/9604.pdf.

372 GovLab interview with Fabrizio Scrollini, September 13, 2016.

373 Oluwabunmi Ajilore "Big Data, Big Prospects: Crunching data for farmers' climate adaptation," *Change for the Better: The CCAFS 2015 Annual Report*, September 12, 2014, https://ccafs.cgiar.org/blog/big-data-big-prospects-crunching-data-farmers-climate-adaptation#.V6jLZpODGkp.

Actors in the civic technology and open source communities in Colombia are, as Oscar Montiel of Open Knowledge International (OKI) puts it, "really small and really disconnected from one another."[374] Esteban Peláez Gómez of Fundación Corona agrees, arguing that while there are some tech start ups and innovators in the country, "they are not part of a community that has the objective of having a social impact."[375]

But while Aclímate Colombia does not require private sector civic tech actors to leverage its tools, Montiel argues that without such an ecosystem, there can be negative impacts on the types of data released by the government. He argues that the immature open data demand and use ecosystem feeds into issues like unwieldy data licensing frameworks that make the reuse of government data more difficult.[376]

A lack of civil society collaborators in the Colombian open data ecosystem

OKI's Montiel and Mor Rubinstein, both of whom worked with Colombia as part of the Open Data Index effort, note that, especially in comparison to other countries in the region, civil society in Colombia is fragmented and not playing a major role in pushing forward open data. As Rubinstein notes, Colombian civil society's role in advancing open data is "a big question mark in a way."[377] So while there are notable exceptions, like CIAT and Fundación Corona, Montiel argues that there is not widespread collaboration between government and civil society, and rather, government "just does what they can the way they know how."[378]

Replicability

The potential for replication of Aclímate Colombia's analytical tools and algorithms appears promising as the algorithms and processes that inform the project's tools are not context-specific, and can be used wherever relevant data is available.[379] As a result, steps are already being taken to scale the project

---

374 GovLab interview with Oscar Montiel, Open Knowledge International, September 8, 2016.

375 GovLab interview with Esteban Peláez Gómez, Coordinator of Social Projects, Fundación Corona, September 13, 2016.

376 GovLab interview with Oscar Montiel, Open Knowledge International, September 8, 2016.

377 GovLab interview with Mor Rubinstein, Open Knowledge International, September 8, 2016.

378 GovLab interview with Oscar Montiel, Open Knowledge International, September 8, 2016.

379 Silvain Delerce, et al., "Assessing Weather-Yield Relationships in Rice at Local Scale Using Data Mining Approaches," PLOS One, August 25, 2016, http://journals.plos.org/plosone/article?id=10.1371%2Fjournal.pone.0161620.

across Colombia, as well as in Argentina, Nicaragua, Peru and Uruguay, in partnership with the Latin American Fund for Irrigated Rice (FLAR).[380]

Looking Forward

Improving the Tools and Expanding the Data Being Used

Beyond strategizing ways to engage unaffiliated farmers, as described above, the CIAT team is working to improve the functionality and expand the use of Aclímate Colombia through the integration of new datasets. Future research for the platform will explore how to leverage data on "soils, pests, diseases, costs and other factors to increase explanatory power."[381] The team is also exploring the "emergent field of remote sensing and satellite energy," which Jimenez feels "could be a more efficient way to collect information in the field."[382]

Scaling to Other Countries in the Region

As described above, CIAT is partnering with the Fund for Irrigated Rice in Latin America. In addition, CIAT researchers plan also to partner with the Fund for Irrigated Rice in Latin America (FLAR), with the support of CCAFS and the World Bank, to introduce new approaches to rice growers' associations in other countries, especially Nicaragua, Peru, Argentina and Uruguay. CIAT is also partnering with the CGIAR-affiliated International Maize and Wheat Improvement Center (CIMMYT) to bring data-driven insight into maize production in Mexico. These new projects in Latin America will serve as additional case studies, potentially laying the groundwork for further replication and scaling.[383]

Fostering the Open Data Ecosystem in Colombia

Looking beyond Aclímate Colombia, CIAT and the other data-driven actors involved in the project are well-positioned to help push forward the nascent open data ecosystem in Colombia. As Fabrizio Scrollini argues: "there is a niche for new organizations to emerge or for some organizations that are a part of

---

380 CTIAR and CCAFS, "Big Data for Climate-smart Agriculture," *Change for the Better: The CCAFS 2015 Annual Report*, https://ccafs.cgiar.org/bigdata#.V6jLT5ODGko.

381 Ibid.

382 GovLab interview with Daniel Jimenez, August 23, 2016.

383 CTIAR and CCAFS, "Big Data for Climate-smart Agriculture," *Change for the Better: The CCAFS 2015 Annual Report*, https://ccafs.cgiar.org/bigdata#.V6jLT5ODGko.

the politics side, or from the more social side to jump into data on the market side. The niche is there."[384] Indeed, Scrollini argues that while the value of data-driven work is gaining a foothold in areas focused on wealth generation, there has not been a similar uptake in the use of data toward social ends. Aclímate Colombia could actually represent a powerful example of how open data can have positive impacts on both the public good and the pocketbooks of those leveraging the data (in this case, farmers).

As Scrollini puts it: "I guess it is time to get these people organized and get some more traditional NGOs that are more well behaved and engage the government and some punks as well so they can shake things up and get the party going. I know there are people in government willing to take that challenge, it's a matter of getting the dance started. That's what data hopefully will contribute."[385]

Conclusion

With regard to open data's provision, use and impact, Colombia represents a fascinating case study in the developing world. Based on a number of international assessments, the country can be considered a leader among Latin American countries in the field of open data. A number of open data projects either already exist or may soon, although it is worth noting that the bulk of these are founded by international organizations, with relatively little activity in Colombia's private sector and among start-ups.

In this atmosphere of open data innovation, CIAT's Aclímate Colombia could act as a standard-bearer and catalyst. The platform is aimed at addressing a clearly defined problem, leverages partnerships across sectors to access data and push for its use, and provides benefits to a wide variety of private sector actors in the agriculture sector, regardless of their size. USAID notably selected Colombia as one of three initial countries to participate in the Climate Services for Resilient Development initiative, likely thanks in part to the innovative capacity demonstrated by the government and civil society actors that made Aclímate Colombia a possibility.[386] While many questions and barriers remain—not the least of which is the challenge of engaging those farmers currently not involved with key intermediaries—if Aclímate Colombia continues to grow and evolve along its current trajectory, it could establish itself as a bright light in the emerging open data space in Colombia, and indeed throughout Latin America.

---

384 GovLab interview with Fabrizio Scrollini, September 13, 2016.

385 Ibid.

386 Climate Services for Resilient Development, http://www.cs4rd.org/.

Ghana's Esoko

Leveling the information playing field for smallholder farmers

François van Schalkwyk, Andrew Young and Stefaan Verhulst

Summary

Smallholder farmers generate much of Ghana's agricultural production. However, they have only limited access to important information that underlies increasingly complex global food chains, and this prevents them from fully maximizing the value of their crops. Esoko, a company operating in Ghana, sought to address this problem by using multiple data sources, including open government data, to permit farmers to secure better prices for their produce and level the playing field in price negotiations between farmers and buyers. The provision of information to smallholder farmers is being replicated by Esoko in other developing countries, and new organizations are entering the market to provide similar services to smallholder farmers.

Context and Background

Problem Focus/Country Context

As global agricultural value chain continues to grow in importance. This is especially true for many developing countries, where a larger proportion of the workforce and economy are reliant on the agriculture sector.

Africa loses billions of dollars due to its inability to produce enough and process its agricultural commodities. In its 2014 report, the Africa Progress Panel, an NGO advocated for sustainable development chaired by Kofi

Annan, estimates that Africa spends US$35 billion per year on food imports. Connecting farm production, processing and distribution could introduce various efficiencies into the value chain, in the process creating numerous jobs and lifting millions of Africans out of poverty.[387]

The importance of agriculture is only likely to increase in coming decades. According to the World Bank, global food demand is set to double by 2050, and Africa's agriculture and agribusiness markets could reach US$1 trillion in 2030 (World Bank 2013).[388] Ghana could potentially be one of the key beneficiaries of this process, given that, according to the Food and Agriculture Organization of the UN, over 53 percent of the Ghanaian workforce is in the agriculture sector.[389] The country had made some progress in recent years: Ghana is one of a few African countries to have achieved its Millennium Development Goal (MDG) hunger reduction target as well as the World Food Summit goal of halving the absolute number of hungry in the country by 2015. The Government of Ghana is currently elaborating a long-term national development plan to steer the country through the next 40 years.[390]

Yet if Ghana—and Africa more generally—is to build on this success, the agriculture sector will have to undergo certain changes. As global food and agriculture chains become increasingly complex and information-driven, there is a need for new, innovative approaches that can adapt to the complexity. Agricultural methods will need to become more information-driven, more adaptable to new trends in technology, and more resilient to withstand climate change. Small landholders, in particular, will need support as they move toward a new agriculture paradigm. According to the International Fund for Agricultural Development (IFAD), there are more than 500 million smallholder farms globally that produce about 80 percent of the food consumed in Asia and sub-Saharan Africa (IFAD 2013).[391] This suggests the vital importance of programs and tools—such as the one under study here—that help smallholder farmers adapt. Their viability is particularly important in Ghana, where the production of key crops like coffee and cocoa is dominated by smallholders.

---

387 Africa Progress Panel, *Grain Fish Money: Financing Africa's green and blue revolutions*. Africa Progress Panel, 2014, http://app-cdn.acwupload.co.uk/wp-content/uploads/2014/05/APP_APR2014_24june.pdf.

388 World Bank, *Growing Africa. Unlocking the Potential of Agribusiness*. Washington DC: World Bank, 2013, http://siteresources.worldbank.org/INTAFRICA/Resources/africa-agribusiness-report-2013.pdf.

389 Food and Agriculture Organization, "Ghana: Country Fact Sheet on Food and Agriculture Policy Trends," FAO, March 2015, http://www.fao.org/3/a-i4490e.pdf.

390 Food and Agriculture Organization, *Ghana and FAO: Partnering for agricultural development and resilient livelihoods*, 2016, http://www.fao.org/3/a-az484e.pdf.

391 International Fund for Agricultural Development (IFAD), *Smallholders, Food Security, and the Environment*, IFAD/UNEP, https://www.ifad.org/documents/10180/666cac24-14b6-43c2-876d-9c2d1f01d5dd.

Technology, open data and agriculture

Technology is already being used in several instances to help African farmers make better decisions and make meaningful forays into national and/or global value chains. For example, in Kenya, the SMS information provision app mFARM gives farmers important evidence to inform decision-making. In Nigeria, the Hello Tractor service is an Uber-like tractor-on-demand service. In Ghana, the USAID Feed the Future Program is working to implement technology-driven efforts to improve competitiveness, sustainability and the transfer of research insights into practice.[392]

But while such applications and services can create new value, they could also lead to the creation of data monopolies and information asymmetries that may ultimately hurt or otherwise limit the potential of African agriculture. The economic concept of asymmetric information is that there is an imbalance of power in a transaction when one party has access to more information than the other.[393] This results in buyers not being able to bid as much or in sellers not knowing how to price a commodity. Open data can play an important role in breaking down such asymmetries of information. It can do so, for example, by introducing greater transparency in agricultural value chains, in the process making actors in those value chains more accountable to attentive citizens, civil society organizations, and to others, including farmers.

Open data also makes possible the entry into agricultural ecosystems of a larger number of intermediaries, adding both complexity and new value propositions to value chains. Research has shown that open data "intermediaries are vital to both the supply and the use of open data ... Intermediaries can create data, articulate demands for data, and help translate open data visions from political leaders into effective implementations."[394] Research that delved deeper into how open data intermediaries are able to link actors in data supply chains found that "intermediation does not only consist of a single agent facilitating the flow of data in an open data supply chain; multiple intermediaries may operate in an open data supply chain, and the presence of multiple intermediaries may increase the probability of use (and impact) because no single intermediary is

---

392 Feed the Future, "Fact Sheet: Feed the future USAID agriculture technology transfer project," IFDC, 2014, https://ifdcorg.files.wordpress.com/2014/12/att-factsheet.pdf.

393 D. Kleine, A. Light and M.J. Montero, "Signifiers of the Life We Value? Considering human development,technologies and fair trade from the perspective of the capabilities approach," Information Technology for Development, 18, no.1, pp. 42–60.

394 T. Davies, Open Data in Developing Countries: Emerging insights from phase 1, Washington DC: World Wide Web Foundation, 2014, http://www.opendataresearch.org/sites/default/files/publications/Phase%20 1%20-%20Synthesis%20-%20Full%20Report-print.pdf.

likely to possess all the types of capital required to unlock the full value of the transaction between the provider and the user."[395]

A growing international consensus regarding the potential of open data in agriculture is evidenced by the Global Open Data for Agriculture & Nutrition (GODAN) initiative, which brings together nearly 500 governments, NGOs and businesses seeking "to harness the growing volume of data generated by new technologies to solve long-standing problems and to benefit farmers and the health of consumers."[396] Also, in this series of case studies, we examine the use of open data to benefit smallholder farmers in Colombia through the Aclímate Colombia initiative.[397]

Open Data in Ghana

Figure 1. Ghana's National Open Data Portal (data.gov.gh)

Ghana, along with Kenya, was one of the early pioneers of open data on the African continent. The Ghana Open Data Portal was launched in November 2012, as a result of a partnership between the Web Foundation, National Information and Technology Agency (NITA), and a number of civil society

395 F. Van Schalkwyk, et al., "Open Data Intermediaries in Developing Countries," *Journal of Community Informatics*, 12, no. 2, 2016, http://ci-journal.net/index.php/ciej/article/view/1146.

396 http://www.godan.info/about.

397 Andrew Young and Stefaan Verhulst, "Aclímate Colombia–Open Data to Improve Agricultural Resiliency," Open Data's Impact, July 2017 http://odimpact.org/case-aclimate-colombia.html.

organizations within the country.[398] The portal launched with 100 datasets available, and a mobile version was released the next year.

Unfortunately, this early success has dampened in some ways. The most recent Open Data Barometer Survey shows a deterioration in the implementation of government open data initiatives relative to Kenya and other African countries such as Mauritius, Nigeria and Rwanda. However, this is mainly attributable to the government open data portal being inaccessible for an extended period of time.[399]

Neither the Open Data Barometer nor the Global Open Data Index has published data on the availability of open data related specifically to agriculture (e.g., weather data or market price data). Currently, the Ghana Open Data portal[400] makes available six datasets in the "Agriculture" category. These relate mainly to financial or economic data from the agricultural sector. The Ghana Statistical Office, CountrySTAT,[401] an initiative to aggregate and increase the interoperability of datasets, also publishes statistical data and metadata on food and agriculture from different sources. In addition, the Ministry of Food and Agriculture publishes data on average crop yields for major crops, production estimates and weekly market prices.[402]

KEY ACTORS

Key Data Providers

Overall, data sourcing by Esoko is structurally complex: open and proprietary data, some self-generated and some from third-parties, are curated and combined to provide information to customers.

Government of Ghana

The Ministry of Food and Agriculture (MOFA) is the primary government source of data. MOFA publishes data on crop yields, production estimates and market prices. Even though agricultural data are obtained from government, the data are extensively

---

398 World Wide Web Foundation, "Ghana Open Data Initiative," http://webfoundation.org/our-work/projects/ghana-open-data-initiative-godi/.

399 The portal might have been done as a result of extended maintenance in preparation for a revamped new offering, but when the Barometer assessment was being conducted no explanation was made available for the outage – so even if the outage was the result of ultimately beneficial work, trust in the platform and Ghanaian open data more generally likely suffered. World Wide Web Foundation, *Open Data Barometer 3rd Edition: Africa Regional Report*, 2016, http://opendatabarometer.org/3rdedition/regional-report/africa/.

400 Website of Uganda Open Data Initiative, http://data.gov.gh/.

401 CountrySTAT, "Ghana," http://www.countrystat.org/home.aspx?c=GHA.

402 Website of the Ministry of Food and Agriculture, Republic of Ghana, http://mofa.gov.gh/site/; and for data on weekly market prices, see http://mofa.gov.gh/site/?page_id=13613.

curated by Esoko. Curation activities include the structuring of the data, its packaging, and its translation into local languages.

Center for Agriculture and BioSciences International (CABI)

An additional source of data is CABI, an international not-for-profit organization. CABI has an extensive repository of information on agricultural issues like invasive species, food security and trade.

aWhere

Esoko is a client of aWhere, an agricultural intelligence firm. It accesses aWhere's weather data via an API service. Esoko translates daily data as well as an eight-day forecast into relevant and accessible weather updates for farmers. Farmers receive information on precipitation, temperature, wind speed, humidity and growing degree days.

Markets and Farmers

Although a portion of the data sourced by Esoko is open, the company also collects its own data. Esoko actively collects data from farmers that may be of interest to agencies and businesses in the agri-sector. In addition, Esoko deploys its own agents in the field to collect price data in about 50 markets in Ghana (some of these agents are in fact employees of the Ministry of Food and Agriculture).[403]

Key Data Users and Intermediaries

Esoko

Esoko is a for-profit private company with private investors, although it should be noted that the company maintains close ties to the public and foreign donor sectors. Managed from its head office in the capital city of Accra, Ghana, Esoko's principal market is agri-business, while individual farmers constitute a secondary market.

Key Beneficiaries

Farmers in Ghana

The principal objective of Esoko has always been to empower smallholder farmers to make farming more profitable. As the company's website states: "Though we'll geek out any day about supply chain efficiencies and organizational cost savings, we live for the human part of this work."[404]

Esoko's clients

In fact, however, smallholder farmers constitute a secondary market for Esoko. In order to develop a more sustainable business model, and because the acquisition of individual farmers is expensive, Esoko principally targets larger agri-business, NGOs, governments and mobile operators with its data collection and communication

---

403 These data are validated by the Council for Scientific and Industrial Research (CSIR).

404 Website of Esoko, https://esoko.com/about-us/our-story/.

products. This allows the company to generate additional revenues, and its mixed business model (targeting both large and small customers) is in many ways critical to its survival and success.

Project Description

Initiation of the Open Data Activity

The origins of Esoko may be traced to TradeNet, a company that was created in 2004 in Uganda, in partnership with FoodNet and with support from the Food and Agriculture Organization of the United Nations (FAO). In 2005, TradeNet entered into the network of regional Market Information Systems and Traders Organizations of West Africa (MISTOWA) project, which seeks to better coordinate regional efforts around the creation, dissemination and use of agriculture and food-security information.

In 2009, Esoko emerged from TradeNet, with the aim of providing a richer and more comprehensive product. One of the key motivating factors in the creation of the company was an identified gap or market failure in the Ugandan agrarian ecosystem. Esoko's founders realized that while information concerning market prices did exist in Uganda, farmers were often unable to access to the information. TradeNet originally tried to bridge this gap by connecting farmers to the available data by means of mobile-phone technology.

Esoko has sought to address similar shortcomings in Ghana. On the one hand, Ghanaian farmers were actively seeking information concerning market prices and weather (in particular, data on rainfall); unable to retrieve such information, they often traded their produce at low prices and were vulnerable to climate variations. On the other hand, the information did in fact exist at a governmental level and from other sources. However, the government 'extension agents' tasked with conveying this type of information to farmers were inefficient and costly. Consequently, Esoko emerged to bridge the gap by connecting farmers to the available information they required.

Currently, there are two main branches of Esoko in Africa, one located in Ghana and one in Kenya. Even though the offices in Ghana and Kenya function under the name Esoko and provide similar products, they constitute two distinct operations managing the two respective markets. In addition, there are resellers and offices in Mauritius, Malawi, Uganda, Mozambique and Benin.

Esoko's main offering to farmers includes automated alerts containing agrarian and economic information, sent to cellphones in the form of SMS

and voice messages. The products offered include information on market prices (58 commodities in 42 markets countrywide, collected at markets daily), weather forecasts, crop price bids, and crop production protocols. Esoko also developed the first call center (called Helpline) for farmers in Ghana to improve communication and usability of the provided information. The messaging and call centers operate in English and 12 local languages (Dagbani, Mampruli, Twi, Kusaal, Frafra, Sissali, Dagaari, Wali, Ewe, Ga, Fante and Hausa). Esoko's non-mobile products include deployment support for surveys in the field (e.g., the deployment of the company's own agents), strategic planning and field training. While farmers do use these services, they are mostly directed at agribusiness clients.

Most products offered by Esoko use mobile technology. In addition to its information products, it offers a number of B2B products aimed at larger, paying customers. These include marketing products, monitoring and evaluation products, as well as goods sourcing products. These products can take the form of bulk messaging, SMS polling, call center monitoring and call surveys.

Funding

The founder and the first CEO of Esoko was Mark Davies. Investors, who provided the bulk of the capital, were the International Finance Corporation, the Soros Economic Development Fund, Lundin Foundation, and Acumen. Currently, Esoko relies on a mix of donor funding and self-generated revenue from the products and services it has developed for agri-businesses, NGOs, governments and mobile operators.

Demand and Supply of Data type(s) and sources

As mentioned, Esoko was born from Ghanaian farmers' need for data on market prices and weather to help inform planting and other market-related decisions. Esoko sources this data from a variety of data suppliers, including the government, international NGOs and agri-data companies such as aWhere. Esoko Ghana also collects its own data from about 50 markets in Ghana and directly from farmers.

Open Data Use

Esoko's offerings and pricing models rely on a combination of data sources and types. Its services are based on a tiered franchise/subscriber model in several sub-Saharan countries, including Ghana, Burkina Faso, Cote d'Ivoire

and Malawi.[405] The company's SMS price alerts, monitoring capabilities and information system management products are all made possible by the use of open government data.

Impact

As with the other case studies included in this series, the impact of Esoko can be measured in a number of different ways, using a variety of quantitative and qualitative information. These include:

Usage Statistics

According to its website, Esoko has reached 350,000 farmers in 10 countries across Africa. It has sent 9.5 million messages on one million prices in 170 markets collected by 150 field agents. In 2014, Esoko operated 29,344 calls in Ghana, of which 40 percent were related to weather data. Although usage is not always a perfect proxy for impact, the breadth of use and interest in Esoko's offerings is clearly evident, and points to real usefulness for the company's intended audience.

Improved Bargaining Power

A key goal of Esoko is to help farmers better navigate the complexity of global value chains, and in particular to improve their bargaining power versus some of the large, global actors in those chains. Although there have been no widespread studies of the value and impact of Esoko's service, the company has done some targeted surveys of farmers who have reported being able to negotiate prices more confidently and sell their harvests in more distant markets.[406]

One empirical research study on the impact of Esoko's market price information was conducted by Pierre Courois and Julie Subervie for the *American Journal of Agricultural Economics*.[407] Courois and Subervie set out to establish how price information affects the balance of power in the bargaining of prices. They found that farmers typically sell to traders at the farm gate rather

---

405 U.S. Agency for International Development, "Using ICT to Provide Agriculture Market Price Information in Africa," Briefing Paper, 2010.

406 U.S. Agency for International Development, "Using ICT to Provide Agriculture Market Price Information in Africa," Briefing Paper, 2010.

407 Pierre Courois and Julie Subervie, "Farmer Bargaining Power and Market Information Services," *American Journal of Agricultural Economics*, 97, No. 3, pp. 953–977, 2014, http://ajae.oxfordjournals.org/content/97/3/953.

than at district markets because of high transportation costs, and are thus at a disadvantage when negotiating prices because they are unaware of what prices are available in markets. The study also found that Northern Ghanaian farmers who are clients of Esoko were able to negotiate better prices for their produce. Specifically, farmers receiving market price information from Esoko received 10 percent more for maize and 7 percent more for groundnuts than those farmers who were not receiving the market price information.

Value Chain Transparency

One important effect of Esoko's activities as an intermediary in the agricultural ecosystem is to increase the transparency of the value chain. Farmers are able to compare prices at various markets in the country, and compare prices to those offered to them by traders at the farm gate. They can also better recognize the structure and the roles of other agents involved in the food production system. As a result, farmers can negotiate higher prices and discover entirely new markets—in short, they can trade more effectively. This transparency also affects the activities of other agents in the ecosystem. For instance, being aware of farmers' understanding of the ecosystem, traders modify their own bargaining and trading strategies. Because all actors are more aware of each others' positions in the ecosystem, the net result is greater transparency.

Seeding the Ecosystem

According to Andrason and Van Schalkwyk,[408] Esoko, along with similar intermediaries such as Farmerline, have stimulated the emergence of new niches in the local information and communication technology (ICT) ecosystem. At least four new (albeit interconnected) niches are identified in the study:

- First, the presence of Esoko has created room for additional research and thus the need for companies dedicated to agri-data capture and processing. Esoko seeks data that goes beyond what is currently available or provided directly from open sources present in the ecosystem. That is, it generates a need for experts, data collectors and data processing personnel.
- Second, Esoko creates a demand for a range of educational and training organizations that can interact with individuals and communities.

---

408 Alex Andrason and François van Schalkwyk, *Open Data Intermediaries in the Agriculture Sector in Ghana*, Research Paper, Washington DC: World Wide Web Foundation, 2016, http://webfoundation.org/docs/2016/12/WF-RP-Open-Data-Intermediaries-in-Agriculture-Ghana-Update.pdf.

- Third, Esoko contributes to technological innovation. By discovering more efficient means of conveying information and connecting agents in the ecosystem, it creates an additional need for technical personnel, for instance programmers and mobile-phone specialists. In fact, the efficiency of the services offered by Esoko may also contribute to a more rapid development of the mobile phone sector.

- Fourth, the emergence of Esoko enables a more adequate use or even a reuse (or relocation) of elements already present in the ecosystem. To be precise, the previously mentioned government extension agents—relatively ineffective in the traditional framework—have seen their roles and objectives reframed to ensure they are better targeted to the real-world needs and opportunities. This relocation has turned out to be successful and beneficial both for these agents themselves and for the data flow.

Risks

Open data offers tremendous opportunities, but also carries certain risks. As with all the case studies included in this series, it is important to balance the potential rewards with the challenges and pitfalls that may also arise as a result of new and potentially disruptive technological interventions.

Marginal short-term gains may jeopardize future benefits

The success of Esoko depends in many ways on balancing short-term and long-term benefits. The risk exists that some farmers may decide that information helping them accrue a 7 to 10 percent increase in farm-gate prices is insufficient to compensate for the cost of subscribing to the market price information service. Should they elect to discontinue their subscription, they may lose out on the future benefits that could accrue from new information made available by Esoko.

There does exist some evidence that non-governmental organizations subsidize the subscription costs of farmers and this lowers the risk of losing out on future benefits. However, the role of NGOs introduces secondary risks: (1) farmers rely on an organization type that in itself does not have sustainable income and may therefore have to discontinue the subsidy scheme at some point, and (2) aggregating access via NGOs may unintentionally exclude some farmers who may not be aware of, or have access to, these NGOs.

New forms of bargaining emerge that negate the benefits that some farmers enjoy

Courtois and Subervie acknowledge the possible risk that the availability of market price information is not uniform. That is, some farming communities, especially larger or otherwise privileged ones, may be informed while others are not. They describe the following scenario:

> *"Specifically, he [the trader] should seek to deal in uninformed communities when the market price is high, because in that case uninformed farmers, who systematically make incorrect estimates of the market price, agree to accept relatively low prices. On the contrary, the trader should visit informed communities when the market price is low, because it allows him to avoid costly negotiation failures."*[409]

Such a scenario does not necessarily correct the pricing information asymmetry in a food supply chain.

Personal data

Esoko collects personally identifiable data from farmers and repackages and sells this data to agribusiness. Details on the levels of aggregation and anonymization of personal data collected and shared could not be found. However, the risk remains that either Esoko or its clients (or both) may use personal data to target smallholder farmers and that any misuse of personal data in this way could damage any trust that may currently exist between smallholder farmers and Esoko. This, in turn, could reduce usage of the Esoko platform in general, and more generally lower trust in and usage of open data products.

Lessons Learned

Lessons learned can be broadly divided into Enablers (positive lessons) and Barriers (negative lessons). Both types of lessons are important in assessing the success of the project, and more generally in assessing the potential and feasibility of other open data products.

---

409 Pierre Courois and Julie Subervie, "Farmer Bargaining Power and Market Information Services," *American Journal of Agricultural Economics*, 97, No. 3, pp. 953–977, 2014, http://ajae.oxfordjournals.org/content/97/3/953.

Enablers

Existing market failures

Esoko came into being due to a propitious combination of phenomena: an inefficient agricultural information and support delivery system (extension agents); pervasive and relatively low-cost communication technologies (mobile phones/SMS); and the availability of data combined with the ongoing demand from farmers for relevant agricultural information. All these factors together created a market failure and thus a genuine opportunity, or niche, that could be occupied by an organization such as Esoko. Organizations seeking to develop similarly successful open data projects may therefore consider beginning by trying to identify similar market failures and niches.

Multi-tier business model

A further enabler was Esoko's business model of providing low-cost, affordable services to smallholder farmers and targeting established agriculture organizations to generate sufficient income to establish itself as a viable business. This mixed revenue model has enabled more farmers to access Esoko's services. It also allows Esoko to collect its own market price data (which is of value to farmers) because it can resell this data as information not only to farmers but also to its business clients.

Emerging ecosystem

Esoko is operating in a maturing ICT for agriculture ecosystem. As research by Andrason and Van Schalkwyk shows,[410] there are at least two other players operating in the same space as Esoko: Farmerline and CacaoLink, both data-driven agriculture businesses seeking to benefit farmers across many African countries. Each of these organizations has been careful to differentiate its particular niche in the Ghanaian agricultural market, but their presence is nevertheless indicative of a maturing data ecosystem.

Lastly, Esoko was endowed with an effective constellation of "capitals"—mainly economic and social—that enabled it to exploit the niche that presented itself. Specifically, reliable funding at the outset, a strong B2B business model, connections to a network of like-minded organizations and a technically proficient team positioned Esoko for success. The lesson is clear: Not all actors

---

410 Alex Andrason and François van Schalkwyk, *Open Data Intermediaries in the Agriculture Sector in Ghana*, Research Paper, Washington DC: World Wide Web Foundation, 2016, http://webfoundation.org/docs/2016/12/WF-RP-Open-Data-Intermediaries-in-Agriculture-Ghana-Update.pdf.

are equal in the ecosystem, and only some possess the requisite capital to make the most of the niches that open up in an ecosystem.[411]

Barriers

Despite its relative success, Esoko faces four main challenges: deployment costs, infrastructure reliability, information quality on the supply side and information quality on the demand side.

- **Costs:** As far as costs are concerned, deployment constitutes the bulk of Esoko's expenses (95 percent) while the actual technology only contributes a small amount (5 percent). The costs of deployment place limits on the extent to which Esoko can provide free and equal access to its information products.
- **Infrastructure reliability:** In terms of infrastructure, the access to mobile network infrastructure is at times difficult, restricting Esoko's ability to provide a reliable, real-time service to its customers. An unreliable supply of electricity places a similar burden on Esoko's operations.
- **Supply-side information quality:** The quality and timeliness of data received from the government's Ministry of Food and Agriculture can also be an issue. While the government published open data on agriculture more regularly and more frequently in the past, it does not appear to be able to sustain the publication of relevant and timely data. At the time of writing, for example, the most recent published data on market prices was for the first week of June 2014.[412]
- **Demand-side information quality:** Certain information provided by Esoko can also be difficult for farmers to understand, and this limits the usability and the potential impact of the information provided. While Esoko does provide telephonic support in local languages to help farmers use the data, providing information in formats that smallholder farmers can understand remains an ongoing challenge.

Looking Forward

The fact that Esoko currently operates in a number of African countries is indicative of the replicability of its product. In addition, the existence of other

---

411 Ibid.

412 Ministry of Food and Agriculture, Republic of Ghana, "Weekly Market Prices of Food Commodities," http://mofa.gov.gh/site/?page_id=13613.

organizations (e.g., Farmerline) offering similar products and services in Ghana suggests the existence of genuine market opportunities in the local ICT ecosystem, and perhaps a sustainable business climate for open data projects. As more data sources become available, and as the needs of smallholder farmers evolve, it seems likely that new information products that rely on data will enter the market and that value chain transparency will continue to change how prices are negotiated in the agricultural sector.

Partnerships between data intermediaries and data owners may also evolve as both intermediaries and the data owners benefit from having access to better quality data. Already Esoko is working with the Ministry of Food and Agriculture to collect data on market prices. In this case, the Ministry has access to human resources in the form of extension officers and other staff that would be financially burdensome for Esoko to retain, while Esoko has the technology and expertise to collect, curate and disseminate the data.

Conclusion

This case study on the use of open data in the agricultural sector in Ghana offers one of the few instances where solid empirical evidence is available to support claims of the positive impact of open data in developing countries. However, it is important to note that the empirical evidence provided by the cited Courois and Subervie study relies on data collected in 2012. Similarly, while the study by Andrason and Van Schalkwyk on open data intermediaries in the agricultural sector is more recent, its findings are inhibited by limited access to primary source evidence from Esoko and from the smallholder farmers themselves. Therefore, while there is strong evidence that open data can make a positive contribution to development, further research is required to build on and further validate the positive findings currently available, and to better understand the risks and barriers identified in this case study.

Jamaica's Interactive Community Mapping

Open data and crowdsourcing for tourism

Andrew Young and Stefaan Verhulst

Summary

Like much of the Caribbean, the Jamaican economy is heavily dependent on the health of its tourism sector. Influenced by the rise of all-inclusive resorts, which create a general disincentive for tourists to stray far from a few highly-trafficked areas, tourists rarely experience much of Jamaica's unique culture, and the economic benefits of tourism tend to be highly concentrated. In order to demonstrate the potential for increasing tourism (and the spread of its economic benefits), a community mapping project launched in November 2015 sought to combine open government data with crowdsourced mapping data to enable a more participatory development of the tourism sector. Built around open tourism data and the efforts of government agencies, civil society organizations, developers, and a group of motivated community mappers, the initiative is providing early insight into how data and collective intelligence can impact an industry that in many ways represents the lifeblood of the country.

Context and Background

Problem Focus/Country Context

Jamaica is a small island nation located about 600 miles from Miami and 100 miles south of Cuba. It is a member of the British Commonwealth of Nations

and has close economic ties to the United States. It gained its independence in 1962 during an era of global decolonization and still grapples with the political, economic, and social legacies left by colonization.

The Caribbean region continues to be a hotbed of tourism activity. From 2005 to 2013, tourist arrivals to the Caribbean grew by 5.4 percent, outpacing the average global growth rate (4.7 percent). In 2014, the Caribbean as a whole received 26.3 million trips (breaking the previous record set in 2013 by 1.3 million). This level of tourism activity represented 2.3 percent of total global tourism arrivals.[413] The Caribbean is also the number one cruise destination in the world.

Jamaica's economy, similar to that of the Caribbean as a whole, is heavily reliant on service industries, which, according to some estimates, makes up as much as 70 percent of the nation's GDP.[414] Most of those services are related to tourism, one of the nation's economic strengths. According to the *Jamaica Observer*, more than 3 million tourists visited the island in 2014, including those from cruise ships.[415] Jamaica has experienced year-to-year growth over recent years—a 3.6 percent increase from 2013–2014 in stopover visitors and 12.5 percent increase in cruise visitors over the same period, continuing a trend observable since 2007.

While the tourism sector is seemingly healthy and evolving rapidly, the need for a more citizen-inclusive model for tourism development is widely recognized, as is the need for a more intelligent, centralized system for collecting and managing tourism data.[416]

The all-inclusive tourism model

Over the past few decades, tourism in the Caribbean has been influenced by the rise of all-inclusive tourism offerings. The paradigmatic example of this model is a central beachside resort that offers, among other services, all-you-can-eat and drink packages for visitors, ensuring that consumers do not have to leave the grounds of the resort for any reason. These resorts tend to cater to preconceived notions held by travellers about Jamaican culture and life— relatively few visitors, for instance, ever explored Kingston beyond the sights seen from a one-day tour bus. The Trench Town Development Association, a

413 Caribbean Tourism Organization, *Caribbean Tourism Review*, 2014, http://www.onecaribbean.org/wp-content/uploads/2014TourismReviewDocumentAmendedFEB11.pdf.

414 Witherbee, Amy, "Jamaica," *Our World, Research Starters*, January 2016, EBSCO*host* (accessed September 21, 2016).

415 "Tourist Arrivals Increased by 3.6 % in 2014," *Jamaica Observer News*, February 5, 2015, http://www.jamaicaobserver.com/news/Tourist-arrivals-increased-by-3-6---in-2014.

416 Caribbean Tourism Organization, *Caribbean Sustainable Tourism Policy Framework*, http://www.onecaribbean.org/content/files/CbbnSustainableTourismPolicyFramework.pdf.

grassroots initiative, has aimed to help visitors experience the famous Trench Town neighborhood of Kingston – the home of Reggae icon Bob Marley, and the acknowledged birthplace of rocksteady and reggae music – by offering a local tour guide, featuring "a museum, a music studio, and a school, as well as interaction with artists, craftspeople, and community elders."[417] Though still wary of inner-city Kingston violence, visitors are somewhat more likely today than ever before to interact with local communities that have proven to be resilient in the face of both violence and poverty

Christopher Whyms-Stone of the Trench Town Development Association argues that while there are many benefits to the all-inclusive tourism model, "it is lazy for a country to say it is going to push this model because crime in the country is too high so we can't let the visitors go outside. ... No wonder we still have not solved crime in Jamaica.... That is the strongest word I will use—lazy. That is the easy way out."[418] Whyms-Stone is careful to point out that the all-inclusive model has very real benefits for Jamaica—including the fact that many Jamaicans are employed by such resorts, and that many visitors to the Trench Town Development Association are based at all-inclusive resorts for much of their stay. Rather than demonizing the all-inclusive approach, he argues that tourists and Jamaican citizens would benefit from additional efforts to advance community-oriented tourism initiatives rather than relying solely on the all-inclusive model.

Tourism and information

The centrality of tourism to the local economy presents various challenges for policymakers and business owners in Jamaica and across the Caribbean, particularly due to the volatility and unreliability of tourism arrivals. Recently, the need for information has become more apparent, for instance to help Jamaican tourism authorities plan their offerings as well as for tourists themselves to better understand the possibilities on offer (especially the possibilities beyond the all-inclusive resort).

Better information is seen as key to opening up new tourist activities and areas. For instance, a tourist may be more likely to engage in a community-based tour of a Kingston neighborhood if there is easily-accessible information about the unique culture, history, and people of the region. Similarly, a local entrepreneur will make more informed decisions if he/she has access to data detailing the interests and activities of tourists visiting his/her region.

417 Eveline Dürr and Jaffe Rivke, "Theorizing Slum Tourism: Performing, negotiating and transforming inequality," *European Review of Latin American & Caribbean Studies*, no. 93, pp. 113–123, October 2012.

418 GovLab Interview with Christopher Whyms-Stone, Trench Town Development Association, September 29, 2016.

The Inter-American Development Bank notes "a general absence of data for [tourism] benchmarking and strategic planning in the region" and argues that "the effective use of Big Data has the potential to transform the tourism sector, delivering a new wave of productivity growth and consumer surplus." As such, it recommends the development of "public policy promoting positive externalities such as knowledge sharing and addressing coordination failures so that the private sector is encouraged to innovate and upgrade, aiming for collective efficiency."[419]

Open Data in Jamaica

Open data could be critical in generating the necessary information. A recent study conducted by the Caribbean Policy Research Institute (CaPRI) concluded that an open data initiative in Jamaica could improve productivity in the tourism industry by 10 percent. Jamaica is well-aware of this potential (and of the need for better information) and has signalled its openness to open data policies and frameworks.[420] In 2014, the Jamaican government partnered with the World Bank to develop a framework for "open data development as a job creation and entrepreneurship option."[421] It is the opinion of the World Bank that Jamaica has "many of the essential prerequisites needed to support a successful program" as well as "the region's most vibrant community of people who could use" the data.[422]

Maurice McNaughton, the Director of the Caribbean Open Institute (COI), a coalition promoting open development, argues that while the Caribbean as a whole was "late to the open data, open government party," the Jamaican open data space is noteworthy in a number of ways. For instance, he notes that, "unlike many of the more celebrated instances which start with governments publishing a lot of data and then trying to simulate activity around that, we've actually started from a demand side perspective in a number of key sectors and have been working our way back towards identifying the most impactful data sources." He continues: "on the demand side, the user capacity and interest in

419 Seggitur and CICtourGUNE, *Compete Caribbean: Improving competitiveness in the Caribbean tourism sector through ICT-based innovations*, InterAmerican Development Bank, 2014, http://competecaribbean.org/wp-content/uploads/2015/04/Improving-Competitiveness-in-the-Caribbean-Tourism-Sector-Through-ICT-Based-Innovations_September_v4_docx.pdf.

420 Maurice McNaughton, "Open Government Data: A Catalyst for Jamaica's Growth and Innovation Agenda," Caribbean Policy Research Institute, October 2014, http://www.capricaribbean.com/documents/open-government-data-catalyst-jamaicas-growth-and-innovation-agenda.

421 "World Bank to Assist Jamaica with Open Data Development," *Jamaica Observer News*. December 9, 2014, http://www.jamaicaobserver.com/latestnews/World-Bank-to-assist-Jamaica-with-open-data-development.

422 Jamaica Ministry of Science, Energy and Technology, "Jamaica Receives Favourable Open Data Assessment Report," Ministry of Science, Energy, and Technology, http://mstem.gov.jm/?q=jamaica-receives-favourable-open-data-assessment-report.

open data is quite high. In fact, it was rated the highest of the 7 pillars in terms of the World Bank's overall readiness assessment."[423,424]

The belief that the Caribbean and Jamaican tourism industry can benefit from increased open data activity is resulting in greater availability of information.[425]

Interactive Community Mapping (ICM)

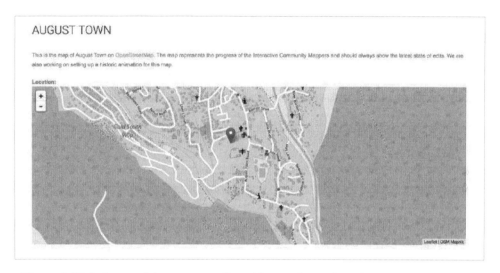

Figure 1. Digital map of August town (http://icm.msbm-uwi.org/content/august-town)

A community map is a map produced by citizens of residents of a particular area. It includes local knowledge and expertise, and is seen by some as a more democratic and people-centric response to traditional cartography.[426] [427] Changes to traditional cartography have been driven in recent years by two main forces: (1) the emergence of critical geographers who have "illuminated the map's crucial and tendentious role in shaping the world" and its relationship to power,[428] and (2) the emergence of freely-accessible data and accessible

---

423 GovLab Interview with Maurice McNaughton, August 24, 2016.

424 Jamaica Ministry of Science, Energy and Technology, "Jamaica Receives Favourable Open Data Assessment Report," Ministry of Science, Energy, and Technology, http://mstem.gov.jm/?q=jamaica-receives-favourable-open-data-assessment-report.

425 Gerard Best, "How Open Data Can Help Caribbean Development, *Caribbean Journal*, October 4, 2015, http://www.caribjournal.com/2015/10/04/how-open-data-can-help-caribbean-development/.

426 Brenda Parker, "Constructing Community through Maps? Power and Praxis in Community Mapping," *Professional Geographer* 58, no. 4, 2006, pp. 470–84.

427 John Pickles, *A History of Spaces: Cartographic reason, mapping, and the geo-coded World*, London: Routledge, 2004; Chris Perkins, "Community Mapping," *Cartographic Journal*, 44, no. 2, 2007, pp. 127–37; and Jennifer Shkabatur, "Closing the Feedback Loop: Can technology bridge the accountability gap?" *Interactive Community Mapping: Between empowerment and effectiveness*, The World Bank, May 2014, pp. 71–106.

428 J.B. Harley, "Maps, Knowledge, and Power," in Denis E. Cosgrove and Stephen Daniels, eds., *The Iconography of Landscape*, Chicago: university of Chicago Press, 1988, pp. 277–312; and J.B. Harley,

mapping technologies."[429] Most community mapping projects are found in developing country contexts.[430]

There are several advantages to interactive community maps. Like many community information projects, they rely fundamentally on open data. Chief among their advantages are the facts that they tend to be drawn quicker, are more dynamic, cost less to produce, and provide more granular information.[431] Successful map projects must carefully consider the particularities of a community being mapped (as well as that community's access to the resulting map, particularly in poorer, marginalized neighborhoods); the existence of civil society actors who can utilize the maps in public campaigns and activist pressure; and the government officials who service the community being mapped (taking care to include their priorities and needs in the mapping project).[432]

There are several examples of ICMs in developing country contexts. ICM efforts have been used for community-driven advocacy (e.g., in Nairobi[433]), and in responses to public health crises (Sierra Leone[434]) or natural and other disasters (e.g., Gulf of Mexico,[435] Haiti[436]). Jennifer Shkabatur, a scholar at the Interdisciplinary Center Herzliya, an Israeli research university, notes that the prevalence of ICMs in fields like disaster response is not surprising. ICM efforts are often successful in such situations because "the incentives are there, you do not have to encourage people. People know they should be there."[437] ICM in less urgent situations, however, are much harder to sustain without similarly clear incentives for participation.

"Deconstructing the Map," *Cartographica*, 26, no. 2, pp. 1–20.

429 John Pickles, *A History of Spaces: Cartographic reason, mapping, and the geo-coded World*, London: Routledge, 2004; and Brenda Parker, "Constructing Community through Maps? Power and Praxis in Community Mapping," *Professional Geographer* 58, no. 4, 2006, pp. 470–84.

430 Chris Perkins, "Community Mapping," *Cartographic Journal*, 44, no. 2, 2007, pp. 127–37.

431 Jennifer Shkabatur, "Closing the Feedback Loop: Can technology bridge the accountability gap?" *Interactive Community Mapping: Between empowerment and effectiveness*, The World Bank, May 2014, pp. 71–106.

432 Ibid.

433 Ibid.

434 Andrew Young and Stefaan Verhulst, "Battling Ebola in Sierra Leone: Data sharing to improve crisis response," GovLab, http://odimpact.org/case-battling-ebola-in-sierra-leone.html.

435 Jennifer Shkabatur, "Closing the Feedback Loop: Can technology bridge the accountability gap?" *Interactive Community Mapping: Between empowerment and effectiveness*, The World Bank, May 2014, pp. 71–106.

436 Wikiproject, "Haiti," http://wiki.openstreetmap.org/wiki/WikiProject_Haiti.

437 GovLab Interview with Jennifer Shkabatur, November 14, 2016.

KEY ACTORS

Key Data Providers

Jamaica's tourism industry is governed by the Ministry of Tourism, which maintains data on the number of visitors who enter the nation and where those visitors stay. Local mappers are also providing data in a crowdsourced manner to supplement official data sources with on-the-ground information.

Key Data Users and Intermediaries

The Caribbean Open Institute (COI) was the lead actor in the ICM effort in August Town. The COI is a "regional coalition of individuals and organizations that promotes open development approaches to inclusion, participation and innovation within the Caribbean, using open data as a catalyst." Its focus areas include spurring "awareness, advocacy and engagement with public sector stakeholders on Open Government and Open Data" and catalyzing "regional capacity building in a core set of technology platforms, tools and standards that are commonly used across the Open Data universe."[438] COI also plays a key role in regional efforts, like the Developing the Caribbean open data conference and Codesprint.

COI's Maurice McNaughton notes that, "we have been very deliberate about picking sectors that are high impact for the Caribbean."[439] As a result, COI's initiatives focus on four main sectors: agriculture, tourism, and marine protected areas.

Key Beneficiaries

The ICM effort is meant to benefit a wide range of actors, including tourists themselves, stakeholders in the local tourism industry, and the country at large, which stands to gain from the economic benefits of a more widely dispersed tourism industry. In a paper describing the initial pilot project studied here, Michelle McLeod, Maurice McNaughton, the drivers of the initiative, note beneficiaries such as, community residents; tourism businesses (to the end of improving the "technology and data literacy skills of tourism businesses to develop innovative tourism products and services); the UWI Mona Source hosting service (which stands to "become a hub for open data and ICM activities"); the Social Development Commission (a government agency that will play a key role in scaling tourism ICM efforts and gain access to new mapping artefacts); and tourism app developers, who stand to gain access to useful new maps and, potentially, new collaboration opportunities with other stakeholders in the space.[440]

---

438 Caribbean Open Institute website, http://caribbeanopeninstitute.org.

439 GovLab Interview with Maurice McNaughton, August 24, 2016.

440 Maurice McNaughton, et al., "Open Data as a Catalyst for Problem Solving: Empirical evidence from a Small Island Developing States (SIDS) context," Paper presented at the 2016 Open Data Research Symposium, Madrid, Spain, October 5, 2016, https://drive.google.com/file/d/0B4TpC6ecmrM7OEN6OVlIUXh1d1U/view.

Project Description

As the potential for crowdsourced mapping efforts (often but not always supplemented with open government datasets) continues to grow in recognition, it is seen as an important enabler of community tourism, which is a "key component of Jamaica's Tourism master plan and efforts to diversify the Tourism product."[441]

In 2015, Maurice McNaughton and Michelle McLeod of the University of the West Indies and Caribbean Open Institute (COI) began a tourism-focused ICM initiative. The project was aimed at leveraging open data and a crowdsourced ICM effort to create new tourism-focused mapping artefacts and build new mapping skills for community members. The initiative was developed to highlight "heritage, culture, ecology, and visitor-community interaction" in a way that enabled the community to generate "its own data and its own intelligence and based on its own indigenous knowledge."[442]

As McNaughton put it in a paper, underlying this initiative was the belief that:

[C]ombining the Internet and new low-cost, interactive, map-based technologies with official Open Government data and indigenous content creates the opportunity for the active engagement of community members in the planning, development and increased visibility of the community tourism product, as well as enhances the interactions between the community, the tourism agencies, and other service providers within the sector; i.e., transportation, larger hotel chains, tour operators, and prospective tourists.[443]

To set the stage for the ICM effort, a team from COI conducted a detailed sector study, looking at the main data sets being put to use in five countries that had important tourism sectors. This effort sought to gain a greater grasp of both the supply and demand sides of the tourism open data ecosystem, the current and potential users of such data and where most of these datasets existed on the open-closed spectrum. The team found that while in some cases data are not fully open, there was "quite a lot of activity both in terms of the demand and supply side in the tourism sector" and available datasets were "being used to make critical strategic decisions in the sector."[444] For example, in an interview,

---

441 Maurice McNaughton, "Open Data and Community Tourism: A strategy for empowering local communities," Paper presented at the Third International Tourism Conference, Jamaica, November 9–11, 2014, http://ocs.msbm-uwi.org/index.php/itc/index/pages/view/abstract-mcnaughton.

442 Ibid.

443 Ibid.

444 GovLab interview with Michelle McLeod, August 24, 2016.

McLeod pointed to Barbados' use of tourist arrival data to enable targeted outreach to new airlines that could benefit from servicing the island and to adjust airline policies to enable growth. She argues that the Barbados case is only one example of how the "openness of the tourism data is critical for timely decision making and strategic adjustments in the sector."[445]

Following these initial research efforts, the ICM pilot project advanced by McLeod and McNaughton began in earnest during an initial meeting in June 2016 with partners from the Centre for Tourism and Policy Research; Mona Social Services, a social and economic development NGO; and The Source, a local resource hub. The goal was to identify potential mappers to take part in the project. The initial meeting was followed by an "intensive 5-day workshop" wherein volunteer mappers were trained on geodata capabilities and, in particular, the use of the OpenStreetMap platform. Upon completion of the workshop, the participating mappers were placed into teams and assigned to different grid areas across August Town, a neighborhood in Kingston. Over a four-week period, the participants mapped landmarks and areas of interest, tour routes and bus stops. They also collected pictures and video for inclusion in mapping artefacts made available to the public.[446]

The ICM initiative was developed with the goal of achieving four main aims. First, it set out to map points of interest and community assets around Kingston and St. Andrew. Second, it sought to provide useful data and information to stakeholders active in the Jamaican tourism sector. Third, it sought to lay the groundwork for future community mapping and community-oriented tourism activities. Finally, the effort sought to provide new skills and entrepreneurial opportunities for community members participating in the mapping initiative.[447] The first output of the initiative was a Virtual August Town tour companion app providing data-driven and community-oriented maps and suggestions for making the most out of visits to the area.

A follow-on initiative was organized shortly afterward, bringing together a number of community leaders in addition to the strategic partners and mappers. This second focus group yielded a "Tourism Related Wish List" that helped to better target the efforts of the community mappers. Some of the items on the wish list included, food festivals, youth sports facilities and local

---

445 Ibid.

446 Maurice McNaughton, et al., "Open Data as a Catalyst for Problem Solving: Empirical evidence from a Small Island Developing States (SIDS) context," Paper presented at the 2016 Open Data Research Symposium, Madrid, Spain, October 5, 2016, https://drive.google.com/file/d/0B4TpC6ecmrM7OEN6OVlIUXh1d1U/view.

447 Ibid.

community tour guides.[448] The two initial pilot mapping projects yielded a number of digital maps and tourist routes described in more detail below.

Demand and Supply of Data Type(s) and Sources

According to the Open Knowledge Foundation's Caribbean census site, a number of open data sets related to tourism are available (even if some of the data is not truly "open" by the strictest definition). Some of these datasets include: tourism arrivals ("aggregate data about tourist stop-over visits, derived from anonymized landing card data"); tourism service providers ("listing of registered service providers including Tour Operators, Transportation / Taxi service, Car rental, Adventure & Entertainment providers"); and tourism assets ("list of registered tourism assets including large/small hotel properties, attractions, craft markets").[449] These datasets represent the core public information on the sector, and provided a foundation for the ICM effort, helping to target mappers' focus toward areas of particular interest.

Funding

COI has five central partners and funders: the International Development Research Center (IDRC), Mona School of Business & Management, SlashRoots, Fundacion Taiguey and Open Data for Development Network. Specifically, the ICM effort was one of four strategic sector initiatives being implemented as part of the Harnessing Open Data to Achieve Development Results in Latin America and the Caribbean program funded by IDRC.[450]

Open Data Use

The ICM effort leveraged the open datasets available listed on the Open Knowledge portal to target mapping efforts and provide the backbone for the crowdsourcing effort. The newly generated, crowdsourced, open data was created through the OpenStreetMap platform, available for access and reuse by anyone, including other tourism-focused actors in Jamaica, demonstrating

---

448 Ibid.

449 "Caribbean Open Data Census," http://caribbean.census.okfn.org.

450 Maurice McNaughton, et al., "Open Data as a Catalyst for Problem Solving: Empirical evidence from a Small Island Developing States (SIDS) context," Paper presented at the 2016 Open Data Research Symposium, Madrid, Spain, October 5, 2016, https://drive.google.com/file/d/0B4TpC6ecmrM7OEN6OVlIUXh1d1U/view.

the value of supplementing open data with crowdsourced – and ensuring the crowdsourced data itself is made open.[451]

Impact

The Jamaican Interactive Community Mapping initiative is still in its infancy, and major on-the-ground impacts have not yet been achieved. The initiative has, however, achieved some early wins – in the form of new deliverables produced, skills provided for community members, and inspiration for similar initiatives in the region aimed at leveraging open and crowdsourced data to benefit the public good.

Encouraging More Diverse, Community-Oriented Tourism

One of the initial outputs of the project, demonstrating the utility and potential of interactive community mapping data, was the design of a virtual August Town tour companion app, which was launched at the 178th anniversary of the August Town community.[452] Some of the key points of interest include the Judgement Yard, the Bedward Church Ruins, the Berry Spring and the culminating food- and craft-focused Artisans' Village.[453] Many other buildings and points of interest are interspersed along the path.[454]

This new community-produced route for tourists stands to be a win-win situation, where tourists are exposed to points of interest that they would be unlikely to experience if they stayed on-site at their all-inclusive hotels (or, indeed, participated in a traditional bus tour), and the local community is exposed to a larger population, with the map helping "to create more business activity in the community."[455]

Skill-Building for Mappers

From the start, McNaughton and McLeod saw the digital maps as only one of the intended outcomes of the project. McNaughton describes the second

---

451 Ibid.

452 Ibid.

453 Carlos Gordon, "A Hidden Gem: August Town Tour Comes to Life!", The Caribbean Open Institute, August 2016, http://caribbeanopeninstitute.org/ATour_pilot.

454 Maurice McNaughton, et al., "Open Data as a Catalyst for Problem Solving: Empirical evidence from a Small Island Developing States (SIDS) context," Paper presented at the 2016 Open Data Research Symposium, Madrid, Spain, October 5, 2016, https://drive.google.com/file/d/0B4TpC6ecmrM7OEN6OVlIUXh1d1U/view.

455 GovLab interview with Michelle McLeod, August 24, 2016.

objective as "more of a process outcome," specifically: "How do we build capacity and a capability for the community to begin to create its own narrative and its story?"[456] As such, the ICM effort was aimed at seeding "the ability of the community to generate its own content and to anchor new tourism products and services around that open map content."[457] Such a focus is common among ICM efforts. Shkabatur notes that "the engagement itself, the skills and the tools that community members gain from the mapping exercise" are often as beneficial as the fruits of their efforts.[458] For McLeod, "It's all about community resilience."[459]

There are several indications that such efforts in Jamaica have borne fruit. McNaughton found that the mappers "developed an energy and enthusiasm and entrepreneurial spirit" as a result of their new-found skills. For example, many mappers have taken it upon themselves to create maps of nature tours, hiking trails and other potential tourist attractions. This entrepreneurial spirit has not gone unnoticed. Other communities in Jamaica with significant Tourism interests such as the Treasure Beach Cluster are keen to explore similar approaches to enhancing their community tourism product.[460] Community leaders, like the President of the Community Development Council have recognized the value and potential of such efforts, and are in the early stages of developing and implementing new opportunities for mappers to leverage their skills, with the goal of further "showcasing the heritage, the music, the art, and just that general community spirit."[461]

Scaling and Replication Across the Region

Maurice McNaughton found that "one of the major emerging insights" from the effort was the fact that the "digital asset and its openness…can be pivoted in many different directions."[462] For example, community mappers are exploring opportunities with local government agencies to support a number of initiatives, including efforts to promote school safety, improve resilience and response to Zika, and to further increase the visibility of Jamaica's tourism offerings.[463]

---

456 GovLab Interview with Maurice McNaughton, August 24, 2016.

457 GovLab interview with Michelle McLeod, August 24, 2016.

458 GovLab Interview with Jennifer Shkabatur, November 14, 2016.

459 Ibid.

460 "The Emergence of Experiential Tourism in Jamaica," Compete Caribbean, http://files.constantcontact.com/825e9e58201/9c460a8f-b801-41ad-85d9-d7a15599a398.pdf.

461 GovLab interview with Michelle McLeod, August 24, 2016.

462 GovLab Interview with Maurice McNaughton, August 24, 2016.

463 Maurice McNaughton, et al., "Open Data as a Catalyst for Problem Solving: Empirical evidence from a Small Island Developing States (SIDS) context," Paper presented at the 2016 Open

Going forward, the COI team hopes to continue to replicate and expand on the initiative across regions and sectors, with a notable focus on education.[464] Future efforts specifically related to tourism could include "spinoffs such as bed and breakfast [mapping] opportunities, and opportunities to even beautify the environment in the community."[465] Shkabatur argues that replication of ICM efforts are often quite easy in terms of technology, especially given the prevalence of OpenStreetMap, but sometimes experience challenges when there is a mismatch in social context or the strength of community groups and organizers.[466] Given the ICM interest and buy-in among both organizers and participants in the Jamaican tourism effort, perhaps these issues will be less challenging than in other contexts.

Risks

As evidenced by the example of the Jamaican ICM effort and various other case studies included in this series, open data holds tremendous potential for positive transformation. But, as we also see throughout this series, open data also poses certain risks. It is important to understand these risks in order to ensure that open data projects are implemented in a way that maximizes the potential upside and limits the downside.

Potential for Negative Publicity

While the ICM effort is premised on the belief that tourists and the Jamaican community both stand to benefit from increased interaction, the impetus for the rise of all-inclusive resorts remains a question. Poverty and crime issues are still present in Jamaica, and on top of the obvious human cost of any crime (violent or otherwise) befalling tourists using the ICM-generated artefacts, the potential negative publicity arising from encouraging tourists to venture off the beaten path could undermine these community tourism efforts.

Data Research Symposium, Madrid, Spain, October 5, 2016, https://drive.google.com/file/d/0B4TpC6ecmrM7OEN6OVlIUXh1d1U/view.

464 GovLab Interview with Maurice McNaughton, August 24, 2016.

465 GovLab interview with Michelle McLeod, August 24, 2016.

466 GovLab Interview with Jennifer Shkabatur, November 14, 2016.

Lessons Learned

Several important lessons with wider applicability emerge from this particular case study. These can broadly be categorized by considering the key enablers of the project, as well as the most important barriers or challenges to its success.

Enablers

Problem definition and context

Tourism is not one of the central areas of focus for open data initiatives in most parts of the developing or developed world. McNaughton notes, however, that while other countries are actively engaged in transportation, government budget, or agriculture open data efforts, "the Caribbean is seen as the most tourism-dependent region in the world. We thought it was important to look at tourism as one of the region's key sectors and what the possibilities or the opportunities were for open data to make an impact...Context matters."[467]

To refine and focus in on the areas of most potential impact, as described above, COI conducted detailed tourism open data and ICM scoping studies, which helped to target mapping efforts and data use. This clear, upfront problem focus also helped to identify gaps in existing open government datasets, and consider other avenues for filling those gaps. It was one of the keys to the project's relative success.

Engaging the press

Upon completion of the initial ICM effort, COI leveraged the press as a key intermediary in spreading the word about the fruits of the project. While many open data efforts—including some in this series of case studies—struggle with raising awareness, COI promoted both the output (i.e., the August Town tour) and the process (i.e., OpenStreetMap-enabled ICM) through the local press.[468] Such an effort could help to ensure that the tourism artefacts, maps and datasets are used by those who stand to benefit the most from them. In addition, such efforts can also promote the use of open data and ICM more generally, potentially pushing forward the approaches in other areas.

---

467 GovLab Interview with Maurice McNaughton, August 24, 2016.

468 Maurice McNaughton, et al., "Open Data as a Catalyst for Problem Solving: Empirical evidence from a Small Island Developing States (SIDS) context," Paper presented at the 2016 Open Data Research Symposium, Madrid, Spain, October 5, 2016, https://drive.google.com/file/d/0B4TpC6ecmrM7OEN6OVlIUXh1d1U/view.

Building partnerships

Brokering partnerships with community groups, intermediaries, NGOs and government was seen as a key factor in allowing for the targeted matching of the supply and demand for data around Jamaican tourism.[469][470] COI is not only well-connected in the local Jamaican community, leading to more buy-in from government actors and volunteer mappers, but also to the global open data community, helping to enable knowledge transfer and collaboration with others doing similar work across the world.

Barriers

Resource challenges

Given the relatively limited availability of open data, as described above, it is little surprise that the availability of resources at the data supply side represented the central challenge for the ICM effort. In reference to the supply side, McNaughton notes that, "I don't think in the Caribbean we have the luxury of just opening up all data and making hundreds or thousands of data sets available and then seeing what happens. We don't have the luxury of that scattershot approach as has characterized many open data initiatives."[471] So while this project could be advanced with relatively little funding (considering the volunteer nature of the mappers and the open source OpenStreetMap platform), resource constraints at the supply side often create barriers to efforts to leverage open data in the country.

To address these types of challenges, McNaughton notes that Jamaican open data efforts often must be "very targeted, starting from sector-specific challenges and opportunities that we perceive and then working from those back towards engaging in partnerships with the supply side to get the data that is relevant to those either problem- or opportunity-centered approaches." [472] [473]

469 Ibid.

470 Carlos Gordon, "Enabling Sustainable Partnerships through Open Data and Interactive Community Mapping," The Caribbean Open Institute, http://caribbeanopeninstitute.org/icm_partners.

471 GovLab Interview with Maurice McNaughton, August 24, 2016.

472 GovLab Interview with Maurice McNaughton, August 24, 2016.

473 Maurice McNaughton, "Problem-Solving with Open Data: A Caribbean Perspective (Part 2), International Open Data Conference Blog, November 19, 2015, http://opendatacon.org/problem-solving-with-open-data-a-caribbean-perspective-part-2/.

Institutional culture challenges

While resource constraints create major challenges, McNaughton believes that "perhaps a larger barrier that we have encountered in much of our work is a cultural barrier to sharing data."[474] While progress is being made—students no longer need to parse static government PDF documents to pull out relevant "open" data as they previously did—shifting the culture remains a slow process with fits and starts. The growing visibility of international open data assessments and shared policies are helping to push for meaningful culture change and institutional recognition of the value of machine-readable open data, and, as a result, the opening of more useful datasets.[475] Important steps forward were taken in 2016 with the launch of Jamaica's Open Data Portal (http://data.gov.jm/) and its entry into the Open Government Partnership.[476]

Supply-side awareness building

As discussed above, the open data ecosystem in Jamaica is largely demand-driven. And while international readiness assessments like those conducted by the World Bank are helping to push forward the supply side, there is still relatively little awareness of the potential value of providing more open data to the public. McNaughton believes that making the case more effectively to government that the issues they face could help to bring more problem-solvers outside of government into the equation could help improve the supply of open data in the country. As it stands, there is little understanding of the types of problems that could be solved through open data, the benefit of allocating the time and resources necessary to make it available, and what open data can do to "enhance what we do in terms of growth and development in the region."[477]

Looking Forward

Due to the importance of tourism to the Jamaican economy, continued development and scaling of open data-driven tourism efforts is likely to continue. As Whyms-Stone of the Trench Town Development Association

---

474 GovLab Interview with Maurice McNaughton, August 24, 2016.

475 Ibid.

476 OGP Support Unit, "Leaders at OGP Summit Call for Greater Government Openness in Response to Worrying Global Trends," Open Government Partnership Blog, December 7, 2016, https://www.opengovpartnership.org/blog/ogp-support-unit/2016/12/07/leaders-ogp-summit-call-greater-government-openness-response.

477 GovLab interview with Michelle McLeod, August 24, 2016.

notes: "we are an island with not a lot of resources…Not a lot of minerals, we don't got oil. But what we do have is a place like Trench Town, a place called Jamaica that people want to come to for whatever reason."[478]

He continues that he "believes in tourism 100%…it is a source, an economy of revenue so your people can have a better quality of life, health, education, housing. And that is why I believe in tourism because it is necessary. People want to come here; we want people to come here. We need an economy, let's make it work."[479]

Current Status

The initial pilot ICM initiative has now concluded, but the insights and resources (including the tourism artefacts) it generated are being put to use in a number of ways. The project is now expanding and evolving across a number of sectors and regions, described more below.

Sustainability

Given the benefits provided to community mappers in terms of skills development, and the limited resources required for spurring an ICM effort, the continued expansion of the Jamaican tourism initiative seems promising. While there are challenges, as described above, especially around the availability of relevant open datasets, the public interest and availability of the open source OpenStreetMap platform bodes well for the sustainability of such efforts. As a cautionary note, it is worth mentioning that in other parts of the world, efforts to sustain ICM interest and engagement over a longer time period have proven difficult after the initial motivation for citizen participation (e.g., a natural disaster or the creation of a specific mapping artefact) became less urgent.[480] The ICM Tourism Pilot in Jamaica has identified the many actors that need to collaborate in order to develop a vibrant, sustainable open data ecosystem in community tourism.[481]

---

478 GovLab Interview with Christopher Whyms-Stone, Trench Town Development Association, September 29, 2016.

479 Ibid.

480 GovLab Interview with Jennifer Shkabatur, November 14, 2016.

481 "Building a Sustainable GeoData Ecosystem," Open Data for Development, Caribbean Open Institute, http://caribbeanopeninstitute.org/sites/default/files/images/Building_geoData_Ecosystem.png.

Replicability

Replicability of the ICM effort across the Caribbean is promising, given the key insights and resources developed as part of the Jamaican effort. Given resource constraints, scaling innovations across the region often rely on the availability of "common resources and common approaches," which this effort has provided.[482] Regarding the replication of the tourism ICM effort, McNaughton notes, "We have packaged it. We have developed approaches and platforms and techniques and quite interesting workshop around mapping. We can easily replicate that in many other contexts so that everybody is not reinventing the wheel, which is a challenge that the Caribbean has had in traditional endeavors."[483]

As McLeod notes, "Of course, we are divided by the sea and that is a barrier, but we want to be able to really replicate it across the islands and ensure that our region can benefit with the whole open data movement."[484]

Conclusion

While the on-the-ground impacts of the Jamaican interactive community mapping effort are still largely aspirational, the initiative provides inspiration and important lessons regarding the use of open data and crowdsourcing to create new economic opportunity and improve social cohesion. Based on a clearly defined problem – i.e., the need for more information on the tourism sector in the country to benefit local stakeholders and tourists themselves – the project organizers were able to identify useful open data sets and fill gaps in the data with a community-oriented data collection effort. By both producing new artefacts to benefit the sector and providing community members with new mapping skills, the initiative stands to create an ongoing impact for those living in the region, as well as those vacationing there.

---

482 GovLab Interview with Maurice McNaughton, August 24, 2016.
483 Ibid.
484 GovLab interview with Michelle McLeod, August 24, 2016.

Open Data's Impact on Solving Public Problems

Nepal Earthquake Recovery

Open data to improve disaster relief

Juliet McMurren, Saroj Bista, Andrew Young and Stefaan Verhulst

Summary

After two devastating earthquakes in 2015, Nepal faced a lengthy and costly relief effort and recovery. Nepali open data activists sought ways to crowdsource and deploy open data to identify the most urgent needs of citizens, target relief efforts most effectively, and ensure aid money reached those in need. A number of initiatives created post-quake maps that were used by relief agencies, alerted rescuers to Nepalis in need of urgent assistance, provided opportunities for citizens to share feedback on the recovery with government, and ensured fiscal accountability for aid money through transparency portals. Data-driven disaster preparedness efforts and the use of local knowledge, expertise and connections greatly enhanced the success of the post-quake open data projects. Natural disasters are human and economic calamities, creating a huge drain on the resources of countries and the international community. The initiatives discussed in this case study show the potential for open data to inform crowdsourced data collection efforts, helping to save lives and make relief efforts more effective.

Context and Background

Problem Focus / Country Context

Nepal is a seismically active country: between 1900 and 2011, there were six serious earthquakes, resulting in a total of around 13,500 deaths.[485] In April and May 2015, Nepal was struck by a series of major earthquakes that killed 8,898[486] people and injured a further 22,300.[487] The first earthquake, measuring magnitude 7.8,[488] struck on April 25, 2015, with an epicenter in Barpak Village, approximately 75km from the capital, Kathmandu. The weeks that followed saw over 300 quakes greater than magnitude 4.0, including a second serious earthquake (magnitude 6.3[489]) on May 12, with an epicenter near Mount Everest.[490]

The effect of the earthquakes was devastating. Thirty-one of the country's 75 districts were affected, of which 14 were declared crisis-hit. Almost half a million homes were destroyed,[491] including entire villages near the epicenter of the earthquakes,[492] and a further 250,000 were damaged.[493] In addition, there was extensive damage to government buildings, schools, hospitals, heritage sites, transport and power infrastructure, and agricultural land. All told, almost 3.5 million people were left homeless by the earthquakes, and 8 million people—almost a third of the country's population—were affected.[494]

The impact of the earthquakes was exacerbated by Nepal's poverty and low levels of development. Although Nepal has been highly successful in reducing its poverty rate from 64.7 percent in 2006 to 44.2 percent in 2011, it remains

485 Wikipedia, "List of Earthquakes in Nepal," Wikipedia.org, https://en.wikipedia.org/wiki/List_of_earthquakes_in_Nepal.

486 Government of Nepal, *Nepal Earthquake 2015: Sector plans and financial projections*, May 2016, http://nra.gov.np/uploads/docs/AStGGdnejZ160823113341.pdf.

487 National Planning Commission of Nepal, *Post Disaster Need Assessment*, Executive Summary, NPC, 2015.

488 Jessica Robertson and Heidi Koontz, "Magnitude 7.8 Earthquake in Nepal and Aftershocks," U.S.G.S., May 12, 2015, https://www2.usgs.gov/blogs/features/usgs_top_story/magnitude-7-8-earthquake-in-nepal/; and Government of Nepal, *Nepal Earthquake 2015: Sector plans and financial projections*, May 2016, p. 47, http://nra.gov.np/uploads/docs/AStGGdnejZ160823113341.pdf.

489 Jessica Robertson and Heidi Koontz, "Magnitude 7.8 Earthquake in Nepal and Aftershocks," U.S.G.S., May 12, 2015, https://www2.usgs.gov/blogs/features/usgs_top_story/magnitude-7-8-earthquake-in-nepal/.

490 "Nepal – Earthquake post disaster needs assessment: sector reports (English)," The World Bank, 2015, http://documents.worldbank.org/curated/en/546211467998818313/Nepal-Earthquake-post-disaster-needs-assessment-sector-reports.

491 Ibid.

492 Sahina Shrestha, "Lang Tang Is Gone," Nepali Times, May 1–7,2015, http://nepalitimes.com/article/nation/langtang-destroyed-in-earthquake,2205.

493 https://www.worldbank.org/content/dam/Worldbank/document/SAR/nepal/PDNA%20Volume%20A%20Final.pdf.

494 Ibid.

one of Asia's poorest countries, with a GDP per capita of $2,573 in 2016.[495] The United Nations Development Program considers Nepal a low human development country.[496]

On the 2015 Global Open Data Index, Nepal is ranked 61st of 122 countries, with a score of 30 percent open.[497] The 2015 Open Data Barometer ranked Nepal 68th with a score of 13.09, well below the global average of 32.96. As of January 2017, Nepal has not joined the Open Government Partnership (OGP), though preliminary steps have been taken toward that eventual end.[498] The 2014 creation of OpenGov Hub Kathmandu, a co-working and collaboration space for open data, transparency and accountability, and civic technology organizations and startups, also points to a continued evolution of open data interest and use in the future.[499] However, Nepal's technical infrastructure and readiness remains limited. According to the ODB, for instance, Nepal has only 15 Internet users per 100 people.[500]

KEY ACTORS

Key Data Providers, Users and Intermediaries

Unlike many of the projects included in this series of case studies, where different actors assumed different roles in the open data value chain, the actors involved in this particular initiative combined roles as data collectors, providers, users and intermediaries. The focus on generating crowdsourced data and putting it to use alongside open government data blurred the lines that typically demarcate traditional roles among open data stakeholders.

With that in mind, the lead actors in the projects examined here are:

495 International Monetary Fund, "Report for Selected Countries and Subjects," IMF, October 2015, http://www.imf.org/external/pubs/ft/weo/2015/02/weodata/weorept.aspx?sy=2015&ey=2016&scsm=1&ssd=1&sort=subject&ds=.&br=1&pr1.x=34&pr1.y=16&c=558&s=NGDPD%2CNGDPDPC%2CPPPGDP%2CPPPPC&grp=0&a=.

496 United Nations Development Program, *Human Development Report 2015*, "Statistical Annex," UNDP, http://hdr.undp.org/sites/default/files/hdr_2015_statistical_annex.pdf

497 Open Knowledge, "Global Open Data Index: Nepal," http://index.okfn.org/place/nepal/.

498 Narayan Adhikari and Pranav Budhathoki, "The OGP Process in Nepal – On the Path of Our Own Choosing," Open Government Partnership Blog, December 1, 2016, http://www.opengovpartnership.org/blog/narayan-adhikari/2016/12/01/ogp-process-nepal-%E2%80%93-path-our-own-choosing.

499 "We've Opened an OpenGov Hub in Nepal!" OpenGov Hub, May 21, 2014, http://opengovhub.org/blog/5/2014/weve-opened-an-opengov-hub-in-nepal.

500 World Wide Web Foundation, "Open Data Barometer, 2015," http://opendatabarometer.org/data-explorer/?_year=2015&indicator=ODB&lang=en&open=NPL.

Kathmandu Living Labs[501] *(KLL)*

A non-profit civic technology company working to create high impact technology to transform the ways government works.

Young Innovations Ltd[502]

A Kathmandu tech company founded in 2007 specializing in solutions for development, their goal is to establish open data as one of the priorities of the Government of Nepal.

Local Interventions Group[503]

Local Interventions Group (LIG) is a non-profit working in the global south to improve governance through data-driven solutions. Founded by participants in a student seminar at the London School of Economics, it has offices in the UK and Nepal. LIG is both data user and provider, having actively sought to expand Nepali open datasets through crowdsourcing and the conversion of static government data to machine-readable format.[504]

Open Nepal[505]

A knowledge hub and learning space for Nepali organizations and people who produce, share, and use data for development. The platform is owned by Young Innovations, NGO Federation of Nepal, Freedom Forum, and Development Initiatives, and was intended to bring together journalists, CSOs and those in the tech industry working with open data.[506]

Code for Nepal[507]

A 501(c)(3) non-profit organization registered in the U.S., dedicated to empowering Nepal through increasing digital literacy and access to open data, building apps to improve lives, service delivery to earthquake survivors and right to information.[508] Cofounded by Mia Mitchell and Ravi Kumar Nepal in 2014, Code for Nepal has pursued projects aimed at bridging the digital divide experienced by women, poor people, rural people, and ethnic minorities in Nepal.[509]

Key Beneficiaries

Most of the open data projects reviewed here were intended to directly benefit the Nepali population affected by the quakes, either through immediate relief work or through a more efficient and effective recovery. This improved efficiency, however, also

---

501 http://www.kathmandulivinglabs.org/.

502 http://younginnovations.com.np/.

503 http://www.localinterventions.org.uk/.

504 Interview with Pranav Budhathoki, CEO, Local Interventions Group, September 7, 2016.

505 http://opennepal.net/.

506 Interview with Bibhusan Bista, CEO, Young Innovations, September 12, 2016.

507 http://codefornepal.org/en/.

508 See: Code for Nepal, http://codefornepal.org/en/.

509 Code for Nepal, "About Us," http://codefornepal.org/en/about-us/.

benefited aid agencies, donors, and government, through better targeting of relief and recovery efforts and funds. Other projects were intended to reach intermediaries such as journalists, so that they could use the data to improve accountability.

Project Description

The effort to leverage open data in response to the Nepal earthquakes was diverse, and spanned a number of initiatives and organizations – with additional examples not covered in this case study involving the use of corporate datasets to inform relief efforts.[510] This case study focuses on a number of these efforts, addressing each in sequence and then trying to draw some cross-cutting lessons.

Among the most prominent of the projects, Kathmandu Living Labs (KLL), arose out of a collaborative effort in the Fall of 2013. Dr. Nama Raj Budhathoki, now Executive Director of KLL, member of the Humanitarian OpenStreetMap Team (HOT), and local organizer of OpenStreetMap, had recently completed a doctorate in crowdsourcing, open data and social and mobile media at the University of Illinois, Urbana-Champaign in 2010.[511] His co-founder, Robert Soden, was working for the World Bank in Washington D.C., and looking for a Nepali partner for a World Bank Open Data for Resilience Initiative (OpenDRI) project in 2012. Robert and Nama met in Kathmandu in Fall 2012, when Nama took on a leadership role on OpenDRI in Nepal. KLL was formed as a not-for-profit civic technology company in the fall of 2013, as a means of continuing the work after the end of the OpenDRI project.[512] This kick-off initiative brought sought to map all the "educational institutions, health facilities, road networks, tangled mesh of *gallies*, religious sites and other geographic features of Kathmandu Valley."[513]

Immediately after the earthquakes, KLL began to build on its pre-earthquake mapping work. Working from desks in the organization's parking lot—it was unsafe to go back indoors[514]—KLL members coordinated the work of about 8,000 local and international volunteers who collaborated to build a detailed map of affected areas. Online volunteers around the world used post-quake

510 Stefaan G. Verhulst, "Corporate Social Responsibility for a Data Age," *Stanford Social Innovation Review,* February 15, 2017, https://ssir.org/articles/entry/corporate_social_responsibility_for_a_data_age.

511 Saira Asher, "How 'Crisis Mapping' Is Helping Relief Efforts in Nepal," BBC News, May 6, 2015, http://www.bbc.com/news/world-asia-32603870.

512 See: Kathmandu Living Labs, http://www.kathmandulivinglabs.org/pages.

513 "Who We Are," Kathmandu Living Labs, http://www.kathmandulivinglabs.org/about.

514 Shreeya Sinha, "Three Ways Nepalis Are Using Crowdsourcing to Aid in Quake Relief, *New York Times*, May 1, 2015, http://www.nytimes.com/2015/05/02/world/asia/3-ways-nepalis-are-using-crowdsourcing-to-aid-in-quake-relief.html?_r=3.

satellite images to update the team's pre-quake maps, while in Kathmandu, KLL staff scraped images of damage from social media and mapped the damaged city on foot.[515] The resulting map was then used by search and rescue teams, emergency services, the Nepal Army, and international relief agencies such as the Red Cross[516] and UN[517] to plan and mobilize their resources. The volunteer mapping efforts were coordinated using the Humanitarian OpenStreetMap Team (HOT) tasking manager,[518] an open source tool that helps to coordinate large-scale mapping efforts by breaking the job into smaller tasks to be assigned to collaborators.[519]

KLL also used its data to develop QuakeMap.org, a website through which users could report their needs to emergency organizations. With phone networks largely inoperative after the earthquakes, the internet became a lifeline for many. Built on the open source Ushahidi platform that had previously been used after the Haiti and New Zealand earthquakes, QuakeMap.org invited people to contribute information in real time about immediate local needs. Observers could note where people were trapped, identify damage to infrastructure, post information on resources such as emergency shelter, or ask for assistance with necessities such as shelter, food, and water.[520] KLL had a small team of volunteers dedicated to validation of reports on QuakeMap.org, via a callback to the poster to verify the facts. The Nepal Army, which took the lead in the relief effort, downloaded reports from QuakeMap.org every two hours, passing on requests for assistance to their relief division. A second level of validation also took place within Army headquarters, where a desk was set up to verify QuakeMap.org reports.[521] Once assistance was received, the database was updated to indicate the problem was resolved and to avoid duplication of resources.[522] QuakeMap.org also included a page called Who's

515 Imogen Wall, "Could Mapping Tech Revolutionize Disaster Response? *The Guardian*, April 25, 2016, https://www.theguardian.com/global-development-professionals-network/2016/apr/25/could-mapping-tech-revolutionise-disaster-response?CMP=share_btn_tw.

516 Shreeya Sinha, "Three Ways Nepalis Are Using Crowdsourcing to Aid in Quake Relief, *New York Times*, May 1, 2015, http://www.nytimes.com/2015/05/02/world/asia/3-ways-nepalis-are-using-crowdsourcing-to-aid-in-quake-relief.html?_r=3.

517 Imogen Wall, "Could Mapping Tech Revolutionize Disaster Response? *The Guardian*, April 25, 2016, https://www.theguardian.com/global-development-professionals-network/2016/apr/25/could-mapping-tech-revolutionise-disaster-response?CMP=share_btn_tw.

518 http://tasks.hotosm.org/.

519 Nirab Pudasaini, "Open Source and Open Data's Role in Nepal Earthquake Relief," OpenSource.com, June 8, 2016, https://opensource.com/life/16/6/open-source-open-data-nepal-earthquake.

520 Saira Asher, "How 'Crisis Mapping' Is Helping Relief Efforts in Nepal," BBC News, May 6, 2015, http://www.bbc.com/news/world-asia-32603870.

521 Interview with Dr Nama Raj Budhathoki, Executive Director, Kathmandu Living Labs, September 10, 2016.

522 Siobhan Heanue, "Nepal Earthquake: How open data and social media helped the Nepalese to help themselves," ABC News, August 17, 2015, http://www.abc.net.au/news/2015-08-16/nepal-earthquake-how-open-data-social-media-helped-rebuild/6700410.

Doing What Where, to help relief agencies view activity in the field and direct their work more effectively.

Open Nepal and Young Innovations

A second prominent initiative, the Earthquake Response Transparency Portal,[523] was launched by Open Nepal and Young Innovations, two organizations involved in technology and development. Soon after the Haiti earthquake in 2010, more than 40 countries ratified the International Aid Transparency Initiative (IATI)[524] standard for publishing development-related data (including budgets, annual reports, and strategic documents for country plans). In 2012, Young Innovations launched AidStream,[525] a platform to help aid organizations publish data in the IATI format, which uses XML.[526] Since then, the format has been adopted by more than 470 organizations, including Oxfam, the Red Cross, and the Bill & Melinda Gates Foundation.[527]

Before the earthquakes, few organizations within Nepal had adopted the standard.[528] However, within 24 hours of the first earthquake, Open Nepal, an online and offline development data knowledge hub, and Young Innovations had partnered to produce the Earthquake Response Transparency Portal, a portal that tracks national and international donations (both cash and in-kind) to earthquake relief efforts. As Bibhusan Bista, CEO Young Innovations, put it:

> *Immediately after the earthquake there was a self-ignited, organic movement among youth in different sectors… to provide whatever assistance they could to earthquake victims. On April 26, the day after the earthquake, five or six of my colleagues and I gathered in the carpark at our office, since the ground was still shaking and we couldn't go inside. And we asked ourselves: what can we do? Instead of rushing to the field, where a lot of people are already active, can we do something based on our expertise? So… we said, let's start tracking the resources coming into Nepal.[529]*

---

523 http://earthquake.opennepal.net/.

524 http://www.aidtransparency.net/.

525 http://aidstream.org/.

526 Jennifer Rigby, "A Year After the Devastating Earthquake, Nepals Young Are Rebuilding Their Country," Quartz.com, April 27, 2016, http://qz.com/670197/a-year-after-the-devastating-earthquake-nepals-young-are-rebuilding-their-country/.

527 "Who's Using It?" AidStream, https://aidstream.org/who-is-using.

528 Amrit Sharma, "Where Is All the Aid Money for Nepal Going? Open data could help lift the veil," Takepart.com, August 6, 2015, http://www.takepart.com/article/2015/08/06/open-nepal-earthquake-aid-money.

529 Interview with Bibhusan Bista, CEO, Young Innovations, September 12, 2016.

The group began with United Nations Office for the Coordination of Humanitarian Affairs (OCHA) Financial Tracking Service (FTS) data, but then began scraping, cleaning and standardizing data as it was reported in the national and international media, as well as from government and non-government sources, to create a centralized portal. As Bista said: "There were a lot of questions being asked: do we have enough resources? Are those resources being used appropriately? We needed a common, accessible repository to track those data."[530]

The portal's intent was "to support the accountable and effective use of funds that are available for relief and reconstruction activities." To achieve this goal, it sought to (1) establish the traceability of funds from donors to intermediaries to implementing organizations; (2) enable inquiries about results of specific relief efforts and projects; and (3) provide a country-wide view of relief efforts to avoid duplication. Attempting to provide a holistic view of relief efforts and their finances, the portal shows both data from primary and secondary sources on funds given and received by all national and international entities, as well as how funds were used by these organizations.[531] Data used to build the portal is available for download in csv format.

The data used for the Earthquake Response Transparency Portal had to be scraped, cleaned and standardized before it could be used. Much of the data came from press releases issued by donors and was in unstructured text format, which had either to be manually entered or scraped using purpose-built tools. Data from the UN was machine-readable, but not fully open. Double counting was common in the days after the earthquake, with numbers reported from donors and implementing agencies working on the same project being added together.[532]

Bista observes that the portal was intended to reduce friction and overcome some of the delays inherent in IATI reporting. In addition, the portal was also designed to address irregularities that often plague the aid and donor ecosystem. Bista notes that irregularities are apparent just by looking at the data at the macro level. For example, he said that despite a promised $4.4 billion in aid, the data only accounted for some $3.85 billion.[533] The Earthquake Response Transparency Portal sought to address such shortcomings by tracking pledge money as it passed from the donors through intermediaries, and by

530 Ibid.

531 Young Innovations, "Earthquake Response Transparency Portal," http://earthquake.opennepal.net/about.

532 Interview with Bibhusan Bista, CEO, Young Innovations, September 12, 2016.

533 Amrit Sharma, "Where Is All the Aid Money for Nepal Going? Open data could help lift the veil," Takepart.com, August 6, 2015, http://www.takepart.com/article/2015/08/06/open-nepal-earthquake-aid-money.

independently verifying aid money's use for intended projects in an open manner. In the process, Young Innovations hopes to improve accountability by uncovering instances of corruption or inefficiencies leading to money failing to reach its intended beneficiaries. "Independently verifying that the pledged money was delivered to the intended project is the biggest challenge for transparency and accountability today," he says. "We want to prevent the Haiti mistakes and serve as a model for how technology can help facilitate transparency and accountability."[534]

The main users of the Earthquake Response Transparency Portal were data-using intermediaries such as journalists. After the post-disaster needs assessment and the donors' conference, as donor pledges began to flow in, media reporting often failed to make a distinction between pledges, commitments and actual disbursement. As Bista put it: "There were reports in the media saying, this is the amount that has been given by India, or the UN. We wanted to educate intermediaries that we have actually not received that money. The pledge has to be converted to commitment, the commitment then has to be converted to disbursement, the disbursement then has to be converted to expenditure on an actual project."[535]

In addition to data intermediaries, Bista identifies three other potential target audiences: the donors themselves, to hold them accountable for gaps between pledges and actual disbursement; CSOs and NGOs, who could use the portal both to investigate donor resources and areas of interest for potential rebuilding projects, and to "follow the money" to ensure projects were carried out; and government policymakers, to enable planning of government contributions to the rebuilding.[536]

Code for Nepal

A third series of projects were launched by Code for Nepal, a Nepal-based nonprofit that seeks to leverage innovation, data and training efforts to improve public life. Soon after the first earthquake, Code for Nepal was looking for ways to provide a humanitarian response in badly affected regions outside Kathmandu. To do this, the team used a low-tech form of crowdsourcing, hoping to encourage the widest possible participation.[537] Within 36 hours of

---

534 Ibid.

535 Interview with Bibhusan Bista, CEO, Young Innovations, September 12, 2016.

536 Ibid.

537 Femke Mulder, et al., "Questioning Big Data: Crowdsourcing crisis data towards and inclusive humanitarian response," *Big Data and Society*, August 1, 2016, http://bds.sagepub.com/content/3/2/2053951716662054.

the earthquake, Code for Nepal developed an open Google document to enlist information about relief agencies, volunteers and victims.[538]

Additionally, Code for Nepal carried out two surveys of earthquake survivors to seek feedback on the kind of aid they had received. Rahat Payo[539] (a Nepali term meaning "did you get relief?") and the Kobo Toolbox[540] surveys were carried out in two phases. The first phase surveyed 776 affected Nepalis in 40 locations across five districts in August 2015. A second phase, conducted in December 2015, focused solely on residents of the village of Barpark, the epicenter of the first major earthquake. The preliminary findings were published on the Code for Nepal website and the data shared in an open format.[541] The results of the surveys were published in the media, and were shared with non-profits working in the field, providing a granular, on-the-ground perspective of the effectiveness and reach of aid distribution. Ravi Kumar reports that more surveys are planned, probably in online format.[542]

Local Interventions Group

Local Interventions Group, governance-focused non-profit with offices Nepal, also used open data to address the post-earthquake situation. This work was built on the foundations and experience of earlier projects in the areas of open governance, crowdsourcing, and smarter city solutions. In particular, the organization had built projects to help Kathmandu citizens report complaints concerning local police; crowdsourced grievances with government in two remote regions of Nepal; and worked with Google to create GIS maps of human trafficking hotspots and routes.

Within 24 hours of the earthquake, Local Interventions Group began partnering with the Nepali Home Ministry to digitize information collected by its post-earthquake emergency telephone hotline. It partnered with Accountability Lab, an incubator aimed at "strengthening systems of accountability,"[543] to send out Mobile Citizen Help Desks into affected areas, identify local needs and linking affected communities to resources. Over subsequent weeks and months, as the recovery progressed, this work developed into #quakeHELPDESK, a four-part earthquake response strategy that not only allowed users to track aid

---

538 Interview with Ravi Kumar Nepal, September 9, 2016.

539 http://codefornepal.s3.amazonaws.com/rahatpayo/index.html.

540 https://1s3ej.enketo.kobotoolbox.org/webform.

541 Interview with Ravi Kumar Nepal, September 9, 2016.

542 Ibid.

543 http://www.accountabilitylab.org/.

data use, but also provided "a platform for affected communities, emergency responders, and volunteers to report gaps at the last mile."[544]

The other components of the project included citizen perception surveys conducted for the UNOCHA InterAgency Common Feedback Project[545] (an open data platform designed to improve the responsiveness of the relief and recovery effort); the Open Mic Project,[546] a partnership with Internews which sought to track and counter earthquake rumors and misinformation; and Follow the Money, an aid tracking and accountability program.[547] All these projects helped the Local Interventions Group close the feedback loop through a communications campaign with the UN, in which town hall meetings with local political representatives to discuss grievances raised through the #quakeHELPDESK were broadcast on local FM radio.[548]

Who's Doing What Where

In addition to these projects, various other organizations also sought to use data to introduce new efficiencies and greater transparency into relief efforts. One notable example arose from the Humanitarian Data Exchange (HDX),[549] an open platform managed by the UN OCHA for sharing humanitarian data to drive analysis. The HDX team set up Nepal—Who's Doing What Where (Housing Recovery and Reconstruction) (HRRP 4W). This tool inventories relief housing efforts in the 14 districts most severely affected by the earthquakes according to what, where, when, and by whom projects are being planned and carried out. Data is supplied every two weeks through self-reporting after training by over 350 partner organizations working in housing recovery and reconstruction. The data are then compiled and cleaned at a national level, and used to develop reports.[550] The current database shows data from January 1, 2016 to the present, and reports continue to be filed as of late August 2016.

Funding

The projects had varied sources (and amounts) of funding. The Earthquake Response Transparency Portal was funded entirely by Young Innovations

---

544 "Our Mission," #quakeHELPDESK, http://www.quakehelpdesk.org/what.php.

545 http://cfp.org.np/.

546 http://www.quakehelpdesk.org/openmic.php.

547 Local Interventions Group, "Interagency Common Feedback Project: Nepal earthquake 2015," http://www.localinterventions.org.uk/programmes.php?post=32.

548 Interview with Pranav Budhathoki, CEO, Local Interventions Group, September 7, 2016.

549 https://data.humdata.org/.

550 Humanitarian Data Exchange, "Nepal—Who's Doing What Where," https://data.humdata.org/dataset/160625-hrrp-4w-national.

from the proceeds of its more commercial activities.[551] Most of the projects, however, were heavily dependent on grants from aid agencies such as the United Nations. Quake Map and the perceptions surveys that formed part of #quakeHELPDESK were both UN funded, for example.[552] The work of Code for Nepal was funded largely through donations, although the second Rahat Payo survey was supported by George Mason University and Tufts University.[553]

Impact

Indicators of success and impact can be divided into two broad categories: metrics and stories of use, and changes to organizational, political and social culture or behavior.

Given that the projects in Nepal emerged from a crisis, efforts to track site metrics or analyze use or traffic were seldom made at the time, although some of those interviewed said that they intended to do so in the future. As a result, it is necessary to rely on more qualitative accounts to gauge the use made of these various projects. It is important to keep in mind that even such accounts are incomplete and conjectural, however, since we can only speculate on how the relief effort would have been different if, for example, KLL's OSM project had never taken place. Nonetheless, the below attempts to assess some illustrative examples of impact across the different initiatives.

Metrics and Stories of Use

Before the earthquake, Dr. Budhathoki and a dozen student interns collectively mapped every educational institution, health facility, road network, and religious site of the Kathmandu Valley, adding these and other important geographic features to OpenStreetMap. The team also gave mapping workshops to university students, government officials, the tech community, NGOs, and youth groups, recruiting volunteers to join their mapping efforts.[554] Through their pre-earthquake efforts, they had collectively created the most detailed map of the Kathmandu Valley available in the country.[555]

---

551 Interview with Bibhusan Bista, CEO, Young Innovations, September 12, 2016.

552 Interview with Pranav Budhathoki, CEO, Local Interventions Group, September 7, 2016.

553 Interview with Ravi Kumar Nepal, September 9, 2016.

554 See: Kathmandu Living Labs, http://www.kathmandulivinglabs.org/pages.

555 Shreeya Sinha, "Three Ways Nepalis Are Using Crowdsourcing to Aid in Quake Relief, *New York Times*, May 1, 2015, http://www.nytimes.com/2015/05/02/world/asia/3-ways-nepalis-are-using-crowdsourcing-to-aid-in-quake-relief.html?_r=3.

After the earthquake, Dr. Budhathoki went from managing a small team of between seven and 100 local volunteers to coordinating the efforts of 9,000 remote volunteers from a situation room. A week after the first earthquake, the team had been able to map 70 to 80 percent of the earthquake-affected areas.[556] International media reported that the OSM map was being used by relief agencies such as the Red Cross. According to Adele Waugaman, a former fellow at the Harvard Humanitarian Initiative, KLL's efforts to map all the health facilities in Kathmandu Valley before the earthquake would "undoubtedly help the relief workers' ability to deliver supplies and help save lives."[557]

QuakeMap.org received 2,035 reports, of which 978 were verified by volunteers and 551 required action.[558] Calculating the true value of the portal is more complicated, however, than looking at the metrics. As Dr. Budhathoki put it: "How many lives were saved by it? How much human suffering was relieved by the use of QuakeMap data? I don't know. I can't give any quantified data about that."[559]

Changing Culture and Behavior

Although the Earthquake Response Transparency Portal had no use case before its launch, Bista's hunch that the target market would be the media proved correct. Within Nepal, the portal has been used by national journalists to provide evidence for their write-ups. Bista reports that international media such as the BBC have also used the portal to track governmental use of funds.

Young Innovations also found an audience among journalists. It found itself being asked to provide training in data journalism to members of the media wanting to know how they could make better use of the platform. In addition, some surprising uses also emerged. For instance, the Nepalese diaspora in the US, which was actively generating and gathering funds and resources for the relief effort, used the portal to screen NGOs to decide where to contribute. There were also requests for increased granularity of data by district, by users who were interested in tracking geographic distribution of aid, although the nature of the data reporting made this difficult to supply.[560]

---

556 Ibid.

557 Ibid.

558 Nirab Pudasaini, "Open Source and Open Data's Role in Nepal Earthquake Relief," OpenSource.com, June 8, 2016, https://opensource.com/life/16/6/open-source-open-data-nepal-earthquake.

559 Interview with Dr. Nama Raj Budhathoki, Executive Director, Kathmandu Living Labs, September 10, 2016.

560 Interview with Bibhusan Bista, CEO, Young Innovations, September 12, 2016.

Improving IATI

The experience of the Earthquake Response Transparency Portal has also illuminated some of the limitations of IATI reporting in emergencies, and in the process perhaps contributed to future improvements in the system. The portal met a clear need by several audiences for immediate, centralized reporting of structured and standardized data during a crisis and its aftermath; these were benefits existing IATI reporting mechanisms could not provide. Bista has been able to feed this experience back into the IATI ecosystem through participation in international conferences on humanitarian data, such as the World Humanitarian Summit in Istanbul in May 2016. "Through this, we are also contributing to the discussion on how data on global humanitarian aid should be standardized," he said. IATI now has a team working on data standardization, including representatives from Young Innovations.[561]

Risks

The proliferation of open data projects in the chaotic environment after a natural disaster presents opportunities to help, but also introduces the possibility of greater confusion and chaos. Untrained volunteers keen to help may swamp relief agencies and hamper their efforts; even where their help is welcome, as with KLL's QuakeMap work, managing volunteers requires the commitment of staff time. Unconscious duplication of effort may also occur: several perception surveys of earthquake survivors were carried out by those organizations interviewed, for example, with surveyors sometimes unaware of one another's work. Finally, crowdsourced emergency information platforms can add to confusion among survivors and waste time among rescuers if information is not carefully verified. Platforms such as Open Mic, which counter rumor among survivors, provide a tool to combat misinformation.

Lessons Learned

Several important lessons with wider applicability emerge from this particular case study. These can broadly be categorized by considering the key enablers of the project, as well as the most important barriers or challenges to its success.

---

561 Ibid.

Enablers

Learning from Haiti

Several of the projects were very consciously built on the experience of Haiti's devastating earthquake of January 2010. Those involved were well aware of the pitfalls of poor preparedness and a lack of transparency for a poor, earthquake-prone country, and sought to find ways to improve the outcome for Nepal, either before the earthquake or immediately after it.[562] This awareness of previous efforts, and willingness to build on lessons learned, was one of the key enablers that contributed to the impact and success of Nepali efforts.

The experience of Haiti motivated Dr. Nama Budhathoki to return to Nepal to begin mapping the country. During his studies, he had observed how open mapping was used to aid relief efforts during the Haiti earthquake. Aware that a serious earthquake would one day hit Nepal,[563] and conscious of the poor quality of Nepal's existing official maps,[564] some of which had not been updated for between 10 and 25 years,[565] he had returned to Kathmandu after graduating to begin building an open mapping community in Nepal. "Nepal sits in one of the most risky zones for earthquakes and other disasters. In Haiti they made [the map] after—I wanted to make the map before the earthquake."[566]

The creators of the Earthquake Response Transparency Portal were also acutely aware of the problematic history of the Haiti earthquake appeal. Nepalis had been concerned about reports of discrepancies in the reporting policies of international aid organizations, particularly after it was revealed that $500 million was missing from Red Cross funds earmarked for Haiti's earthquake recovery. According to Bibhusan Bista, CEO of Young Innovations, "[The portal] empowers people with a snapshot of how money is flowing into Nepal's rebuilding and reconstruction projects and promotes transparency at a time of great need.... We don't want to repeat the mistakes of Haiti."[567] He continues:

---

562 Amrit Sharma, "Where Is All the Aid Money for Nepal Going? Open data could help lift the veil," Takepart.com, August 6, 2015, http://www.takepart.com/article/2015/08/06/open-nepal-earthquake-aid-money.

563 Shreeya Sinha, "Three Ways Nepalis Are Using Crowdsourcing to Aid in Quake Relief, *New York Times*, May 1, 2015, http://www.nytimes.com/2015/05/02/world/asia/3-ways-nepalis-are-using-crowdsourcing-to-aid-in-quake-relief.html?_r=3.

564 Saira Asher, "How 'Crisis Mapping' Is Helping Relief Efforts in Nepal," BBC News, May 6, 2015, http://www.bbc.com/news/world-asia-32603870.

565 Interview with Dr. Nama Raj Budhathoki, Executive Director, Kathmandu Living Labs, September 10, 2016.

566 Saira Asher, "How 'Crisis Mapping' Is Helping Relief Efforts in Nepal," BBC News, May 6, 2015, http://www.bbc.com/news/world-asia-32603870.

567 Amrit Sharma, "Where Is All the Aid Money for Nepal Going? Open data could help lift the veil," Takepart.com, August 6, 2015, http://www.takepart.com/article/2015/08/06/open-nepal-earthquake-aid-money.

After Haiti, there were a lot of concerns about the relief and rehabilitation funds being misused and misallocated. To avoid that, it is critical to first see who is giving what money to whom. To us, that was an interesting case to be made, that openness could avoid the mistakes that were made in Haiti. That was, for us, the internal incentive to go on with the project.[568]

Permission to innovate

The government also played a central role in the success of these various Nepali open data projects. Immediately after the earthquake, Bista says that crucial government actors including the National Planning Commission and the then Prime Minister of Nepal embraced the importance of transparency and accountability. Crucially, they supported such efforts not merely within the government, but also through independent, non-state initiatives like the Earthquake Response Transparency Portal.[569] This type of high-level buy-in can play a key role in pushing forward innovation and experimentation with open data.

International organizations and tapping into existing ecosystems

Many of the projects discussed in this case also relied on data and infrastructure provided by international organizations like UN OCHA. This case demonstrates the importance of such organizations in enabling open data efforts in developing countries through access to tools and funding, and in helping to fill gaps in national government databases by opening relevant datasets in their possession.

Pranav Budhathoki also points to an existing ecosystem of data users as a potent enabler in gaining the necessary traction to get results from the data they collected and opened. Because of their funding connections within the UN, they were connected to an international open data system that responded quickly and enthusiastically to their bulletins.[570] Activating this global, distributed network of problem-solvers brought to bear a diversity of skill and experience that would otherwise have remained untapped.

---

568 Interview with Bibhusan Bista, CEO, Young Innovations, September 12, 2016.
569 Ibid.
570 Interview with Pranav Budhathoki, CEO, Local Interventions Group, September 7, 2016.

Relationships, trust, and access

Several interviewees commented that Nepal is a highly hierarchical society in which relationships, and the nature of those relationships, strongly condition access to people and institutions. Making effective use of data may involve creating relationships with key actors before a disaster strikes, when, as Dr. Budhathoki notes, government agencies and relief organizations may have no time or inclination to meet open data groups, no matter the potential value of their data. Demonstrated expertise, and a product in hand, are also helpful in putting to rest doubts. Dr. Budhathoki found his past career in government mapping, his expertise with OSM, his publications, and his qualifications helped overcome institutional suspicion and mistrust of crowdsourced data, while the map data OSM had already generated in Nepal allowed him to demonstrate its value and robustness.[571]

Pranav Budhathoki, CEO of Local Innovations Group, noted that the organization made a point of hiring the most senior journalist they could find as district coordinators for #quakeHELPDESK, since these people would already have unfettered access to government agencies and established relationships with decisionmakers. Social connections with legislators were even more helpful. "That's the sort of access we needed to ensure the information we produced got the audience that so many other agencies were struggling to get."[572] At the same time, Budhathoki cautions that depending too much on personal connections—and perhaps becoming too cozy with those in power—can hamper the ability to effect real change on the ground.[573]

Volunteers: Both barrier and enabler

Several of the interviewees spoke of the benefits of working with local volunteers. Once trained, a team of committed volunteers can take possible projects beyond the means of a relatively poor country, as Nepal's OSM community has shown. For crisis mapping, local volunteers bring a depth of detailed knowledge that remote contributors, however experienced or careful, cannot.[574]

At the same time, training volunteers represents a significant and uncertain investment. There is no guarantee that, once trained, volunteers will continue to participate, as life circumstances change and interest wanes. Sometimes the

---

571 Ibid.
572 Interview with Pranav Budhathoki, CEO, Local Interventions Group, September 7, 2016.
573 Ibid.
574 Interview with Dr Nama Raj Budhathoki, Executive Director, Kathmandu Living Labs, September 10, 2016.

supply can be overwhelming, as Dr. Budhathoki describes in the aftermath of the earthquakes, when he found himself managing thousands of remote crisismappers. "There was chaos on the ground, but the chaos was also there in the online community," he says. "How do we effectively coordinate and channel that desire to help Nepal?"[575]

Nonetheless, Dr. Budhathoki believes that Nepal was better positioned to harness the potential of mapping than previous countries in crisis because of the existence of a robust and skilled group on the ground, who were able to direct, coordinate and guide international volunteers, and ensure that efforts went where they were most needed. "Without that local knowledge—the in-country capacity—[remote mapping] doesn't take us too far."[576]

Barriers

Connectivity and tech literacy

As with many case studies in this series, a lack of technical capacity and readiness was one of the most commonly cited barriers to success. Many of the intended beneficiaries and users of these portals lacked even a simple Internet connection. Adele Waugaman, a former fellow at the Harvard Humanitarian Initiative, notes that a tool's capacity to function offline can make the difference in determining its usefulness in hot zones during a crisis.[577] One doctor interviewed by the *New York Times* working in Gorkha District said he would have used the work by Code for Nepal and Kathmandu Living Labs if he had Internet connectivity. For those like him without a reliable connection, use may be impossible, or limited to screenshots of maps for later use offline.[578] The production of the maps also relies on a viable Internet connection, since even pencil and paper maps must be uploaded to OSM at some point.[579]

Those with an internet connection must also be comfortable using technology. Dr. Budhathoki observed a certain discomfort with the technical aspects of mapping among potential volunteers.[580] As Code for Nepal has noted, there is a clear digital divide in Nepal that negatively affects the capacity

---

575 Ibid.

576 Ibid.

577 GovLab interview with Adele Waugaman, September 16, 2016.

578 Shreeya Sinha, "Three Ways Nepalis Are Using Crowdsourcing to Aid in Quake Relief, *New York Times*, May 1, 2015, http://www.nytimes.com/2015/05/02/world/asia/3-ways-nepalis-are-using-crowdsourcing-to-aid-in-quake-relief.html?_r=3.

579 Interview with Dr Nama Raj Budhathoki, Executive Director, Kathmandu Living Labs, September 10, 2016.

580 Ibid.

of women, poor people, rural people, and Nepal's ethnic minorities to partake in the benefits of the Internet.[581]

Data creation vs. data use

Dr. Budhathoki observes that one of the barriers confronted was a preoccupation with simply creating data rather than with ensuring that data is actually useful or used. "We need to emphasize the use of the data from day one," he says. "It's very important not just to create the data, to make maps, but to ensure that the data is being used by relief organizations. … Creation is the easy part. The harder part is to talk to the relief organizations and ensure they use the maps."[582]

Institutional culture

Institutional culture—in government, in civil society, among the public—always plays a key role in determining whether open data projects are successful or not. Bista reports that his organization would like to increase the granularity of its data to show giving at different levels. For instance, he says it would be helpful to show how money is apportioned to secondary donors who subsequently disburse it to others. However, this kind of granularity is not supported by current reporting practices or by an institutional culture, both of which have yet to embrace openness and transparency. "The organizations are not responsive," he said. "They feel their obligation is to their donors and to the government authorities and what they demand, instead of feeling that they need to release data for public consumption. That lack of accountability and transparency, to me, is the biggest challenge—and it's not just people in Nepal, it's international organizations."[583]

Ravi Kumar agrees that institutional and political culture is a major brake on the impact of open data in Nepal:

> When there's a lack of capable, responsive institutions on the ground, there's only so much you can do to leverage open data, civic tech, or ICT4D. Nepal hasn't had local elections in more than a decade. There's no local capacity—or if there is local capacity, they were not ready to be responsive, equitable and fair. Even though we have the results, we can't get a response to these things.[584]

---

581 Interview with Ravi Kumar Nepal, September 9, 2016.

582 Ibid.

583 Interview with Bibhusan Bista, CEO, Young Innovations, September 12, 2016.

584 Interview with Ravi Kumar Nepal, September 9, 2016.

Looking Forward

Current Status

Most of the projects were short- or medium-term, and were not intended to persist beyond the relief or recovery phases. The relief projects, such as QuakeMap and Code for Nepal's Google Doc, have largely been shut down. QuakeMap.org is no longer actively soliciting new reports as of July 13, 2015, although new reports could still be filed and would be followed up. Dr Budhathoki reports, however, that the site is being held in readiness in case it is needed for future emergencies.[585]

Those projects tracking the experiences of survivors through the recovery period are still ongoing, although surveys occur less frequently. Interviewees from LIG and Code for Nepal hope to continue their respective surveys into a third phase if funding permits.

As of September 2016, the Earthquake Response Transparency Portal continues to be active. "The rebuilding and reconstruction will go on for the next five years," says Bista. He adds: "After the early, chaotic relief and rescue phase, we are moving towards a tangible reconstruction effort and structured rebuilding of schools and health centers. If we can structure the data and get it into the portal, 'follow the money' activities become much easier. As we see it, this is where the real value of the portal [lies], and centralized open data on fiscal flows for rebuilding and reconstruction becomes even more crucial."[586]

Sustainability

The projects surveyed are, with few exceptions, supported by commercial ventures or aid funding and carried out by teams of paid staff, sometimes with volunteer help. Furthermore, Nepal's recovery and reconstruction is the nation's highest priority, so demand for projects to facilitate the process continues to be high. Bista emphasizes the sustainability of his project will depend on maintaining both supply and demand sides—the openness of the data from the government side, and the community of users—but the project's funding has been provided by Young Innovation's commercial projects, whose profits are reinvested to support its civic tech activities. Bista hopes, however, that it will be possible to sync the portal with other projects on evidence for development, and in the process diversify its funding sources.[587]

---

585 Interview with Dr Nama Raj Budhathoki, Executive Director, Kathmandu Living Labs, September 10, 2016.
586 Interview with Bibhusan Bista, CEO, Young Innovations, September 12, 2016.
587 Ibid.

Replicability

Many of the projects use platforms or models that have been successfully deployed after disasters in the past, and clearly could be again. For example, OSM HOT and Ushahidi-based crowdsourcing platforms were both used successfully after the Haiti and Christchurch earthquake, and are now an established part of the humanitarian open data toolbox.

Bista feels that the experience of the Earthquake Response Transparency Portal would be highly replicable in other places. "We would need to do a little work to create an open source model, because the software we've created is not quite ready to just take and use elsewhere," he says. "But the concept itself is highly replicable." Bista says Young Innovations are currently in discussion with the UN OCHA FTS about the possibility of incorporating some components of the portal's software into FTS. "[R]eplication could involve not just using the software as a whole, but the standards and the concepts that we have could be brought in to make another system that's working elsewhere even better," he says.[588]

Surveys of the kinds carried out by LIG and Code for Nepal could also be successfully deployed in other locations to oversee the responsiveness and accountability of the recovery process. Their efficacy would be greater, however, if agencies conducting such surveys carried out environmental scans to ensure they were not duplicating one another's work. Currently, there is no equivalent of Ushahidi's crowdsourcing platform for humanitarian surveys. The emergence or creation of a dominant technology might help reduce such duplication.

Conclusion

The response of Nepal and the international community to the earthquakes of 2015 was greatly enhanced by the efforts of its open data community. In some cases, their activities provided vital information that would otherwise have been unavailable to rescuers, as with KLL's OSM work. In other cases (QuakeMap.org and Code for Nepal's Google doc) the work they did offered a lifeline to survivors, who could use the new platforms to reach out for assistance.

All this work continues to be significant through the recovery phase, as organizations like LIG, Young Innovations, and Code for Nepal seek to ensure that survivors' voices are heard, that their needs are met, and that donor money

---

588 Ibid.

is received and responsibly spent. Despite the important role such institutions played in enabling the projects discussed in this case study, interviewees often spoke with frustration about the challenges a lack of responsiveness from international organizations and national government could introduce into open data efforts. These experiences make clear that although open data can have major impacts in crisis relief efforts, open data proponents must continue to advocate for open governance to obtain the full benefit of humanitarian open data.

Paraguay Dengue Prediction
Forecasting outbreaks with open data

Juliet McMurren, Andrew Young and Stefaan Verhulst

Summary

Dengue Fever has been endemic in Paraguay since 2009. Recognizing that the problem was being compounded by the lack of a strong system for communicating dengue-related dangers to the public, the National Health Surveillance Department of Paraguay opens data related to dengue morbidity. Leveraging this data, researchers created an early warning system that can detect outbreaks of dengue fever a week in advance. The data-driven model can predict dengue outbreaks at the city-level in every city or region in Paraguay— as long as data on morbidity, climate and water are available.

Context and Background

Problem Focus / Country Context

Paraguay is a tropical to subtropical country of 6.7 million inhabitants, of whom almost a third live in the capital, Asunción.[589] Following several decades of rapid economic growth, the 2015 UN Human Development Index classifies it as a country of medium human development,[590] and the World

---

589 Wikipedia, "Paraguay," https://en.wikipedia.org/wiki/Paraguay.

590 United Nations Development Program, "Human Development Index," *Human Development Reports*, http://hdr.undp.org/en/content/human-development-index-hdi.

Bank now considers it an upper middle income nation.[591] The percentage of the Paraguayan population living below the poverty line has declined sharply over the last two decades, from 49 percent in 2002 to 22.2 percent in 2015.[592]

While most of Paraguay's urban population has access to clean drinking water, rural and/or indigenous communities are frequently reliant on surface or rainwater, raising the risk of water- and mosquito-borne disease.[593] In 2013, the Millennium Development Goals Fund reported that only 6 percent of Paraguay's indigenous households had access to drinking water, and only 3 percent had adequate sanitation. Furthermore, only 10 percent of Paraguay's sewage was treated.[594]

Dengue is a mosquito-borne tropical infection caused by four viruses (DENV-1, DENV-2, DENV-3, and DENV-4) in the *Flavivirdae* family. These viruses are transmitted by infected female *Aedes aegypti* and *Aedes albopictu*s mosquitoes that feed diurnally both indoors and outdoors, and breed in settings with standing water (including in puddles, water tanks, containers and old tires), poor sanitation, and a lack of garbage collection. The mosquitoes that transmit dengue are endemic in parts of Central and South America, Africa, Asia, and Oceania, with most cases occurring during the rainy season or warmer months in urban and suburban areas.[595] Up to 100 million people worldwide contract dengue each year, with 500,000 developing severe illness and 22,000 dying. Some 2.5 billion people live in dengue-endemic areas. Worldwide, cases of dengue have increased thirtyfold since 1960, driven by urbanization, population growth, increased international travel, and climate change.[596]

Dengue fever is asymptomatic in as many as 50 percent of those infected, while a further minority, particularly among the young and those contracting dengue for the first time, experience an undifferentiated fever only.[597] Symptoms of dengue, which appear four to seven days after a bite, include a sudden high fever lasting two to seven days; headache and pain behind the eyes; muscle, joint, and bone pain; and skin rash and bruising. Treatment

591 World Bank, "World Bank Country and Lending Groups," https://datahelpdesk.worldbank.org/knowledgebase/articles/906519.

592 World Bank, "Data: Paraguay," http://data.worldbank.org/country/paraguay.

593 Natalia Ruiz Diaz, "Paraguay: Clean Water Out of Reach for Native Peoples," *Inter Press Service*, June 29, 2010, http://www.ipsnews.net/2010/06/paraguay-clean-water-out-of-reach-for-native-peoples/.

594 Millennium Development Fund Achievement Goals, "Paraguay," http://www.mdgfund.org/country/paraguay.

595 International Association for Medical Assistance to Travellers, "Country Health Advice: Paraguay," https://www.iamat.org/country/paraguay/risk/dengue.

596 Wikipedia, "Dengue Fever Outbreaks," https://en.wikipedia.org/wiki/Dengue_fever_outbreaks.

597 Centers for Disease Control and Prevention, "Clinical Guidance: Dengue Virus," Updated September 6, 2014, http://www.cdc.gov/dengue/clinicallab/clinical.html.

consists of supportive care, and no antiviral treatment is available.[598] In severe cases, patients may progress to Dengue Hemorrhagic Fever (DHF), with severe abdominal pain, vomiting, diarrhea, convulsions, bruising, and uncontrolled bleeding. Complications can lead to potentially fatal circulatory system failure and shock, also known as Dengue Shock Syndrome (DSS). Dengue infection confers immunity to future infections with the same virus serotype, and a transient immunity to other serotypes. Once that transient immunity passes, however, patients contracting other dengue serotypes are at increased risk of developing DHF.[599]

Dengue has been declared endemic in Paraguay since 2009.[600] The Pan American Health Organization reported that there were over 173,000 probable cases of dengue for the year 2016, with 48 cases of severe dengue and 16 deaths.[601] The Direccion General de Vigilancia de la Salud (DGVS) (National Health Surveillance Department of Paraguay) heads up the country's prevention and response efforts.

Open data in Paraguay

Paraguay ranked 62nd in the 3rd Open Data Barometer, ahead of Venezuela but behind the majority of Latin American countries, including Argentina (52nd), Peru and Costa Rica (44th), and Colombia (28th). Paraguay's ranking is largely the result of low scores regarding government policies and government action related to open data.[602] The Open Knowledge Foundation's Open Data Index ranked it 50th worldwide in 2015, moving down from its previous ranking of 41 in the 2014 Index. Its open data on procurement tenders and government budget information received high marks, but many other datasets from sectors like the environment and company registers were non-existent or low quality.[603]

---

598 International Association for Medical Assistance to Travellers, "Country Health Advice: Paraguay," https://www.iamat.org/country/paraguay/risk/dengue.

599 Ibid.

600 Juan Pane, Julio Paciello, Verena Ojeda, Natalia Valdez "Enabling dengue outbreak predictions based on open data," Open Data Research Symposium Draft Paper, October 5, 2016, https://drive.google.com/file/d/0B4TpC6ecmrM7Q1lpQ0xoNlJnZlU/view.

601 "Number of Reported Cases of Dengue and Severe Dengue (SD) in the Americas, by Country: Figures for 2016," Pan American Health Organization, World Health Organization, February 6, 2017, http://www.paho.org/hq/index.php?option=com_docman&task=doc_download&Itemid=270&gid=37782&lang=en.

602 World Wide Web Foundation, Open Data Barometer, Third Edition, WWWF, April 2016, http://opendatabarometer.org/3rdedition/regional-report/latin-america/.

603 "Paraguay," Global Open Data Index 2015, http://index.okfn.org/place/paraguay/.

KEY ACTORS

Key Data Providers

Direccion General de Vigilancia de la Salud (DGVS) (National Health Surveillance Department of Paraguay)

DGVS is the agency responsible for the prevention and control of epidemic disease in Paraguay. It collects and publishes data on disease outbreaks and morbidity.[604]

Key Data Users and Intermediaries

Juan Pane

A researcher at the Facultad Politecnica-Universidad de Asuncion with an interest in open data and open government, Juan Pane leads a team seeking to develop data models to provide early warning of dengue outbreaks in Paraguay. He also works for a democracy initiative funded by USAID assisting the Paraguayan government with transparency portals. Paraguayan by birth, Pane completed a doctorate in computer science at the University of Trento, Italy in 2012, followed by a postdoctoral fellowship. He returned to Paraguay with his family in 2013, just as the country was experiencing a dengue epidemic, with 150,000 reported cases and 233 deaths.[605] Pane reports that the probability of acquiring dengue in some Asunción neighborhoods that year was as high as one in four, a rate that filled him with alarm for his family, but also motivated him to find ways to address the problem of dengue.[606]

Iniciativa Latinoamericana por los Datos Abiertos (ILDA)

ILDA, a network of NGOs and research organizations focused on Latin America, played a key enabling and funding role for the initiative studied here. ILDA's "overarching objective" is to "strengthen the accountability and legitimacy of public institutions, improve public services, and fuel economic growth in Latin America and the Caribbean through research and innovation on open data initiatives."[607]

Key Beneficiaries

The direct key beneficiary was DGVS itself, since the data model provided an early warning system of future demands on the healthcare system. Beyond that, Pane intended to help the people of Paraguay: "Dengue doesn't distinguish between a government minister and my child. Mosquitoes don't care who they bite. I don't want *anyone* to get dengue."[608]

---

604 Juan Pane, Julio Paciello, Verena Ojeda, Natalia Valdez, "Enabling dengue outbreak predictions based on open data," Open Data Research Symposium Draft Paper, October 5, 2016, https://drive.google.com/file/d/0B4TpC6ecmrM7Q1lpQ0xoNlJnZlU/view.

605 World Bank, "The Dengue Mosquito Bites and Makes Latin America Sick," *World Bank News*, April 7, 2014, http://www.worldbank.org/en/news/feature/2014/04/07/dengue-en-latinoamerica.

606 GovLab interview with Juan Pane, September 9, 2016.

607 "About ILDA," Iniciativa Latinoamericana por los Datos Abiertos, http://idatosabiertos.org/about-ilda/.

608 Ibid.

Project Description

Initiation of the Open Data Activity

DGVS collects and publishes incidence and morbidity data on dengue outbreaks in Paraguay. Despite the presence of this data, DGVS lacks an automated predictive tool to enable it to predict dengue outbreaks. In 2013, shortly after returning to Paraguay from his doctoral studies in Italy, researcher Juan Pane and his colleagues at Facultad Politecnica-Universidad de Asuncion noted that there was no open source tool available that could be adapted for this purpose by DVGS, nor had any work been done to examine the correlation between incidence of dengue in Paraguay and variables such as climate, cartography, and population.[609]

Pane's initial hope was to build dynamic maps using the published data to show the origin and spread of outbreaks. He quickly found, however, that the available data would not support this type of granular geospatial tracking.[610] Looking to other dengue-affected countries in Latin America for examples of disease modeling, he found that the few other countries where data was collected, such as Brazil, had similar problems with inadequate granularity and comparability of data, creating major obstacles to longitudinal analysis that could inform predictive modeling. He successfully applied to Iniciativa Latinoamericana por los Datos Abiertos (ILDA), a Latin American open data research, funding and advocacy network, for a research grant to study data modeling of dengue. He and his colleagues then defined the required epidemiological variables and co-variables such as climate, geographic and demographic information, and surveyed 30 dengue-affected countries to assess the availability and format of published dengue data, as well as relevant government agencies responsible for publishing such data.[611] Pane and his team surveyed the reporting forms used throughout Latin America, identifying 285 variables collected across the 30 countries. Finally, Pane's team reviewed literature to identify those variables necessary to model dengue incidence.[612]

Pane's team then correlated the dengue incidence data with open climatic, geographic, demographic, and sanitation data, and produced a prototype model which was shared with DGVS. The open source web application allowed DGVS

609 Juan Pane, Julio Paciello, Verena Ojeda, Natalia Valdez, "Enabling dengue outbreak predictions based on open data," Open Data Research Symposium Draft Paper, October 5, 2016, https://drive.google.com/file/d/0B4TpC6ecmrM7Q1lpQ0xoNlJnZlU/view.

610 GovLab interview with Juan Pane, September 9, 2016.

611 GovLab interview with Juan Pane, September 9, 2016.

612 Ibid.

to incorporate collected data on a weekly basis and produce early warning maps of predicted dengue incidence for the following week.[613]

Demand and Supply of Data Type(s) and Sources

Pane's team used existing DGVS data on dengue incidence. The data, which was being collected on forms to report confirmed or probable cases of notifiable diseases to DGVS for subsequent reporting to the World Health Organization, provided information on number of cases, incidence of the four dengue serotypes, and demographics and location of patients. Some of this data was published in PDF format on a weekly basis, but was spread across multiple documents and tables, and did not follow a standard format in each publication. In order to access the raw data, Pane made an agreement with DGVS to supply them with the data model and training in data collection in exchange for granting his team access to the data itself.[614] This arrangement demonstrates how a clear problem definition and understanding of specific datasets that could help address the problem can enable progress even while government open data efforts lag behind standards and expectations.

Funding

As noted, the project was partially funded through a research grant from Iniciativa Latinoamericana por los Datos Abiertos (ILDA). Aside from this funding, however, the project has been conducted entirely on of the university research team.

Open Data Use

Data on dengue morbidity that feeds into the prototype application was already opened by DGVS. Additional data accessed by the research and development team was also opened as part of the process of developing the data model. Additionally, all source code used to build the predictive tool is open on. As described above, however, much of the data was provided to the researchers in a reciprocal arrangement, rather than broadly opened to the public by the government itself.

---

613 Ibid.
614 Ibid.

Impact

The dengue prevention tool exists as a prototype and proof of concept on how open data can be used to inform the fight against dengue in Paraguay. As such, the principal success indicator to date is successful prediction of future outbreaks, with a secondary indicator of adoption of the data model by the intended key user, DGVS.

Accurate Forecasting

The research and development team's preliminary results indicated that the open data-driven model was able to predict dengue outbreaks a week ahead with an accuracy of 94.78 percent.[615] The prototype data model was given to DGVS after the first round of research to enable their uptake of the tool and its continued development. The follow on impacts of providing this type of predictive capacity to the government entity responsible for managing dengue prevention and response remains to be seen. As of early 2017, there is little indication that this new predictive capacity has fundamentally shifted the intervention strategy at DGVS, but with this newly developed and demonstrably accurate tool in their dengue-prevention toolkit, there is significant potential for impact going forward. Any such impact, however, will be largely dependent on DGVS's responsiveness, especially in the form of a commitment to act on insights generated through the tool; readiness for change and commitment to ensuring sustainability for the effort through consistent resource allocation and data provision.

Risks

The potential for privacy harms is likely the central risk of the use of open data to predict dengue outbreaks in Paraguay. As is the case with any data-driven efforts focused on public health concerns, the possibility exists for personally identifiable information to made accessible, open information to be mashed up with other accessible datasets to create new privacy concerns and disease history to inform future decisions (e.g., insurance, housing or hiring) in an unacceptable way.

Additionally, countries affected by dengue are tropical and subtropical, often with a substantial economic dependence on tourism. As a result, they

---

615 Juan Pane, Julio Paciello, Verena Ojeda, Natalia Valdez, "Enabling dengue outbreak predictions based on open data," Open Data Research Symposium Draft Paper, October 5, 2016, https://drive.google.com/file/d/0B4TpC6ecmrM7Q1lpQ0xoNlJnZlU/view.

stand to see their economies suffer as a result of full disclosure of the true incidence of dengue and other mosquito-borne viruses. Many of the data-driven efforts to fight dengue and mosquito-borne illnesses focus on mapping high-risk areas and encouraging additional vigilance.[616] Although important for minimizing the spread of such diseases, such interventions could lead to a downtick in tourism and greater reluctance to inform this type of openness from government.[617]

Finally, the initiative is being driven by a small team and championed by a single individual. While this structure helped enable agility in the project development, the project's large dependence on one individual introduces risks to its longer-term sustainability.

Lessons Learned

Several important lessons with wider applicability emerge from this particular case study. These can broadly be categorized by considering the key enablers of the project, as well as the most important barriers or challenges to its success.

Enablers

Leveraging existing relationships

The research team behind the effort found success not only thanks to data science capabilities, but also the ability of Pane to leverage contacts from his various professional roles as a researcher and transparency consultant to the Paraguayan government to advance the project. For example, Pane's ability to broker an agreement with DGVS to access their unpublished data, despite their initial concerns about the privacy status of the data, was critical to the tool's launch; he was only able to reach such an agreement because of his preexisting relationship of trust. Dedicated data champions outside government (the demand side of open data) can play a central role, especially if they are able to leverage pre-existing relationships, networks and associations within government.

---

616 Andrew Young, David Sangokoya and Stefaan Verhulst, "Singapore's Dengue Cluster Map: Open data for public health," GovLab, http://odimpact.org/case-singapores-dengue-cluster-map.html.

617 GovLab interview with Juan Pane, September 9, 2016.

Clear problem definition and understanding of data needs

As described above, important data that feeds into the prototype dengue prediction tool was only made available to the researchers as a result of a reciprocal data-sharing arrangement. While this arrangement would likely not be possible were it not for the existing relationships just discussed, the clear problem definition and granular understanding of the specific datasets that could be brought to bear to help solve the problem also played a key enabling role. Rather than being driven exclusively by the data already available, the university research team developed a clear understanding of the objective of their data use (i.e., a longitudinal understanding of incidences of dengue in Paraguay toward the development of a predictive tool for DGVS), which led to a clear understanding of which datasets needed to be accessed and the development of a strategy to loosen the government's grip on them.

Barriers

Reluctance to share

Pane identifies an unwillingness to share data—manifested both as data hugging and exaggerated fears about personal privacy violations—as the single greatest barrier to the project's success.[618] Before he built his tool, the data published by DGVS was in static rather than machine readable format, and was of limited usability for automatic data processing.[619] Better, more complete and more usable data existed, but was being withheld. "The biggest issue is not the technology: it's convincing people to do transparency based on open data," says Pane. [620] Pane also adds that the World Health Organization and Pan American Health Organization could play a more pro-active role, arguing that they too sometimes withhold or otherwise restrict the free flow of data.[621] "We need good data," he says. "The more people publish the data, the better we all collectively will be."[622]

---

618 GovLab interview with Juan Pane, September 9, 2016.

619 Juan Pane, Julio Paciello, Verena Ojeda, Natalia Valdez, "Enabling dengue outbreak predictions based on open data," Open Data Research Symposium Draft Paper, October 5, 2016, https://drive.google.com/file/d/0B4TpC6ecmrM7Q1lpQ0xoNlJnZlU/view.

620 GovLab interview with Juan Pane, September 9, 2016.

621 Ibid.

622 Ibid.

Other mosquito-borne priorities

The dengue data model benefitted in part from growing awareness of and concern about not just dengue, but a host of related mosquito-borne illnesses, such as Zika and Chikungunya. On the other hand, the rapid emergence of these multiple illnesses, with often overlapping symptoms, has also created challenges for the team. For example, Pane reports that DGVS is currently withholding data updates while it struggles to come to terms with the impact of Zika on its dengue data. He adds that the new viruses make identifying and modeling dengue much more complex, in large part because the symptoms being reported that previously indicated probable cases of dengue are the same as those for Zika and Chikungunya.[623]

Looking Forward

Current Status

In 2016, Pane's team released preliminary results and a prototype open source web application that makes use of their data model as proof of concept. In collaboration with another group of researchers, Pane is currently modifying the existing model to enable it to predict the number of dengue cases. The current model merely predicts whether there will be an outbreak or not, but Pane is dissatisfied with the subjective nature of the prediction, since there is no accepted definition of what constitutes an outbreak other than disease incidence beyond what would normally be expected.[624]

Pane notes that the rules of engagement have changed dramatically since the emergence of two new mosquito-borne viruses, Zika and Chikungunya. "The world changed. We don't have just dengue now," he says. "Here we have two more diseases that we don't understand."[625] For example, he says that in the past, if a region had 10 confirmed and 40 probable cases of dengue, it was reasonable to assume that the probable cases were also dengue. That assumption can no longer safely be made. Pane and his team are now trying to determine whether to continue to attempt to model dengue, or to attempt to model the suite of symptoms common to all three viruses.[626]

---

623 Ibid.
624 Ibid.
625 Ibid.
626 Ibid.

At the same time, Pane acknowledges that the crisis of Zika may catalyze change, forcing the Paraguayan government and other affected countries to embrace greater openness in order to contend with the threat the disease poses. "We should use this momentum to boost the conversation about openness," he says.[627]

Sustainability

The project's results are preliminary, but the fact that an apparently successful open source model has already been developed suggests that it is sustainable. Future use would depend on the development of an immediately replicable open source model.

Pane identifies a number of potential risks to the project's longevity. Like other open data projects, the Paraguay data model is being driven by the passion and conviction of a single individual, and could therefore fall victim to changes in his time and circumstances. Pane also acknowledges the possibility that his model could fail to attract international attention, languishing in obscurity while other researchers attempt to produce similar models. In an attempt to prevent this, he has spoken about the project at several international open data conferences, and all the source codes are open, so that other researchers can benefit from the work already done.[628]

Replicability

Although it is not yet ready for immediate adoption elsewhere, Pane's intent is to produce an open source model that can be readily adapted for use in other countries and with other diseases. Within Paraguay, he hopes to extend its use beyond dengue to include other mosquito-borne viruses such as Zika and Chikungunya.[629]

Potential barriers to replicability outside Paraguay foreseen by Pane include national data privacy legislation; varying definitions of dengue infection; lack of technical infrastructure and national data collection and management; and political reluctance to jeopardize tourism revenue by exposing the true incidence of dengue. [630]

---

627 Ibid.

628 Ibid.

629 Ibid.

630 Juan Pane, Julio Paciello, Verena Ojeda, Natalia Valdez, "Enabling dengue outbreak predictions based on open data," Open Data Research Symposium Draft Paper, October 5, 2016, https://drive.google.com/file/d/0B4TpC6ecmrM7Q1lpQ0xoNlJnZlU/view.

Conclusion

While it remains a work in progress, Pane and his team have demonstrated that it is possible to use open health data to build a highly accurate early warning system for dengue. Although its continuance has been cast into doubt by the confounding variables of Zika and Chikungunya, Pane remains optimistic that these challenges can be overcome, and that his predictive model could be useful both within Paraguay and abroad.[631]

Pane has sometimes been exasperated by the reluctance of Paraguayan authorities to share data with his team of researchers. He emphasizes the need for governments to consider the usefulness of the data they publish— and withhold: "If there's a message I could send to disease authorities around the world, it is that you are not on your own. There are people around who are smart, who could help you understand what is going on. But for that to happen, you need to publish your data in a way that is actually useful for researchers."[632]

---

631 GovLab interview with Juan Pane, September 9, 2016.
632 Ibid.

PART 3
Conclusion

Leveraging Open Data as a New Asset for Development

The preceding discussion has relied on a wide variety of emergent evidence to better understand how, when, and under what conditions open data projects succeed and fail in developing economies. Our goal, as indicated at the outset, has been neither to champion nor denigrate the potential of open data. The available evidence indicates a mixed picture, with open data resulting in meaningful impact in some cases, and less so in others. Identifying the signal in current research and practice is challenging since the field is still largely built around a belief in the potential of open data and a few compelling yet anecdotal success stories. Our effort here has been to understand specific pathways—using a logic model—by which open data operates in developing economies. This logic model can inform future research and evidence gathering toward a more conclusive understanding of open data's true impacts on development.

Our broad conclusion, supported by the literature, stories, and examples contained in the case studies, are that the theory of change being advanced in the field of open data for development is built around the premise that open data can:

- *Improve governance*, specifically by enhancing transparency and accountability, introducing new efficiencies into service delivery, and increasing information sharing within government departments
- *Empower citizens* in developing countries by improving their capacity to make decisions and widen their choices, and also by acting as a catalyst for social mobilization
- *Create economic opportunity*, notably by enabling business creation, job creation, new forms of innovation and more generally spurring economic growth
- *Help solve complex public problems* by improving situational awareness, bringing a wider range of expertise and knowledge to bear on public problems, and by allowing policymakers, civil society, and citizens to better target interventions and track impact

Again, none of these impacts are inevitable; they are currently better understood as intended rather than realized impacts. As part of our broader logic open data model, we have identified a number of enabling conditions and disabling factors—phenomena or aspects that may spur the potential of open data in developing economies. In particular, the impact of open data in developing economies depends upon:

- *Problem and Demand Definition*: whether and how the problem to be addressed and/or the demand for open data are clearly defined and understood
- *Capacity and Culture*: whether and how resources, human capital and technological capabilities are sufficiently available and leveraged meaningfully
- *Partnerships*: whether and how collaboration within and, especially, across sectors using open data exists
- *Risks*: whether and how the risks associated with open data are assessed and mitigated
- *Governance*: whether and how decisions affecting the use of open data are made in a responsive and legitimate manner

The accompanying Periodic Table of Open Data Impact Elements, outlined in Part II details the enabling conditions and disabling factors that must be taken into account. The list can be used as a checklist of elements that are essential to keep in mind whenever designing or funding open data projects since they may determine the difference between success and failure.

We conclude this book with six takeaways and subsequent recommendations for open data practitioners and decision makers, such as donor agencies, on how to leverage open data as a new asset for development. They represent an initial effort to operationalize the above discussion, and are derived from the empirical evidence in the case studies conducted as part of this project. Considered together, they amount to something of a "roadmap" of open data project design, implementation, and monitoring within developing economies.

Focus on and define the problem, understand the user, and be aware of local conditions. The most successful open data projects are those that are designed and implemented with keen attention to the nuances of local conditions, have a clear sense of the problem to be solved, and understand the needs of the users and intended beneficiaries. Projects with an overly broad, ill-defined, or "fuzzy" problem focus, or those that have not examined the likely users, are less likely to generate the meaningful real-world impacts, regardless of funds available. Too often open data projects have less impact because they

are overly focused on leveraging newly available technology or datasets rather than being problem- and user-focused.

Recommendations for open data practitioners

- Articulate the issue to be addressed with as much granularity as possible.
- Identify and seek to understand the needs of the intended users and beneficiaries (including data intermediaries/partners such as NGOs or journalists) of the open data effort (potentially using user-centric design methods).
- Clearly define why the use of data for addressing the problem matters.
- Explore existing work that seeks to address the problem (locally or otherwise) and how your open data efforts are complementary.

Recommendations for decision makers (including donor agencies)

- Seek to promote problem- or demand-focused open data policies and strategies where open data can provide value.
- Seek ways to strengthen the capacity toward problem definition and user-centric research, for instance, by developing common problem definitions or user research tools and decision trees that can be used by practitioners.
- Develop and integrate—or ask your partners or grantees to conduct—regular exercises that identify how open data could contribute to the problem(s) one seeks to address (as to generate a data-demand culture).
- Invest in research that maps and seeks to create a better understanding of the demand side of data that can or could be matched with the current or future supply side of open data (including, for instance, a list of questions and problems that can complement the list of data-sets released).
- Invest in the development of data-capturing tools that can be used toward specific ends (such as opening information on results-based financing efforts) but have the flexibility to be applied in varied contexts.
- Require grantees to complete a "canvas" or diagnostic of open data project design to demonstrate that the problem and theory of change have been well-defined and to provide the basis for conversation between donor and recipient about the use of data.

Focus on readiness, responsiveness, and change management. Implementing open data projects often requires a level of readiness among all stakeholders, as well as a cultural transformation in the way governments and institutions collect,

share, and consume information. For development funders, this important determinant of success can imply difficult decisions regarding high-potential open data initiatives in developing economies that lack clear institutional readiness or demonstrated responsiveness to feedback. The existence of a robust ICT4D sector, such as that found in Ghana, can act as a catalyst for the quick and effective development of open data capabilities. Moreover, commitment and buy-in from international development agencies themselves can play a key role in establishing the readiness necessary for impact, as evidenced in cases like Burundi's Open RBF efforts.

Recommendations for practitioners

- Consider the institutional culture(s) and "readiness" of the relevant data providers, data intermediaries, and data users that may impact both the supply of data and the response to or use of the insights generated.
- Explore partnerships with providers, partners, or intermediaries with capabilities that could help fill existing capacity gaps.
- Develop internal data literacy training opportunities.

Recommendations for decision makers (including donor agencies)

- Develop and/or fine-tune data-readiness assessment tools that can help determine the true potential of releasing and leveraging open data in developing economies.
- Invest in the generation and dissemination of evidence that can strengthen the value proposition of open data toward increasing political will to open up datasets.
- Invest in or develop coaching efforts that can nurture data-readiness and a data-driven culture at the supply, demand, and use sides of the open data ecology.
- Consider the creation of new "data intermediaries" and/or seek to support existing intermediaries (such as journalists or libraries) that can bridge the data-gap.
- Develop roadmaps to prevent or address the growing divide between those who have access and capacity to leverage data and those who do not.

Nurture an open data ecosystem through collaboration and partnerships. Data does not exist in isolation. The success of open data projects relies on collaboration among various stakeholders, as well as collaboration with data scientists and topic or sector experts. During the problem definition and initial design phase,

practitioners and funders should explore the types of collaborations that could increase uptake and impact. Such partnerships could, for example, take place with other data providers (perhaps from different sectors), like-minded international or local organizations, as well as established intermediaries such as journalists or industry groups.

Recommendations for practitioners

- Conduct due diligence on important actors in the field relevant to the initiative.
- Explore, in particular, private-sector data holders that could be incentivized to participate in a data collaborative (complementing open government data).
- Build bridges with cross-sector stakeholders in the problem and solution (i.e., open data) spaces, for example, by attending conferences or meetups.
- Establish mechanisms and agreements to enable ongoing collaboration between identified partners.

Recommendations for decision makers (including donor agencies)

- Promote collaboration and dialogue among and between the supply (including national statistical agencies and corporate actors) and demand side of open data.
- Develop methodologies that can help identify different demand segments and/or constituencies that can leverage open data toward their mission.
- Invest in "labs" and creating those structures in which different partners can freely collaborate and exchange expertise toward solving hard problems.
- Develop and/or strengthen problem-solving and expert networks seeking to address sustainable development challenges with open data.
- Develop and/or fine-tune common agreements that can accelerate partnerships and exchange of data and expertise.
- Support the organization of and participation in events where different actors (global, regional, and national) can connect and identify common solutions toward improving the open data ecosystem.

Have a risk mitigation strategy. Open data projects need to be mindful of some of the important risks associated with even the most successful projects. Notably, these risks include threats to individual privacy (for example, through insufficiently anonymized data) and security. Funders should ensure

that projects dealing in information that is potentially personally identifiable (including anonymized data) have audited any data risks and developed a clear strategy for mitigating those risks before proceeding with the partnership.

Recommendations for practitioners

- Assess how the data will be accessed and used, including ways that might not represent the central intended use case(s).
- Conduct a data inventory to determine how the data will be stored and monitored, and who can gain access to the data.
- Consider risk-producing scenarios or use cases to help target a mitigation strategy.
- Develop risk counter-measures based on these scenarios, such as data handling policies, training, technological solution (for example, to de-identify personal information) and a data ethics framework.

Recommendations for decision makers (including donor agencies)

- Seek ways to complement the value-proposition of open data with a broader awareness of the risks involved— for instance, through an effort to collect (learn-by-failure) case studies or stories that illustrate what can go wrong.
- Support or develop "data responsibility" models, including decision trees or expert systems that enable responsible decision making at each stage of the data life cycle (collecting, processing, sharing, analyzing, and using);

Secure resources, build evidence, and focus on sustainability. Open data projects can often be initiated with minimal resources, but require funding and additional sources of support to sustain themselves and scale. It is important to recognize that access to funding at the outset is not necessarily a sign that open data projects are destined for success. A longer term, yet flexible, business model or strategy is a key driver of sustainability, and should be developed in the early stages of the design process.

Recommendations for practitioners

- Identify local and international funders active in the sector or vertical problem area to be addressed, or in the use of data and technology to solve public problems.

- Determine how long current funding streams will be sufficient for sustainability.
- Explore and learn about additional funding or revenue generation options (e.g., tiered pricing models for open data-driven business offerings).

Recommendations for decision makers (including donor agencies)

- Develop assessment methodologies that can help identify the cost and resources necessary to sustain open data initiatives, such as the World Bank's Open Government Data Toolkit, the Open Governance Costing project being advanced by the World Bank and Research Consortium on the Impact of Open Government Processes.[633]
- Coordinate and increase funding resources—for instance, by allocating an (open) data line in each budget proposal.

Build a stronger evidence base and support more research. This book sought to capture the narratives, practice, and evidence around open data's uses in developing economies. Although there are some early, often muted signals pointing to the impacts of open data for development, the field is still largely built on a belief that open data is creating demonstrable positive outcomes. To move to a more evidence-based understanding of open data in developing economies, we distilled a theory of change and analytical framework informed by the current practice, not to further entrench faith in the positive narrative surrounding open data, but to create a flexible analytical framework that can inform future research and impact assessment. We identified a number of premises—in the form of apparent enabling conditions and disabling factors for open data initiatives—but these premises need further study (and scrutiny) by the research field to determine whether or not they hold water in practice. Thus we end with a call for more research; if open data is to reach its significant, and much-discussed, potential for spurring development, we need to move beyond ideology to create a systematic understanding and evidence base regarding what open data's impacts have been to date and how positive impacts can be enabled.

---

633 Stefaan Verhulst, "Research Consortium on the Impact of Open Government Processes," *The GovLab Blog*, February 11, 2016, http://thegovlab.org/research-consortium-on-the-impact-of-open-government-processes/.

Recommendations for open data practitioners

- Embed research and analysis of what works in the design of the open data initiative allowing for both more iterative approaches and long-term insights into how to improve certain variables.
- Integrate lessons learned and research findings into the design and development of open data initiatives (toward a more evidence-based design process).

Recommendations for decision makers (including donor agencies)

- Support more research and the further development and implementation of assessment frameworks (as provided in this book) that can help identify what works and what doesn't; as well as what can be used to scale open data initiatives across developing economies (including the possible creation of "what works labs" in different regions).
- Seek ways to translate and disseminate existing research and evidence into an "open data canvas" (akin to the GovLab Public Projects Canvas[634]), using the Periodic Table we developed in this book, that can guide more informed approaches to leverage scarce resources and ensure that interventions do not reinforce existing power or economic inequities.

Finally, given the nascent nature of existing open data initiatives, the signals of open data's impact in developing economies are still largely muted, as evidenced in the examples discussed in our paper. Our goal in this book was not to use these examples as the ultimate proof of open data's importance for development; rather, we have picked up these signals and placed them into an analytical framework to enable further practice and analysis going forward. It is only with this type of structured analysis that we can gain a systematic and comparative evidence base of whether and how open data is meaningfully impacting on-the-ground conditions in developing economies.

Remaining Questions and Evidence Gap

Although much research has contributed to our understanding of how and when open data works, there remain several questions that could benefit from more evidence and research. For instance:

---

634 The GovLab Academy Canvas, http://canvas.govlabacademy.org.

- Matching supply and demand:
  - How can we identify and unlock currently closed datasets that are likely to have a real-world impact, while avoiding "open-washing"— i.e., the tendency of governments to characterize data releases of questionable impact as examples of "open data" as a means for improving reputation?
  - How can we better match the supply of open data to the demonstrated demand for data among communities of use, and, as a result, minimize instances of scarce resources being used to open data with low potential for use and impact?

- Building capacity and an institutional open data culture:
  - How can developing countries build open data capacity, e.g., technical readiness, culture change, and training, necessary to maximize positive impacts and avoid potential harms?
  - How does the average cost of building open data capacity differ between developing and developed countries?
  - How does one establish a data-driven mindset and sense of responsibility among decision makers in developing economies that would generate a commitment and willingness to act upon the insights gained from open data?
  - How can development agencies accelerate the supply and responsible use of open data and share their own data with a broader range of constituencies, including governments, NGOs, educational institutions, business hubs, and other donor organizations?
  - How can we strategize and implement institutional and cultural change, including within international development organizations, to amplify the impact of open data in developing economies?

- Building an open data ecosystem:
  - How can we better capture the direct effects of impact enablers—like intermediaries—to help practitioners target efforts?

- Risks and challenges:
  - How can we avoid entrenching existing power asymmetries and inequalities—both socioeconomic and digital—when much of the marginalized community in developing countries is not represented in official datasets?
  - How can we minimize the potential privacy and security harms resulting from the opening of more government data?

Interviewees

Experts and stakeholders interviewed during the development of the 12 Open Data in Developing Economies Case Studies:

- Bibhusan Bista, Young Innovations
- Nama Raj Budhathoki, Kathmandu Living Labs,
- Pranav Budhathoki, Local Interventions Group
- Penhleak (Pinkie) Chan, Open Development Cambodia
- Dr J. Cunningham, Doctor in the Public and Private Healthcare Sectors, South Africa
- Aidan Eyakuze, Twaweza
- Adi Eyal, Code for South Africa
- Miryam Patricia Guzmán García, Fedearroz
- Dr R. Henry, Doctor in the Public Healthcare Sector, South Africa
- Elena Ignatova, BlueSquare, Belgium
- Priya Jadhav, Assistant Professor, Indian Institute of Technology—Bombay
- Daniel Jimenez, International Center for Tropical Agriculture (CIAT)
- Vincent Kamenyero, Burundi
- Verena Luise Knippel, World Bank
- Swheta Kulkarni, Research Associate, Prayas Energy Group
- Antoine Legrand, BlueSquare, Belgium
- David Lemayian, Code for Africa
- Anca Mantioc, The Engine Room
- Michelle McLeod, Caribbean Open Institute / University of the West Indies
- Maurice McNaughton, Caribbean Open Institute / University of the West Indies
- Arnold Minde, Developer of Shule.info
- Oscar Montiel, Open Knowledge International
- Mulle Musau, Elections Observation Group (ELOG), Kenya
- Ravi Kumar Nepal, World Bank, Code for Nepal
- Dr. Etienne Nkeshimana, Burundi
- Jean Claude Nshimirimana, Open RBF Programs, Ministry of Health, Burundi

- Muchiri Nyaggah, Local Development Research Institute, Kenya
- Juan Pane, National University of Asunción, Paraguay and Latin American Open Data Initiative
- Esteban Peláez Gómez, Coordinator of Social Projects, Fundación Corona
- Ashok Pendse, Authorised Consumer Representative with the Maharashtra Electricity Regulatory Commission (MERC)
- Mor Rubinstein, Open Knowledge International
- Priyadarshan Sahasrabuddhe, Vishwadeep Pressparts Pvt. Ltd
- Fabrizio Scrollini, DATA Uruguay
- Jennifer Shkbaktur, IDC Herzliya
- Simone Soeters, Cordaid, The Netherlands
- Thy Try, Open Development Cambodia
- Daniel Uribe, Fundacion Corona
- Samhir Vasdev, ICT Sector Unit, World Bank Group
- Adele Waugaman, USAID
- Christopher Whyms-Stone, Trench Town Culture Yard

Open Data in Developing Economies Advisory Committee

- Izabela Corrêa, Former Coordinator for the Promotion of Ethics, Transparency, and Integrity, Directorate for Corruption Prevention, Brazil
- Elena Ignatova, BlueSquare
- André Laperrière, Executive Director, Global Open Data Initiative for Agriculture and Nutrition (GODAN)
- Maurice McNaughton, Director of the Centre of Excellence for IT Enabled Innovation, Mona School of Business and Management, University of the West Indies, Jamaica
- Jean Philbert Nsengimana, Minister of Youth and Information Communication Technology, Rwanda
- David Selassie Opoku, Open Data for Development (OD4D) Africa Lead, Open Knowledge International
- Fernando Perini, International Development Research Center, Canada
- Nii Narku Quaynor, Chairman, Network Computer Systems, Ghana
- Nicole Stremlau, Programme in Comparative Media Law and Policy, University of Oxford, UK

Recognized Peer Reviewers of the Open Data in Developing Economies research

- Patrick Enaholo, Pan-Atlantic University, Nigeria
- Sara Fernandes, University of Minho and United Nations University
- Claudia Frittelli, Carnegie Corporation
- Silvana Fumega, University of Tasmania, Institute for the Study of Social Change
- Shurland George, World Wide Web Foundation
- Felipe Gonzalez-Zapata, University of Manchester
- Julina Hooks, Teachers College Columbia University
- Alicia Johnson, San Francisco Emergency Management
- Antonio Almansa Morales, Diputación Provincial Málaga (Málaga City County Council)
- Freddy Oswaldo, Independent Consultant
- Iris Palma, DatosElSalvador
- Mohamed Salimi, HCP
- Juliana Taylor, Start Smart
- Julia Roberto Herrara Toledo, Red Ciudadana
- Mariam Rafique Vadria, Delivery Associates
- Christopher Wilson, University in Oslo
- Ken Zita, Network Dynamics Associates

Participants to Workshop at the International Open Data Conference in Madrid, Spain (Wednesday, October 5, 2016) on "Getting to Grips with the Impact of Open Data" (The Open Data in Developing Economies Project)

Facilitator: Stefaan Verhulst, The GovLab
Participants:
- Laura Bacon, Omidyar Network
- Mark Cardwell, USAID
- Patrick Enaholo, Pan-Atlantic University, Nigeria
- Adi Eyal, Code for South Africa
- Feng Gao, Open Data China
- Silvana Fumega, University of Tasmania, Institute for the Study of Social Change
- Mohammad Hossein Ichani, Open Data for Iran
- Michael Jelenic, World Bank
- Michelle McLeod, University of the West Indies
- Maurice McNaughton, University of the West Indies

- Indanna Minto-Coy, University of the West Indies
- Jean Claude Nshimirimana, Ministry of Health, Burundi
- David S. Opoku, Africa Lead, Open Data for Development, Open Knowledge International
- Juan Pane, National University of Asunción, Paraguay and Latin American Open Data Initiative
- Alán Ponce, University of Southampton
- Brandon Pustejovsky, USAID
- Lorna Seitz, Legis Institute
- Tanya Sethi, AidData
- Ilham C. Srimarga, University of the Western Cape
- Kat Townsend, MCC
- Mireille van Eechoud, University of Amsterdam
- Roza Vasileva, World Bank
- Julian Walcott, University of the West Indies
- Natalie Widmann, Max Planck Institute for Intelligent Systems